T0231549

AVIATION RESOURCE MANAGEMENT

## Dedication

**These volumes are dedicated to the memory
of the following fine aviators**

Mike Birks
Paul Carter
Mark Duncan
Tim Ellis
Steve Erskine
Mark Fallon
Ross Fox
Mark Lewin
Jeff Radbone

# Aviation Resource Management

## Volume two

Proceedings of
The Fourth Australian Aviation Psychology Symposium

*Edited by*
ANDREW R. LOWE AND BRENT J. HAYWARD

Routledge
Taylor & Francis Group

LONDON AND NEW YORK

First published 2000 by Ashgate Publishing

Published 2016 by Routledge
2 Park Square, Milton Park, Abingdon, Oxon OX14 4RN
711 Third Avenue, New York, NY 10017, USA

*Routledge is an imprint of the Taylor & Francis Group, an informa business*

**British Library Cataloguing in Publication Data**
Aviation resource management
    Vol. two : Proceedings of the Fourth Australian Aviation
    Psychology Symposium
    1.Aeronautics - Human factors - Congresses
    I.Hayward, Brent J. II.Lowe, Andrew R. III.Australian
    Aviation Psychology Association
    629.1'3252

**Library of Congress Control Number:** 00-132597

ISBN 13: 978-1-8401-4974-6 (hbk)

# Contents

## PART 2: TRAINING

## PART 3:   HUMAN FACTORS

## PART 4:   AIR TRAFFIC CONTROL

# Foreword

This collection of papers from the *Fourth Australian Aviation Psychology Symposium* provides a broad view of contemporary research and thinking in aviation psychology and human factors. It is particularly impressive to see the breadth of the applied and research work reported here and to see Africa, Asia, Australia, Europe, and North and South America represented. Aviation psychology and its application are truly becoming global.

In applying the *Resource Management* title to these volumes, the editors, Brent Hayward and Andrew Lowe, acknowledge the impact that Crew Resource Management programs have had on aviation and aviation psychology. Their choice of title is significant also in light of the fact that CRM has recently come under attack by some who claim it has failed, since human error persists and human error accidents continue to occur. Critics of CRM fail to recognise two vital points – (1) that humans are inherently limited in their capabilities making error inevitable, and (2) that complex systems such as aviation will necessarily experience failures. Given these characteristics, the users of the system must make most effective use of all available resources, including the findings and solutions that psychology can supply. Lowe and Hayward have also expanded the list of resources to include the basic content domains of aviation psychology and human factors. Resource management is a useful phrase. It avoids the flavour of psychobabble and intrusive invasion of the psyche that many associate with psychology and at the same time it doesn't imply a restricted focus on 'knobs and dials' technology that the term human factors may convey.

When we look at the topics addressed in these volumes, we see not only the familiar concerns of psychology and human factors, but also some new additions that show the increasing sophistication of the field. Culture has taken its place as a central influence on the global aviation system. Papers address the concept of the safety culture as well as the influence of national, organisational, and professional cultures on behaviour and training. Issues surrounding multi-cultural organisations are also addressed. Also on the cultural front, the diversity of author origins is a reassuring sign that the cultural hegemony of the United States in aviation research may be diminishing.

Safety and safety investigations are central topics including new methodological approaches and strong awareness of the importance of cultural factors for understanding system accidents. We are far beyond the era of 'blame and punish' into a multivariate world that recognises the multiple contributory factors in system failures.

Automation is also addressed with a healthy recognition of its limitations. As with other resources, automation design and use are influenced by culture and pose new challenges for the operator and the researcher.

Not surprisingly, CRM itself continues to be a significant research topic, but with extensions to organisational issues, cultural factors, and extensions not only to other sub-units such as the cabin and maintenance but even to the company level. The cabin, air traffic control, and maintenance are recognised as worthy research topics in their own right. At the same time, classic topics in human factors and psychology such as selection, training, fatigue, stress, and human-machine interfaces continue to receive needed attention.

The issues addressed at the Symposium and within these proceedings are of critical import for the aviation system. However, many of the approaches and concepts are equally applicable to other environments where teams interact with technology. This point is addressed in a paper showing how methods of aviation safety investigation can be applied in medicine. One of the challenges for the research community is to make the findings from aviation available to other domains to avoid the re-invention of the wheel.

The Symposium was more than a collection of papers. The organisers designed a series of six developmental workshops to engage participants in the discussion of critical issues. These included human factors training, safety investigation, cabin safety, air traffic control, maintenance, and situation awareness. The workshops allowed participants from the diversity of cultures and companies to exchange best practices and seek consensus. They provide the reader with a sense of the interplay between the research and operational communities.

Each of the four Australian symposia has been a landmark in aviation psychology. One can only wonder where the field will be at the Millennium.


*Robert L. Helmreich*
*Austin, Texas*

# Preface

The effective management of available resources has been a catch-cry of aviation in the 1990s. The meanings of this statement are, however, wide and varied. Initially the reference was to aspects of operational safety following the catastrophic mismanagement of resources on some of our more infamous flight decks (including the Everglades, Tenerife, and Portland). Subsequently, the call has gradually and rightly spread to other areas of the aviation system, and to contexts other than safety.

If we consider the resource management catch-cry as a metaphor for the growth in human factors applications within the aviation domain, the spread to other areas of the aviation system has been notably positive. Over the last decade we have witnessed an increasing emphasis on the adoption of human factors principles within many previously neglected components of the aviation system. Where much of our early effort in human factors research and applications was focussed on the cockpit, we now see an increasing emphasis on applied research and work to do with the aircraft cabin, air traffic control, maintenance, ramp, and even some of the corporate and support components of the aviation system.

The conventional wisdom of the early 1980s suggested that around 70 percent of aircraft accidents were attributable to human error. As thinking on this has gradually matured to a realisation that humans are involved in conceiving, designing, constructing, maintaining and managing the aviation system, as well as operating it, there is now a growing recognition that human error/s of some kind underlie virtually *all* accidents. Indeed, most accidents and incidents are not caused by a single human error, but by combinations of multiple errors and factors, as evidenced by concepts such as the *error chain* and the *Reason model* of systems safety.

The more positive flip-side of this coin is that a far greater number of accidents are averted by human action than are caused by them. Human beings are primary contributors to the excellent safety record enjoyed by the greater part of our commercial jet transport industry.

It is the work of these human beings, be they practitioners or researchers, which is the subject of the two volumes of this book. Each chapter within represents a presented paper or workshop held at the Fourth Australian Aviation Psychology Symposium in Manly, Australia in March 1998. These volumes thus reflect not only the unique experience and expertise of individual authors, but also the collective knowledge and convictions of delegates from the variety of nationalities, airlines, service providers, universities, manufacturers, aviation safety agencies, consultants and research establishments who attended and participated so actively in the Symposium.

The foundation stones of the Symposium, and thus these volumes, are the invited chapters contributed by a "flock" of industry stalwarts, including: Dan Maurino (ICAO), Bob Helmreich (University of Texas Team Research Project), Jean Pariès and Ashleigh Merritt (Dédale) Ron Westrum (Eastern Michigan University), Azmi Radzi (Malaysia Airlines), Nicole Svátek (Virgin Atlantic), Patrick Hudson (Leiden University), Sherry Chappell (Delta Technology), Nick McDonald (Trinity College Dublin), Jan Davies (University of Calgary), John Bent (Cathay Pacific Airways), Carol Manning (FAA), Manfred Barberino and Anne Isaac (Eurocontrol), Drew Dawson (University of South Australia), Rebecca Chute (NASA Ames Research Center), Gavan Lintern (Aeronautical and Maritime Research Laboratories), Bert Ruitenberg (IFATCA), and Mica Endsley (SA Technologies).

The presentations by these eminent practitioners provided a solid foundation for the submitted papers and Developmental Workshops which followed and which make up the remaining chapters of these books.

Volume 2 is divided into seven parts. The first six of these represent areas of vital and enduring importance in today's complex aviation system: Selection; Training; Human Factors; Air Traffic Control; Maintenance; and Situational Awareness. Part 7 contains reports from three Developmental Workshops conducted during the Symposium, in Air Traffic Control, Maintenance, and Situational Awareness.

The Fourth Australian Aviation Psychology Symposium was staged by the Australian Aviation Psychology Association (AAvPA), a not-for-profit association established with the objective of increasing the contribution of aviation psychology and human factors to the safety and efficiency of the aviation industry. The Symposium was attended by over 250 delegates from the global community of aviation, including those from Argentina, Australia, Brazil, Canada, Fiji, France, Germany, Guatemala, Hong Kong, Indonesia, Ireland, Japan, Malaysia, the Netherlands, New Zealand,

Norway, Papua New Guinea, the Philippines, Portugal, Saudi Arabia, Singapore, South Africa, Sweden, the United Arab Emirates, the UK and the USA.

We were once again delighted to welcome such a culturally diverse array of participants, whose presence provided a truly international perspective to the Symposium and to the contents of this book.

The Symposium, and thus this book, were made possible by the generosity of our major sponsors, including: Air New Zealand, Airservices Australia, Ansett Australia, Ashgate Publishing, the Aviation Information Centre, Canadian Airlines International, Cathay Pacific Airways, the Civil Aviation Safety Authority, Malaysia Airlines, Psytech Ltd, Qantas Airways, and Selector PAS Ltd. Further generous support was provided by the Aviation Safety Foundation of Australia, the Bureau of Air Safety Investigation, Cullen Egan Dell, Lawrence Erlbaum Associates, and Systems Analysis - A Division of Take 2 Ltd.

Particular thanks are due to Chris Kriechbaum from Air New Zealand, John Guselli from Airservices Australia, Trevor Jensen from Ansett, John Hindley from Ashgate, John Bent from Cathay Pacific, Azmi Radzi from Malaysia Airlines, Ken Lewis from Qantas, and Rob Lee from BASI for their efforts in facilitating such generous support from their respective organisations.

Our sincere gratitude is offered to the speakers, authors, workshop leaders and participants whose endeavours generated the expert, practical content for the Symposium and for these books, and who have been so patient in awaiting their publication.

Special recognition is reserved for our families, for their extraordinary tolerance and understanding during the seemingly interminable process of editing and delivering these volumes.

Our final appreciation is once again extended to our publisher, John Hindley of Ashgate, for his enduring patience and understanding as successive deadlines were overtaken by other commitments, and for his ever optimistic encouragement to complete the task.

*Andrew Lowe and Brent Hayward*
*The Australian Aviation Psychology Association*
*<www.vicnet.net.au/~aavpa>*

*Melbourne*
*June 1999*

# Invited contributors

**Captain John Bent** is Flying Training Manager (Development) for Cathay Pacific Airways in Hong Kong. Between 1993 and September 1995, he was the launch Flying Training Manager for the Airbus A340 and A330 aircraft introduction to the company. For many years he has researched airline training methods, and pioneered the introduction of a new concept of "Seamless" Training for the Airbus. Since 1989, he has been actively involved in a major re-alignment of flying training policy and processes in Cathay Pacific Airways, engaged in the research and development of future training programmes. His first step in this process, between 1989 and 1992, was the development of an in-house *Train-the-Trainer* Workshop Programme aimed at improving flying training skills, in conjunction with Professor Telfer of the University of Newcastle, Australia. This workshop used broad industry research as the basis for design, with a strong human factors emphasis. Together with many other active projects, he is currently leading the establishment of a Computerised Reporting and Analysis System for the Flying Training Section. The last half of John's 21 years in Cathay Pacific Airways have been spent in the Check and Training Section and he has held Training Management positions for eight years. John was born in the UK, and has been flying for 35 years, with the Royal Air Force and three airlines in civil aviation. His early flying days (on two of the three "V"- bombers) quickly instilled the need for effective crews rather than just effective individuals. His instructional experience has included military flying instruction (single and multi-engine), management of a flying school in Germany as Chief Flying Instructor, and the development and launch of a new multi-cultural pre-school and Primary School in Hong Kong, the latter as founding Chairman of the Board of Governors in his free time over a period of five years. Captain Bent has a keen interest in the man-machine interface in modern aviation and human factors in flight operations. He continues to strive for more effective training methods, appropriate to the technology of today.

**Dr Sherry Chappell** is the Program Manager for Human Factors Services and Research in Delta Technology's Usability Engineering Department. Delta Technology is the information technology division of Delta Air Lines. She manages the Human Factors Services for Delta's Flight Operations, In-Flight Services, Technical Maintenance Operations, and Dispatch/Flight Control. Projects include user task analyses, user requirements specification, training program design, procedure design, user interface design, and usability testing. Prior to joining Delta Technology, Dr Chappell spent 17 years at the NASA Ames Research Center, Moffett Field, California. She was the Principal Scientist of the Aviation Safety Reporting System. She had responsibility for the research program that utilized incident reports voluntarily submitted by pilots and air traffic controllers. Areas of investigation included: the proper allocation of automation in the cockpit, the management of information in cockpit and air traffic control tasks, and the development of error-tolerant systems and procedures. Sherry worked with organisations world wide to solve aviation safety problems and to develop reporting systems. Previously at NASA Sherry was Deputy Project Manager of the Aviation Performance Measurement System Research Program. This project examined Flight Operations Quality Assurance (FOQA) programs world wide. Dr Chappell developed scientific methodology to evaluate safety trends and human performance using flight data. These techniques are being implemented in domestic and international airlines. She also designed and performed user requirements studies to determine specific requirements of decision-makers throughout an airline. In addition, Sherry designed the information system and interface for accessing safety data with minimal user actions and performed usability testing. Dr Chappell was the principal investigator for NASA's human factors evaluation of the Traffic Alert and Collision Avoidance System and Data Link / Information Transfer Programs. She was responsible for ensuring that pilots are able to correctly interpret the TCAS and data link information and make the required responses to the information being portrayed, conducting many simulation studies evaluating cockpit traffic displays. Sherry also designed a suite of tools for analysing flight operations quality assurance data to detect developing safety trends and provide baseline safety and efficiency measures for airlines. Sherry holds a PhD in Cognitive/Experimental Psychology from the Ohio State University. She has published over 40 articles and chapters on Aeronautical Human Factors, and has served two terms as president of the Association of Aviation Psychology. Sherry is a certified Human Factors engineer and an instrument-rated commercial pilot and flight instructor. She has also flown over 6000 hours as flight deck observer on US and foreign airlines.

**Dr Jan Davies** is a Professor in the Department of Anaesthesia at the University of Calgary, Canada. She has had a long-standing interest in all aspects of anaesthetic safety, including unexpected postoperative deaths, quality assurance and risk management. In 1989 she moved out of operating room practice. Her clinical time is now spent in the Preoperative Assessment Clinic. There she sees patients who are booked to have an operation and who require consultation from a specialist anaesthetist. She also sees patients who are not booked to have an operation but who believe that they (or some member of their family) have suffered an anaesthetic complication. She acts as a consultant for various provincial medical examiners and coroners, the Canadian Medical Protective Association (the mutual defense organisation which looks after the medico-legal concerns of some 97% of all Canadian doctors), plaintiff's lawyers and an aviation safety organisation. Her association with the aviation system began when she attended an anaesthetic conference at which Dr Rob Lee and Mr Larry Sheehan (now flying for Ansett International) were also speaking. Since then, she and Rob Lee have collaborated on number of projects, including a systematic method for the investigation of anaesthetic deaths. She has collaborated with Professor James Reason, in the first application of the Reason Model to a medical complication. She is also working with Professor Bob Helmreich, in the area of simulation in the operating room and with Captain Norm Dowd of Air Canada, on the topic of decision-making.

**Dr Drew Dawson** is an Associate Professor in the School of Psychology, at The University of South Australia. He is based at The Queen Elizabeth Hospital, where he is the Director of the Centre for Sleep Research. The studies undertaken by The Centre For Sleep Research include investigations into the relationship between hours of work, fatigue and work performance; exploring the impact of shiftwork on organisations, employees and the community; and the neuroendocrine determinants of sleep and sleep disorders, particularly in the elderly. The Centre is funded through grants from various government agencies and industry. Current granting agencies include ARC, NH&MRC and WorkSafe Australia. In addition, Drew has extensive consulting practices with industry and government on the design and evaluation of shiftwork. He specialises in the negotiation of shift systems as part of enterprise bargaining agreements in a variety of industries, including transport, manufacturing and service.

**Dr Mica Endsley** is President of SA Technologies based in Marietta, Georgia, where she specialises in situation awareness issues in advanced aviation systems. She recently left her post as a Visiting Associate Professor at MIT in the Department of Aeronautics and Astronautics and Associate Professor of Industrial Engineering at Texas Tech University. Prior to joining Texas Tech she was an Engineering Specialist for the Northrop Corporation, serving as Principal Investigator of a research and development program focused on the areas of situation awareness (SA), mental workload, expert systems and interface design for the next generation of fighter cockpits. She holds a PhD in Industrial and Systems Engineering from the University of Southern California. Dr Endsley has been conducting research on SA, decision making and automation in aircraft, air traffic control and aviation maintenance for the past 12 years. She is the author of over 90 scientific articles and reports on numerous subjects including the implementation of technological change, the impact of automation, the design of expert system interfaces, new methods for knowledge elicitation for AI system development, pilot decision making, and situation awareness.

**Brent Hayward** is Managing Director of Dédale Asia Pacific, an Australian-based company providing consultancy services in organisational safety, aviation psychology and human factors. Brent is a professionally qualified and registered psychologist, with more than 20 years of experience within the aviation industry. Previous full-time employers include the RAAF Psychology Service, Australian Airlines, and Qantas Airways. His work and research interests include aviation selection and training, the development and implementation of applied human factors training, and the impact of national, organisational and professional culture on performance. Brent is founding President of the Australian Aviation Psychology Association, and also holds Membership of the Australian Psychological Society, the Association of Aviation Psychologists (USA) the European Association for Aviation Psychology, the Human Factors and Ergonomics Society, and the International Society of Air Safety Investigators.

**Robert L. Helmreich** is Professor of Psychology at The University of Texas at Austin. He is also Director of the University of Texas Team Research Project. He received his BA, MS, and PhD degrees from Yale University and served as an officer in the US Navy. He studies team performance in many groups including pilots, astronauts, and surgical teams. He has been involved with the definition and implementation of CRM training for some 20 years. In 1994 he received the Flight Safety

Foundation/Aviation Week and Space Technology Distinguished Service Award for his contributions to the development of CRM. He has authored many papers and chapters, is co-editor with Earl Wiener and Barbara Kanki of *Cockpit Resource Management* (1993), and co-author with Ashleigh Merritt of the recently published book *Culture at Work in Aviation and Medicine* (Ashgate, 1998).

**Alan Hobbs** is a Human Performance Investigator with the Bureau of Air Safety Investigation in Canberra, where his responsibilities include accident and incident investigation and research. He currently manages the research section of BASI. His research interests include the investigation of human and organisational factors which contribute to maintenance errors in aviation. He is a member of the International Society of Air Safety Investigators and the Australian Aviation Psychology Association.

**Professor Patrick Hudson** began his study of psychology at Edinburgh University and received his PhD from the University of St Andrews in 1977. He earlier worked building flight simulators (Boeing 707-720 and DC9) for General Precision Systems, who later became Redifon. In 1975 he moved to Amsterdam, Department of General Linguistics and became visiting professor of Artificial Intelligence in 1976. He moved to Nijmegen University in 1976 and then to TNO, Institute for Perception, in 1979. During this period he worked on flight operations in Maritime Control and anti-aircraft systems with Stinger. In 1985 he moved to Leiden University, becoming Reader in 1987. In 1990 he also became part-time professor of Computer Science at Maastricht University. He has been project leader for Shell International's research work on human error, developing the Tripod system together with Professor Jim Reason and Willem-Albert Wagenaar. More recently he has been working on violations of procedures and is currently involved in a major project relating to safety motivation in a broad cross-cultural setting.

**Dr Gavan Lintern** completed Bachelors and Masters degrees in Psychology at the University of Melbourne before beginning work at the Aeronautical Research Laboratories (Human Factors Group) of the Defence Science and Technology Organisation in 1971. In 1974 he went to the University of Illinois to pursue a degree in Engineering Psychology, and completed a dissertation on the use and evaluation use of special instructional strategies for teaching flight skills in a simulator. From 1978 to 1985 he worked for Canyon Research Group, a private company, on a US

Navy contract based in Florida. The research was focussed on evaluating the contributions of high cost simulator features with a high fidelity and wide field of view visual systems to flight training. Gavan returned to the University of Illinois in 1985 to join the faculty of the Aviation Research Laboratory. He continued to work on instructional strategies for flight simulation with support from the Federal Aviation Administration, the (US) Naval Air Warfare Center, the (US) Office of Naval Research and the (US) Army Research Institute. In 1997 Gavan now returned to the Defence Science and Technology Organisation at Fishermen's Bend to assist with flight simulation and training research programs. The goal over the next several years is to establish a systematic and principled procedure for assessing the design parameters of flight training simulators and for developing instructional programs to be used with them.

**Dr Andrew R. Lowe** is a management consultant with the Melbourne office of Mercer Cullen Egan Dell. Until 1997 he was Senior Psychologist at the Royal Australian Air Force Headquarters Training Command, Point Cook, near Melbourne. His 20 years of experience with the RAAF included air crew selection, training, selection validation research, and safety and management education. As the RAAF's human factors specialist he investigated a number of military aircraft accidents. Andrew holds an Honours Degree in Psychology from the University of Melbourne, and in 1997 he completed a PhD at Monash University on the relationship between pilot personality and operational performance.

**Dr Carol Manning** is an Engineering Research Psychologist in the Human Factors Research Laboratory at the FAA's Civil Aeromedical Institute (CAMI), located in Oklahoma City, USA. Carol has a Ph.D in Experimental Psychology from the University of Oklahoma (1982), with an emphasis in Decision Theory. She has been with CAMI since 1983. She has conducted research on validation of Air Traffic Control Specialist (ATCS) selection procedures, evaluation of ATCS field training programs, and identification of aptitude requirements for ATCSs who will operate future automated systems. More recently, she has worked to identify potential impacts on ATCSs of converting from paper to electronic representations of flight progress data. She was involved in developing criterion measures for validation of a new selection procedure for ATCSs. Carol is currently involved in developing objective measures of ATCS taskload and performance using available National Airspace System data and FAA Academy simulation data. She is also working with Air Traffic Operations to investigate how to help controllers transition away from using paper flight progress strips. Carol participated in the Scientific Task Planning Group that developed the ATC portion of the FAA's National Plan for Aviation Human Factors in 1990.

**Captain Daniel E. Mauriño** is Coordinator of the Flight Safety and Human Factors Programme with the International Civil Aviation Organisation (ICAO). After obtaining a degree in education, he started his flying career in the late 1960's. In 1974 he joined Aerolineas Argentinas, where in addition to his flying duties he held several management positions, including Flying Training Manager. In 1988 he joined CAE Electronics in Montreal to participate in a flight simulator research programme. The following year he was seconded by Aerolineas to ICAO and tasked with the responsibility of developing and implementing the Organisation's Human Factors Programme. Dan is a member of the International Society of Air Safety Investigators (ISASI) and the Human Factors and Ergonomics Society (HFES). He sits representing ICAO at the IATA Human Factors Task Force. He is also a member of the Flight Safety Foundation's ICARUS Committee and the ISASI Human Factors Working Group. Dan is co-author (with James Reason, Neil Johnston and Rob Lee) of the book *Beyond Aviation Human Factors*. He has also contributed to the books *Applied Aviation Psychology, Aviation Instruction and Training, Aviation Psychology in Practice*, and *Aviation Human Factors*.

**Dr Ashleigh Merritt** completed her early education and undergraduate studies in Brisbane, Australia. She later undertook doctoral studies at the University of Texas at Austin. Her dissertation was a cross-cultural study of commercial pilots' attitudes and work values across 15 countries. She continued her post-doctoral work at the University of Texas Aerospace Crew Research Project, and recently co-authored a book with Professor Robert Helmreich entitled *"Culture at Work in Aviation and Medicine: National, Organizational, and Professional Influences"* (Ashgate, 1998). In late 1997 Ashleigh moved to Paris to work for the Dédale human factors and safety consulting group, under the leadership of Jean Pariès. She is currently involved in several safety and training development projects, including Human Factors distance learning using web technology, organisational safety models, and cultural customisation of training. Ashleigh has been an invited speaker at aviation conferences around the globe, hosted by ICAO, IATA, the Royal Aeronautical Society, the Orient Airlines Association, and the Australian Aviation Psychology Association. Her interests include cultural influences on safety attitudes and performance, the cockpit-cabin interface, issues of face, work and communication, modernisation and national culture, and attitudes towards stress.

**Jean Pariès** is Managing Director and leader of the Dédale company, based in Paris, France. Jean graduated from ENAC, the French National School of Civil Aviation as a civil aviation engineer in 1973. He then joined the French civil aviation authority, the DGAC, where he took several positions dealing with aviation safety. He was involved in airworthiness regulation, operational regulation, and pilot licensing and training regulation. He has been a member of several ICAO and European Joint Aviation Authority working groups and was the chairman of the JAA Professional Pilot Licences Working Group. In 1990, Jean joined the French air accident investigation body, the Bureau Enquêtes Accidents (BEA) as Deputy Head, and Head of Investigations. He was Rapporteur General of the Commission of Investigation into the 1992 Air Inter A320 Accident at Mont Saint-Odile, France. In 1994, Jean left the BEA to be a founding member and Managing Director of the Dédale company. Dédale activity focuses on the human factors dimensions of safety, for aviation as well as for maritime operations, medicine, nuclear power, and the like. Jean has been a member of the ICAO Human Factors & Flight Safety Study Group since its creation in 1988. He is the author of several communications on human factors in aviation safety, and co-author of the *"Briefings"* © pilot training course in Human Factors developed by Dédale. Jean holds a Commercial Pilot Licence with Instrument, Multi-engine, Turboprop, and Instructor ratings and a Private Pilot Licence for helicopters.

**Captain Azmi Radzi** trained as a cadet pilot with Qantas Airways and graduated in 1972 with an Australian Airline Transport Pilots' Licence. He flew as a co-pilot with Malaysia Airlines on the Fokker F-27 and Boeing 737, and became a commander on the F-27 in 1979. He has since been a captain and check pilot on various fleets, including the B737, Airbus A-300, B747-200, and –300, and is now flying the Boeing 747-400. Always keeping busy, Azmi graduated from the University of Hull/Malaysian Institute of Management with a Master's degree in Business Administration in 1995, majoring in Human Resource Development. He was recently promoted to oversee all aspects of Human Resource Management for Malaysia Airlines cockpit and cabin crew.

**Bert Ruitenberg** began his career in Air Traffic Control in 1976, when he entered training in the Royal Netherlands Air Force. In 1980 he transferred to the Dutch CAA as a TWR/APP controller at Schiphol Airport, and has worked there ever since. He has instructed on ATC simulators since 1988, and from 1983 till 1989 was a member of IFATCA's Standing Committee 4, the Federation's working-group dealing with Professional matters, including working conditions, medical matters, selection and training, licensing, and human factors. In 1994 Bert was re-elected as IFATCA's Executive Vice President Professional Affairs, representing IFATCA in ICAO's Human Factors and Flight Safety Study Group. Bert has made presentations on human factors at various seminars, symposia and conferences, including the 1994 (W)EAAP Conference in Dublin and the International Symposium on Aviation Psychology held in Columbus, Ohio.

**Nicole Svátek** is Manager of Human Factors at Virgin Atlantic Airways, where her remit includes the Flightdeck, Cabin Crew and Engineering human factors training programmes. One of the original members of the IATA Human Factors Committee, she was an IATA representative to the ICAO Human Factors Working Group and developed the first CRM course for a commercial Airline in Canada, (Wardair). Since returning to the UK in 1993, Nicole has worked extensively with the RAF, the Fleet Air Arm and has lately been involved with adapting Virgin's Human Factors programme for medical resuscitation teams and Anaesthetists. A member of the Royal Aeronautical Society Human Factors Group, she also serves as advisor to the UK Operators Technical Group (Engineering). Notwithstanding all of the above, Nicole's first loyalty and prime responsibility is to Virgin Aircrew.

**Peterlyn Thomas** is a Cabin Safety Investigator with the Australian Bureau of Air Safety Investigation (BASI). Peterlyn commenced flying in 1968 and has been involved in cabin safety issues and training for more than 20 years. She spent an extended period as the Flight Attendant Safety Supervisor with Ansett Australia, and retired from line flying duties with Ansett in 1994. She has since worked on cabin safety issues with the Southern California Safety Institute, and is a member of the Australian Aviation Psychology Association.

**Ron Westrum** is Professor of Sociology and Interdisciplinary Technology at Eastern Michigan University. He has an undergraduate degree from Harvard University in Social Relations (honors) and both master's and doctoral degrees from the University of Chicago in Sociology. He is a sociologist of science & technology, and also complex organisations. He is particularly interested in how organisational cultures shape the design and use of technology. He has published two books: *Complex Organizations: Growth, Struggle, and Change* (1984) and *Technologies and Society: The Shaping of People and Things* (1993). He is now completing a third book, on the development of the Sidewinder Missile at China Lake Naval Weapons Center. He is co-editor of the newsletter *Social Psychology of Science*. In addition, he has published numerous articles in books and journals. He belongs to seven professional societies, including the American Association for the Advancement of Science and the Human Factors and Ergonomics Society. Professor Westrum has presented talks on aviation and systems safety to many national and international bodies, including the National Transportation Safety Board, the International Civil Aviation Organization and NATO advanced seminars. As the Principal Consultant for his firm Aeroconcept he has worked with many clients in the United States. His work in the aviation field has revolved around the idea of "generative corporate cultures", those that support high information flow and cooperative arrangements in advancing safety. He has also been active in the field of corporate creativity, notably in developing and managing a long-running seminar on technical creativity for General Motors. He lives in Beverly Hills, Michigan.

# List of abbreviations

| | |
|---|---|
| AAIB | Air Accident Investigation Branch (UK) |
| AAvPA | Australian Aviation Psychology Association |
| ADI | Attitude Director Indicator |
| ADSO | Airways Data Service Officer |
| AFA | Association of Flight Attendants |
| AFCAC | African Civil Aviation Conference |
| AGL | Above Ground Level |
| AIDA | Automated Instructional Design |
| ALPA | Airline Pilots' Association |
| APU | Auxiliary Power Unit |
| ARL | Aviation Research Laboratory |
| ARP | Airfield Reference Point |
| ASD | Acute Stress Disorder |
| ASM | Air Space Management |
| ASR | Air Safety Report |
| ASRS | Aviation Safety Reporting System |
| ATA | Air Transport Association |
| ATC | Air Traffic Control |
| ATCARDS | ATC Automated Display System |
| ATCO | Air Traffic Control Officer |
| ATIS | Automatic Terminal Information Service |
| ATM | Air Traffic Management |
| ATPL | Airline Transport Pilot's Licence |
| ATS | Air Traffic Services |
| BA | British Airways |
| BASI | Bureau of Air Safety Investigation |
| CAA | Civil Aviation Authority |
| CAO | Civil Aviation Order |
| CASA | Civil Aviation Safety Authority |
| CASPS | Computer Aided Strip Printing System |

| | |
|---|---|
| CATIS | Computerised Airport Terminal Information Service |
| CBT | Computer Based Training |
| CC | Cognitive Compatibility |
| CDM | Critical Decision-Making |
| CFIT | Controlled Flight Into Terrain |
| CIRP | Critical Incident Response Program |
| CISD | Critical Incident Stress Disorder |
| CISM | Critical Incident Stress Management |
| CMAQ | Cockpit Management Attitudes Questionnaire |
| CNS | Communications, Navigation, Surveillance |
| CPDLC | Controller Pilot Datalink Communication |
| CRM | Crew Resource Management |
| CRT | Cathode Ray Tube |
| CTA | Cognitive Task Analysis |
| DFDR | Digital Flight Data Recorder |
| DSTO | Defence Science and Technology Organisation |
| EAAP | European Association for Aviation Psychology (formerly WEAAP) |
| ECAC | European Civil Aviation Conference |
| EPC | Emergency Procedures Course |
| ETA | Estimated Time of Arrival |
| FA | Flight Attendant |
| FAA | Federal Aviation Authority |
| FANS1 | Future Air Navigation System - Version 1 |
| FAR | Federal Aviation Regulation |
| FCU | Flight Control Unit |
| FIS | Flight Information Service |
| FISOR | Flight Information Service On Request |
| FMAQ | Flight Management Attitudes Questionnaire |
| FMC | Flight Management Computer |
| FMS | Flight Management System |
| FO | First Officer |
| FPS | Flight Progress Strip |
| FSF | Flight Safety Foundation |
| FSO | Flight Service Officer |
| GA | General Aviation |
| GPS | Global Positioning System |
| GPWS | Ground Proximity Warning System |
| HCD | Human Centred Design |
| HCI | Human-Computer Interface |

| | |
|---|---|
| HF | Human Factors |
| HFR | Human Factors Reporting |
| HMD | Helmet Mounted Display |
| HSI | Horizontal Situation Indicator |
| HUD | Head-up Display |
| IATA | International Air Transport Association |
| ICAO | International Civil Aviation Organization |
| IFALPA | International Federation of Airline Pilots' Associations |
| IFATCA | International Federation of Air Traffic Controllers' Associations |
| IFR | Instrument Flight Rules |
| IGS | Instrument Glide Slope |
| ILS | Instrument Landing System |
| IMC | Instrument Meteorological Conditions |
| IRDS | Interim Radar Display System |
| IRE | Instrument Rating Instructor |
| ISASI | International Society of Air Safety Investigators |
| ISPACG | Informal South Pacific ATC Coordination Group |
| JAA | Joint Airworthiness Authority |
| JAR | Joint Airworthiness Requirement |
| JDM | Judgement and Decision Making |
| KLM | KLM - Dutch Airlines |
| LLC | Line/LOS Checklist |
| LOFT | Line Oriented Flight Training |
| LOS | Line Oriented Simulation |
| MANOVA | Multiple Analysis of Variance |
| MCDU | Multi-purpose (/function) Control and Display Unit |
| MDA | Minimum Descent Altitude |
| MEDA | Maintenance Error Decision Aid |
| MEI | Maintenance Error Investigation |
| MEL | Minimum Equipment List |
| MSAWS | Minimum Safe Altitude Warning System |
| NASA | National Aeronautical and Space Agency |
| NASA/MAC | NASA/Military Airlift Command |
| NATO | North Atlantic Treaty Organization |
| NDB | Non-directional Beacon |
| NM | Nautical miles |
| NTSB | National Transportation Safety Board |
| NWA | Northwest Airlines |
| OAA | Orient Airlines Association |

| OPQ | Occupational Personality Questionnaire |
| ORMAQ | Operating Room Management Attitudes Questionnaire |
| PAL | Philippine Airlines |
| PCT | Perceptual Control Theory |
| PD | Power Distance |
| PDD | Partial Dome Display |
| PDP | Parallel Distribution Processing |
| PFD | Primary Flight Display |
| PLPQ | Pilot Learning Processes Questionnaire |
| POB | Persons on Board |
| PPL | Private Pilot's Licence |
| PTSD | Posttraumatic Stress Disorder |
| QAR | Quick Access Recorder |
| QFI | Qualified Flying Instructor |
| RAAF | Royal Australian Air Force |
| RMI | Radio Magnetic Indicator |
| ROM | Read Only Memory |
| RPD | Recognition Primed Decisions |
| RPT | Regular Public Transport |
| RT | Reaction Time |
| RTO | Rejected Take-off |
| SA | Situational Awareness |
| SAFAC | Safety Advisory Committee (of IATA) |
| SAIT | Situational Awareness Information and Training |
| SAR | Search and Rescue |
| SART | Situational Awareness Rating Technique |
| SCSI | Southern California Safety Institute |
| SD | Standard Deviation |
| SEAT | Situational Experiential Awareness Training |
| SHEL | Software-Hardware-Environment-Liveware |
| SIV | Survey of Interpersonal Values |
| SMC | Surface Movement Controller |
| SOP | Standard Operating Procedure |
| SRK | Skill-Rule-Knowledge |
| SSR | Secondary Surveillance Radar |
| TAAATS | The Australian Advanced Air Traffic System |
| TAF | Terminal Area Forecast |
| TCAS | Traffic Collision Advisory System |
| TMA | Terminal Manoeuvring Area |
| TOQ | (CRM) Technical Operators Questionnaire |

| | |
|---|---|
| TRE | Type Rating Examiner |
| TSO | Technical Standing Orders |
| UAL | United Airlines |
| ULH | Ultra Long Haul |
| UNSW | University of New South Wales |
| VACBI | Video and Computer Based Instructional System |
| VASI | Visual Approach Slope Indicator |
| VDU | Visual Display Unit |
| Vfe | Flap speed limit |
| VFR | Visual Flight Rules |
| VOR/DME | VHF Omni Range/Distance Measuring Equipment |
| WAC | World Aeronautical Chart |
| WEAAP | Western European Association for Aviation Psychology (now EAAP) |

# Part 1
# SELECTION

# 1 Job requirements of airline pilots: Results of a job analysis

*Peter Maschke, Klaus-Martin Goeters, Andrea Klamm*
*German Aerospace Center (DLR)*

## Introduction

A systematic selection process in combination with good training is the best guarantee for having excellent airline pilots. In this connection selection is the basic element combined with which qualified training can lead to a successful proficiency standard.

There are several ways of improving the quality of selection systems, e.g., development of reliable methods (Goeters et al., 1993), or validity studies (Hörmann & Maschke, 1996). An important precondition for the application of suitable selection methods is the definition of the job requirements. These requirements are by no means invariable. They can change depending on the technical and environmental conditions of the job. Moreover we cannot definitely assume that there is only one requirement-profile for airline pilots, since there might be different job demands for captains, first officers, etc. Considering the dramatic changes in flight guidance technologies the question is even more interesting as to how the increasing computerisation of cockpit systems changes the requirements. All these issues call for a review of the basic personal capabilities needed by airline pilots.

## Method

### Instrument

The method used was the Job Analysis Survey F-JAS by Fleishman (1992). With the F-JAS, job holders are asked to rate their jobs on 7-point rating scales with respect to the level of the ability required. One main advantage of the Fleishman system is that it provides a list of tests to measure the identified abilities. Thus it is possible to transfer the results of the job analysis directly into assessment methods (Fleishman & Reilly, 1992). Although the F-JAS is a general method for analysing all kinds of jobs, particularly in aviation, experience with the application has been good (Eissfeldt, 1997).

The F-JAS consists of 72 behaviourally-anchored rating scales, mainly focusing on aptitudes, knowledge and skills. There are also nine interactive/ social scales, which were supplemented in our study by nine additional scales developed by the German Aerospace Center (DLR) in order to cover this area more comprehensively. This was done in order to take into account prior research indicating the importance of attitude and personality for a successful career of airline pilots (Chidester et al., 1991; Hörmann & Maschke, 1996). Five knowledge/skills scales were not used for this study, because they were obviously not related to the professional activities of an airline pilot, eg., "Typing". This was done in order to increase the acceptance of the survey by pilots. In the applied version the survey consisted of 76 scales: 21 cognitive, 10 psychomotor, 9 physical, 12 sensory, 18 interactive/social, and 6 knowledge/skills scales.

*Sample*

Participants in the study were 141 airline pilots of Lufthansa German Airlines (both captains and first officers on different types of jet aircraft). The mean age was 37 years (standard deviation 8.5 years), the average number of flight hours was 6900 in all, and on current type 2100 hours.

*Procedure*

The study was conducted by the German Aerospace Center (DLR). The modified version of the Fleishman Survey was administered to the sample of 141 airline pilots of Lufthansa German Airlines in fleet meetings. This guaranteed standardised instruction and application. Moreover this meant a somewhat randomised sample, because the meetings were arranged according to the availability within the airline operation. None of the participants refused to fill in the questionnaire. F-JAS data were collected anonymously in two steps. In a first step the pilots were asked to rate the required level of a particular factor for airline pilots in *general*. In a second step they were asked to rate the level of each factor required for their *specific* position and aircraft type (e.g., as a first officer on A320). This was done to focus attention on the specific requirements related to different cockpit positions and aircraft types.

## Results

*General ratings.* Regarding the general ratings, differences concerning cockpit positions and type of aircraft were mainly insignificant. Therefore the ratings of the 141 pilots could be analysed together.

As the Fleishman system consists of 7-point rating scales (scale-mean = 4) and the ratings scores in our study were distributed with a standard deviation of about 1, abilities rated with a mean of more than 5 were interpreted as "important" and those with a mean of more than 6 were interpreted as "very important", as they clearly exceed the scale average.

Table 1.1 shows the results of the general ratings in order of importance. Time sharing and spatial orientation (cognitive abilities), rate control (psychomotor abilities), map reading (knowledge/skills scales), and stress resistance, cooperation, and communication (interactive/social scales) received the highest ratings (mean > 6). Most of the scales rated as important (> 5) were cognitive, psychomotor and sensory abilities as well as interactive/ social capabilities. The majority of the knowledge/skills and all physical abilities were rated as less important for the job.

*Specific ratings.* The specific ratings were evaluated regarding the cockpit position (first officer/captain) and the degree of computerisation (high/low). Senior first officers were included in the group of first officers. As Lufthansa maintains a modern fleet and does not operate real conventional aircraft, we differentiated between a low degree of computerisation (eg., B747-200) and highly computerised cockpits (e.g., A320). Four pilots could not be included in the evaluation concerning the degree of computerisation, since they had two ratings on different types.

Table 1.2 (left column) shows the differences between specific mean ratings of the captains and the first officers. Only significant differences in those scales which were rated as at least important (> 5) in the general ratings (altogether 42 scales, see Table 1.1) are presented.

Only in 10 out of these 42 scales were significant differences regarding the cockpit position observed in the specific ratings; in 32 scales the differences were not significant. All significant differences showed higher ratings for captains than for first officers. The highest difference in mean ratings between captains and first officers was found in the interactive/social scale "Leadership", which clearly reflects the differences in responsibility of both positions.

3

## Table 1.1
## Job analysis of airline pilots: Factors rated as very important (M>6) and important (M>5), N = 141 airline pilots

| Scale | Area | Mean Rating M |
|---|---|---|
| Map Reading | Knowledge/Skills | 6.38 |
| Stress Resistance | Interactive/Social | 6.36 |
| Cooperation | Interactive/Social | 6.30 |
| Communication | Interactive/Social | 6.28 |
| Time Sharing | Cognitive | 6.23 |
| Decision Making | Interactive/Social | 6.20 |
| Spatial Orientation | Cognitive | 6.13 |
| Rate Control | Psychomotor | 6.09 |
| Leadership | Interactive/Social | 5.94 |
| Situational Awareness | Interactive/Social | 5.94 |
| Self Awareness | Interactive/Social | 5.86 |
| Resistance to Premature Judgment | Interactive/Social | 5.85 |
| Behavior Flexibility | Interactive/Social | 5.79 |
| Problem Sensitivity | Cognitive | 5.75 |
| Control Precision | Psychomotor | 5.71 |
| Resilience | Interactive/Social | 5.69 |
| Speed of Closure | Cognitive | 5.67 |
| Selective Attention | Cognitive | 5.66 |
| Response Orientation | Psychomotor | 5.66 |
| Auditory Attention | Sensory | 5.63 |
| Speech Recognition | Sensory | 5.58 |
| Assertiveness | Interactive/Social | 5.52 |
| Multilimb Coordination | Psychomotor | 5.50 |
| Flexibility of Closure | Cognitive | 5.38 |
| Perceptual Speed | Cognitive | 5.34 |
| Night Vision | Sensory | 5.34 |
| Motivation | Interactive/Social | 5.33 |
| Far Vision | Sensory | 5.32 |
| Number Facility | Cognitive | 5.31 |
| Glare Sensitivity | Sensory | 5.29 |
| Reaction Time | Psychomotor | 5.28 |
| Written Comprehension | Cognitive | 5.27 |
| Social Sensitivity | Interactive/Social | 5.26 |
| Depth Perception | Sensory | 5.23 |
| Reading Plans | Knowledge/Skills | 5.22 |
| Peripheral Vision | Sensory | 5.21 |
| Oral Fact Finding | Interactive/Social | 5.19 |
| Information Ordering | Cognitive | 5.19 |
| Memorization | Cognitive | 5.10 |
| Visualization | Cognitive | 5.09 |
| Deductive Reasoning | Cognitive | 5.09 |
| Oral Defense | Interactive/Social | 5.05 |

## Table 1.2
**Differences in specific ratings regarding cockpit position and level of computerisation (only in scales rated as generally important)**

| Scale | Area | Significant Mean Scale Differences (p < .05) | |
|---|---|---|---|
| | | Cockpit Position Capt n=49, FO n=92 | Computerisation High n=62, Low n=75 |
| Map Reading | Knowledge/Skills | .31 | n.s. |
| Stress Resistance | Interactive/Social | n.s. | n.s. |
| Cooperation | Interactive/Social | n.s. | n.s. |
| Communication | Interactive/Social | n.s. | n.s. |
| Time Sharing | Cognitive | n.s. | n.s. |
| Decision Making | Interactive/Social | .34 | n.s. |
| Spatial Orientation | Cognitive | n.s. | n.s. |
| Rate Control | Psychomotor | n.s. | n.s. |
| Leadership | Interactive/Social | 1.12 | n.s. |
| Situational Awareness | Interactive/Social | n.s. | n.s. |
| Self Awareness | Interactive/Social | n.s. | n.s. |
| Resistance to Premature Judgment | Interactive/Social | .41 | n.s. |
| Behavior Flexibility | Interactive/Social | n.s. | n.s. |
| Problem Sensitivity | Cognitive | n.s. | n.s. |
| Control Precision | Psychomotor | n.s. | n.s. |
| Resilience | Interactive/Social | n.s. | n.s. |
| Speed of Closure | Cognitive | n.s. | n.s. |
| Selective Attention | Cognitive | n.s. | n.s. |
| Response Orientation | Psychomotor | .50 | n.s. |
| Auditory Attention | Sensory | n.s. | n.s. |
| Speech Recognition | Sensory | .34 | n.s. |
| Assertiveness | Interactive/Social | n.s. | n.s. |
| Multilimb Coordination | Psychomotor | n.s. | n.s. |
| Flexibility of Closure | Cognitive | n.s. | n.s. |
| Perceptual Speed | Cognitive | n.s. | n.s. |
| Night Vision | Sensory | n.s. | n.s. |
| Motivation | Interactive/Social | n.s. | n.s. |
| Far Vision | Sensory | n.s. | n.s. |
| Number Facility | Cognitive | n.s. | n.s. |
| Glare Sensitivity | Sensory | n.s. | n.s. |
| Reaction Time | Psychomotor | .51 | n.s. |
| Written Comprehension | Cognitive | .46 | n.s. |
| Social Sensitivity | Interactive/Social | .59 | n.s. |
| Depth Perception | Sensory | n.s. | n.s. |
| Reading Plans | Knowledge/Skills | n.s. | n.s. |
| Peripheral Vision | Sensory | n.s. | n.s. |
| Oral Fact Finding | Interactive/Social | n.s. | n.s. |
| Information Ordering | Cognitive | n.s. | n.s. |
| Memorization | Cognitive | n.s. | n.s. |
| Visualization | Cognitive | n.s. | n.s. |
| Deductive Reasoning | Cognitive | .36 | n.s. |
| Oral Defense | Interactive/Social | n.s. | n.s. |

5

In regard to level of computerisation, Table 1.2 (right column) shows no significant differences were observed in the scales generally rated as important. Only in scales with a mean general rating of the required level of less than 5, and therefore not given in Table 1.2, were some differences statistically significant. Pilots working in highly computerised cockpits rated finger dexterity, persistance, manual dexterity, visual color discrimination, sound localisation, and electrical knowledge as more important and static strength as less important than pilots working in cockpits with a lower level of computerisation.

## Discussion

Which conclusions should be drawn for airline pilot selection? The results of the general ratings emphasise the importance of most of the classical pilot selection criteria, especially regarding cognitive and psychomotor factors. Nevertheless some traditional criteria were rated surprisingly low, e.g., mathematical reasoning, electrical and mechanical knowledge.

Besides the traditional aptitude factors, the results underline the importance of personality factors for a successful career as an airline pilot. Nowadays working as an airline pilot means not only being a manager of the technical systems, but also being integrated in a complex interaction of different crew members. Considering this, it is surprising that airline pilot selection is often still focussed only on individual aptitudes, whereas personality evaluation is still under-represented in most current selection systems. A lack of suitable personality methods may be a reason for this. More activity should be carried out to develop reliable and valid personality assessment instruments (Goeters et al., 1993; Hörmann et al., 1997).

The results of the *specific* ratings concerning the cockpit position are not of particular relevance with regard to selection, not only because few significant differences between captains and first officers were found, but also because major airlines do not look for applicants who will always fly as first officers. Normally an airline wants a first officer to fulfil all necessary requirements for being upgraded to a captain when appropriately experienced. Nevertheless the results for cockpit position are interesting as to the specific tasks within the cockpit crew. The requirements needed for being a successful first officer are in most cases not significantly different from those of captains. First officers perform an important function within the cockpit crew with a high level of responsibility. Therefore the similarity between the ratings of captains and first officers may also be a result of progressive CCC and CRM philosophies in the airline.

The specific results due to computerisation are even more surprising, since no significant differences in the important factors were found between less and highly computerised cockpits. In particular there appears to be no general reduction of the level of demands due to computerisation. On the contrary, if at all, there is a trend towards slightly higher requirements in highly computerised cockpits. Altogether the consequences of cockpit-computerisation for job requirements should not be overestimated. This result is very important with regard to selection, because the selection decision should normally be valid for the whole of the pilot's career, which usually covers some decades. Although there is no garantee for stable demands in the long run, there is hope that the basic requirements in modern airline pilot selection will not dramatically change in the near future.

## References

Chidester, T.R., Helmreich, R.L., Gregorich, S.E. & Geis, C.E. (1991). Pilot personality and crew coordination: Implications for training and selection. *The International Journal of Aviation Psychology, 1*, 25-44.

Eissfeldt, H. (1997). Ability requirements for different ATC positions. In *Proceedings of The Ninth International Symposium on Aviation Psychology*, Columbus, Ohio.

Fleishman, E.A. (1992). *The Fleishman Job Analysis Survey (F-JAS)*. Palo Alto: Consulting Psychologists Press, Inc.

Fleishman, E.A. & Reilly, M.E. (1992). *Handbook of human abilities. Definitions, measurements, and job task requirements*. Palo Alto: Consulting Psychologists Press, Inc.

Goeters, K-M., Timmermann, B. & Maschke, P. (1993). The construction of personality questionnaires for selection of aviation personnel. *The International Journal of Aviation Psychology, 3*, 123-141.

Hörmann, H-J. & Maschke, P. (1996). On the relation between personality and job performance of airline pilots. *The International Journal of Aviation Psychology, 6,* 171-178.

Hörmann, H-J., Manzey, D., Maschke, P. & Pecena, Y. (1997). Behavior-oriented assessment of interpersonal skills in pilot selection: Concepts, methods, and empirical findings. In *Proceedings of The Ninth International Symposium on Aviation Psychology*, Columbus, Ohio.

# 2 Pilot selection: Getting more bang for the buck

*Eugene Burke, People Technologies, UK*
*Alan Kitching and Colin Valsler, Psytech Ltd., UK*

## Introduction

Although the business of pilot selection has been going for several decades now, it is only since the early 1990s that a clearer picture of what constitutes a valid pilot selection process has begun to emerge (Burke, 1995a and 1995b). This is due to three significant advances in recent years: a clearer understanding of the links between cognitive abilities, personality and work behaviours; a clearer picture of the validity of various pilot selection measures; and the advances in human assessment technology facilitated by the development of computer based assessment (CBA) methods. The purpose of this paper is to describe recent results from one line of research and development (R&D) that has sought to capitalise on these three advances; namely, the development of the **PIL**ot **AP**titude Tester or **PILAPT** system (Burke, 1996a & 1996b; Burke, Kitching & Valsler, 1995, 1997).

The most significant feature of this programme is the explicit use of a *confirmatory* rather than *exploratory* approach to constructing predictors of pilot training and job performance. An exploratory approach is essentially a *look-see* approach in which tests or other measures are loaded into a R&D programme on a *good-idea-at-the-time* basis. Subsequent analysis of the relationship between these measures and outcomes in training tends to rely on a *hope-for-the-best* philosophy. While such a characterisation may appear to do an injustice to the intent of many past pilot selection R&D programmes, Hunter and Burke (1994, 1995) have commented that this approach to R&D has tended to be the case in the history of pilot selection.

How does a confirmatory approach differ from an exploratory one? Essentially it does so by planning out R&D with very clear research pursued within a clear structure for defining what is to be measured, how

9

such measures are to be constructed, and the types of data required to demonstrate whether R&D objectives have been met. This has been possible within the PILAPT programme given the knowledge we have now of those domains that are consistent in predicting pilot training success (Hunter and Burke, 1994, 1995), and the development of CBA technologies for both constructing and administering pilot aptitude measures (Burke, 1987, 1992, 1993, 1997a; Burke, Kitching & Valsler, 1995; Burke, Kokorian, Lescreve, Martin, Van Raay & Weber, 1995). Building on the meta-analysis results reported by Hunter and Burke and combining these with taxonomies of human performance, it is possible to clearly identify domains with higher probabilities of pay-off for use in pilot selection.

Having specified these domains, the next step is to design CBA tools for constructing the relevant measures within those domains. In the PILAPT programme, this process can be accomplished through computer-based test generation software. A clear model for the test is first specified by the test author and then represented within the test generation software. In human factors parlance, the knowledge of the author is elicited and then engineered into the software. The vagaries of individual item writers are then engineered out since the software takes over control of the production of the test (see Burke, Kitching & Valsler, 1995, for an example of how this approach was applied to developing the PILAPT information processing test Hands). Again, test generation software provides a clear example of a confirmatory approach to constructing valid pilot selection measures.

The PILAPT design cycle described by Burke (1996b) takes the following steps:
- Specification of Key Domains of Pilot Aptitude (Step 1)
- Construction of Test Design and Generation Tools (Step 2)
- Design of CBA Systems (Step 3)
- Evaluation of R&D Objectives (Step 4)

The first three of these steps are described in more detail elsewhere (Burke, 1996a, 1996b; Burke, Kitching & Valsler, 1995). Results obtained from two recent studies involving the PILAPT tests will be described next to provide evidence of the extent to which the PILAPT design philosophy has achieved its objectives to date.

**The proof of the pudding**

In 1995, the first large field trials of PILAPT tests were undertaken by the Royal Air Force (RAF) University Air Squadron (UAS) organisation. The UAS provides facilities for those attending UK universities who express an interest in a military aviation career. These include a fixed wing training course similar to that for a private pilot license (PPL). Prior to these trials, those wishing to enter the UAS were screened via a structured interview modelled on the interview used for RAF officer entry.

Given that no aptitude tests were then in use and that large numbers apply to join the UAS, the UAS trials provided a unique opportunity for gathering validity data on flying training cadets. The UAS trials were undertaken between August and October 1995 involving real applicants, although the PILAPT scores were not used in UAS selection decisions. Distributed test stations were established around the UK by installing PILAPT systems on UAS personal computer platforms equipped with standardised interfaces and response peripherals. Three of the PILAPT tests were selected by the UAS for the trials. These tests are:

- **Deviation Indicator (DI)** which is a compensatory tracking task requiring the candidate to keep a horizontal and a vertical line simultaneously centred on the screen using a joystick. The candidate is given two practice trials with feedback prior to a scored run of the task. The format of the test is modelled on the flight path deviation indicator cockpit instrument.

- **Trax** which is a pursuit tracking task requiring the candidate to cope with changes in three-dimensional dynamics much as in real flight. As per DI, the candidate is given two familiarisation runs with performance feedback to facilitate task learning prior to a third scored flight.

- **Hands** which presents the candidate with audio messages via headphones giving a required search sequence. After a short delay, images are presented and the candidate has to state within a timed response window how many of the images meet the audio search message presented earlier. This test was designed to measure information processing capacity and is scored in terms of speed and accuracy of responses.

More recently, a fourth test **Patterns** has been added to PILAPT which combines measures of perceptual closure (identified by CRM researchers as a factor related to situational awareness) with speed and accuracy. This is a short test of ten complex items that have to be completed under strict time constraints. Given that it was still in development, this test was not included in the original UAS trials, but has been researched through development for the Royal Norwegian Air Force (RNoAF) and for United Kingdom air training schools.

## Reliability

One of the standard quality checks of the psychometric properties of any test is the reliability of the test scores. Reliability indices provide a coefficient which estimates the amount of variation in test scores that can be attributed to true measurement as opposed to error either in test design or test administration. As such, reliability data also provide evidence against which the output of test generation software can be judged. Where a test generated by such software displays high reliability (approaching a maximum of +1.0), then support is given for the consistency of the test generation programme in producing the test. Two reliability indices will be reviewed from the UAS data. The first , which is referred to as the test-retest or stability coefficient, is obtained by administering a test twice to the same person, preferably with several weeks between administrations. This coefficient tells us how stable the ranking of people from highest to lowest scores is over time. This type of coefficient can be used with most types of test, but is particularly suitable for tests such as DI and Trax which involve dynamic tasks rather than discrete items presented independently.

Subsequent to selections into UAS squadrons and following a four month period following entry, 109 UAS cadets were retested at six UAS sites. The stability coefficients obtained for the DI and Trax tests were 0.803 and 0.837 respectively, while the retest reliability for Hands was 0.766, which compare favourably with retest reliabilities reported for UK and US psychomotor tests which tend to fall in the 0.60 to 0.70 ranges (Burke & Van Raay, 1993). It is also worth noting that the second administration of the tests took place after the cadets who participated had undergone several hours of flying instruction, suggesting that the differences between cadets test scores are relatively robust to such training, a point that will be taken up later in relation to selecting self-sponsored candidates for CPL and type training. As will also be described below, the three PILAPT tests have been combined into an overall aptitude score referred to as UAS. The retest reliability for this composite score was 0.905.

Given that Hands is a discrete item test, another measure of reliability can be applied. The internal consistency coefficient estimates the extent to which questions or items in a test contribute consistently to variation in people's overall scores on a test. Two estimates of internal consistency were calculated from data obtained on 585 UAS applicants. One approach taken was to split the test into odd and even items and create two sub-tests from these groupings of items. These two parts were then correlated and the Spearman-Brown Split-Half correction applied. As mentioned above, Hands generates scores for speed (time taken from presentation of the visual image to response) and accuracy (whether the response is accurate or not) which are combined into an overall speed accuracy score. The internal consistency coefficients for these three scores have all been found to exceed 0.9 for UAS applicants (N = 585) and for Norwegian fast-jet applicants (N = 210), both representing ab initio applicant pools, but also for UK self-sponsored pilot applicants holding both PPLs and CPLs (N = 107).

Similar analyses of Patterns for UK non ab initio and Norwegian fast-jet applicant samples have shown this short test to yield internal consistency reliabilities of 0.7.

## Construct validity

Another source of evidence on the validity of a test is it's correlation with other tests having known predictive validity. Data of this type were made available through the RNoAF study. Included in this study are five tests taken from the RAF aircrew battery which have shown consistent validity in predicting pilot training success (Burke, Bradshaw & Hobson, 1994; Burke, Hobson & Linsky, 1997; Hobson & Burke, 1993). The RAF battery comprises two psychomotor tasks, an aircraft instrument comprehension test and two information processing tests (one a continuous vigilance task and the other a short-term memory digit recall task). Both RAF and PILAPT test instructions have been translated into Norwegian and are administered at the RNoAF's aircrew selection centre at Varnes using a networked system of 12 personal computers. Two sets of regression analyses were conducted between the two test batteries for a sample of 382 applicants: Regression A = the RAF composite score on the four PILAPT tests (administration time 40 minutes); Regression B = the PILAPT composite on the five RAF tests (administration time 60 minutes plus). The Multiple Rs obtained were 0.882 (78% of the variance in the RAF composite explained) for Regression A, and 0.699 (49% of the variance in the PILAPT composite explained) for Regression B. While these results clearly show that PILAPT is strongly correlated with an older test battery with established validity, it also shows that PILAPT is a better predictor of the RAF score that the other way round. Why? The answer lies in the aviation psychology (knowledge of pilot aptitude domains and their respective validities) and the design technology (item generation and control software) underpinning the PILAPT tests, and again provides supporting evidence that PILAPT R&D is meeting its quality assurance targets.

13

## Predictive validity

The evidence that most people are interested in is whether a test actually predicts training or job performance. Since 1995, those entering the UAS as cadets and undertaking flying training have been followed up. Cadet performance on each stage of UAS flying training is assessed using a 1 (low) to 5 (high) grading scale. By the summer of 1996, data were available on the performance of 165 UAS cadets over their first six months of flying training. Each cadet's average training grade over all stages of training to this point was calculated and used as an initial criterion for evaluating the predictive validity of the three PILAPT tests. Correlations with this criterion were 0.457 for DI ($p < 0.001$), 0.509 for Trax ($p < 0.001$) and 0.255 for Hands ($p < 0.001$). Regression analysis suggests that, despite the lower correlation between Hands and training performance, a best fit prediction equation can be formed by giving standardised scores on all three tests equal (unit) weight. This is supported by comparing the Multiple R of 0.564 obtained from regression weights with the correlation of 0.548 obtained by simply summing the standardised scores on the three tests. Furthermore, despite what might appear a modest validation sample of 165, the statistical power or expected reproducibility of this validity estimate is extremely high at over 100% for a one-tailed test of significance at 0.01 (Cohen, 1977).

Some commentators have suggested that there is something amiss with pilot aptitude tests given their low validities (e.g., Damos, 1995). Indeed, in their meta-analytic review of pilot test validities, Hunter and Burke did find a trend over recent decades such that validities appeared to be in decline. Hunter and Burke gave various suggestions for this trend, one of which was increasingly small percentages of pilot applicants being selected resulting in statistical reductions in validities due to range restriction (see Thorndike, 1949, for a fuller discussion of this effect). More recently, Burke, Hobson and Linsky (1997) have shown the impact of range restriction on observed validities calculated directly from data on highly selected pilot trainees. The data presented here for the PILAPT tests were relatively free of any such effects and therefore provide a purer set of validity estimates than is commonly possible in pilot selection research. Indeed, given that the composite validity of 0.548 is considerably higher than the validities reported by Hunter and Burke, and given that Hunter and Burke point out that their data were subject to a number of statistical artifacts that they were unable to include in their analysis, the PILAPT data suggest that Hunter and Burke's results may substantially underestimate the true validity of pilot selection tests.

Figure 2.1 provides a graphical summary of the strength of the PILAPT prediction of flying training success. This is a box plot that shows the mean and range of flying performance ratings for each of five aptitude bands based on the PILAPT composite score (1 = low and 5 = high). UAS headquarters also requested an analysis using a flying grade of 3 as a criterion marker. Figure 2.2 shows the percentages within each aptitude band which met that requirement.

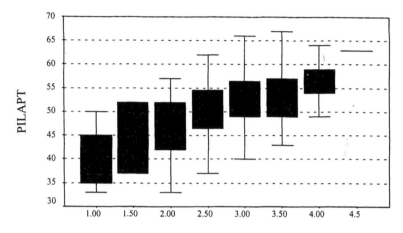

Flying Training Rating

**Figure 2.1 - PILAPT by flying grade**

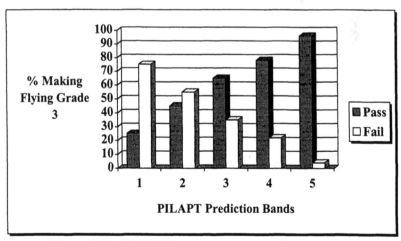

**Figure 2.2 - PILAPT by percentage meeting the grade**

## Robustness of PILAPT predictions

One common concern throughout the military and civilian aviation worlds is the security of pilot selection tests and the extent to which their validity may be compromised by applicants having had prior practice with them. Burke (1997b) has shown that the simple experience of taking a test once before does result in substantial gains in test scores which persist for five years or more. Data on the extent to which such practice influences the predictive validity of tests, particularly the effect on pilot selection tests, are rare.

Such data were however obtained through the UAS retest study described above. Of the 109 UAS cadets retested in 1996, complete training performance data were available for 79 cadets. Using norms taken from the sample of 585 UAS applicants, initial UAS and retest UAS score composites were computed.

The respective validities of these composites against flying training grades were 0.534 ($p < 0.001$) for initial scores and 0.454 ($p < 0.001$) for retest scores. While there is around a 0.08 difference in these validity estimates, statistical testing of this difference shows it to be non-significant (t-test for correlated samples = 0.987, df = 76, p = n.s.; Ferguson, 1976). As such, and bearing in mind that retesting was undertaken after cadets had received flying training, these data suggest that PILAPT predictions are robust to practice and gains in test scores (the average gain in the composite score was quite substantial at 8.55 T-score units or 0.855 of a standard deviation in line with Burke's 1997b findings).

## Results for non ab initio pilot applicants

Last year saw a series of applications of the PILAPT testing system in screening UK self-sponsored pilot candidates. One trend in the UK is the delegation of pilot selection to training schools for certain streams of applicants such as the self-sponsored route. Data thus far obtained on 132 such applicants shows that, while means are higher for this type of applicant when compared to ab initio applicants, there is still sufficient range in scores for the PILAPT tests to offer discrimination and validity. Indeed, as a form of quality check, the use of systems such as PILAPT go a long way to answering the question of what skills development has been achieved in the hours a self-sponsored candidate has spent in flying training thus far. Table 2.1 below provides some comparisons by ab initio and non ab initio training groups.

**Table 2.1**
**Comparisons between ab initio and non ab initio applicants**

|  | RAF UAS | RNoAF FJ | UK Self-sponsored |
|---|---|---|---|
| Trax | Mean 66.09<br>SD 41.31 | Mean 90.56<br>SD 31.80 | Mean 96.71<br>SD 41.49 |
| DI | Mean 37.59<br>SD 10.73 | Mean 59.29<br>SD 12.44 | Mean 50.89<br>SD 10.78 |
| Hands | Mean 7666.19<br>SD 2713.83 | Mean 7836.96<br>SD 2357.53 | Mean 8511.58<br>SD 2841.06 |
| Patterns |  | Mean 214.66<br>SD 122.24 | Mean 268.07<br>SD 137.02 |

## Full CBA and more general apects of pilot applicant assessment

The validity of a test is not merely a matter of research evidence and depends on how test scores are used in making selection decisions. Such decisions often involve integrating test scores with other information regarding an applicant's suitability. However, when applicant volume is high or a selector's time is both precious and expensive, there is a clear need to support the valid use of test scores. This is possible through CBA with the provision of on-line diagnostic and decision aids for use by selectors once test administration and scoring have been completed (Burke, 1997a). Accessed through a Windows dialogue box that permits the selector to move from one applicant's scores to the next using the up and down arrow keys, an instant snapshot of the applicant's performance on the tests is provided. Scores are coded into levels of training risk for each test, with a short narrative report emphasising the overall level of training risk associated with that pattern of scores. A graphical summary enables the selector to evaluate in more detail relative strengths and weaknesses as indicated by scores on specific tests, and, accessed through a desktop computer, this applicant profiler can be used on-line to guide selection decisions and provide feedback to an individual applicant.

As such, the strength of a CBA system such as PILAPT is that, in addition to greater control over the generation and administration of tests, it can serve to guide test users in the interpretation and use of test scores in selection decisions. As suggested at the outset of this paper, it may well be that, rather than the validity of pilot selection tests being put into doubt, it is only now as our knowledge and technological capabilities mature that the full value of tests for selecting pilots and other aviation personnel will be better understood.

17

## References

Burke, E. (1987). *Current trends in pilot selection: Introduction and examples from current RAF research* Proceedings of the 29th Annual Conference of the Military Testing Association. Ottawa: Directorate of Military Occupational Structures and Directorate of Personnel Selection, Research and Second Careers.

Burke, E. (1992). *On the validation of rather a lot of computerised tests.* Paper presented at the British Psychological Society Annual Conference, April, Scarborough.

Burke, E. (1993). *Pilot selection in NATO: An overview.* Proceedings of the 7th. International Symposium on Aviation Psychology. Columbus, OH: Ohio State University.

Burke, E. (1995a). *Pilot selection I: The state of play.* Proceedings of the 8th International Symposium on Aviation Psychology. Columbus, OH: Ohio State University.

Burke, E. (1995b). *Pilot Selection II: Where do we go from here?* Proceedings of the 8th International Symposium on Aviation Psychology. Columbus, OH: Ohio State University.

Burke, E. (1996a). *Pilot selection: Where do we go from here?* Proceedings of the 7th. International Training Equipment Conference (ITEC), The Hague, Netherlands. Warminster: ITEC Ltd.

Burke, E. (1996b). *The power of contemporary pilot selection.* Paper present at the Four Forces Symposium on Pilot Selection and Training, London, September.

Burke, E. (1997a). *Computer-based assessment: Old chestnuts and new thorns.* Proceedings of the British Psychological Society Occupational Psychology Conference, 1997. Leicester: British Psychology Society.

Burke, E. (1997b). A short note on the persistence of retest effects on aptitude scores. *Journal of Occupational and Organizational Psychology, 70,* 295-301.

Burke, E., Bradshaw, J., & Hobson, C. (1994). *Designing and implementing a large scale computer-based testing system.* Paper presented at the British Psychological Society 1994 Occupational Psychology Conference, Birmingham, January.

Burke, E., Hobson, C., & Linsky, C. (1997). Large sample validations of three general predictors of pilot training success. *International Journal of Aviation Psychology, 7*, 225-234.

Burke, E., Kitching, A., & Valsler, C. (1995). Computer-based assessment and the construction of valid aviator selection tests. In N. Johnston, R. Fuller, & N. McDonald (Eds.) *Aviation psychology: Training and selection*. Aldershot: Avebury Aviation.

Burke, E. Kitching, A., & Valsler, C. (1997). *The Pilot Aptitude Tester (PILAPT): On the development and validation of a new computer-based test battery for selecting pilots*. Proceedings of the 7th International Symposium on Aviation Psychology. Columbus, OH: Ohio State University.

Burke, E., Kokorian, A., Lescreve, F., Martin, C.J., Van Raay, P., & Weber, W. (1995). Computer-based assessment: A NATO survey. *International Journal of Selection and Assessment, 3*, 75-83.

Burke, E., & Van Raay, P. (1993). *Computer-based assessment in NATO: Final report of Research Study Group 15*. Brussels, NATO Headquarters: AC/243 (Panel 8) TR/12.

Cohen, J. (1977). Statistical power analysis for the behavioral sciences. New York: Academic Press.

Dwyer, J.H. (1983). *Statistical models for the social and behavioural Sciences*. Oxford: Oxford University Press.

Damos, D. (1995). Pilot selection batteries: A critical examination. In N. Johnston, R. Fuller, & N. McDonald (Eds.) *Aviation psychology: Training and selection*. Aldershot: Avebury Aviation.

Dillon, W.R., & Goldstein, M. (1984). *Multivariate statistics: Methods and applications*. New York: John Wiley & Sons.

Ferguson, G.A. (1976). *Statistical analysis in psychology and education (4th Edition)*. Tokyo: McGraw-Hill Kogakusha.

Hobson, C., & Burke, E. (1993). *Pilot test battery: Validation study*. London, UK Ministry of Defence: Directorate of Science (Air) Report No. 15/93.

Hunter, D.R., & Burke, E. (1995). *Handbook of pilot selection*. Aldershot: Avebury Aviation.

Hunter, D.R., & Burke, E. (1994). Predicting aircraft pilot training success: A meta-analysis of published research. *International Journal of Aviation Psychology*, *4*, 297-313.

Jackson, D.N. (1967). *Personality Research Form Manual*. Port Huron, Mich.: Research Psychologists Press.

Thorndike, R.L. (1949). *Personnel selection: Test and measurement Techniques*. New York: John Wiley & Sons.

# 3   The DMT downunder: An Australian validation of the Defence Mechanism Test

*Andrew R. Lowe*
*William M. Mercer Cullen Egan Dell* [1]

## Introduction

In 1986 a research project was implemented in the Royal Australian Air Force (RAAF) to investigate the potential utility of the Defence Mechanism Test (DMT) for pilot selection in the Australian military forces. Further information on the DMT project methodology, and preliminary results showing the relationship between DMT scores and performance in *ab initio* flying training, are provided in Lowe, Hayward, and Neuman (1989).

This paper reports a second stage of the DMT validation study, which evaluated the relationship between DMT scores and the operational performance of pilots who graduated from training. It was predicted that personality measures would be associated with incidents attributed to pilot actions, but not with incidents attributed to external influences (environmental conditions or mechanical failure). The possible influence of individual differences in flying ability was controlled for, by comparing incident rates for pilots with different tested aptitude. Background to this phase of the project and preliminary findings have been reported previously (Lowe, 1989: Lowe & Hayward, 1990).

The research reported here is derived from the author's Doctoral thesis on the relationship between a range of ability, aptitude and personality measures and the performance of Australian military pilots in initial training and in subsequent operational flying (Lowe, 1996).

[1] At the time the research for this paper was undertaken the author was employed by the Department of Defence as Senior Psychologist, Royal Australian Air Force Headquarters Training Command, Melbourne.

## The DMT and pilot performance

The Defence Mechanism Test (DMT) is a projective personality test developed in Sweden over thirty years ago (Kragh, 1955; 1960), and subsequently adapted for pilot selection in the Royal Swedish Air Force (RSwAF) by Neuman (1971, 1978). In this test, stimulus pictures depicting for example, a "hero" figure being threatened by an older person, are shown tachistoscopically at varying exposure times. The respondent reports and sketches their perception of each picture. The theory of perceptual defence suggests that perceptions will be modified in the unconscious to reduce anxiety provoked by the stimulus. Differences between each stimulus and the subject's reports are coded according to psychoanalytic theory, to produce measures of personality defensiveness. The DMT also draws on percept-genetic theory to propose that the *series* of test presentations reveals the developing percept, and thus exposes information about important historical life events. Further information on the theory underlying the DMT is provided by Kragh and Smith (1970).

Although the DMT has seen broad application in experimental psychology and clinical practice (see Lowe, Hayward, & Neuman, 1989, for a review), its major application has been in military pilot selection (Neuman, 1982). The hypothesis is that operators in high risk, high threat environments like military flying must maintain an accurate perception of reality. Those affected by personality defences in response to anxiety provoking situations are posited to be less likely to cope with the demands of training, and to perform less capably in operational flying (Cooper, 1988a; Vaernes, 1982). Neuman (1971, 1978) demonstrated the predictive validity of the DMT in the RSwAF, where it contributed to a reduction in training failure rate from over 60% in the early 1970s, to less than 40% in the 1980s (Carlstedt, 1981) and subsequently to below 10% (Neuman, 1986; Sandahl, 1988).

The DMT has been applied with similar success in the Air Forces of Norway (Torjussen, 1987; Martinussen & Torjussen, 1993); Denmark (Termohlen, 1981; Byrdorf, 1987); and Greece. A Royal Air Force (RAF) evaluation (Stoker, 1982) did not support the validity of the DMT, possibly attributable to methodological differences in the testing procedure (Cooper, 1988b). This finding was contradicted by Cooper and Kline's (1989) study of RAF aircrew, using an "objective" system to score the DMT (based on G-analysis). They reported a significant difference ($p < .05$) on mean DMT factor loadings between pilot trainees who passed and those who failed.

In the RAAF trial of the DMT, over 500 pilot trainees were tested between 1985 and 1989 (see Hayward & Lowe, 1988 for an overview of the project). Initial results were positive (Lowe, Hayward, & Neuman, 1989), suggesting potential cost saving if the DMT were introduced at selection (Lowe, 1990b). Subsequent analysis of a further sample failed to reproduce significance differences in pass rate across DMT values (Lowe & Hayward, 1990). The scoring system was revalidated using the test scores and training results of the first 400 pilots tested (all previous protocols had been scored using normative data from the RSwAF), and the revalidated system applied to a further sample of 105 pilot trainees. Comparison of pass rates for different DMT scores revealed a pass rate of 44% for trainees with a "low" DMT score, and 70% for those with a "good" score, $\chi2$ $(1, N = 105) = 6.96$, $p < .01$ (Lowe, 1994). DMT scores in combination with the RAAF Pilot Index (an aptitude stanine) showed a capacity to differentiate trainee groups with graduation rates of 40% at one extreme, to 75% at the other (Table 3.1). Aptitude and personality measures in unison offered the best prospects of accounting for pilot training results in this study.

**Table 3.1**

**Pass rates on RAAF pilot course for combinations of high versus low Defence Mechanism Test (DMT) scores, and high versus low Pilot Index ($N$ = 105; from Lowe, 1994)**

|  |  | Pilot Index | |
| --- | --- | --- | --- |
|  |  | 4 - 7 (Low) | 8 - 9 (High) |
| DMT score | 1 - 5 (Low or "poor") | Pass rate 40% (failed 12) (passed 8) | Pass rate 47% (failed 10) (passed 9) |
|  | 6 - 9 (High or "Good") | Pass rate 65% (failed 12) (passed 22) | Pass rate 75% (failed 8) (passed 24) |

Lowe (1996) explored two analytical approaches to investigate the relationship between predictor variables (aptitude, personality) and incident involvement. In the first, two criterion groups were defined for each incident category: pilots not involved in an incident, the *incident-free* group, and pilots involved in one or more incidents, the *incident-involved* group. Group means on numerous aptitude and personality measures were examined for significant difference using the *t* test procedure for independent samples. This methodology followed that of Alkov and Borowsky (1980) where accident and non-accident involved pilots were compared (retrospectively) on selected biographical and personality dimensions.

These incident-free and incident-involved group comparisons made no distinction between pilots involved in one incident, and those involved in many. The accident-proneness hypothesis suggests that some pilots are likely to be involved in repeated incidents by virtue of fundamental personality dispositions, while others will remain relatively safe. Previous DMT research (Neuman, 1986; Lowe, 1989, 1990) supports this view, that pilots affected by extreme defence mechanisms are accident-prone, and more likely to be involved in multiple incidents or eventually a more serious accident. The present study tested the specific prediction that the incident rate for pilots with high or "good" DMT scores would be lower than for pilots diagnosed with a low or "bad" DMT score. Similar analyses of the incident rate across different scores on numerous other aptitude and personality variables found no meaningful differences (Lowe, 1996).

**Methodology**

*Subjects*

The subjects for this study were graduates from *ab initio* pilot training courses at the RAAF's No. 1 Flying Training School (1FTS), Point Cook, Victoria. RAAF Pilot Course students include direct entrants into the RAAF as aircrew (pilot) cadets, graduates of the Australian Defence Force Academy, or Royal Australian Navy (RAN) Officers and Midshipmen. Of the 505 pilots tested on the DMT between 1986 and 1991, 286 or 56.6% graduated on to operational conversion courses. These 286 pilots formed the sample for this study using the operational performance criterion of involvement in reported flying incidents.

*Measures*

Predictor scores were obtained through administration of the DMT by trained RAAF Psychologists using the standard individual testing approach developed in the Royal Swedish Air Force (Neuman, 1986). Test protocols were scored according to the system developed and validated on Swedish pilot samples. All protocols were scored "blind", without knowledge of training outcomes or other test data.

Criterion data came from Air Incident Reports submitted to the RAAF Directorate of Flying Safety (DFS) by aircrew to describe "events affecting the potential or actual safety of aircraft or personnel". Incidents are categorised by DFS according to type and cause. Five primary causal categories are used: *Human* ("*HUM*"), *Materiel* ("*MAT*"), *Environmental* ("*ENV*"), *Undetermined*, and *Under Investigation*. As in previous reports (Lowe, 1989, 1990), the latter two categories were combined into an *Other* classification ("OTH"). As *human* cause incidents are of cardinal interest, other incident types served as comparative criteria. Incident classifications were accepted as assigned by DFS, with the exception that *human* causes attributed to ground personnel or non-pilot crew members (and obviously therefore outside the pilot's control) were recoded as *Other*. Consistent with the principles of aircraft captain responsibility, some "errors" committed by a co-pilot are classified against the pilot in command.

The hypothesis that DMT scores would be associated with incident involvement was tested by calculating incident rates across nine levels of the DMT predictor as an independent variable, and comparing rates using one-way Analysis of Variance (ANOVA). This procedure was considered suitably robust, even though the incident data are not normally distributed.

## Results

Table 3.2 shows the breakdown of incident-involved and incident-free pilots for each incident type. *Human, Environmental* and *Other* cause incidents affected similar proportions of the pilot group. Around 60% of pilots had experienced no such incidents. Over 80% of the sample had experienced one or more *Materiel* failure incidents.

### Table 3.2
### Distribution of incident-involved and incident-free pilots for each incident type

| Incident Category | HUM f | HUM % | MAT f | MAT % | ENV f | ENV % | OTH f | OTH % |
|---|---|---|---|---|---|---|---|---|
| No incidents | 167 | 58.4 | 49 | 17.1 | 182 | 63.6 | 164 | 57.3 |
| Some incidents | 119 | 41.6 | 237 | 82.9 | 104 | 36.4 | 122 | 42.7 |
| Total | 286 | 100.0 | 286 | 100.0 | 286 | 100.0 | 286 | 100.0 |

Incident causes: HUM - Human; MAT - Materiel; ENV - Environmental; OTH - Other

The total number of pilots at each DMT level was divided by the total incident frequency for the group to produce the incident rate, which was converted to rate per hundred pilots. Table 3.3 shows the incident rates across nine DMT levels. Rates for Human, Environmental and other cause incidents are plotted for comparison in Figure 3.1.

### Table 3.3
### Incident rates at each DMT level on four incident categories

|  | DMT value | | | | | | | | | |
|---|---|---|---|---|---|---|---|---|---|---|
|  | 1 | 2 | 3 | 4 | 5 | 6 | 7 | 8 | 9 | Total |
| Pilot n | (22) | (20) | (28) | (24) | (50) | (33) | (26) | (15) | (5) | (223) |
| HUM freq | 19 | 24 | 24 | 17 | 38 | 27 | 16 | 8 | 1 | 174 |
| Rate[a] | 86 | 120 | 86 | 71 | 82 | 81 | 61 | 53 | 20 | 78 |
| MAT freq | 86 | 107 | 152 | 117 | 298 | 173 | 119 | 87 | 19 | 860 |
| Rate | 390 | 535 | 543 | 487 | 596 | 524 | 458 | 580 | 380 | 386 |
| ENV freq | 15 | 14 | 18 | 12 | 33 | 22 | 18 | 16 | 4 | 146 |
| Rate | 41 | 70 | 64 | 50 | 66 | 67 | 69 | 107 | 80 | 65 |
| OTH freq | 14 | 10 | 21 | 26 | 43 | 34 | 15 | 12 | 4 | 179 |
| Rate | 64 | 50 | 75 | 108 | 86 | 103 | 58 | 80 | 80 | 80 |

Incident causal classifications: HUM - Human; MAT - Materiel; ENV - Environmental; OTH - Other

[a] Rate = incidents per 100 pilots

As predicted, there is a clear trend indicating lower human cause incident rates at higher DMT values. Pilots with a DMT score of 7, 8 or 9 had a significantly higher human cause incident rate than pilots with a DMT score of 1, 2 or 3, $F(1, 114) = 3.97$, $p < .05$. The incident rate for these "poor prognosis" DMT pilots is 97 per hundred, approaching twice that of the "good prognosis" DMT group at 54 incidents per hundred pilots. Interestingly there is also a non-significant tendency for more Environmental cause accidents to be experienced and reported by pilots with higher DMT scores. This is consistent with the notion that lower personality defence allows greater situational awareness and attention, such that unusual environmental events might be perceived and interpreted correctly, and reported more frequently.

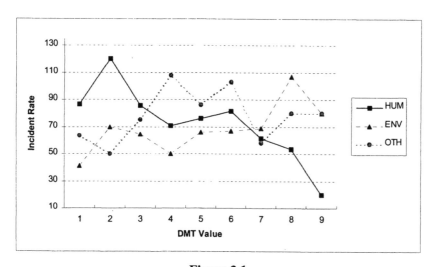

**Figure 3.1**
**Human, Environmental, and Other cause air incident rates at each DMT value**

A composite DMT score, "Accident Proneness" (AP), has been validated using actual air accident involvement of pilots in the RSwAF. Given the low frequency of incidents in this study involving pilots with high Accident Prone scores, the AP variable was collapsed into two categories: *not accident prone* (value of zero) and accident prone (*low* through to *extreme* accident proneness, values 1 to 6). Cross-tabulating this dichotomy with Human cause incident involvement showed a significant association between the DMT Accident Prone assessment and involvement in one of more human incidents, $\chi2 = 4.75$, $p < .03$ (Table 3.4). This relationship could be progressively confirmed as further incident data become available.

**Table 3.4**
**DMT Accident Proneness and involvement in Human cause incidents**

|  |  | Human Cause Incident Involvement | |
| --- | --- | --- | --- |
|  |  | None | Some |
| DMT Accident Prone Assessment | Not Accident Prone | 124 (62.6%) | 74 (37.4%) |
|  | Accident Prone | 43 (48.9%) | 45 (51.1%) |

$\chi2 = 4.75$, $df = 1$, $p < .03$

**Conclusion**

The essential goal of personality research in regard to aviation safety was summarised by Biesheuvel (1949) more than 45 years ago:

> The real touchstone of safe flying is not the ability to maintain an accident free record under normal conditions of flight, but at all times, and for an indefinite period. It is for this reason that personal attributes which increase or decrease the probability that a pilot will be equal to the demands which may be placed on him, cannot be ignored. (p. 27).

An extensive analysis of Australian military flying incidents (Lowe, 1996) showed no evidence that the aptitude measures which predict training outcome convey any influence into the sphere of operational pilot performance, measured by air incident involvement. In the same study, standard personality inventories showed no meaningful association with incident involvement, which might be predicted for example from individual stress-breakdown interpretations of accident predisposition (Chappelow, 1989; Green, 1985). The most likely explanation is that self-report personality inventories are ill-equipped in content and sensitivity to anticipate responses to life-threatening events which fortunately occur very infrequently during a non-combat flying career.

The global measure of personality quality obtained from the DMT was the only variable showing significant linear association with incident involvement in this sample of Australian military pilots. This finding is important from three perspectives. First, the observed empirical link between test behaviour and operational flying supports the theoretical contentions underlying the DMT, that perceptual defences are likely to influence pilot capacity to respond effectively under threat. Second, up to six years may have passed between DMT personality assessments in this RAAF research project, and subsequent incident experience. This supports a second DMT theoretical assertion, that the personality structures being identified through this projective test are fundamental and enduring ones. Finally, it has been proposed that the DMT only "works" in Scandinavia (Martinussen & Torjussen, 1993), where its special predictive power derives from clinical impressions during testing, and skilled scoring and interpretation. The findings reported here demonstrate that the DMT is able to cross cultural boundaries, and that it is a valid and potentially beneficial predictor of safe flying behaviour in this sample of 286 Australian military pilots, if not in other spheres of Australian aviation.

# References

Alkov, R.A., & Borowsky, M.S. (1980). A questionnaire study of psychological background factors in U.S. Navy aircraft accidents. *Aviation, Space, and Environmental Medicine, 51*(9, Section 1), 860-863.

Byrdorf, P. (1987). *Practical use of the DMT in Denmark.* Paper presented at the 1987 DMT Conference, Vienna, Austria.

Carlstedt, L. (1981). *Improved pilot training through modification of selection procedure and training climate* (FOA Report 1981-05-13). Stockholm: Swedish National Defence Research Institute.

Chappelow, J.W. (1989). Causes of aircrew error in the Royal Air Force. In AGARD Conference Proceedings No. 458, *Human behaviour in high stress situations in aerospace operations* (pp. 1-1 to 1-9). Neuilly-sur-Seine, France: NATO Advisory Group for Aerospace Research and Development.

Cooper, C. (1988a). Predicting susceptibility to short-term stress with the Defence Mechanism Test. *Work and Stress, 2,* 49-58.

Cooper, C. (1988b). The scientific status of the Defence Mechanism Test: A reply to Kline. *British Journal of Medical Psychology, 61,* 381-384.

Cooper, C., & Kline, P. (1989). A new objectively scored version of the Defence Mechanism Test. *Scandinavian Journal of Psychology, 30,* 228.

Green, R.G. (1985). Stress and accidents. *Aviation, Space, and Environmental Medicine, 56,* 638-641.

Hayward, B.J., & Lowe, A.R. (1988). Selecting safely: New directions in pilot selection. *Human Resource Management, 26*(2), 89-98.

Kragh, U. (1955). *The actual-genetic model of perception-personality: An experimental study with non-clinical and clinical groups.* Unpublished thesis, University of Lund, Sweden.

Kragh, U. (1960). The Defense Mechanism Test: A new method for diagnosis and personnel selection. *Journal of Applied Psychology, 44,* 303-309.

Kragh, U., & Smith, G. (1970). *Percept-Genetic Analysis.* Lund: Gleerups.

Lowe, A.R. (1989). *Relationship between Defence Mechanism Test score and reporting of aircraft incidents amongst Australian military pilots.*

Royal Australian Air Force Report. Melbourne: Headquarters Training Command.

Lowe, A.R. (1990). *Relationship between Defence Mechanism Test score and reporting of aircraft incidents amongst Australian military pilots: Follow up study*. Royal Australian Air Force Report. Melbourne: Headquarters Training Command.

Lowe, A.R. (1994). *Validation of a measure of coping potential with Australian military pilots*. Paper presented at the Australian Aviation Psychology Association Seminar "Emerging Trends and New Technologies", Melbourne, Australia, Aug 10.

Lowe, A.R. (1996). *Predicting Military Pilot Performance*. Unpublished doctoral dissertation, Monash University, Melbourne, Australia.

Lowe, A.R., & Hayward, B.J.H. (1990). *Personality assessment and pilot selection*. Paper presented at the First Australian Aviation Psychology Symposium, Melbourne, 25 September.

Lowe, A.R., Hayward, B.J., & Neuman, T. (1989). Defense mechanisms and the prediction of performance. In B. J. Fallon, H. P. Pfister, & J. Brebner (Eds.), *Advances in Industrial Organisational Psychology* (pp. 247-260). Elsevier Science Publishers B.V. (North-Holland).

Martinussen, M., & Torjussen, T. (1993). Does DMT (Defence Mechanism Test) predict pilot performance only in Scandinavia? *Proceedings of the Seventh International Symposium on Aviation Psychology* (pp. 398-403). Columbus, OH: Ohio State University.

Neuman, T. (1971). Perceptual defence organisation as a predictor of the pilot's adaptive behaviour in military flying. In J. D. Anderson (Ed). *Reports of the 9th Conference for Aviation Psychology*. Cambridge, UK, 21-24 September.

Neuman, T. (1978). Dimensioning and validation of percept-genetic defence mechanisms. A hierarchical analysis of pilot's stress behaviour *(FOA Report C-55020-H6)*. Stockholm: Swedish National Defence Research Institute.

Neuman, T. (1982). Influence of DMT on economy of training and flight safety. *Interpersona Report for the RSwAF*, Stockholm.

Neuman, T. (1986). Influence of DMT on economy of training and flight safety in the RSwAF 1970/71 - 1985/86. *FOA Report C-5153751-2.* Stockholm: Swedish National Defence Research Institute.

Sandahl, F.P. (1988). The Defence Mechanism Test DMT as a selection instrument when testing applicants for training as military pilots. Stockholm: Sartryck ur Kungl Krigsvetenskapsakademiens. *Handlinger och Tidskrift 4/88.*

Stoker, P. (1982). An empirical investigation of the predictive validity of the Defence Mechanism Test in the screening of fast-jet pilots for the Royal Air Force. *British Journal of Projective Psychology and Personality Study, 27*(1), 7-12.

Termohlen, J. (1981). Experiences with a projective test (DMT) as an instrument for selection of pilot candidates to the Royal Danish Air Force. Copenhagen. Unpublished paper.

Torjussen, T. (1987). Validation of the DMT amongst Royal Norwegian Air Force Pilots. Reported in B. J. Hayward, *Report on the 1987 DMT Conference, Vienna, Austria.* RAAF Departmental Minute, March, 1988.

Vaernes, R.J. (1982). The Defence Mechanism Test predicts inadequate performance under stress. *Scandinavian Journal of Psychology, 23,* 37-43.

# 4 A personality test for aircrew selection: Goats or sheep?

*Martyn Roast, Helen Muir and John Harris*
*Cranfield University*

## Describing the problem

> *"...because the first officer was unable to recall what he saw on the instruments, it has not been possible to determine why he made the mistake of believing that the fault lay with the No. 2 engine. When asked which engine was at fault he half formed the word 'left' before saying 'right'. His hesitation may have arisen from genuine difficulty in interpreting the reading."*

Air Accidents Investigation Branch (1990).

What cockpit voice recorders cannot record are the personalities of crew members - personalities that form the building blocks for a working relationship acquired over the hours, days, months and even years before the 30 minutes of a CVR tape. Such a relationship can have a profound effect on how the crew operate together.

I can remember a captain who was legendary because of his intimidatory behaviour. He would often take control from a first officer if he thought the aircraft was not being operated quite how it should be. A favorite comment of his was "I suppose that it will be left up to me to knock the first officers into shape", despite the fact he had never been given a training position. The hapless first officer would know that he had made a mistake because control of the aircraft was taken from him. First officers rarely disappointed him by giving a faultless performance.

## Solving the problem: Selection or training?

If an organisation wishes to ensure that aircrew operate together effectively as teams then two of the options available are training or selection. Training can be expected to change *attitudes* to flight deck behaviour but success is not guaranteed in the time available. Where stable personality characteristics are influencing negative attitudes then only selection can deal with the untrainable (Helmreich, 1984). Traditional personality screening methods focus on selecting out psychopathology but do not give sufficient fidelity to enable the desirable factors associated with effective group performance to be selected in. What is needed is a means to positively identify those personality types that are likely to be most effective in multi crew aircraft.

## Personality testing with the Personal Characteristics Inventory (PCI)

For such personality testing of aircrew to be validated there must be a demonstrable link between personality and sustained pilot performance on line (Helmreich, Sawin, & Carsrud, 1986). In what has now become a milestone in aircrew personality research Tom Chidester et al. (1990) have shown how certain groups of personalities can be predicted to perform during simulator LOFT exercises. Using the self-response questionnaire known as the Personal Characteristics Inventory (PCI) aircrew were grouped together using a statistical procedure known as cluster analysis. Three different clusters or groups of personalities were found:

- *"The Right Stuff"* (IE+ve) is considered the preferred cluster that returns the best performance. The Right Stuff possess both goal orientation (positive instrumentality) and have a high level of interpersonal awareness (positive expressivity).

- *"The Wrong Stuff"* (I-ve) although possessing goal orientation are associated with high levels of arrogance, egotism and an autocratic approach.

- *"No Stuff"* (EC-ve) have low scores on any of the positive instrumentality and expressivity scales and high scores on the less desirable negative scales. The performance of those known as "no stuff" is consistently disappointing, characterised by a complaining trait (C-ve).

## Study aims

Whilst recognising the significance of the NASA findings few studies of a similar nature have been carried out on British crews. This study aims to validate the use of the PCI with aircrew on the opposite side of the Atlantic. In addition the study hopes to take a second look at those personalities known to possess high levels of goal orientation and known as the "Wrong Stuff". From the author's own experience as a line captain, effective crew performance is not contingent on pilots belonging to the single personality cluster known as the right stuff. A high goal orientation without high expressivity or interpersonal warmth is not necessarily indicative of poor team performance. So the main aim of this study is to find a fourth cluster that is high in goal orientation, scores neutral on interpersonal awareness yet nevertheless returns a commendable performance.

It is intended that the results of this investigation be used to develop a psychometric assessment for the selection of aircrew. As the data for this study come from aircrew already working for a major airline it is hoped that the results will reflect the attributes of pilots with minimal motivation to fake the results (Helmreich, Sawin & Carsrud, 1986). Having a tool that taps into sustained achievement and motivation has considerable potential.

## The Personal Characteristics Inventory as a methodology for research

The Personal Characteristics Inventory is a collection of three self-response questionnaires composed of the Extended Personal Attributes Questionnaire (EPAQ; Spence, Helmreich & Holahan, 1979), the Work and Family Orientation Questionnaire (WOFO; Spence & Helmreich, 1978) and the Achievement Striving and Impatience/Irritability scales (Pred, Spence & Helmreich, 1986). The PCI is a 72 item Likert scale that focuses on the core dimensions of instrumentality and expressivity. High positive instrumentality scores (I+ve) represent high levels of goal orientation, self-reliance and independence. Other dimensions in the PCI are a desire to master challenging tasks, meeting internal standards of excellence and a desire to work hard at developing competence. High positive expressive scores (E+ve) represent warmth, kindness and awareness of others feelings.

The EPAQ also taps into more negative attributes with negative instrumentality (I-ve) representing a more autocratic, dictatorial competitive and egotistical orientation. An orientation towards verbal aggression, a nagging or fussy disposition is scored as negative expressivity (E-ve) along with subservience and gullibility.

35

## Method

The PCI was issued to pilots working for a British airline in January 1997. The airline has three bases and five aircraft types with pilots from a variety of military and civilian backgrounds. The subjects were issued the PCI through their company mail file and given a Freepost envelope to return the completed questionnaire to the University of Cranfield. Of the 281 questionnaires distributed 117 were returned with 115 valid responses, giving a response rate of 41%.

Cluster analysis was carried out on the EPAQ variables using Wards method, combining clusters with the smallest increase in the overall sum of the Euclidean distance. The technique allows for the number of clusters to be specified and a three cluster solution was sought so that the previously determined personality groups of Right Stuff, Wrong Stuff and No Stuff could be validated.

## Results

*Three personality clusters*

As can be seen from Figure 4.1, clusters similar to each of the three groups of personalities described by Chidester were found; the right stuff possess higher than average levels of people and goal orientation, the wrong stuff with higher than average levels of goal orientation but low levels of people orientation and high levels of arrogance and egotism and the no stuff cluster with low scores in goal and people orientation and high scores in verbal aggression and gullibility. This would seem to validate the use of the PCI as a means of personality assessment within a British Airline.

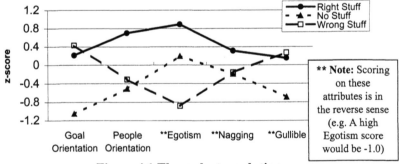

**Figure 4.1 Three cluster solution**

In Figure 4.1 the scoring on these attributes is in the reverse sense (i.e., a high Egotism score would be -1.0.

*A closer look at the wrong stuff*

Using the same statistical procedure a four cluster solution was then sought to find out how the groupings would respond. After cluster analysis the two clusters referred to as the right stuff and no stuff did not change and it was only the group referred to as the wrong stuff that disappeared to form two other clusters, as shown in Figure 4.2 below.

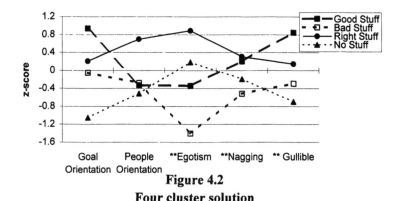

**Figure 4.2**
**Four cluster solution**

The results in Figure 4.2 show a fourth cluster that is goal orientated with a neutral relationship orientation but with low levels of egotism, verbal aggression and gullibility; the more negative attributes of other goal orientated types. This cluster was given the title of "Good Stuff" after a favourite catch phrase from one of my flying instructors. The remaining cluster was given the name of "Bad Stuff" to reflect the higher scores on the more negative aspects of goal orientation.

*Achievement motives and personality*

To confirm the consistency of the personality clusters the performance of each cluster was measured on the remaining scales of the PCI; that is, the work and achievement scales and Impatience/Irritability scale. Each cluster responded in a way that could be predicted from a knowledge of the scores from the above as can be seen in Figure 4.3 Both the positive clusters

(Good Stuff and Right Stuff) showed elevated positions when compared to the others. The motivation for working at developing competence and mastering new skills was marked in these two groups. The No Stuff grouping came out particularly badly with low levels of work, mastery and achievement striving but a degree of competitiveness.

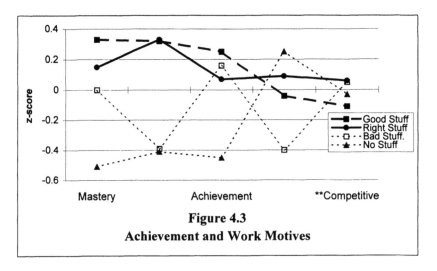

**Figure 4.3**
**Achievement and Work Motives**

**Measuring aircrew performance**

*Attitudes to CRM as performance criteria*

Further performance measures were needed to confirm the hypothesis that successful goal orientated groups do not necessarily depend on a high level of interpersonal awareness. Previous work using the Flight Management Attitudes Questionnaire (FMAQ) has recorded the link between attitudes to cockpit management and effective behaviours on the flight deck (Helmreich, Foushee, Benson & Russini, 1986). Three scales are measured: *Communication and Co-ordination*, which taps into communication of intent, delegation of tasks and monitoring of crew members; *Recognition of Stressors*, which deals with the response to fatigue, workload and personal problems; and *Command Responsibility*, which deals with attitudes to the captain's autocracy and responsibilities. To obtain an indicator for effective cockpit behaviour, the FMAQ 2.1 was included with the PCI and issued to the population of aircrew discussed above. Although the low sample size proved to be a problem, the Good Stuff cluster had the highest score on all three scales.

*Attitudes to organisational culture as performance criteria*

To successfully select aircrew for a particular airline account should be taken of the correspondence between organisational culture and an individual's values. Attitudes to CRM are particularly vulnerable to the influence of culture (Merritt, 1993). The FMAQ has a section devoted to attitudes surrounding organisational culture but there was a requirement for the development of scales that could contour the organisational culture. Data from the FMAQ were used to develop four scales for use with the organisational culture section of the FMAQ.

- *Organisational Climate* deals with the issues surrounding how a pilot feels about the organisation. If the pilot is proud to work for the organisation and feels a high degree of trust towards senior management then the score will be high.

- The *Management Relationship* deals with how the pilot perceive the consideration that management displays when dealing with the concerns and difficulties encountered by pilots.

- Positive attitudes to safe practices and a confidence in the safety standards would be reflected in the *safety culture*.

- *Training/Standards* deals with the respect and confidence with which the training and operations department is held.

Again the small sample size proved to be a problem for statistical significance but the good stuff cluster scored the highest in three of the four scales. Only the Training and Standards score was lower than that for other clusters.

## A case study of personality and performance criteria

During the course of my studies I was approached by one of the organisations' training captains and asked if I could prepare his profile. The individual concerned is widely regarded as an expert pilot and respected as a proficient and popular training captain. The profile is reproduced below (Figure 4.4). The statistical analysis allocated case 054 to the good stuff cluster and the average score on person orientation confirms the grouping. Knowing the individual concerned it is quite likely he would also have a high score on any performance measure designed for pilots.

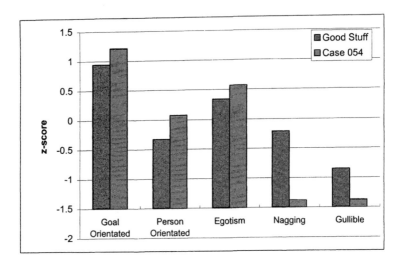

**Figure 4.4**
**Case study (Case 054)**

## Conclusion

The study achieved its objective of demonstrating that personality testing can be an indicator for effective aircrew performance. A group of personalities that were goal orientated but with less than average interpersonal awareness were shown to nevertheless demonstrate effective performance, contrary to previous expectations. This finding has a number of implications for both training and selection. Whilst recognising the benefits of interpersonal sensitivity those personalities without a preference for such behaviour may well have other strengths that enable effective performance. A training and selection strategy that recognises the strengths and ameliorates the weaknesses of the different personalities is likely to be more widely accepted.

Perhaps the answer is that aviation needs both goats and sheep.

## References

Air Accidents Investigation Branch, (1990). Report on the accident to Boeing 737-400 G-OBME near Kegworth, Leicestershire on 8th January 1989. Aircraft Accident Report No. 4/90 (EW/C 1095).

Chidester, T.R., Kanki, B.G., Foushee, H.C., Dickinson, C., & Bowles, S. (1990). *Personality factors in flight operations: Leader characteristics and crew performance in a full-mission air transport simulation* (NASA TM102259). Moffett Field, CA: NASA-Ames Research Center.

Helmreich, R.L. (1984). Cockpit management attitudes. *Human Factors*, 26(5), 583-589.

Helmreich, R.L., Foushee, H.C., Benson, B.A., & Russini B.A. (1986). Cockpit resource management: Exploring the attitude-performance linkage. *Aviation, Space and Environmental Medicine, 57*, 1198-1200.

Helmreich, R.L., Sawin, L.L., & Carsrud, A.L. (1986). The honeymoon effect in job performance: Temporal increases in the predictive power of achievement motivation. *Journal of Applied Psychology, 71*(2), 185-188.

Merritt, A. (1993). The influence of national and organisational culture on human performance. *Proceedings of the Australian Aviation Psychology Association Industry Seminar*, Sydney.

Spence, J.T., & Helmreich, R.L. (1978). *Masculinity and femininity: Their psychological dimensions, correlates and antecedents*. University of Texas Press, Austin.

Spence, J.T., Helmreich, R.L., & Holahan, C.K., (1979). Negative and positive components of psychological masculinity and femininity and their relationships to self-reports of neurotic and acting out behaviours. *Journal of Personality and Social Psychology, 37*(10), 1673-1682.

Spence, J.T., Helmreich, R.L., & Pred, R.S. (1987). Impatience versus achievement strivings in the Type A pattern: Differential effects on students' health and academic achievement. *Journal of Applied Psychology, 72*(4), 522-528.

# 5 Pilot selection procedures: A case for individual differences in applicant groups

*Melissa M. Monfries and Phillip J. Moore*
*Faculty of Education, The University of Newcastle, Australia*

## Background

The selection procedures for occupations requiring a high degree of technical skill and subject specific expertise have, to date, placed minimal emphasis on interpersonal skills. Yet, contemporaneous research suggests that skills in the interpersonal domain may have a substantial impact on outcomes related to a number of high profile professions. Currently the media is focussing on the importance of doctors' interpersonal skills and have suggested that deficits in the area can have a substantial impact on a patient's diagnosis. Moreover, organisational psychologists report floundering productivity if interpersonal constructs such as individual personalities, teamwork capabilities and leadership skills are ignored when groups of people are brought together (Rosene, 1997). Consequently, there is growing interest in the role that interpersonal skills play in a pilot's performance and the success of cockpit crew management. The aims of this paper were primarily to assess the extent to which interpersonal skills affected pilot selection for an international airline, and to gauge the role interpersonal skills might play in subsequent selection procedures.

The training and selection of pilots cover a diverse area of skills assessment. Generally it is considered essential that pilots possess technical expertise, aptitude and training (Helmreich, 1993). These skills rely heavily on intellectual ability and include decision making abilities, aviation knowledge, spatial reasoning, mechanical reasoning, and a variety of verbal, numerical and diagrammatic abilities which are assessed using traditional intelligence tests (Doat, 1995; Stead, 1995). In addition to these skills, a number of psychological factors are also examined. These have included: personality variables (Stead,1995); biographical inventories (Damos, 1995); levels of self confidence and risk taking (Carretta & Ree, 1993); and motivation, leadership style and social relations (Bartram & Baxter, 1995).

Despite the apparent diversity of selection criteria, Damos (1995) has posited that pilot selection batteries have remained relatively unchanged over a fifty year period and differ very little from the World War II battery used for US Army Air Corps selection (Guildford, 1947; cited in Damos, 1995). Moreover she asserts that the predictive ability of the these tests across different countries remains relatively low. Consequently, the area of pilot selection is not mature and is in need of stronger theoretical foundations.

Some researchers suggest that selection procedures need to be adjusted to suit evolving technology (Doat, 1995), because it is acknowledged that an understanding of the effects of automation on human activities is rather limited (Lambrios & Giannacourou, 1995). Effective aviators need strong interpersonal skills in addition to their intellectual and technical skills (Helmreich, 1993), but it has been suggested that pilots may be lacking in such "people skills" (Ross, 1992). Consequently, the importance of interpersonal skills in an automated environment needs to be addressed, so that its importance for selection procedures can be ascertained. Indeed, recent research has addressed the areas of automation and interpersonal skills by investigating the effects of automative and technological trends in the commercial aviation industry on the quality of interpersonal communications on the flight deck (Billings, 1991; Moore & Telfer, in press; Mouloua & Parasuraman, 1994).

An over-riding feature of the pilot selection procedure has been the interview. Its usefulness in pilot selection procedures has been acknowledged but largely neglected in the multivariate analyses of who is selected to be a pilot. Nevertheless, the nature and effects of the interview have been the focus of a number of other occupations' selection procedures and its importance in these contexts has been acknowledged and analysed in depth. Research into these other contexts suggests that the interview offers the opportunity to examine among other things, a complex array of interpersonal factors.

Our previous work on selection criteria relationships (Monfries & Moore, 1995) and success in being selected for airline operations (Moore &

Monfries, 1997) focussed on interpersonal skills, cognitive skills, and performance in simulated situations. In our 1997 study, 29 experienced commercial airline pilots with commercial instrument ratings and multi-crew experience were examined for their performance on a number of typical selection criteria including mental reasoning ability, specific abilities (e.g., mechanical), interpersonal values, attitudes to cockpit operations, simulator, and an extensive interview. The findings showed significant and positive relationships between experience and both interview scores and valuing Support (from Gordon's 1993 Survey of Interpersonal Values). Comparisons of performance scores for those finally selected and those not selected showed statistically reliable differences on the interview measure with those selected scoring higher.

Recognising the problems of univariate analyses, we conducted a multivariate stepwise discriminant function analysis with all variables being entered to ascertain which variable or collection of variables best predicted those who were selected by the airline. This analysis selected three contributing variables: Interview; Conformity; and Co-ordination and Communication attitudes. These variables explained 27% of the variance and overall the model correctly classified 65.3% of all cases, and 68.4% of pilots who were selected. Those selected scored higher on both the interview and Conformity measures, but lower on their attitudes to cockpit co-ordination and communication. It should be noted that all selected pilots met the airline's criterion cut-off points for each of the major selection criteria, suggesting that the three variables emerging from the discriminant function analysis played a more substantial role than the others in the final determination.

This paper continues the above line of research by examining similar patterns in another group of experienced pilots who were seeking selection to an international carrier. Again, the prime focus is on the relevance of interpersonal skills.

## The study

*Subjects*

The sample for this study consisted of 37 experienced commercial pilots with commercial instrument ratings and multi-crew experience. They had been short listed for further assessment from a larger pool of applicants by airline management and consequently the group represents a highly selected group of individuals.

*Materials and measures*

*Reasoning*: The ACER Test of Reasoning Ability (1984) was used to assess reasoning ability. This adult scale includes 70 items designed to assess numerical and verbal reasoning skills in a timed situation (45 mins.). The manual reports satisfactory test characteristics. The maximum score is 70, the minimum, zero.

*Specific mental abilities*: The airline Human Resources Unit utilised a Mechanical Reasoning Test and Spatial Relations Test as part of selection. Both tests are time limited, with the Mechanical test consisting of 68 multiple choice items (each related to a specific mechanical operation) and the Spatial test consisting of 60 multiple choice items (each related to a two dimensional unfolded figure and its appropriate three dimensional representation). Each correct answer scored one point, with 68 and 60 being the maximum possible score for the respective tests.

*Interpersonal Values:* Gordon's (1993) Survey of Interpersonal Values was used to provide an index of Conformity. It will be recalled that Conformity (doing the correct thing, following regulations) was one of the positive attributes observed in our previous study. The manual reports satisfactory reliability and validity.

*Approaches to learning:* Moore, Smith and Telfer's (1994) Pilot Learning Processes Questionnaire was used to assess pilots' preferred approaches to learning. The 30 item Likert scaled questionnaire examines three dominant approaches: Deep, Surface, and Achieving (10 items for each with a maximum score for individual scales being 60). Deep oriented learners are internally motivated and seek understanding. Surface oriented learners focus on details and facts by using rote learning and reproducing strategies. Achieving oriented learners are keen to succeed and are organised for learning. Satisfactory reliabilities and validity are reported in Moore, Smith and Telfer (1994).

*Crew Resource Management:* To examine pilots' knowledge of crew resource management principles, the airline developed a written scenario based upon an actual accident in North America. The text was 10 pages and included background information, actual cockpit voice recordings and other relevant information. Forty minutes were allocated for applicants to read and make written responses to two items: To identify any factors that influenced the decisions made by the crew; and to suggest an alternative, more appropriate course of action for the crew. The written responses were examined, against a template developed by CRM experts, for organisational factors (5 points), environmental/task factors (5 points), and crew factors (5 points). Five points were allocated for alternative suggestions making 20 the maximum possible score for the exercise.

*Interview schedule:* A 32 item interview schedule developed by the airline and consultants was used to examine personal attributes, expectations and knowledge of the airline, flying abilities/experiences/incidents/, ways of learning, crew resource management, and stress management. Each of the items was scored on a three point scale from Unsatisfactory (1) to Very Satisfactory (3). Scores were obtained by averaging the scores of the five panel members, each of whom held a managerial position in the airline. For the purposes of this paper, only the total interview score was entered for averaging. A higher score represents a more favourable appraisal of the applicants by the panel.

*Flight simulator rating:* Subjects were required to multi-crew a flight simulator on a flight sector out of a capital city using instruments. The scenario was scheduled for one hour per pilot in command. Two experienced airline check and training pilots assessed applicants using 10 criteria, each rated on a 5 point scale. The criteria included technical skills, accuracy of flight under instruments, cockpit procedures, cockpit management and crew co-ordination. A higher score represents a better performance in the simulator.

**Procedure**

As part of the assessment centre, all pilots undertook testing over a period of 10 days. During this time all questionnaire data were gathered from group testing situations. Pilots were randomly assigned in pairs for the simulator component and all were advised that revealing details of the scenario to others would jeopardise their selection chances. The interviews were similarly randomised across the latter days of the assessment centre. At the conclusion of all assessment activities, the panel considered the profiles of each applicant against the company profile for the major measures. The outcome of this process was that 19 pilots were selected to be offered a position in the airline.

## Results and discussion

The major analyses consisted of comparisons of those who were selected and those who failed to meet the company criteria. The means for the respective groups revealed very little difference on the three approaches to learning scores (i.e., Deep, 50.47 vs 50.47; Surface, 21.05 vs 22.93; Achieving, 41.32 vs 43.40) but higher (though non-significant) scores by selected applicants on Conformity (24.05 vs 21.00), Mechanical ability (59.10 vs 53.60), Spatial ability (47.26 vs 37.00), Reasoning (51.00 vs 38.13), CRM knowledge (15.76 vs 10.43), Interview (74.97 vs 70.43) and Simulator (33.21 vs 26.66).

Univariate analyses of variance showed five variables reliably differentiating the two groups of candidates: Mechanical ability; Spatial ability; Reasoning; Interview; and Simulator rating. In each case, superior scores were associated with those selected. In other words, comparisons between those selected and those not selected showed three mental ability measures, one technical/communication skills measure and the interview as statistically significant discriminators. These factors could be categorised as intelligence, interpersonal and performance variables.

As in our previous work, these univariate analyses were followed by multiple discriminant function analysis to ascertain which combination of variables best predicted those who were selected. This analysis showed a significant discriminant function of three variables (Simulator rating, Mechanical ability, Reasoning) which accounted for 64.7 percent of the variance. The percentage of cases correctly classified by the function was a reasonably high 88.24 percent with 89.5 percent correct classification for the selected group. For each variable in the discriminant function, applicants who were selected by the airline scored higher than those not selected.

Comparisons between the findings of this current study and those of the previous cohort selected for the airline (see Moore & Monfries, 1997) show certain consistencies. For example, in both studies, performance at interview significantly predicted selection, though in the second study it was significant in the univariate analysis and not the multi-variate analysis. In addition Conformity scores of selected applicants were consistently higher for those selected. Therefore the integral role of interpersonal measures is highlighted by the differentiating capacity of interview skills and interpersonal measures. In our first study, however, both Interview and Conformity entered into the discriminant function whereas in this study neither variable gained such prominence. In this study, the emphasis detected in the multivariate procedures was one of intelligence and technical performance.

An examination of the mean scores in both of our studies shows some interesting differences between the cohorts. For example, the cohort for this study showed higher mechanical and reasoning abilities, higher values for regulations and following procedures, and produced higher interview scores than the Moore and Monfries (1997) cohort. Further investigation showed substantial differences in the cohorts when selection was the criterion. Here the differences were of a reasonable magnitude with, for example the reasoning scores of those selected in this study some 18 percent higher than for the previous study. The two groups were less able to be differentiated by their simulator score, with the present cohort scoring only 7 percent higher than the previous cohorts.

Do these current findings with their emphasis on mental abilities and flying skills suggest that interpersonal skills are unimportant in the operational environment? We would argue against such a proposition on several grounds. One, there is a literature substantiating the role of interpersonal skills in aviation beyond that described in this paper (e.g., Hörmann, Manzey, Maschke & Pecena, 1997; Ross, 1992). Two, in both of our studies and in others (e.g., Bartram & Baxter, 1995) the personal interview predicted selection, and in both studies the interpersonal measure of conformity was positively highlighted. Three, the simulator rating also incorporated aspects of interpersonal skills such as communicating and while we have not examined that particular dimension at this stage, such qualities are reflected in the overall simulator rating.

Perhaps most importantly, we feel that our combined results highlight the way in which variables interact within different cohorts. Clearly the cohort for this study was more "intelligent" and also more adept at operating the simulator than the Moore and Monfries' (1997) cohort and while those selected in both studies met the company requirements, these mental abilities and technical skills emerged above and beyond the other criteria in the final analysis, the interpersonal dimensions continuing to play their roles as important background variables.

We have begun following both cohorts as they progress through their endorsements and check and training. Such longitudinal follow-ups should allow us to determine which variables, individually and in concert, contribute to longer term operational performance. In addition, we would like to see an extension of the selection process to include closer examination of interpersonal skills in operation. Work by Hörmann (1997) highlights the positive relationships between interpersonal skills such as

49

empathy and actual cockpit performance. However, Hörmann also notes the difficulties in reliably assessing such skills and the need to train selection personnel in such procedures.

## References

Bartram, D., & Baxter, P. (1995). Cathay Pacific Airways pilot validation. examination. In N. Johnston, R. Fuller, & N. McDonald (Eds.), *Aviation Psychology: Training and selection* (pp. 194-201*)*. Aldershot: Avebury Aviation.

Billings, C. (1991). Towards a human-centred aircraft automation philosophy. *International Journal of Aviation Psychology, 1,* 261-270.

Damos, D. (1995). Pilot selection batteries: A critical examination. In N. Johnston, R. Fuller, & N. McDonald (Eds.), *Aviation Psychology: Training and selection* (pp. 165-169). Aldershot: Avebury Aviation.

Doat, B. (1995). Need of new development in Air France selection. In N. Johnston, R. Fuller, & N. McDonald (Eds.), *Aviation Psychology: Training and selection* (pp. 182-187). Aldershot: Avebury Aviation.

Gordon, L.V. (1993). *Survey of interpersonal values.* SRA Macmillan/McGraw.

Helmreich, R.L. (1993). Whither CRM? Directions in crew resource management training in the cockpit and elsewhere. In R. Jensen (Ed.), *Proceedings of the Seventh International Symposium on Aviation Psychology.* Columbus: Ohio University Press.

Hörmann, H-J. (1997). Behaviour oriented assessment of interpersonal skills in pilot selection, Part 11: Empirical findings. *Paper presented at the Ninth Symposium on Aviation Psychology.* Columbus, Ohio. April 27-May 1.

Hörmann, H-J., Manzey, D., Maschke, P., & Pecena, Y. (1997). Behavior-oriented assessment of interpersonal skills in pilot selection concepts, methods and empirical findings. *Paper presented at the 9th international Symposium on Aviation Psychology,* Columbus, Ohio, April 28- May 2.

Lambrios, L., & Giannacourou, M. (1995). Human factors issues in advanced ATC systems. In R. Fuller, N. Johnston, & N. McDonald (Eds.). *Human factors in Aviation Operations* (pp. 108-116). Aldershot: Avebury Aviation.

Monfries, M.M & Moore, P.J. (1996). Human resource management: An interpersonal skills approach. In B.J. Hayward & A.R. Lowe (Eds.), *Applied aviation psychology: Achievement, change and challenge* (pp. 361-369). Aldershot: Avebury Aviation.

Moore, P. & Monfries, M. (1997). Interpersonal skills in airline pilot selection. *Paper presented at the Industrial and Organisational Psychology Conference*, Melbourne, June.

Moore, P.J., & Telfer, R.A. (1997). Learning for new technologies. In R.A. Telfer & P.J. Moore (Eds.), *Aviation training: Learners, instruction and organisation* (pp. 87-96). Aldershot: Avebury Aviation.

Moore, P.J., Smith, M., & Telfer, R.A. (1994). Learning for automation: Generic versus specific approaches. In M. Mouloua (Ed.), *Human performance in automated systems: Current research and trends* (pp. 307-312).

Mouloua, M., & Parasuraman, R. (1994). *Human performance in automated systems: Current research and trends.* Hillsdale: Erlbaum.

Ross, M.J. (1992). *The integrated commercial flying school: An evaluation of commercial flight training and flight simulator effectiveness.* Unpublished doctoral dissertation, University of Newcastle, Australia.

Rosene, L.R. (1997). Team personality. *American Psychological Association Monitor,* September (pp. 5).

Stead, G. (1995). Qantas pilot selection procedures: Past to present. In N. Johnston, R. Fuller, & N. McDonald (Eds.), *Aviation psychology: Training and selection* (pp. 176-181). Aldershot: Avebury Aviation.

# 6 Alternative approaches to gathering information in air traffic control selection research

*Greg Hannan*
*University of Tasmania*

## Introduction

Air traffic control selection research, like pilot selection, has traditionally employed statistical regression models such as multiple linear regression to validate the tests used to select trainees. A few selection studies have reported the use of other regression models such as discriminant analysis (Collins, Nye & Manning, 1990) and logistic regression (Raju, Steinhaus, Edwards & DeLessio, 1991) to validate a selection test programme.

The procedure of multiple linear regression allows for a number of predictor (selection) variables to be regressed against a single criterion (performance) variable: in the case of an ATC validation study, some measure of performance on either a simulated session or operational task. It may also be the simple dichotomous measure of success/failure in training and/or licensing examinations.

There are, however, several limitations of the multiple linear regression model not widely appreciated by researchers and reviewers. Issues such as the normality of variables and the number of predictor variables entered into a regression model in comparison with the number of cases in the validation cohort, are rarely considered by researchers, raising questions as to the accuracy of the regression equations upon which subsequent selection decisions are made.

While selection research using regression techniques have certainly assisted in choosing candidates, and bought some rigour to validation of selection programmes, there has been little increase in the correlations of weighted predictor composite scores and training outcomes since this type of research commenced in the aviation industry in the early 1950s (Bartram,1992). According to Bartram, "a continued effort will be needed simply to maintain validities in the 0.3-0.4 region...as training needs and demands change".

It is argued here that regression modelling on a large scale fails to capitalise on the subtleties of the data that are fed into them because of the nature of the "number crunching" involved, and perhaps because of the violations of good practice in the use of such statistical models. However, individual cases, or groups of cases, may shed particular light on the complexities of predicting future success of trainees. Hannan (1996) argued the standard validation approaches fail to take account of other relevant factors such as the interaction of the individual with the nature of the course and other cognitive/affective factors that may assist or detract from their progress on course.

For these reasons the author decided to apply some additional analyses to a medium sized data set from Flight Service Officer (FSO) and Airways Data Service Officer (ADSO) conversion course trainees (1992-1995) to determine if such approaches do assist in understanding which candidates may have more or less success in graduating from a training course and obtaining an ATC license. This data set, and a preliminary analysis of data from it, have previously been described in Hannan (1996). The selection programme involved five aptitude tests from the Saville and Holdsworth advanced test battery and the Occupational Personality Questionnaire (OPQ). In addition to these measures the author gathered data from a small group (N=58) of the 198 trainees on learning styles, using a modified version of a descriptive instrument developed by Butler (1986), based on the work of Gregorc (1982). Butler argued that individuals may perceive the world in either concrete or abstract terms and approach the ordering or information in a systematic (linear) fashion or in a random (non-linear) way. The result of this conceptualisation is four channels of cognitive operation: "concrete sequential", "abstract sequential", "concrete random" and "abstract random". Each of these four channels is associated with a group of set characteristics and behaviours, that is, a style. Butler described the concrete sequential style as "practical, predictable, to-the-point, organised and structured"; the abstract sequential style as "intellectual, logical, conceptual and studious"; the abstract random as "emotional, interpretative, holistic and thematic"; and the concrete random style as "original, experimental, investigative, option-oriented and risk-taking".

The remainder of this paper reports on the additional analyses based on some of the instruments referred to above and some conclusions reached from them.

## The alternative approaches

As argued above, the analysis of individual cases or groups of cases has not featured in the air traffic control selection literature. Case study as an approach is used in a range of settings to glean detailed qualitative and/or quantitative information about a phenomenon. The information gathered may then be used in either theory building or evaluation. In the author's experience of working closely with air traffic control trainees, in both training and operational environments, it is apparent that numerous factors not directly used in the selection of candidates (but nevertheless available in the existing selection data), and other characteristics evident from trainees' interactions with their course and instructors (situational factors), play a significant role in some candidates' success or failure. The case study approach may be more able than the regression type validation, at unravelling these factors, and hence providing useful information for selection specialists in organisations.

Having decided to use case or special group studies, the next question to be addressed is what groups and individuals have the potential to shed light on factors which may contribute to success/failure. There is a danger in choosing unique individuals in a random fashion in that they may make for interesting analysis, but may not provide any useful insights into selection factors, and in fact may be misleading. To maximise the chances of these approaches being fruitful it is necessary to examine groups, and individuals from groups, that have some significance in selection and performance outcomes. A useful means of targeting these can come from the regression models of validation studies. A regression model provides a predicted score $y'$, if based on multiple linear regression, or a probability of success value, $p$, if based on logistic regression. These values can then provide the basis for choosing useful groups or cases to examine.

The groups that are of particular interest to the organisation and selection researcher are:

- those predicted to have a high chance of success and do perform well (hits);
- those predicted to perform well but failed training (false positives);
- those predicted to have a low chance of success but who passed their course and became efficient controllers (false negatives).

The first of these groups is important because it represents trainees who are presumably the most able in terms of the abilities and characteristics entered in the regression analysis. If this group can be examined in terms of available data it may provide some evidence of the characteristics which might typify a first rate controller rather than an intuitive view. The second group is of particular interest as these are the trainees who cost an organisation dearly and create for themselves and trainers a high degree of anxiety and frustration. If common characteristics can be gleaned from an examination of this group an organisation and the potential trainees would benefit from that information. The last group is interesting in that there is always doubt about excluding candidates who show up poorly from a statistical model but who selectors may believe have what it takes to do the job.

In the analysis of the FSO and ADSO conversion course selection programme described in Hannan (1996), logistic regression was used with the performance criterion (pass/fail), a dichotomous rather than continuous variable of some composite performance score. The probabilities of success generated from this model were then used to target two groups of trainees. These were:

| Hits: | N = 24 with an average probability of success of p = 0.97 |
| --- | --- |
| False positives: | N = 10 with an average probability of success of p = 0.86 |

The other group (false negatives) was not used in this analysis as the number of trainees in the group was considered insufficient to achieve any reasonable comparison.

Some summary descriptive statistics were then generated to compare these two groups on measures that were available from the initial selection testing programme. As would be anticipated there was little difference between the two groups on the aptitude test measures. This is because all aptitude measures used to select the candidates were also used in the logistic regression model. If both groups show a high probability of success, the aptitude measures would be expected to be similar for the two groups. However, some interesting trends were evident from the personality traits measured by the Occupational Personality Inventory (Saville and Holdsworth) and age of trainees, the average age for the success group being 26 years compared with an average of 30 years for the failure group.

The concept version of the OPQ measures 31 traits in three broad categories: relationships, thinking style and feelings/emotions. The success group were clearly higher than the fail group in most of the relationship scales with a profile emerging of the success group as more socially confident and outgoing, more "affiliative" and "democratic", less "modest" and reserved than the failure group. Although a similar consistent pattern did not emerge in the other two broad categories, three traits from thinking style revealed interesting differences between the two groups. These were in the traits referred to in the OPQ as "data rational" and "conceptual" (in which the failure group were substantially higher than the success group), and "forward planning" (in which the success group was substantially higher than the failure group). This gives the impression of this particular group of failed trainees as overly analytical and focussed on data, but less organised and systematic. It is relevant to note here that apart from the significant personality trait of "forward planning" no other trends were evident from just the preliminary descriptive analysis of the whole data set and the subsequent logistic regression analysis.

**Case study analyses**

To conclude this approach of more specifically examining groups and individuals, three separate cases were chosen at random from the interest groups articulated above. A brief overview of aptitude scores and OPQ scales is offered, along with notes from interviews and anecdotal evidence gathered during the course of their training. A synthesis is then offered to argue the usefulness of this approach.

*Case 1 (High probability of success and passed licensing assessment)*

The case chosen from this group was a male trainee, 30 years of age at the commencement of the course. His aptitude scores were on average quite high (average sten = 6.4), with lower scores on the DT8 (abstract reasoning) and higher scores on the DA5 (diagramming) and ST7 (spatial reasoning). His overall personality profile showed some strong points in relation to the criteria specified by Airservices, particularly in thinking style areas such as "forward planning" and "conscientious", from a subset described as "structure". From the Learning Style Inventory this trainee showed a consistent pattern of successful trainees of considerably higher scores in the sequential dimension (than the random) with concrete sequential style higher than the abstract sequential. At an orientation interview he gave the impression of being a quietly confident individual, who was well organised and had developed some specific study strategies he was comfortable with. In relation to the personality profile the trainee showed high scores on social scales such as "democratic", "socially confident" and "outgoing". The overall impression of this person was a likeable, well respected individual who was always conversant and comfortable in social, as well as classroom settings. While not an extrovert he was clearly a socially competent and well adjusted individual.

During the course of his training he excelled in both theoretical and simulation classes. Instructors found him to be a cooperative learner even though he showed considerable skill and understanding of the processes from an early stage of training. He was often sought after by peers for assistance.

### Case 2 (High probability of success but failed licensing assessment)

This trainee was 35 years of age at the commencement of training. His aptitude scores were again reasonably high (average sten = 6.6). He had high scores on the numerical estimation task (sten = 9) and the abstract reasoning test (sten = 7), but a lower score on the diagramming test (sten = 5). From the OPQ scales there were areas that gave the selection panel some cause for concern. In particular, high scores on the "relaxed" scale and low scores on "worrying" and "forward planning" matched the impression of an individual who was very confident in his own ability, but who at a later stage did not seem to cope with adjusting to the demands of a course that required diligence and organisation. In the relationship group there was generally a lower pattern of scores indicting a less than socially competent person. This was particularly apparent from low scores in "democratic", "caring" and "affiliative".

On the Learning Style Inventory he had a much higher score on the abstract sequential scale than on the concrete sequential scale, which again matched the impression of a person who was not organised, practical or conscientious in his approach but rather, analytical and laisez-faire. From the OPQ a similar pattern was evident with high scores on "data rational" and "conceptual" scales from the thinking style group. In simulation classes he regularly argued with instructors about the wisdom of their advice on ATC strategies and the logic of some procedures and practices he was asked to use, and generally adopted something of an individualistic approach to learning.

The overall impression is of a trainee in the age bracket that is known to be problematic in terms of acquiring ATC skills, with a learning approach high in the abstract and lower in the concrete domain, and not all that socially adaptable.

*Case 3 (Low probability of success but passed licensing assessment)*

This case is a male trainee who was 28 at the commencement of his training. His aptitude scores were slightly below the sten average of six that was considered desirable (average sten = 5.9) and showing a higher score on the abstract reasoning test than the diagramming test. This would have been the basis of the his lower probability of success derived from the logistic regression model along with a lower score on OPQ scale "forward planning". However from the Learning Styles Inventory he showed the typical pattern of successful trainees alluded to above, that is higher on the sequential, rather than the abstract dimension and higher in the concrete sequential than the abstract sequential.

While the OPQ score on the "forward planning" scale was low, two other score on scales that are indicative of a more structured approach ("conscientious" and "detail conscientious") suggest that he had the kind of leaning approach suited to the type of course and profession he was training for. He was also high in some of the social scales shown to be typical of the group of trainees represented by Case 1; that is high "affiliative", "democratic" and "caring". This was consistent with anecdotal reports of an individual who was cooperative and eager to relate to instructors and peers alike, without being extroverted. Some instructors related that he had expressed high personal motivation to become an air traffic controller.
In summary this trainee shows quite a few of the traits and learning style characteristics evident in the high probability/successful group.

**Summary**

The approach advocated in this paper, of using more descriptive research approaches in selection research, in addition to the standard multivariate regression techniques, has shown some promise in advancing the understanding of the characteristics necessary to be successful in training and gaining an ATC license. In particular this approach has confirmed age as significant factor, but also demonstrated that a more structured and concrete learning style (rather than an abstract) and a more positive social outlook, are ingredients of success in ATC training. Specific measures and scales that can detect these characteristics have also been identified.

**References**

Bartram, D. (1992). *The development and validation of the Micropat Battery*, paper presented to the BPS Occupational Psychology Conference, Liverpool, 1992.

Butler, K.A. (1986). *Learning and teaching style in theory and practice.* Australia: Hawker Brownlow Education.

Collins, W., Nye, L., & Manning, C. (1990). *Studies of post-strike Air Traffic Control Specialist trainees: III. Changes in demographic characteristics of academy entrants and biodemographic predictors of success in air traffic controller selection and academy screening.* DOT/FAA/AM-90/4. Washington, DC: US Department of Transportation, Federal Aviation Administration.

Gregorc, A. (1982). *An adult's guide to style.* Maynard, MA: Gabriel Systems Inc.

Hannan, G.J. (1996). Selecting air traffic controllers: Airservices Australia's ATC conversion course selection program. In B.J. Hayward and A.R. Lowe (Eds.), *Applied aviation psychology: Achievement, change and challenge.* Aldershot: Avebury Aviation.

Ackerman, P.L., Schneider, W., & Wickens, C.D. (1984). Deciding the existence of a time sharing ability: A combined methodological and theoretical approach. *Human Factors, 26*(1), 71-82.

Park, K.S., & Lee, S.W. (1992). A computer-aided aptitude test for predicting flight performance. *Human Factors, 34*(2), 189-204.

Raju, N.S., Steinhaus, S.D., Edwards, J.E., & DeLessio, J. (1991). A logistic regression model for personnel selection. *Applied Psychological Measurement, 15*(2), 139-152.

Saville & Holdsworth, Ltd. (1988). *Civil Aviation Authority predictive validation study: The selection of air traffic control cadets.* Report to the CAA-UK, London: SHL.

# 7 Selecting and training air traffic controllers ab initio: Validation of a 1990s selection-testing program

*Richard E. Hicks, Bond University*
*Brian Keech, Airservices Australia*

## Synopsis and introduction

A review of the Civil Aviation Authority's air traffic control selection and training processes in Australia was carried out in 1992 by the Training Review Project Team (Keech, Maher, Donato & Sutherland, 1992). This review recommended change to the selection process then in place and the commencement of the College for Air Traffic Controller Training now based in Melbourne. The College took its first trainees based on the new selection procedures in 1994. This move to in-house selection and training mirrored to some extent the situation applying in the 1970s and early 1980s when the Australian Civil Aviation Authority (CAA, now Airservices Australia), conducted training through its Henty House facility in use at the time. The 1990s Airservices Australia selection processes and college facilities are more extensive and comprehensive than was the case in the 1970s and 1980s.

In between the two "in-house" approaches, from the mid-1980s to the mid-1990s, a combined university and CAA approach in air traffic control training was used. Emphasis was placed on a university diploma program combined with a college-based practical experience field training. A success rate of just under fifty percent had been achieved for the combined university and final field training ratings. At the time the opportunity was taken to develop air traffic controllers through a purpose oriented, vocational ATC training college. New selection processes were introduced at the same time for college entrants and involve an overall three-stage selection program. By mid-1997 the majority of those selected through the extensively advertised Campaign 1 had completed their training and ratings processes. A successful graduation rate of 70-75% as against the previous rates of around 50% has been achieved.

## Background

There is much national and international interest in and about air traffic control. It is an area that has far reaching impacts on the lives of many people and across many areas including political, legal, social and community areas and matters of environment and safety. Effective and efficient air traffic control selection programs play a significant part in contributing to the needs of the industry.

There have been a number of reported international studies on selection tests and processes in use. These include recent studies as well as those available to the 1992 review. Examples are those by Broach and Manning (1994, 1997); Collins, Schroeder and Nye (1989); Haglund (1994); Manning (1991); Manning, Rocco and Bryant (1989); Schroeder, Broach and Young (1993); Stoker, Hunter, Batchelor and Curran (1987); Wing and Manning, 1991; Wise, Hopkin and Garland (1994); and Young, Broach and Farmer (1996).

Findings from these studies or earlier related information underpinned many of the decisions made concerning tests to use in the Australian Air Traffic Control selection process. Specific tests were identified as likely to assess elements of the major ability and skill clusters involved in air traffic control performance (see later discussion). These were incorporated into the Primary Test Battery and the Assessment Centre programs. The choice of tests included local adaptation or development of the tests and simulations (Keech, 1992).

This current article gives special attention to the 1994 primary test battery used as the major initial screen and to the assessment centre tests used as the final screen for training course entry. A number of the tests then used were experimental and more tests were used than anticipated would be the case in due course, when the most successful of the tests would be selected for ongoing use. This paper gives attention to the overall selection process, not to the individual tests as such, though reference to the tests used will be made.

**Selection prior to the new processes**

Prior to the changes, selection processes emphasised specific recruitment standards and criteria, including:

- initial academic standing sufficient to meet CAA and university diploma entry requirements (for entry to the University of Tasmania's course),
- medical fitness,
- successful completion of an interview process (assessing motivation and background relevance), and
- successful completion of ability tests and general suitability questionnaires (including personality assessments).

On meeting the initial educational screen requirements the remaining applicants completed the tests and questionnaires and subsequently undertook the interview. The tests and questionnaires included five paper and pencil measures:

- a test of computational speed and accuracy,
- a map reading test (ability to measure distance between points on a map),
- a test of spatial visualisation ability (the Minnesota Paper Form Board test, in which applicants identify which one of five simple geometric shapes can be formed from several smaller given shapes),
- a questionnaire assessing study attitudes and personal style, and
- a self report inventory on aspects of anxiety (the State Trait Anxiety Inventory).

These tests were similar to those used in the 1970s and early 1980s. Hobbs and Luke (1985) of the Department of Aviation Psychological Services Division (as cited in the ATC Review Report) had reported on the success of the earlier tests in use. Essentially the same kinds of measures continued in use until the early 1990s, until the new comprehensive procedures put in place following the recommendations of the ATC Report Review.

The 1992 review members surveyed overseas practices in air traffic control selection and training and carried out an extensive job analysis and study of the air traffic controller in Australia. On the basis of the information gathered and analysed recommendations were made on those tests and procedures thought to be the most effective and relevant. The recommended new approaches included the use of a variety of paper and pencil, audio and computerised tests and job simulations, going well beyond the emphases in the earlier selection programs.

## Basic recommendations concerning testing and assessment: The underlying competencies

In summary the selection of tests was based on

- key attributes and competencies required in the work of the air traffic controller in Australia, identified following completion of a detailed job analysis, and
- extensive information gathering, including contact with overseas aviation agencies and test distributors in the UK, US and elsewhere.

The job analysis and review of overseas data indicated four main clusters of skills and competencies as being of importance for air traffic control trainee selection.

These four clusters were:

- visualisation (three dimensional spatial aptitude including problem solving ability),
- pattern management (planning, sequencing, prioritising and traffic problem solving),
- general problem solving (e.g., computational, convergent and divergent thinking) and
- human factor aspects (e.g., inter-personal, communication, team skills, decision making and stress management skills).

In addition ability to deal with organisational factors impacting on and interacting with the four clusters was also seen to be essential (see ATC Review Report, 1992, p. 7, on the "intelligence- ability cluster profile").

The approach to selecting new tests and strategies included giving specific attention to meeting *ten ATC competencies* reflecting the four clusters and the organisational context. At the time, Australian strategies were seen to emphasise only four of these ten, with the four in *italics* in the list below (from Attachment 1 of the 1992 Review Report, p. 63):

- ability to utilise logical analysis through the ability to follow complex instructions
- ability to reason with diagrams and utilise logical rules governing sequences
- ability to listen to audio instructions, check and carry out appropriate responses
- ability to check data
- *ability to visualise and manipulate three dimensional stimuli (develop mental pictures)*
- *ability for spatial relations, estimating lengths, angles and shapes*
- general intellectual orientation, verbal and numeric ability
- *arithmetic and/or mathematical ability*
- basic problem simulation to test multi-task ability
- *personality function, stress/anxiety core profile.*

In the review report, recommendations concerning selection were made to incorporate much more extensive assessment across the ten competencies (and other related attributes) and to investigate other approaches (tests or processes) among the four competency areas currently assessed.

*A recommended model of selection-training-career (professional) development based on identified competencies.* As a base an integrated selection, training and career development model was designed and recommended, based on the major competencies identified for air traffic controllers. This model was to enable selection and training decisions to be linked with the overall professional vocational goal: to produce competent qualified (en-route) air traffic controllers "ab initio"; that is, from aviation-inexperienced but interested and motivated applicants. In addition the model allowed for these controllers to continue career development to "full-performance" air traffic controller status, with career development planning based on the required competencies. (Of course, a number of aviation experienced individuals such as former pilots also apply for consideration; these are often able to complete course aspects quickly or receive credits where appropriate. They are not included in the validation figures reported in this article, which gives attention to the "ab initio" candidates).

The model has been able to be implemented directly with respect to the selection tests in use, and partially with respect to the training college programs (which use multiple competency simulations and study to achieve the end goals). The model with emphasis on the identified competencies has been implemented in a limited way with respect to changes in performance appraisals for licensed air traffic controllers. Such changes, with tailoring of assessments and assessment systems to include some competencies not previously addressed directly, take time, especially when current systems work soundly. Nevertheless, the model has been applied in detail to the first part of the process; it is this selection process which is the focus of this paper.

The application of the integrated model *to the selection process* can be demonstrated in part by reference to one competency area: personal or personality attributes. The heart of the recommendation is to examine the various selection strategy options available in each of the ten competency areas. For example, among the personality and related assessments a number of options were available besides or in addition to the State Trait Anxiety Inventory then used. Thus, the UK authorities used the Occupational Personality Questionnaire (OPQ), the US was using the 16PF, and New Zealand was using the Personality Research Form. There were other questionnaires assessing related and also possibly relevant personal qualities, such as Belbin's Team Roles Inventory and learning styles inventories. These were open for consideration in any intensive programs of selection. Thus, decisions on strategies and specific tests to use in a renewed selection process were to be made in line with the integrated, competency oriented model. In the event, with respect to personal quality measures, the new CAA-Airservices Australia program opted to use the OPQ, Belbin and the Learning Styles Inventory and also gathered other data related to personal history. This approach expanded on the earlier approach and made more data available for use in the selection process.

Methods of assessment and stages in assessment vary from country to country but all major authorities used cognitive paper and pencil aptitude testing (mostly comprehensive). Some used intensive "assessment centre" or other formal 2-3 day assessment approaches, while others used early screening via initial application blanks. Interviews were a standard part of procedures sometimes within the advanced testing or assessment centre stages. Screening during early stages of training, for example via ability demonstrated on simulators, was also a feature of US selection approaches. It was noted that those authorities using the more extensive selection programs were obtaining benefits in increased throughput (with attrition rates markedly lowered).

The scene was thus set for change in ATC selection and training in Australia. The new *selection* approach involves a three-stage "hurdle" process before commencement of training.

## The new selection processes from 1994 onwards

The new three-stage selection process now involves:

- the initial primary test battery stage and screening stage (Stage 1, following pre-screening of the applications to ensure the required educational qualifications),

- an interview stage (Stage 2) and

- comprehensive assessment centre testing stage (including work related simulation tests, personality measures and further interviews - Stage 3).

The primary test battery stage (PTB stage, Stage 1) of the program involved five tests with just three used in the early phase to obtain a total score. Subsequently all five tests were (are) used to give a total score on which progression to the next stage is based. These tests assess a number of the ten general competencies listed above, including diagrammatic logic and reasoning, three-dimensional spatial ability, ability to follow instructions dealing with spatial and other materials, numerical facility and multiple performance measures (e.g., implementing oral "interrupt" instructions while carrying out numerical tasks).

At the interview stage (Stage 2) background factors such as knowledge of the air traffic control environment and understanding of the demands and pressures of the work, were given emphasis. Expressed motivation and preferences, social skills and other factors such as self-awareness and self understanding are also examined. In Campaign 1 the interview made use of personality and personal questionnaires administered early in the process. In subsequent programs these questionnaires were part of assessment centre testing. The interview is not explored further in this report and is the subject of further study. Early results, however, demonstrate partial correlation with selected assessment centre outcomes but rather lower correlations (than for the cognitive tests) with subsequent training and field ratings.

At the assessment centre stage (Stage 3), comprehensive testing to assess all major competencies is carried out. This testing mirrors or checks some of the earlier testing and in addition incorporates assessments of general problem solving, dynamic memory, accuracy and speed in response, time pressure reaction and following directions. Performance on simulations of complex traffic movement (computer based, multi-task scenario performance tests), and personal, social and team preferences and skills are also assessed.

The overall success of the new process, assessed at the ratings stage (70% to 75% success rate vis-a-vis the early 50% success rate), has already been indicated.

## Validation review: General comments

This new selection process was examined with respect to its progress outcomes in 1997 (Hicks, 1997) and this current paper summarises the results. First over 2,400 applications and many more enquiries were received from the start of the Campaign. Some 2,283 Campaign 1 candidates met the educational screen and underwent the primary test battery. Of these some 550 underwent interviewing and 148 attended the Stage 3 assessment centre testing. Just over 100 of the assessment centre candidates were offered places in the ATC Training College courses. At the stage of writing results were available for some 60 who had attended one of the first four training college courses and, where successful, subsequently attempted the field ratings examinations required for licensing as an air traffic controller. Each course normally took around 16 candidates.

The recruitment rate (over 2,400 applications) was more than eight times the annual attraction rate over the previous 5-6 years of university-CAA joint venture and reflected in part the more extensive advertising and the shorter but very intense and more vocationally targeted program. The increased numbers also meant a wider pool from which to assess and choose the best applicants, and most likely a larger number of high quality applicants. These aspects impact on technical validity studies, increasing restriction of range effects. These effects were taken into account in the validation analyses of the tests and total criteria used.

## Tests in the Primary Test Battery (PTB)

The five PTB tests were aimed at assessing the selected core cognitive attributes (visualisation, problem solving, pattern and interruption-stress management capacity). Two of the five tests reflect emphases present in the earlier testing (spatial and numerical). Short term memory, planning skills, numerical facility, logical sequencing and spatial recognition as well as other specific skills are assessed by the five PTB tests.

### DIT5 "Diagramming DIT5"

This test was developed by Saville and Holdsworth (SHL) and is from the Information Technology Test Series. It involves the use of symbols representing complex instructions to be followed (for example, a diagram such as a letter within a circle may require a set of data to be re-ordered in some way; multiple instructions may be given). Ability to follow instructions, attention to detail and logical processing are involved.

*DT8 Diagrammatic reasoning and logic*

This test, also developed by the SHL group, involves general reasoning skills based on symbolic information.

*SIT7 Spatial test*

This spatial ability test developed by SHL is designed to measure the ability to visualise and manipulate shapes in three dimensions, given a two-dimensional drawing.

*NRT "Test NRT": Numerical Reasoning Test*

This 60-item test was locally developed for Airservices Australia. The Instructions page indicates that the test assesses numerical reasoning skills incorporating information of the type regularly used by Air Traffic Controllers and that it is to be completed concurrently with the Test IT. The questions range from simple questions involving one aircraft to more complex questions involving two or more aircraft; for example:

> "An aircraft arrived at Airport B at 9:37. If its flight time was 47 minutes, what time did it depart Airport A?"

*IT "Test IT"- Interrupt Test*

This 25-item test was developed for Airservices Australia. This is a 40-minute test completed at the same time as Test NRT. Instructions are given at varied times as set on the audio-tape.
    An example of the kind of interrupt item would be:

> *"Attention please. Look at 8 (a set of interlocking shapes on the separate answer sheet given to candidates). When I say "Go" but not before, make a figure T in the space which is in shape A but not in Shape B or C, and also make a figure M in the Shape to the left of Shape B.... Go."*

### Use of the tests in the Primary Test Battery: The PTB Total Scores

The predictor used as the basis for ranking performance on the Primary Test Battery results from summing the standard scores for each of the tests, though initially the first three tests alone were used. Total scores on the PTB3 (three tests) and PTB5 (five tests) were used as the basis for selection to the next stage. In turn these can be considered to be predictors of subsequent stages, that is, of the assessment centre total score, training college success and ratings success and failure. An outline of the tests used in the Assessment Centre and details on the training college subjects are given in later sections.

### Table 7.1
### Stage 1 PTB Total Test Scores correlated with later Criterion Stages #

| Criteria | AC Comb T | Course Theory | Course CR, SA, C | Course 9 units | FFT Rating |
|---|---|---|---|---|---|
| N | 148 | 57 | 57 | 57 | 57 |
| *Predictors* | | | | | |
| Primary test battery | .52 ** | .16 ns | .22 * | .09 ns | -.17 ns |
| PTB3 Total (3 tests) | (.29) | (.08) | (.12) | (.04) | (-.09) |
| Primary test battery | .48 ** | .53 ** | .48 ** | .40 ** | .31 * |
| PTB5 Total (5 tests) | (.22) | (.25) | (.22) | (.18) | (.14) |

*Coefficients corrected for restriction of range (uncorrected in parentheses).*
*\* indicates significance level $p < .05$; \*\* indicates significance level $p < .01$*
*# The criterion stages are:*

| | |
|---|---|
| AC Comb T | Stage 3 Assessment Centre Combined T score |
| Course Theory | Stage 4 Training course Phase 2 Theory units |
| Course CR, SA, C | Stage 4 Training course - sum of three main subjects (Conflict Recognition, Separation Assurance, Coordination) |
| Course 9 units | Stage 4 training course- sum of other 9 core subjects |
| FFT Rating | Stage 5 to final field training- Rating Success or Failure |

The PTB scores did not predict interview outcomes but as indicated in Table 7.1, the summed total scores (both PTB3 and PTB5) predict strongly and significantly subsequent success in the assessment centre stage, the next major stage. Then the PTB5 score (but not the PTB3 score) successfully predicts course success and the final field ratings for licensing as an air traffic controller. Though not indicated in Table 7.1, the numerical facility and interrupt tests among the five tests were the most successful and the three-dimensional spatial ability test was the least successful in predicting subsequent outcomes. Follow-up cross-validation research is underway, to confirm these findings (subject to the small sample size involved) and to determine whether (and which) three or four tests may be most valid and efficient in the initial testing stage.

**Tests in the Assessment Centre stage**

*The Assessment Centre stage* involves a test battery comprising measures related in general to spatial conceptualisation, memory, logical processing, and problem solving and includes computerised job sample tests simulating aspects of the work of air traffic controllers.

**Tests in the Assessment Centre testing**

As for the PTB tests the tests used in the assessment centre assessed the selected core cognitive attributes and also gather non-cognitive data. The cognitive tests used each assess multiple competencies and include:

- tests used by the UK Civil Aviation Authority (Saville and Holdsworth tests): the Sort test, the Directions test and the Moving Objects test, including time-pressure responses and ability to handle information from different sources including interruption sources

- tests used by the US Federal Aviation Administration: Safety and Efficiency tests, Pattern Recognition tests, a Continuous Memory test and a Static Vector test, and a Job Sample test with speed and accuracy, scanning, prioritising, interruption-coping and memory skills all significantly involved

- tests from Embry Riddle Aeronautical University: the Manikin, Absolute Differences, Dynamic Memory and Grid tests, involving verbal and spatial memory, left/right handedness, and arithmetical and spatial ability, and

- a job sample test developed/adapted by the Australian Civil Aviation Authority, assessing coordination, prioritisation, vectoring and working memory skills (a Tracon simulation).

Results on these tests were weighted and combined to give a 24-weight overall AC *Combined T Score*. The Safety and Tracon tests received 5 weights each, and 1 or 2 weights were assigned to each of the response time, continuous memory, pattern recognition, job sample efficiency, speed-accuracy trade-off and other tests or sub-tests, but not the Embry-Riddle test initially). Subsequently a 34-weight Combined T score was used, incorporating 10 additional weights from the Embry-Riddle tests. These included weightings of 1-3, on the four sub-tests with emphasis on accuracy and speed-accuracy trade-off. These 24-weight and 34-weight scores reflected assessment of aspects of the four major competency groups: visualisation, pattern management, problem-solving and human factors.

Table 7.2 gives the corrected correlation coefficients for the Combined T Score (24 weight) compared with success in the training course (three measures) and in the final field ratings (pass/fail) for licensing as an air traffic controller. The coefficients are each highly significant and indicate the success of the assessment centre tests (combined) in prediction of subsequent training and ratings outcomes. The 34-weight Combined T Score including additional tests produced similar and in one or two instances slightly improved coefficients as shown in the Table.

**Table 7.2**
**Stage 3 Assessment Centre Combined T Score correlated with later Criterion Stages #**

| Criteria | Course Theory | Course CR, SA, C | Course 9 units | FFT Rating |
|---|---|---|---|---|
| *Predictors* | | | | |
| *Assessment Centre* | | | | |
| Combined T Score T-24 (for N = 57) | .44 ** (.22) | .51 ** (.26) | .39 ** (.19) | .33 ** (.16) |
| *Assessment Centre* | | | | |
| Combined T Score T-34 (for N = 50) Including Embry-Riddle | .43 ** (.24) | .53 ** (.37) | .49 ** (.29) | .27 ** (.19) |

*(Coefficients corrected for restriction of range- uncorrected in parentheses).*
\* *indicates significance level: p < .05;* \*\* *indicates significance level: p < .01*
\# *The criterion stages are* listed at the foot of Table 7.1

The performance of the individual tests are not discussed in detail in this article, though the most effective tests appear to be the Safety, Sort, Continuous Memory, Time-wall pattern recognition and, among the Embry-Riddle sub-tests, the Dynamic Memory (accuracy) and Absolute Difference (speed-accuracy trade-off) tests. All specific tests and sub-tests are being examined in a cross-validation study (including the second half of the college trainees). The Moving Objects test was used as a trial test in the Assessment Centre and analysis of its results will take place during this further study..

As indicated in Table 7.2, the predictive validity coefficients of the tests in the Combination weighted T scores are at significant levels, but economies of operation are needed and the best pattern of weights and of tests to use are yet to be determined. These will be reported in due course when the question of a three-stage hurdle process versus a one or two stage process leading to training will also be examined.

*Other, non-cognitive assessments*

In addition to the cognitive test battery in the assessment centres, non-cognitive assessments were also made. These included personal and interpersonal skills, personality qualities, preferences and styles. The role of these assessments was to provide additional information for the interviewers and assessors carrying out final grading and the scores were not incorporated directly into the Combined T score. While several of the non-cognitive tests were administered earlier in the Campaign 1 programs these tests and questionnaires are now administered during the assessment centre phase. Further research is proposed concerning the use and predictive validities of the non-cognitive attributes.

**The training course**

The Training Course stage involves more than twelve months study and simulation work, over four phases. These phases are:

- an initial short phase not examined in this study because of its introductory nature,

- a theoretical grounding phase (Phase 2),

- a procedural simulation phase involving twelve subjects (Phase 3) and

- a radar simulation phase also again including the related twelve subjects (Phase 4).

The four phases are followed by the Final Field Training (this is essentially "Phase 5"). A final practical examination follows, and success leads to initial licensing (Rating) as an air traffic controller.

The nature of the training course is clearly vocational and career oriented with limited attention to general education subjects not directly related to air traffic control (though general problem solving, numerical facility, communication skills and teamwork approaches are involved in the subject areas). The twelve subjects studied in the Procedural and Radar Simulation phases (3 and 4) are:

> Conflict Recognition
> Separation Assurance
> Coordination
> Work and Time Management
> Traffic Planning
> Radar Techniques in the Radar Simulations
> IFER- Emergency Response
> Strip-work
> Phraseology and Communication
> Equipment Handling
> Airspace Knowledge and
> Hand-over/Takeover (with respect to coordination between en-route air traffic controllers handling adjacent routes).

Subject results were available for the three main phases of training. Using these results three overall course criterion variables were calculated. The first of the three criteria was: "Phase 2 Theory", essentially giving a ranking on success in this phase emphasising the theoretical underpinnings of the course. The second was a "Combined 3" criterion, based on the sum of the percentages obtained in three central subjects over Phases 3 and 4 (the first three in the above list). The third was a "Combined 9" criterion: based on the sum of the grades assigned to each of the remaining nine core subjects (the remaining nine in the above list).

In the study reported in this paper a total of 57 candidates had completed the PTB tests, assessment centre testing, and the training course and ratings stages. While some 64 trainees were enrolled in the four courses, a small number of these had been granted special entrance because of relevant related ATC experience or had been transferred to later courses and scores were not available for comparison.

The results of the PTB and assessment centre stages in predicting success in combinations of these occupation-relevant subjects have been presented in Table 7.1 and have already been discussed. The correlations between training course success and success in the final field examination are also high as would be expected, reflecting the "virtual reality" of the simulation experience used in training.

Nevertheless a few trainees need a little time to settle down into the "real world" of real planes and real time lines; the supervision in the preliminary periods of the final field practice exposure is especially important in these cases. Some individuals who have passed the training course aspects but at marginal levels carry on to be successful in the practical field training. A few of these, however, fail at this stage. In terms of overall course progress nearly 75% make it successfully through the full training and ratings program. Of the 25% who fail, 15-20% are failed before they get to the final field exposure; just 5-10% fail at the final examination.

These figures of around 70-75% are much improved on the earlier throughput rates of around 40 to 50%. Examination of the performance of individual tests has identified ways in which the failure rates during the training course might be further reduced, hopefully yielding success rates in due course at and over the 80% level. In the meantime the new selection processes have been shown to be working in the direction desired. The changes to the in-house selection processes have seen a marked improvement overall. These results of the selection process also need to be seen in company with the changed training location and approach (where emphasis is placed on specialised vocational training and experience). The success of the new selection and training processes have more than justified the changes made and the returns in terms of financial savings and safety, efficiency and effectiveness in control of the airways are substantial.

On the wider front in the Australian scene, significant changes may be set to occur in the aviation industry. For example, extensive radar coverage across major parts of Australia via a new TAAATS system is ready for implementation and in addition a more streamlined, "commercial" and business orientation is being introduced, leading to structural changes and changes to selection and training administration. Ongoing research will help inform the decision making process in relation to selection and training needs. That the current selection system has been changed to meet the changing demands as assessed in the early 1990s and has taken into account some of the known future needs, suggests that the Airservices Australia's selection processes are in sound order to face the challenges ahead. The results presented in this paper have demonstrated that sound selection processes exist and these should continue to prove valuable in screening potential air traffic controllers in the monitoring and the safety of Australia's skies.

**References**

ATC Training Review Project Team (1992). Report on the review of the ATC Training system. CAA Central Office Library, Canberra.

Broach, D., & Manning, C.A. (1997). *Review of air traffic controller selection: An international perspective.* US Federal Aviation Administration report: DOT/FAA/AM-97/15. National Technical Information Service, Springfield, Virginia.

Broach, D., & Manning, C.A. (1994). *Validity of the air traffic control specialist nonradar screen as a predictor of performance in radar-based air traffic control training.* Federal Aviation Administration Report: DOT/FAA/AM-94/9.

Collins, W., Schroeder, D., & Nye, L. (1989). *Relationships of anxiety scores to academy and field training performance of air traffic control specialists.* Federal Aviation Administration report: DOT/FAA/AM-89-7.

Haglund, R. (1994). Presentation of a Swedish study program concerning recruitment, selection and training of student air traffic controllers: the MRU Project Phase 1. In J.A. Wise, V.D. Hopkin, & D.J. Garland (Eds.), *Human factors certification of advanced aviation technologies.* Embry-Riddle Aeronautical University Press.

Hicks, R.E. (1997). *Validation of the ab initio ATC selection program.* Report to Airservices Australia. Air Traffic Services Human Resources Branch, Airservices Australia, Canberra.

Keech, B. (1992). *Selection Model - New ATC National Training System: Aptitude/Ability - Competency Continuum.* (Internal memorandum and report, Air Traffic Services Human Resources Branch, Airservices Australia, Canberra, ACT).

Keech, B., Maher, P., Donato, R., & Sutherland, P. (1992). *Review of air traffic services training system.* Report to Civil Aviation Authority (now Airservices Australia), Canberra.

Manning, C.A. (1991). Individual differences in air traffic control specialist training performance. *Journal of the Washington Academy of Sciences, 81,* 2, 101-109.

Manning, C., Rocco, P., & Bryant, K. (1989). Prediction of success in FAA air traffic control field training as a function of selection and screening test performance. FAA Report: DOT/FAA/AM-89-6.

Schroeder, D., Broach, D., & Young, W. (1993). *Contribution of personality to the prediction of success in initial air traffic control specialist training.* Federal Aviation Administration report: DOT/FAA/AM-93-4.

Stoker, P., Hunter, D.R., Batchelor, C.L., & Curran, L.T. (1987). *Air traffic controller trainee selection.* Air Force Human Resources Laboratory, Brooks Air Force Base, Texas.

Wing, H., & Manning, C. (Eds.) (1991). *Selection of air traffic controllers: complexity, requirements, and public interest.* Federal Aviation Administration: DOT/FAA/AM-91/9.

Wise, J.A., Hopkin, V.D., & Garland, D.J. (1994). *Human factors certification of advanced aviation technologies.* Embry-Riddle Aeronautical University Press.

Young, W., Broach, D., & Farmer, W. (1996*). Differential prediction of FAA Academy performance on the basis of gender and written air traffic control specialist aptitude test scores.* Federal Aviation Administration report: DOT/FAA/AM-96-13.

# Part 2
# TRAINING

# 8 The foundations of Crew Resource Management should be laid during ab initio flight training

*Steven J. Thatcher*
*University of South Australia*

## Introduction

Airline passenger safety has increased substantially since the 1950s. However in relatively recent times the accident rate has plateaued. The previous gains in airline safety have been largely due to the increased mechanical reliability of the turbo-jet, and on-board systems. At present it has been calculated that about 70% of accidents are caused by pilot error (Helmreich & Foushee, 1993). Cooper, White, and Lauber (1980) and Murphy (1980) (cited in Cooper et al., 1980) suggest that human error, or pilot error, was more likely the result of failure in team communication and coordination than failure in technical flight proficiency. In an effort to further reduce the accident rate many airlines have introduced crew resource management (CRM) which focuses on crew coordination, communication and effectiveness.

Hackman (1993) is concerned that CRM programs tend to focus on improving the attitudes and performances of individual pilots in the crew in order to improve team functioning, rather than improving the behaviours, attitudes and performances of the crew as a whole. This suggests a belief that improved team functioning will come about naturally if individual crew members becomes familiar with their own personal style of leadership /followership, and understand that there is a need for good communication and coordination within the cockpit. However, team skills are learned most effectively in actual team situations. It should not be assumed that team skills are necessarily innate or learned during traditional flight training (Hackman, 1993).

So why shouldn't team skills be learned during basic flight training? There are two important arguments for learning team skills at the ab initio level.

- The student pilot is a relatively "clean slate". Therefore pilots can construct a "cognitive picture" of potentially desirable team behaviours during basic flight training when student pilot repertoires of flight behaviours are relatively small (Thatcher, 1997).

- Team skills are learned in the cockpit during flight in the same context in which the skills will later be utilised (Thatcher, 1997). Lintern (1995) has also argued from the field of situated cognition that learning will be ineffective if removed from the context in which the behaviours must subsequently be deployed.

Learning team skills early in flight training is important because they form the foundation for later development. But of more importance to CRM is the realisation that a person in a highly aroused condition will tend to revert to well learned behaviours, exhibiting whatever response is most dominant for that person in that particular situation (Zajonc, 1965).

Research by Li and Baker (1994; 1995) in two separate studies found that pilots who were previously involved in commuter aircraft or air taxi accidents or violations have a significantly higher risk of subsequent accident or violation than their counterparts. Their research suggests that initial flight training influences a pilot's future flying career and that attitudes and behaviours learned at an early stage in a pilot's career are highly resistant to decay, despite major learning events such as accidents or incidents.

If a crew-centred flight training (CCFT) curriculum were adopted team skills could be learned naturally during flight training (Thatcher, 1998). The attitudes learned in CCFT would become entrenched and eventually form part of a pilot's personality. CRM courses could use these team skills as a foundation for further development and would not have to assist pilots modify team-destructive behaviours.

## Crew-Centred Flight Training (CCFT)

*Aim of Crew-Centred Flight Training*

The aim of Crew-Centred Flight Training (CCFT) is to provide a nurturing environment in which a pilot can learn to be safe and proficient in the technical aspects of flying, and more importantly, learn the educational and team processes, embodied in the training, which will provide a foundation for further development (Thatcher, 1998).

The central principle of CCFT is the establishment of a student-instructor team that takes responsibility for the student's learning. Traditionally flight training has been mediated using an instructor-centred approach with the instructor taking responsibility for the student's progress. As a consequence very few students have adequately learned the educational and team processes embodied in the flight training.

The traditional or pedagogical (that is child education) approach is based on two assumptions about student pilots (Table 8.1):

"1) *The need to know.* Learners only need to know that they must learn what the teacher teaches if they want to pass and get promoted; they do not need to know how what they learn will apply to their lives.

2) *The learner's self-concept.* The teacher's concept of the learner is that of a dependant personality; therefore, the learner's self concept eventually becomes that of a dependant personality." (Knowles, 1990).

These assumptions are instructor-centred. A student's prior experience is not considered relevant to the learning task and a student's motivation and readiness to learn is largely dependent on the instructor. The skill or knowledge learned is taught as a discrete component, and it is assumed that it will be applied sometime in the future.

Furthermore, an instructor-centred approach assigns to the instructor (or the flying school) the full responsibility for decisions about what will be learned, how it will be learned, and indeed, even the assessment as to whether it has been learned or not. The educational relationship is instructor-focused and instructor-directed rather than student-focused or student-directed. The student pilot is relegated to taking a submissive or dependent role in the relationship. A role predominantly based on following an instructor's directions in order to elicit an instructor's reward and advance to the next lesson.

## Table 8.1
### Educational assumptions of instructor-centred and crew-centred flight training

| | Educational Assumptions | |
|---|---|---|
| *Flight Training Type* | **Instructor-Centred** | **Crew-Centred** |
| *The need to know* | Dictated by instructor, credit learning (Extrinsic) | Mutually ascertained by team, student research (Intrinsic) |
| *Self-concept* | Dependency | Assertive Self-directing |
| *Student's prior experience* | Irrelevant | Used as foundation for further learning |
| *Readiness to learn* | Instructor dependent Social pressure (Extrinsic) | Student's developmental level (Intrinsic) |
| *Motivation to learn* | Instructors reward Credit learning | Self fulfilment |
| *Time line for application of learning* | In the future | In the present |
| *Orientation to learning* | Subject-centred curriculum | Problem-centred curriculum |

A CCFT or andragogical (that is adult education) approach assumes that student pilots are assertive and self-directing, that the "need to know" will be determined by the crew based on the student's requirements. A student's prior experience is regarded as a valuable input to the learning process and the crew's assessment of the student's readiness and motivation to learn is based on the student's developmental level and desires. The skill or knowledge learned is taught as solutions to real-life problems or situations, which have application in the present rather than the future. Therefore in CCFT the instructor-student crew has a mutual responsibility for decisions regarding what, how and when knowledge and skills are learned. Student performance, assessment and further training is mutually negotiated by the crew. In CCFT the flight instructor adopts the role of flight facilitator and facilitates student learning within the flight environment.

### CCFT Curriculum Design

A CCFT curriculum encompasses more than training in the technical aspects of flight proficiency. It provides an education in both crew dynamics and educational processes. Training in crew dynamics will enable students to develop more favourable team attitudes and behaviours, whereas training in educational processes will enable students to learn effectively in the absence of the instructor. This last point is important because learning to fly is a life-long education with the majority of learning taking place away from the flight training environment (Table 8.2).

**Table 8.2**
**Curriculum design characteristics of Instructor-centred flight training and crew-centred flight training**

| | Curriculum Design Characteristics | |
| | Instructor-centred Flight Training | Crew-centred Flight Training |
| --- | --- | --- |
| *Climate* | Authority-oriented Flying School-centred Instructor-centred Competitive | Mutually respectful Crew-centred Student-centred Collaborative |
| *Planning* | By Flying School | Mutual, negotiation Between interested groups |
| *Diagnosis of needs* | By Instructor By Flying School | Mutual negotiation By crew Self-diagnosis |
| *Formulation of objectives* | By Instructor By Flying School | Mutual negotiation By crew |
| *Design* | Training syllabus dictated order Subject dictated order Content units | Sequence based on student readiness Problem units |
| *Activities* | Based on content and information transmission | Based on experience transmission Process learning |
| *Evaluation, assessment* | By Instructor By Flying School | Mutual negotiation By crew |

*Climate*. The atmosphere or climate that evolves during the training must be mutually respectful and collaborative. The student must feel comfortable and safe to convey any attitude or ask any question. Individuals in the crew must not feel that they are being judged, evaluated or held up to ridicule. In short they must not feel threatened. They should feel that they are accepted as valid individuals of the crew, and that they are being listened to and understood. The instructor's role is to establish a supportive atmosphere where instructor and student act as a disciplined crew and not as individuals. For example, an instructor must facilitate a cockpit climate conducive to checklists and briefings being completed in a disciplined fashion.

*Planning.* In order for the crew to reach its maximum potential both instructors and students must feel that they have had the opportunity to participate in all matters that will affect them. They must feel that they have been represented by their respective representative bodies in the planning stage of the curriculum.

*Diagnosis of needs.* A CCFT curriculum should consider real flight situations and problems, and the sequence should be dictated by a student's readiness to learn. This is in contrast to the traditional flight training curriculum based on strict adherence to the flight syllabus and presented with a task or subject orientation. For example, traditionally a student is taught the following basic sequence before first solo: Taxying and Effects of Controls, Straight and Level, Climbing and Descending, Turns and Circuits. The instructor assesses the student, and if judged satisfactory, passes the student to undertake the next lesson in the flight sequence. This design is very much syllabus dictated and instructor-focussed. A more CCFT approach would be to discuss circuits with the student and determine, with the student, what is required to be learned before a circuit can be flown. That is the crew determine that the student needs to know how the controls operate, how to taxi the aircraft, how to fly straight and level, how to climb and descend and how to turn. This approach is problem based and the student is continually reminded of the primary objective, to fly a circuit.

*Formulation of objectives, design and evaluation.* The primary objective can be divided into a series of mutually negotiated secondary objectives, as previously discussed, which form the individual lessons in the flight sequence for that particular student. During the individual lessons in the flight sequence the student is evaluated, in terms of assessment and remedial training, by mutual negotiation between the instructor and the student. The student plays an interactive role during the debriefing sessions. Progress sheets should be designed to include sections for both instructor and student comment. Further training is then designed by mutual negotiation.

*Activities.* Lessons should be planned such that the student learns from the past experiences of the instructor in a flight environment which reinforces beneficial team behaviours.

Instructors and flying school management can evaluate their own attitudes and behaviours to see if they are compatible with CCFT by recognising the crew-centred answers to the following seven questions (Rogers, 1948).

1. Do I trust the capacities of the crew, and of the individuals in the crew, to meet the problems encountered, or do I basically trust only my self?
2. Do I create an atmosphere that frees the crew for creative discussion by being willing to understand, accept, and respect *all* attitudes, or do I find myself trying to subtly manipulate crew discussion so that it comes out my way?
3. Do I, as instructor, participate by honest expression of my own attitudes, but without trying to control the student's attitudes?
4. Do I rely on basic attitudes for motivation, or do I think surface procedures motivate behaviour?
5. Am I, as instructor, willing to be responsible for those aspects of action which the crew has delegated to me?
6. Do I trust the student to actively engage in the learning environment?
7. When tensions occur, do I try to make it possible for them to be brought out into the open?

**Discussion**

Traditionally flight instruction has been mediated using a pedagogical approach, with students having little, if any, input into what, how and when knowledge and skills will be learned. Students (and indeed instructors) have come to understand that students must know their place, that they must learn discipline. However, this traditional type of discipline is based on an instructor-centred, autocratic leadership style, rather than the self-discipline of a self-directing student pilot. Traditional flight training has achieved a high level of technical proficiency and has, therefore, remained relatively unchanged and unchallenged. However, the success of this approach has been mainly due to the individual attention received by the student and the importance of situated cognition to learning a skill. Unfortunately, given the multi-crew environment in modern airline operations, it is no longer sufficient for an individual to be technically competent, it is also necessary for an individual to have learned positive crew attitudes and behaviours. It is important for pilots to develop these attitudes early in flight training, where they can become well established and used as the foundation for further learning. These attitudes are best learned naturally, in an atmosphere of mutual respect and trust, where student pilots feels "safe" to explore their learning environment. The creation of this training environment is the essential element of CCFT. The flight instructor becomes a flight facilitator.

Furthermore, because these behaviours and attitudes have been learned at an early stage in a pilot's cognitive and psychomotor development these attitudes and behaviours are likely to resist decay and be manifested at times of high arousal in emergency situations. Using CCFT it is possible to lay the foundations for CRM during basic flight training.

## References

Cooper, G.E., White, M.D., & Lauber, J.K. (Eds.), (1980). *Resource management on the flightdeck: Proceedings of a NASA/industry workshop. (NASA CP-2120).* Moffett Field, CA: NASA-Ames Research Center.

Hackman, J.R. (1993). New directions for CRM training. In E.L. Weiner, B.G. Kanki, & R.L. Helmreich, (Eds.), *Cockpit Resource Management.* San Diego: Academic Press.

Helmreich, R.L. & Foushee, H.C. (1993). Why crew resource management? In E.L. Weiner, B.G. Kanki, & R.L. Helmreich (Eds.), *Cockpit Resource Management.* San Diego: Academic Press.

Li, G., & Baker, S P. (1994). Prior accident and violation records of pilots in commuter and air taxi crashes: A case study. *Aviation, Space, & Environmental Medicine, 65*(11), 979-985.

Li, G., & Baker, S.P. (1995). Crash and violation experience of pilots involved in prior commuter and air taxi crashes: A historical cohort study. *Aviation, Space, & Environmental Medicine, 66*(12), 1131-1135.

Lintern, G. (1995). Flight instruction: The challenge from situated cognition. *The International Journal of Aviation Psychology, 5*(4), 327-350.

Rogers, C.R. (1948). Some implications of client-centered counseling for college personnel work. *Education & Psychol. Measurement, 8*, 540-549.

Thatcher, S.J. (1997, April). *Flight instruction or flight facilitation: A foundation for crew resource management.* Paper presented at the Ninth International Symposium on Aviation Psychology, Columbus, OH.

Thatcher, S.J. (1998*). Towards crew-centred flight training.* Manuscript submitted for publication.

Zajonc, R.B. (1965). Social facilitation. *Science, 149*, 269-274.

# 9 A new way to deliver an old message

*Barrie Hocking*
*Australian Aviation College*

## Introduction

The traditional method of training pilots was developed originally by the RAF/RAAF and was adopted by the general aviation industry many years ago. Those people who know about flight instruction will recognise the terms "Effects of Controls" and "Straight and Level". These are lesson structures that have remained effectively unchanged since the 1950's. The lesson structures were designed for aspiring pilots who were working in their first language, were from a Western culture and had background exposure to technology. These training structures have been broadly accepted as 'the grail' by most training organisations with only small modifications to suit specific requirements.

The challenge of improving early identification of airline cadets lacking in background experience as opposed to those unable to perform these skills meant old ways of training had to be critically examined and challenged in order to improve effectiveness, efficiency and flexibility of the training process.

The Australian Aviation College (AAC) has set out to improve the method of delivering flight training for ab initio airline cadet pilots. These changes impact most on cadets from different cultures and those who have English as a second language. The purpose of this paper is to overview the modified method of flying training now in use at the AAC, specifically up to first solo.

## Background

The AAC is an airline training college based in Adelaide, South Australia. The College conducts ab initio pilot training for airline organisations from around the world. Since 1988 the College has graduated over 1000 cadets with a large number of these being from Asia.

Airline cadets in training at the AAC are from a wide variety of backgrounds, cultures and language levels. The average AAC airline training program entails 50 weeks of intensive integrated ground and flight training. Clearly, the airline client's investment in each cadet is substantial. The AAC's ability to deliver a syllabus easily adapted to the varying backgrounds of the cadets without compromising the development of sound flying skills is fundamental to the provision of customer service.

The diverse backgrounds of the cadets require that an understanding of a broad range of cultures be part of the process. With this in mind a system was needed where the teaching process was clear and the rate of delivery could be adapted to match the individual's ability to rapidly absorb knowledge, particularly in the early flights. This system would need to assist early identification of those students who, despite an improved training delivery, still would fail to complete the course of training due to a lack of ability.

**Discussion**

*Attitude flying - essential to basic flight training*

Attitude, in a training context, is the position of the aeroplane relative to either a natural or artificial horizon. Attitude is measured in terms of pitch (nose up or down) and roll (angle of bank). In level flight, in a climb, a descent or whilst turning the performance required is achieved by setting an attitude, either by relation to the natural horizon through the windscreen or to the artificial horizon which is an instrument on the control panel. The attitude is used in conjunction with a power setting to achieve the required flight path and the performance parameters.

The alternative to attitude flying is performance flying. This occurs when the pilot uses the indication of the performance instruments, especially air speed and altimeter to dictate the selection of attitude. A pilot who flies by "chasing performance" will tend not to stabilise the aircraft attitude. He/she will be over-referencing the performance indicators and will make attitude changes indirectly through the performance indicators. This process is inherently less stable and as a result requires much greater attention from the pilot to keep the aircraft flying within the required parameters. In periods of high work load, for example during take off and landing in poor conditions and during emergencies, it is recognised that the pilot who flies by performance rapidly becomes overloaded and has reduced ability to safely perform the required tasks.

A pilot who flies using the attitude information correctly will select an attitude first, hold the attitude for a period of time sufficient for the aircraft's performance to become observable and reliable, assess the performance and then adjust the attitude to make any corrections necessary. He/she will repeat this process throughout all phases of the flight. There will also be periods of time (albeit sometime very short) where the attitude remains constant.

It is essential for the fundamental difference between the "correct" and the "incorrect" techniques to be understood by the student within the first few hours of flight. This concept of attitude flying is then practiced and reinforced throughout the rest of the cadet's training.

### Identification of the core competencies including attitude control

*Problem:* The traditional syllabus veiled the emphasis of sound attitude control amongst aspects of a less critical nature. Historically, there were many 'nice to knows' obscuring the critical elements of early flight training. The single most critical aspect of initial ab initio training is the concept of attitude flight. The non-essential language and technical requirements of these early sorties was sufficiently complicated to hinder total understanding by a cadet who has English as a second language.

*Solution:* A careful analysis was made of the skills necessary to fly an aircraft safely using the correct technique. The concept of introducing attitude aspects at the very beginning of flight training required a restructure of the training objectives. The planning began by producing a list of critical core competencies required for flying an aircraft, up to the point at which the cadet is first able to fly solo. For example:

- How to recognise an attitude
- How to hold an attitude
- How to change an attitude, etc.

With the restructuring, each objective's requirements became simple to explain and for the student to understand.

### A structural comparison of the two systems

Table 9.1 compares the structure of the old method of delivery and the new. The new method does not have predetermined objectives for each flight. Teaching begins where it left off in the last flight. For comparison, the lessons have been divided up into reasonably typical groupings that would apply to the average cadet.

**Table 9.1**

**Example of some of the structural changes made to the syllabus**

| Old Syllabus | New Syllabus |
|---|---|
| **Effects of Controls**<br>• Primary Effects of Controls<br>• Secondary Effects of Controls<br>• Effect of Changing Power and Flap<br>• Ancillary control | **Flight One**<br>• How to hold the Cruise Attitude<br>• How to hold the Climb Attitude<br>• How to hold the Descent Attitude<br>• Without Trim<br>• With Trim<br>• How to change power by sound<br>• How to maintain an attitude while changing power |
| **Straight and Level/Turning**<br>• Introduce Straight and Level<br>• Flight including the use of performance instruments<br>• Review Trim<br>• Effect of Changing Power and<br>• Flap on Straight and Level<br>• Turning Flight including the use of performance instruments | **Flight Two**<br>• How to maintain an attitude while changing power<br>• Climbing, descending and turning attitudes |
| **Climbing and Descending**<br>• Climbing Flight<br>• Descending Flight<br>• The effect of power and flap on descents | **Flight Three**<br>• Introduction of performance instruments<br>• Review all attitudes and add performance checking.<br>• Teach checking the correction process after assessment of trend and value |

*Timing of the introduction of performance instruments*

*Problem:* The conventional lesson structure introduced the assessment of performance indicators at a stage where the student was struggling with simply holding an attitude.

*Solution:* During the first flights the performance instruments are covered. This focuses the student (and instructor) on the skills of selecting and holding attitudes. Once the instructor considers the student is ready the instruments are uncovered and the appropriate scan taught. At this point the student has developed a focus on attitude flying and has also developed the skill of attitude control necessary to make the adjustments.

## Subdivision of training

*Problem:* Within the conventional syllabus the logical subdivision of each sequence was not clear. Instructors usually identified the main objectives, but since it was not spelt out in the syllabus material the process of meeting training objectives in an efficient way was sometimes "hit and miss" and varied amongst instructors.

*Solution:* Each objective is subdivided into a series of simple tasks. Each task is introduced individually, in order to overcome the problems of language and the problem of students becoming intimidated by the complexity of the objective. This also makes the assessment of the core competencies more obvious for instructors.

This incremental skill development uses a building block process. The process of ensuring that each new task is a logical progression from the last also increases the rate of retention and reduces the need to reteach tasks at a later date. Ancillary tasks are introduced when the information is relevant.

There is a comprehensive training guide which clearly identifies each objective and how to teach it most effectively. This helps standardisation and guides each instructor towards effective teaching methodology.

## Progressing when student is competent

*Problem:* Using the old syllabus, instructors were prone to move to new syllabus items before the student was competent to do so.

*Solution:* At the beginning of each lesson the material covered in the last sortie is reviewed. This is a check that the student has retained the skills and gives the instructor the opportunity to revise one or more of the tasks if necessary. The instructor is then able to introduce new objectives confident that the prerequisite skills are sound. This is fundamental to the success of the system.

The instructor then demonstrates each new task then hands over to the student and talks him or her through the task. The student is then allowed to practice without further input from the instructor. The instructor checks that each task can be performed to a satisfactory standard before moving on to the next. At the end of each sortie the instructor will briefly demonstrate the tasks to be introduced in the next sortie.

## *Cultural considerations affecting attitude technique*

*Problem:* The traditional lesson structure expects from the outset that the cadet pilot will easily understand the intricacies of attitude flight. It demands that the student be quickly able to build the required "workcycles" to accurately set attitude and then critically scan the performance instruments to assess whether or not the attitude is correct. (Workcycles are a series of repetitive tasks that need to be performed during the flying process. A classic example would be "Attitude-Lookout-Performance". The idea behind a workcycle is that it helps cue the required actions using a cyclical process. So in this example the student would check Attitude, then move to the lookout for other aircraft and then crosscheck performance to determine whether the attitude is correct.)

Students from many cultures try to please the instructor (perceived, in some cultures, to be all-important). In order to please the instructor they make every effort to fly as accurately as possible from the beginning. This desire to perform accurately quite naturally encourages incorrect use of the performance instruments.

*Solution:* With the amendment of the syllabus we recommended two major changes in the cockpit. The student takes a photocopied picture of the aircraft windscreen when he/she goes flying in the first few sorties. As the instructor introduces each new attitude to the student it is recorded on the windscreen picture. The student is compelled to think about how the attitude looks in order to draw it and takes with him/her a record of the attitudes that he/she can refer to after the flight.

Secondly, any temptation to use instruments prematurely to measure performance is prevented. During the initial introduction of attitude only, the instructor covers all of the flight instruments after a safe distance from the ground has been achieved. These remain covered until the instructor is satisfied that it is time to start to develop the scan of the performance instruments. Correct scan is taught by uncovering the appropriate performance instrument for a short time. This enables the student to assess the need for an attitude change but then, as the instrument is recovered, compels the student to look back to the attitude in order to make any appropriate changes. Once the student has developed the correct scan the instruments may be uncovered permanently. The instructor must, however, remain aware of the student's scan and if any evidence of performance flying is detected should re-cover the instruments to draw the attention of the student back to the attitude.

*Assessment of training progress - by sortie*

*Problem:* In the old system each lesson was given a pass/fail grading on completion. During a one-hour flight exercise there are usually numerous individual training objectives covered. Some will be assessed as satisfactorily completed and some not. However, at the end of the flight the instructors were faced with the difficulty of awarding a suitable overall grade. In the purely theoretical sense this should be easy, however, not in practice. For example, at the end of a sortie most of the objectives performed were judged to have been to a satisfactory standard, although some were not. Does the instructor award a pass grade for the flight despite the fact that a critical competence might not have been achieved? Or does he fail the sortie, requiring a repeat, discouraging the student, diminishing recognition of any elements of achievement within the sortie and, in some cultures, causing the student a serious loss of face.

*Solution:* At the end of each sortie the instructor records only those objectives satisfactorily achieved. Interestingly, for the first time, instructors became focussed on how well a student was achieving the specific flying tasks and so were quick to report any problems early.

*Assessment of training progress – overall*

*Problem:* As indicated earlier there were difficulties in assessing student progress, particularly in the early stages, using the traditional syllabus.

*Solution:* From experience we knew at what rate an average pilot acquired flying skills, and were able to calculate hour markers for groups of objectives. The relationship between hours flown and the number of training objectives achieved now provide the basis for cadet assessment.

Cadet assessment is plotted graphically against three criteria. The first curve represents the expected number of hours that it should take to achieve the syllabus objectives. The second represents the number of hours that the contract with the airline allows. The third curve represents the number of hours that the student has required to achieve the syllabus objectives. This curve indicates whether or not the student is accumulating hours in excess of the contract (overfly). Data is produced for each cadet and forms part of the monthly report of progress to the cadet and to the sponsoring airline. This data also increases the Training Manager's ability to make early assessment of a given cadet's ability and his potential to succeed.

The use of hour markers enables the Training Managers to more clearly differentiate between slow adaptation to the flying environment and language related learning difficulties and a lack of natural flying ability. The Training Managers are able to create a focussed remedial plan for students having difficulty and recommend prompt termination of those with insufficient natural ability.

### Student fault analysis

*Problem:* Instructors tended not to report a difficulty early. Often the first time any problem was realised occurred when a student could not achieve first solo. This happens when instructors are not focussed sufficiently on the fundamentals of flight – power and attitude.

*Solution:* The restructuring of the syllabus placed the appropriate focus on flying skills early in the training and within one or two flights it was evident to the instructor when a student had difficulties with the basics of attitude selection.

With the difficulties more obvious the instructors were quicker to report problems.

### Increasing effective training time with a flexible lesson structure

*Problem:* The lesson structure had insufficient flexibility to cater for unsuitable weather or delayed solo due to English difficulties. For example, when the cadet first starts to practice take offs and landings (circuits), he will normally progress more quickly in calm conditions. Under the conventional structure there is no provision to practice other more advanced skills (that do not pre-require circuit skill) when conditions are unsuitable for circuits or when language ability was below the required standard.

*Solution:* In cases of English difficulty or poor weather the syllabus has an option to delay solo until a later stage. It is critical that this option not be taken to give the student extra practice to compensate for a lack of ability.

The advanced aspects that can be trained are any items that develop handling skill. For example, Steep Turns, Advanced Circuits and Practice Forced Landings. Once conditions or English language level is suitable the student would than go back and achieve first solo. This is accomplished as soon as practicable.

*The introduction of CRM principles*

*Problem:* The syllabus needed to begin early integration of CRM principles despite the single pilot environment.

*Solution:* Like attitude control, this is such a fundamental concept that it should be introduced at the outset of a pilot's training. One of the primary aspects of CRM is effective communication among the flight crew.

The challenge is to create awareness among flight crew of the factors that can compromise error management. The instructor/student team is an ideal environment to introduce the concepts of effective communication and error management in general.

A list of the required CRM competencies was created and these were introduced through the syllabus. The CRM training consists of airborne training and evaluations as well as a small amount of support ground training. Each sortie has an associated group of CRM qualities that are assessed.

This serves as a reporting by exception method and enables instructors and Training Managers to identify students that are likely to be weak in these areas.

## Conclusion

It is now a little over three years since the beginning of these changes took place. There has been sufficient time to objectively review the changes and note further improvements to be implemented.

Since inception of the new syllabus, students have an increased ability to apply themselves (up to about 1.5 hours) without loss of interest or reducing their ability to absorb knowledge effectively. The students are able to achieve more per lesson and feel a greater sense of accomplishment. This process has provided a sound platform on which instructors can operate but, like any teaching system, is highly dependent on the skill and judgement of the instructor.

This change is not an endpoint. There will continue to be evolution of the methods of training. It is important that the process of flight instruction be challenged daily. Instructors must remain open minded and prepared to adapt to the changing needs of their role. The AAC has benefited greatly from challenging old methods and being able to respond to the needs of the customers.

# 10 Evaluating student pilots' proficiency

*Thomas Bluhm*
*Lufthansa Consulting, Germany*

## Introduction

The appraisal of human performance is only uncritical up to the point that the rater hands out compliments. If the rater finds the performance to be weak or even inadequate, then either the qualification of the rater, the appraisal system or even both are understandably subject to criticism.

During flight training where the appraisal of learning progress and flight performance is indispensible, the question must be raised as to how an appraisal system must be conceived to withstand such criticism. In addition, it must be ensured that flight instructors are enabled to carry out appraisals which are as valid, reliable and objective as possible. Finally, the appraisals must be unbiased in relation to the student pilot's belonging to a certain population group, such as age, gender, etc.

The following presentation illustrates the experience made by Lufthansa Consulting, the consulting company of Lufthansa German Airlines, during more than a dozen years at the flight schools in Arizona. Most of our experience is also valid for the appraisals of pilots on the line.

## Failure policy

The basis for the appraisal of flight performance in the ab initio LOFT training of the Lufthansa flight schools is, of course, the performance criteria for ground schools and the flight instruction. Curriculum and syllabus define the performance criteria at every level of the instruction.

The structure of these curricula result both from the requirements of the flight instruction and from the realistic possibilities to meaningfully convey specific contents in a logical and economic way. Theory and flight instructors must be continually aware of the extent to which the performance of the student pilots develops according to the syllabus and whether the material learned has been internalized. The student pilot himself will also want to know at every step of the way whether his performance is "normal" for the program and how his chances are of finishing the program.

Flight school and the student pilot, therefore, are both interested in a continual learning progress observation and a performance measurement in order to take corrective steps, if necessary. Appraisal systems at flight schools are thus essential for achieving the training and learning objectives. Beyond this pedagogical purpose, appraisal systems also constitute the basis for individual staff measures at this early stage of the pilot's career development, if his performance is insufficient. If, despite a good staff selection process, the performance shows extreme deficits, then flight training becomes a further selection instrument to remove unsuitable pilots from the cockpit.

The elementary requirement for an accepted appraisal system is therefore a failure policy which makes the criteria for eventually ending the training transparent. This transparency of failure criteria creates a security for the flight school as well as for the student pilot. Of course, pedagogical measures (such as additional training or a different instructor) will first be undertaken before a training contract is terminated. Experience shows that an early and intensive performace control can correct selection mistakes, ensuring that only suitable staff can acquire licences. Transparency of performance requirements and failure criteria for ending the training as well as the clear regulation of procedures are the decisive prerequisite for ensuring that later appraisals during flight training are accepted. When the student pilot knows in advance what is required of him, then he can better understand why the performance of pilots is tested with a frequency like very few other professional groups. The failure policy should thus be announced to all participants on the first training day.

**Performance appraisal system design**

While many approaches to measuring performance are discussed in the literature (Mohrman et al., 1989, Dobbins, 1993), the following procedures have proved to be successful for cockpit training:

1.  In the company failure policy the learning objectives are operationalised and listed for every single mission.
2.  From the total of all learning objectives appraisal sheets are constructed for the instruction program which contain appraisal dimensions relevant to the learning objectives.

3.  For every appraisal dimension behaviorally anchored rating scales (BARS) are developed.
4.  For the single appraisal items the rater should be provided with a seven-step appraisal scale.

Although reaching agreement in the development of learning objectives in flight instruction generally presents no problems, the crucial task can be seen in the development of an appraisal sheet which should precisely cover all necessary appraisal criteria items while being easy to handle in practical flight operations. Flight schools have found appraisal systems containing not more than 50 items to be practical, whereby 30 single evaluations per mission are submitted as a rule.

More difficult than the development of a knowledge and skills inventory is developing the agreement in the definition of the BARS. Putting together the BARS is a large task. Because flight performance evaluation in the instruction period is carried out daily at Lufthansa, this "relative appraisal system" requires at every stage of the program the definition of what constitutes an average performance, what exceeds the average and what is regarded as inadequate.

## Rater training for flight instructors

Regular training on appraisal matters for the flight instructors is therefore indispensible. After the system has been accepted as such, details of the failure policy, the system of the appraisal sheet, BARS and application questions still have to be taught and trained. The goal is the standardisation of all flight instructors to achieve appraisals as objective as possible. In the literature a distinction is made between "rater error training" and "rater accuracy training" (Gerpott, 1985). In order to integrate an appraisal system in flight instruction in a pedagogically meaningful way, it is necessary to consider the avoidance of rater errors and an accurate observation, evaluation and appraisal. In addition the flight instructor must learn in an interaction-oriented training to present the appraisal results in a way that they are usable for the student. Repeated training lasting several days and with the following contents have met with the best response:

1.  description of the Lufthansa failure policy
2.  comprehensive discussion of typical rater errors
3.  detailed standarisation exercises in which flight instructors must rate filmed presentations of flight performance independent of each other,

while learning to apply BARS with differentiation by means of a video film
4. interactive trainings in which flight instructors systematically prepare their appraisal results in a debriefing, making them available to the student pilot in order to reach the desired behavioral change in the learning process. This prevents appraisal systems from being considered as a mere ritual which is irrelevant for the user as long as his performance is sufficient. As the debriefing is based on a written appraisal with a seven-step scale, even smaller deviations can be discussed and can serve as a basis for performance improvement.

## Feedback systems for instructors

Besides the wide range of measures such as mutual coaching among colleagues in the initial stages, rater discussions with standarization experts as well as student appraisals of the flight instructors, it has proved to be especially helpful when the flight instructor regularly receives a statistical evaluation summary of his rater behavior.

The daily appraisals of missions and check-rides for an anonymous group of students are prepared for the flight instructor. While appraising a group of students, the flight instructor becomes aware of how his rater behavior compares to the total group of instructors and whether his appraisals of certain items are stricter or milder in comparison. In Lufthansa flight schools this personal feedback is given only to the instructor; the school management only receives a total evaluation of all instructors in order to assess whether the ratings as a whole are normally distributed. Such total evaluations enable corrections in the ground schools or in the syllabus to be made, if necessary, if continually bad performances are noted for individual criteria.

## Training movies for rater training

For standardisation purposes a number of training films have been produced which demonstrate bad performance in a certain point of the training. To achieve this, scenes from a series of missions were edited for the movie in such a way that the total performance of the student pilot was borderline. Scripts in which a student and his instructor were asked to create flight errors intentionally have proved unsuccessful. In contrast the editing of combined scenes from various flights has proved to be helpful in standardising flight instructor behaviour. Some films were edited in such a way that the performance in a check-ride was "just barely" acceptable, whereas others showed a performance which was 'just below' the acceptable level. In addition to these standardisation films, video demonstrations of especially successful debriefings and films illustrating rater errors were also made.

## Conclusion

Performance appraisals play a significant role during and after flight training. Their acceptance by those rated and rating can only be ensured through a number of systematic elements that build on each other and a consistency throughout the system. Besides the further development of all components of a scientific appraisal system, the task remains of ensuring a fair consideration of the interests of the pilots concerned as well as the organisation. New tendencies in this field include the necessity to more precisely assess team performance instead of individual performance (Graber et al., 1992) and the heavier emphasis on process evaluation (Persico, 1990) which results in a stronger connection of the appraisals with the employee's career development.

## References

Cardy, R.L., & Dobbins, G. (1993). *Performance appraisal: Alternative perspectives.* Cincinnati: South-Western Publishing.

Gerpott, T.J. (1985). Training von Beurteilern zur Verbesserung von Leistungsbeurteilungsprozessen in Organisationen. *Psychologie und Praxis*, N.F. 3, 116 - 128.

Graber, J.M., Breisch, R.E., & Breisch, W.E. (1992). Performance appraisals and Deming: A misunderstanding? In D.G. Shaw (Ed.), *The performance measurement, management, and appraisal source book* (pp. 57 - 62) Amherst: HRD Press.

Mohrman, A.M., Resnick-West, S.M., & Lawler III., E.E. (1989). *Designing performance appraisal systems.* San Francisco: Jossey-Bass.

Persico, J. (1990). Process evaluation: A new paradigm for managing organizational performance. In G.N. McLean et al., (Eds.), *Performance appraisal: Perspectives on a quality management approach* (pp. 61 - 67). Alexandria: American Society for Training and Development.

# 11 Learning by example: Results from a global Internet study

*David O'Hare and Richard Batt*
*University of Otago*

## Introduction

It is sometimes claimed that there are no new accidents in aviation, merely the repetition of previously experienced events. If this is the case, then it follows that if people fully learned the lessons from these previous experiences then a considerable number of accidents could be avoided in the future. Indeed, the explicitly stated purpose of aircraft accident investigation is "the prevention of accidents and incidents" (ICAO, 1981, p. 12). The results of accident investigations of civil aviation accidents are generally made publicly available and in a growing number of cases can be accessed via the world wide web.

In addition to official reports of accident investigations there are numerous other sources of reports about accidents and incidents in the aviation press and on aviation web sites, through in-house and publicly available magazine articles, books and stories of the "I-learned-about-flying-from-that' kind, as well as much informal talk about flying experiences. Probably more than any other technological activity, aviation has generated a huge publicly accessible store of examples of successful and unsuccessful endeavours.

It is perhaps somewhat remarkable that there has been virtually no scientific investigation of the role of these previous examples in aviation safety and accident prevention. From the perpetual re-occurrence of most accident types one might conclude that very little is learnt from the well-documented and often painful previous experiences of others. Do pilots take any interest in reading about the experiences of other pilots? What do they remember from what they have read? Are these previous examples of any value when facing a difficult situation for real? Are the answers to any of these questions affected by the experience levels and training backgrounds of pilots?

There is certainly anecdotal evidence that pilots may recall and use information from previous examples when confronted by a critical situation of their own. For example, Martensson (1995) presents a detailed analysis of the crash of an MD-81 at Gottrora, Sweden. The aircraft crashed shortly after take-off when ice broke away from the surface of the wings and badly damaged the fans of both the rear-mounted engines. "During the Gottrora flight the captain and the copilot recalled a particular accident and did their very utmost to avoid making the same mistakes as the pilots in that accident" (Martensson, 1995, p. 315). The episode which both pilots recalled was the fatal B737-400 crash at Kegworth, England in 1989. Despite the loss of both engines, the MD-81 was landed in a field with no loss of life.

The present study was designed to gather empirical data on the questions outlined above. The medium of the Internet was chosen as a means of gathering as much information as possible from a large and diverse group of pilots across the globe. One advantage of this approach is that the results should transcend any national or geographic boundaries. As well as providing some initial evidence on the question of learning from previous examples, the study reported here demonstrates the usefulness of the Internet as a resource for research in aviation safety.

The study was conducted in two parts; an initial survey was posted on the Internet and responses invited; a follow-up questionnaire was then sent to respondents from the first survey and was also distributed to an additional 1,143 pilots contacted via Internet listings. Further details are provided in the method section below.

**Method: Initial survey**

*Participants*

One hundred and thirty-eight people responded to the survey. Six were non-pilots, the remainder were pilots of varying ages and experience levels. The survey was essentially designed to stimulate discussion on the central issue - whether pilots do in fact recall previous specific examples at critical times. No detailed information regarding pilot characteristics was requested, although many pilots did indicate their age, experience levels, and training background (e.g., airline, military, glider etc) in their responses. These indicated that respondents ranged from recreational pilots with less than 100 hours total time, to airline and military pilots with many thousands of hours.

*Materials*

A statement outlining the aims of the project was drawn up. Headed "Do we remember all those stories when it counts?", the statement went on to indicate that we were interested in hearing from pilots "about whether they have recalled previous cases at a critical time ... equally interested in hearing from pilots who feel that in spite of being exposed to case studies from various sources they have not consciously brought them to mind when it mattered most". The example of the Gottrora MD-81 crash was mentioned. Pilots were asked to provide details of any experiences that bore on the issues raised.

The statement was distributed via various Internet resources, some of which are indicated in Table 11.1. In all, the statement was distributed to 19 newsgroups, 8 web sites, 8 mailing lists, and 4 Compuserve forums.

**Table 11.1**
**Examples of Internet resources used to distribute survey**

| Resource | Name | Location |
|---|---|---|
| Newsgroup | rec.aviation.misc | |
| Newsgroup | can.aviation.rgs | |
| Web Site | Aviation Safety Connection | www.aviation.org |
| Web Site | The Canadian Aviation Web | www.cavok.com |
| Mailing List | Flyer | flyer@avnet.co.uk |
| Mailing List | Av Rotor | av-rotor@rotor.com |
| Compuserve Forum | Aviation Week Group | AWG |
| Compuserve Forum | Women in Aviation | WIAONL |

**Results: Initial survey**

The survey generated 138 responses ranging in length from 49 to 1,020 words (mean = 320). There were seven categories of comments that addressed the question of whether the details of specific examples are

107

recalled by pilots at critical flight times. These are shown in Table 11.2 together with the percentage of respondents making each point. Fifty-seven respondents (41.3%) described incidents where they had recalled a specific example at a critical flight time. The exact nature of the information recalled varied in a number of ways. In some cases, the examples were very general in character, often relating to well-known hazardous flying situations. In other cases, the examples recalled bore specific similarities to the current flight operation, aircraft type, or geographical location. In some cases the recalled example had been seen only a short time before the critical event, while in other cases the respondent had encountered the example many years previously.

**Table 11.2**
**Comments relating to the recall of previous examples**

| Comment | N | % |
| --- | --- | --- |
| Recalled specific example at critical time | 57 | 41.3 |
| Recalling examples enables avoidance of critical incidents | 23 | 16.7 |
| Information abstracted from examples and stored | 16 | 11.6 |
| Specific examples are not recalled at critical time | 14 | 10.1 |
| Composite examples recalled at critical time | 11 | 8.0 |
| Time available affects what is recalled | 7 | 5.1 |
| Examples recalled after critical time | 5 | 3.6 |

These data show that the percentage of respondents who indicate that they have used specific examples either to avoid getting in to critical flight situations or to guide their response to critical flight situations (58%) far exceeds the proportion who claim not to have been guided by specific examples (10.1%). One respondent in the former category, whose takeoff run was slowed by encountering a large puddle of water suddenly recalled an example in Ernest Gann's book *'Fate is the Hunter'* where Gann found his overloaded aircraft reluctant to leave the runway:

*"He ordered his co-pilot to dump full flaps, which increased lift enough for him to clear the building. Rapidly running out of runway, I dumped flaps and managed to become airborne. It was STUPID...of me to continue that takeoff. Still, I'm glad that I read Gann's book!"*

From the other group, one pilot wrote:

*"I was involved in one bailout accident and two incidents (in an A-1 fully loaded with bombs) and in all cases I did not recall previous accident briefs"*

*Summary*

This informal survey drew a large number of responses from a wide range of pilots. Many respondents reported being interested in reading accident and incident reports and other examples of successful and unsuccessful performance in aviation. The majority of respondents cited examples where their actions before, or during, flight were affected as a direct result of these previously encountered examples. Overall then, there was strong support for the thesis that case-based accident and incident material plays an important role in pilot decision making. To understand some of the issues raised by this survey, a second study was initiated. The second study involved the development of a more formal questionnaire based on the more common responses to the first survey. In addition some background demographic information was gathered so that differences between groups of respondents could be more fully explored.

## Method: Questionnaire study

*Participants*

The questionnaire was emailed to 123 of the 138 people who responded to the first survey (15 were not pilots, or had changed email addresses). To extend the range of the study, the questionnaire was emailed to all pilots listed on the Internet resources shown in Table 11.3.

**Table 11.3**
**Sources of pilot email addresses**

| Source and URL | N |
| --- | --- |
| Four 11 Directory Service<br>http://www.Four11.com | 444 |
| Women in Aviation Resource Centre<br>http://www.aircruise.com/aca/wia | 73 |
| UK Charlie Alpha Web Site<br>http://www.hiway.co.uk/aviation/aviation.html | 626 |

*Materials*

The questionnaire asked for basic demographic information (age, gender etc) and for information about years and hours of experience, licences and ratings held, types of aircraft flown, and training background. The next section asked for details of particular sources of case-based materials (e.g., ASRS, NTSB accident reports etc) that they read and how recently they last read that type of material. Finally, a series of statements was presented which asked whether respondents agreed or disagreed with the more commonly held views expressed by respondents to the first survey (see Table 11.2).

**Results: Questionnaire**

*Response rate.* Eighty-eight responses were received from the original survey respondents for a response rate of 71.5%. Of the 1,143 questionnaires emailed to pilots from the sources shown in Table 11.3, 302 replies were received, giving a response rate of 26.4%. An additional 19 questionnaires were completed by pilots who became aware of the study by other means, so that a grand total of 409 questionnaires were received for analysis.

*Demographics.* Most of the respondents were from the UK (47%) or North America (42%) with 4% from Australia or New Zealand. The majority were males (93%) between the ages of 30 and 50 years (range 18-75). A large majority (84%) had received some form of tertiary education. In terms of category of pilot licence held, 63% held a private certifcate, 20% a commercial certifcate, and 13% an ATPL. The remainder were student pilots. Respondents had been flying for an average period of 12 years (range 3mths - 55yrs) with a mean of 1,720 hours (range 3 - 24,000). Over half the respondents held an Instrument Rating, 32% held a multi-engine rating, and 20% held a flight-instructor rating. Forty-three pilots (10.5%) had flown for airlines and 15% had some military aviation background.

Overall, respondents were predominantly well-educated, middle aged and male with a wide range of backgrounds, ratings, and experience levels. These data are very similar to those reported by Hunter (1995) and O'Hare and Chalmers (in press) in large scale nationwide surveys.

*Exposure to case-based information.* Pilots reported a high degree of exposure to case-based aviation information with 90% of respondents having viewed some such material within the previous month. Seventy-four pilots (19%) reported reading this kind of information within the past two days.

*Are examples recalled at critical flight times?* Respondents were asked to indicate agreement or disagreement with each statement using a five point scale from 'Strongly agree' (5) to 'Strongly disagree' (1). Although the mean response to the statement " The specifics of accident and incident reports do come to mind at critical flight times" was a relatively neutral 3.4, more than 50% of respondents 'agreed' or 'strongly agreed' with the statement compared to less than 20% who 'disagreed' or 'strongly disagreed' with the statement.

Interestingly, there was a significant interaction between total experience and the recency of reading case-based materials. For pilots with fewer than 200 hours total time, those who had read case-based materials within the past two days indicated more agreement with the statement than those who had not read such materials so recently ($F$ (1,391) = 3.81, $p$ = 0.052). For pilots with more than 200 hours total time there was no such difference.

The strongest levels of agreement was shown for the statement that "Recalling specific case histories has enabled me to avoid critical incidents in the first place" (mean = 4.05, $SD$ = 0.94). There was also a high level of agreement with the statement that the recall of specific case histories depends on the time available for action (mean = 3.93, $SD$ = 0.88).

**Discussion**

The present study obtained data from both an unstructured survey and a more formally constructed questionnaire distributed to pilots throughout the world by means of the Internet. Responses in both cases were supportive of the role that examples or case-based information play in aviation safety. The main conclusion is that the beneficial effect of case-based safety material will most likely occur through the avoidance of potentially critical situations rather than by helping pilots to deal with critical events that have already occurred. In part this reflects the fact that critical events are relatively low frequency occurrences - many airline pilots will never experience an engine failure in flight for example. However, in general aviation hazards are more commonplace - surveys by Hunter (1995) and O'Hare and Chalmers (in press) showed that substantial proportions (> 20%) of respondents had run low on fuel, had a mechanical failure, or inadvertently entered IMC (Instrument Meteorlogical Conditions) at least once in their career.

The importance of case-based material is two-fold. Firstly, and most importantly, it assists pilots to proactively plan and monitor their flying activities so as to avoid situations which have been shown to be hazardous. Secondly, it may assist pilots to deal with critical situations if and when they arise. Depending on the time available, pilots may either recall specific instances or more generalised 'composite' examples.

We have experimentally investigated the usefulness of exposure to examples in a simulated flying task (see O'Hare, 1997). In this paradigm, we found an effect of exposure to a simple set of four cases on willingness to 'press-on' in a visual flight task, but only if participants had also been exposed to information about the basic rules of the task. This provides some preliminary experimental evidence for the role of concrete examples in 'tuning' our experience. The present results suggest that knowledge of previous examples is widely used by pilots and that a more systematic approach to utilising this resource might have significant safety benefits.

## References

Hunter, D.R. (1995*). Airman research questionnaire: Methodology and overall results*. Report DOT/FAA/AM-95/27. Washington, DC: Office of Aviation Medicine.

Martensson, L. (1995). The aircraft crash at Gottrora: Experiences of the cockpit crew. *The International Journal of Aviation Psychology, 5*, 305-326.

O'Hare, D. (1997). Expertise by example. In M. Wiggins, I. Henley, & P. Anderson (Eds.), *Aviation education beyond 2000*. Sydney: Department of Aviation Studies, UWS Macarthur.

O'Hare, D., & Chalmers, D. (In press). The incidence of incidents: A nationwide study of flight experience and exposure to accidents and incidents. *The International Journal of Aviation Psychology*.

# 12 Motivation and expectations in pilots and instructors regarding recurrent pilot training

*Jens Rolfsen, Braathens*
*Grete Myhre, RNoAF, Institute of Aviation Medicine*

## Introduction

For pilots, training is an everlasting process. During their careers, pilots have to go through initial training in order to get their first certificate, transition training to operate new aircraft and proficiency training to qualify for new positions in the cockpit. In addition, a professional pilot regularly spends time in the training department to accomplish recurrent training. Training requires a lot of time and money, and it is highly legitimate for the aviation industry to ask if all these resources are spent justifiably and lead to the expected results. In addition, several other factors such as the growing need for new pilots and the recognition of the importance of human factors in aviation have lead to an increased focus on training and instruction during the last 15 years. As a result, we now see the contours of a specific theory of aviation instruction derived from psychological and educational research (Telfer, 1993). There is also a strong emphasis on training and instruction from aviation authorities, like JAA in Europe and the new JAR OPS.

*Recurrent training*

When reviewing the literature on aviation training and instruction, it seems that while ab initio and transition training have received a lot of attention, less consideration has been given to recurrent training. Recurrent training for airline pilots is supposed to cover several purposes: Firstly ensure that the pilot has maintained the proficiency, skills and knowledge required to fly a specific type of aircraft, and secondly to reinforce knowledge about the latest operational information affecting the equipment involved (Orlady, 1993). A third purpose is to help the pilot maintain and develop technical and non-technical skills. Recurrent training is traditionally accomplished on two occasions a year.

Recurrent training is crucial. The aviation industry is characterised by frequent changes in procedures, rules, regulations and technical equipment, in which the pilot needs to be continuously updated. In addition, we know that emergency procedures on board an aircraft involve numerous complex cognitive and motoric processes. The ability to accomplish such skills decays rapidly and extensively without regular training (Childs & Spears, 1986). We also know that CRM-related skills and knowledge continuously have to be reinforced and developed in order to have an optimal effect. Because of these factors, recurrent training is vital to flight safety.

**The present study**

The purpose of the present study was to gain better understanding of instructors' and pilots' expectations and motivation regarding recurrent training. We approached these problems by focusing on two areas.

Firstly, what do the instructors and pilots expect from the training session? Do they see it primarily as an opportunity for learning, or do they see it primarily as a skill test? We examined this by focusing on the role of the instructor, as perceived by the pilot and instructor group. Further, we focused on pilots' and instructors' expectations regarding the use of video in debriefing LOFT-sessions.

Secondly, we wanted to look at the different motivational factors surrounding recurrent training. In this study, motivation is defined as the trainee's willingness to attend, participate, learn, and transfer training to the workplace (Cohen, 1990). It is widely accepted that learning and transfer will occur only when trainees have both the ability and the motivation to acquire and apply new skills, and present research has identified several factors that do influence trainee motivation (see for example, Tannenbaum & Yukl, 1992).

Pilots have the ability to learn from recurrent training, but it is important to question their motivation for the task. We hoped to examine this by asking if the way recurrent training was organised and accomplished could influence pilots' motivation.

*Method*

The study was carried out in cooperation with the training department of a major helicopter carrier. All the 160 pilots in the carrier accomplished their half-annually recurrent training during the first 6 months of 1995, and received at the same time a questionnaire. The questionnaire was designed by the authors, based both on a pilot survey among pilots in the company and as a result of interviews with pilots and instructors. In addition, several of the questions came from reviews of relevant literature, especially those concerning motivational factors. The questionnaires sampled different demographic data, expectations and reactions to the accomplished training, and to recurrent training in general.

At the end of the recurrent training period, the 19 recurrent training instructors in the company received a questionnaire. This questionnaire also contained items about the instructors background in education. The response rate for the pilots was 76.3 percent, giving a sample of 122. The response rate of the instructors was 89.4 percent, giving a sample of 17. Distribution of experience for pilots and instructors is shown in Table 12.1.

**Table 12.1**
**Flying hours for the pilot sample (n = 122) and**
**instructor sample (n = 17)**

| Flying Hours | % of Pilots | % of Instructors |
|---|---|---|
| 2500 – 4999 | 13.1 | 0.0 |
| 5000 – 7499 | 19.7 | 11.8 |
| 7500 – 9999 | 16.4 | 11.8 |
| 10000 – 12499 | 26.2 | 35.2 |
| 12500 – 14999 | 18.0 | 29.4 |
| Above 15000 | 6.6 | 11.8 |

**Results and discussion**

*The perception of instructor role*

When asked what they considered as their primary role during recurrent training, 32 percent of the instructors answered "to help the pilots learn as much as possible". The rest, 68 percent of the instructors, saw their primary role as an examiner to make sure the pilots' qualifications are up to date.

The pilot group was asked almost the same question, regarding what they perceived as the most important role of the instructor. Twenty-two percent answered "to help me learn as much as possible", 50 percent answered "to check that my qualifications are up to standard". The rest of the pilot-group, 28 percent, gave different answers.

These results are interesting, in that they reflect differences both within the pilot and the instructor groups with regard to expectations. Some of the instructors and some of the pilots feel that recurrent training first and foremost is an opportunity for learning. The majority of the rest of the groups perceive recurrent training primarily to be a situation for checking knowledge and qualifications. This incongruence may lead to frustration in both pilots and instructors, when their expectations regarding the training session are not met.

Another important point is that the pilots' expectations about what recurrent training is, also will influence their attitude towards the training itself. In this study, only 30 percent of the pilots agreed upon the statement "I look forward to recurrent training". This lack of enthusiasm can be explained by the impression of recurrent training as being a test. It is therefore important to clarify for both the instructors and pilots what recurrent training is, and this has to be signaled by the management of each airline company. Telfer and Moore (1995) have pointed out that it is the management and organisational level that has the greatest influence on the quality of training. It can not be up to each individual pilot and instructor to set expectations for recurrent training.

*Instructor background*

If we accept that recurrent training is and should be a learning situation, can we expect the present instructors to fulfil the learning potential? When asked what background they had for the instructor task, 10 of 17 answered that they had received formal instructor training, while the rest had "on the job training", observing recurrent training sessions before starting out on their own. Although 59 percent of the instructors in the present company had formal instructor training, 41 percent had no such training. We believe this exemplifies a well-known problem: It has been a credo in aviation that the main criterion for being a flight instructor is to be a good pilot. It has not been widely recognised that a good instructor also needs to know how to instruct, and that this knowledge may be independent of pilot skills and knowledge about flying (Elshaw, 1993). We welcome new rules from the aviation authorities, making it necessary to undergo formal training before taking on the role as an instructor.

## Use of video during Line Oriented Flight Training (LOFT)

Incomplete formal instructor training and knowledge were particularly evident when we looked upon the instructors' and the pilots' expectations toward the use of video-recordings in debriefing line oriented flight training (LOFT) during recurrent training. Although this helicopter carrier clearly states in its training manual that video-recordings should be used during debriefing LOFT-sessions, only 31 percent of the pilots reported that the recording was used. There are several possible explanations to why the video-recordings were not used, but in this context, the most interesting explanation is that neither the instructors nor the pilots fully comprehended the relation between use of video and the learning process. Several of the comments made by both the pilots and the instructors implied that video-recordings were used only if the pilots did not agree on the instructors impression of what had really happened in the simulator. One instructor stated "I brought along the video recording if I knew that the particular crew had a tendency not to agree on what had actually taken place"; another "there is no purpose in using the video if the crew acknowledges mistakes without looking at the recordings." One pilot remarked "there was no doubt about what happened, so we did not see any point in using the recordings".

These comments, along with several others, suggest that video-recordings in this company were used as a penalty or a proof that the instructor could fall back on if the pilots did not agree with him. This penalty-principle is unfortunate. When video-recordings are used to "nail" the pilots, it stops being a tool for learning and instead becomes something both instructors and pilots detest.

LOFT, and especially the use of video-recordings are a new challenge for most instructors. A study carried out in four American carriers revealed that nearly all the instructors fell short on debriefing and facilitation techniques (Butler, 1991). The present study suggests that one of the reasons for the instructors reluctance to use video, is a lack of understanding of the instructional paradigm governing its use. This may lead to expectations in the instructor and pilots group toward video that is not in accordance with learning. It is therefore of vital importance that any training department makes sure that the instructors understand why they should use video as a part of LOFT-debriefing.

*Motivational factors*

The second area of interest in this study was that of motivation. We wanted to know if the way recurrent training is organised and accomplished may influence the pilots motivation for learning.

In general, before starting any training program, most organisations should carry out an analysis. The purpose of this analysis is to examine the trainee's strengths and weaknesses, in order to decide on the training program and how to perform the training. Research has shown that this kind of analysis is important for trainee motivation (Noe, 1986; Noe & Schmitt, 1986). If the trainees feel that the analysis has given useful information, they will to a larger degree consider the training useful, and their motivation will increase. On the other hand, the motivation in trainees who don't have this understanding will be low. The content of most recurrent training programs is not primarily a result of such analysis, since the training traditionally is planned to fulfil demands from the company and from the aviation authorities. In theory, we would therefore expect that motivation among the pilots could be influenced in a negative way since no individual analysis of training needs exist. Several questions in the questionnaire were designed to sample pilots reactions on choice of training items. We assumed that pilots who found the included training items relevant, useful and valuable, for example, would be more motivated than pilots who questioned the choice of training items.

A majority of the pilot group (between 86 and 93 percent) agreed upon statements describing the simulator part of the current training program as useful, relevant, realistic and fitting to individual needs. This indicates a high degree of satisfaction among the pilot group to the content of the simulator part of the training program, and indicates a high level of motivation. These results are somewhat puzzling in light of theory – no individual analysis of training needs exists, still the results indicate that motivation for learning among the pilot group is high. The answer to the puzzle could be that most pilots seldom or never experience a serious in-flight emergency. At the same time, they know that safety depends upon their ability to cope should an emergency occur. Training emergency procedures in the simulator is therefore in itself highly motivating.

It is important to notice that although the pilots were very pleased with the simulator part of the training, 20 percent thought recurrent training did not leave enough room for theory and questions. In addition, different pilots had different needs with regard to which theoretical items they felt due for refreshment. This provides an opportunity for introducing a new factor to recurrent training. Several studies have demonstrated that choice and influence with regard to content of training programs increases motivation for learning (Tannenbaum & Yukl, 1992).

## Conclusion

The purpose of the present study was to gain a better understanding of instructors' and pilots' expectations and motivation regarding recurrent training.

Both pilots and instructors had different expectations with regard to the purpose of the training session. It is important to clarify what recurrent training is, both for the pilots and the instructors. This should be found in the company's policy.

- The instructor group lacked knowledge about the theory behind using video-recordings as a learning tool, and this influenced the expectations toward the use of video-recordings. Recordings were thus used as a penalty instead of as a learning instrument. This as a very serious matter. Without using recurrent training and the tools that are known to be effective for training and developing CRM-related knowledge and skills, one can hardly expect CRM to be successful.

- Motivational factors should to a greater extent be taken into consideration with regard to recurrent training. Adults don't learn unless they are motivated to do so, and we feel the airline industry should to a larger extent accept theory and research that demonstrates the relationship between motivation and learning.

The present results may not represent recurrent training in other airline companies. We still believe that the results can be a valuable contribution to the discussion on recurrent training.

## References

Butler, R.E. (1991). Lessons from cross-fleet/cross airline observations: Evaluating the impact of CRM/LOFT training. *Proceedings of the Sixth International Symposium on Aviation Psychology.* (pp. 326 – 331). Columbus: Ohio State University.

Childs, J.M., & Spears, W.D. (1986). Flight-skill decay and recurrent training. *Perceptual and Motor Skills, 62,* 233-242.

Cohen, D.J. (1990). What Motivates Trainees? *Training & Developmental Journal*, Nov., 91-93.

Elshaw, C. (1993). Preparing better flight instructors. In R.A. Telfer (Ed.), *Aviation Instruction and Training*. Vermont: Ashgate.

Noe, R.A. (1986). Trainees' Attributes and Attitudes: Neglected Influences on Training Effectiveness. *Academy of Management Review*, *11*, (4), 736-749.

Noe, R.A., & Schmitt, M. (1986). The influence of trainee attitudes on training effectiveness: Test of a model. *Personnel Psychology*, *39*, (3), 497-523.

Orlady, H.W. (1993). Airline Pilot Training Today and Tomorrow. In E.L. Wiener, B.G. Kanki & R.L. Helmreich (Eds.), *Cockpit resource management*. San Diego: Academic Press.

Tannenbaum, S.I., & Yukl,. (1992). Training and development in work organizations. *Annual Review of Psychology, 43*, 399-441.

Telfer, R.A. (Ed.). (1993). *Aviation Instruction and Training*. Vermont: Ashgate.

Telfer, R.A., & Moore, P.J. (1995). Learning, Instruction and Organisation in Aviation. In *Proceedings of the Eighth International Symposium on Aviation Psychology, Vol II,* (pp. 1183 - 1188). Columbus: Ohio State University.

# 13 Structural knowledge concepts in airline pilots

*Simon Henderson and Joey M. Anca*
*Ansett Australia*

## Introduction

This paper presents the results of a Cognitive Task Analysis (CTA) undertaken at a major Australian airline during late 1997. The study was carried out as a precursor to more extensive task analysis related to methods employed under the Advanced Qualification Program (AQP). The methods adopted relied heavily on the published works of Seamster, Redding and Kaempf. Fifty-six (56) declarative knowledge concepts were isolated from Flight and Technical Training manuals, State Regulations and company standard operating procedures. These concepts were items that the pilots had to know. Sorting and rating techniques were used to analyse the structural relationships. Four groups of pilots were identified for the study; new intake First Officers, recent initial commands, senior training Captains, and check Captains. These groups essentially covered an experience range from novice to expert. The paper reviews the methodology used in analysis, isolates differences between pilot groups, and draws some conclusions about the application of the results to the design of training curricula and the presentation of written material in manuals.

## Why Cognitive Task Analysis (CTA)?

Ansett Australia is adopting several Advanced Qualification Program (AQP) principles in its review of pilot training. Task analysis is a central element of AQP. Investigations and benchmarking activities carried out during the previous year had led the project development team to the conclusion that the more traditional style of instructional systems design used in the AQP left out several vital cognitive elements essential for a analysis of a pilot's role.[1] This position is widely supported in the available literature about Cognitive Task Analysis (CTA) and expert decision making. Neil Johnson in the forward to Seamster et al., 1997 makes this point quite eloquently and is supported by researchers in a variety of fields (Gordon & Gill 1997; Erricsson, 1996). Ansett intends to carry out more detailed task analysis of generic first officer and captain duties in the future. This trial allowed the researchers and the training development section of the Flight Department to gain experience in CTA and in research techniques.

The trial was also seen as a stepping stone to being able to establish a basis for validating the acceptance of certain experienced personnel as Subject Matter Experts (SMEs). Additionally, it was an opportunity to examine the impact of a newly produced generic policy and procedures manual and to explore the acceptance of recent CRM training initiatives.

## Fundamental concepts

The following fundamental concepts were assumed from the literature review and used to construct the study:

- Knowledge is organised with an underlying structure (Seamster, Redding & Kaempf 1997; Chase & Simon 1973; Richman et al., 1996).
- There is strong evidence supporting the notion that experts exhibit some form of structural advantage in the way that declarative knowledge is arranged (Chi, Glaser & Rees, 1982.
- Expert - novice differences can be determined by examining structural arrangement of domain specific knowledge (Olson & Biolsi, 1991).

These assumptions have implications for training and the assessment of training effectiveness.

## Research goals

The research trial had the following goals and objectives:

- Elicit generic airline and domain specific knowledge concepts.
- Represent the structural characteristics of differing groups
  (Check Captains, Training Captains, Initial Commands and First Officers).
- Validate the results with expected outcomes from literature.
- Evaluate representations to determine training strategies and requirements.

---

[1] For a more detailed explanation of the differences between task analysis and cognitive task analysis in its application to pilots see Seamster et al., 1997.

**Methodology**

After reviewing the available and accepted CTA methodologies the research team elected to carry out a sorting and associated rating exercise (see Olson & Biolsi, 1991 for a more detailed explanation of available CTA methodologies). A generic listing of knowledge concepts was elicited from domain specific training and reference documentation. Examined sources included Ansett Australia's Generic Policy and Procedures manual, flight crew training manuals, Civil Aviation Regulations, Civil Aviation Orders and Jeppesen Airway Manual documentation. Where possible these concepts were stated as nouns in as few a words as possible and were reviewed by an extended team of experienced management pilots to remove ambiguity and confusion. More than 180 concepts were established. A smaller group of so called "Super SMEs" examined this list and combined numerous elements sharing common concepts and discarded others as irrelevant to the goals of the study. The culling process reduced the concepts to 56 (see Table 13.1).

*Research protocols*

The research program was overseen by a Steering Committee that was also involved in AQP program development within Ansett Australia. The research proposal did not undergo any formal ethics approval, however, support was sought and found from Flight Department Management. Future research programs involving Flight Department personnel will now undergo an ethics approval process. The following protocols and principles were used to recruit participants into the trial:

- Complete anonymity was maintained after the initial collection of biographical information and career aspirations as all forms were de-identified. Data collected from the various rating and sorting tasks undertaken were then linked to this de-identified data via a randomly generated participant number.
- Subjects were only to participate in the trial following completion of flying duties for that day.
- A variety of scripts were produced to manage the initial contact, recruitment into the trial and experimental procedure. These forms were approved by the Steering Committee and are attached.
- Subjects were randomly recruited based on a sign-off window of opportunity. Essentially, research staff determined their own personal availability and then used the crew computer system to determine the eligible potential subjects who would be completing duties at that location during that specific period.

## Table 13.1
## Knowledge concepts

| Knowledge Concepts | | | |
|---|---|---|---|
| Chain Of Command | Authority, Duties and Responsibilities | Operating Priorities - Safety, Pax Comfort, Schedule Economy | Licensing/Currency Requirements |
| Powers Of Arrest and Restraint | Aircraft Limitations | Aircraft Systems | Performance Figures |
| Crew Management | Automation | The Support Process | Decision Making |
| Flight Planning | Fuel Requirements | Application of CARs And CAOs | Aerodrome Minima |
| Crew Briefings | Approach / Departure Briefing | Sterile Flightdeck | Handover/Takeover |
| Standard Calls | Altimetry | Terrain Clearance | Speed Control |
| Tolerance Calls | Autopilot and/or FMS | Reduced Visibility Minima | Checklists Usage |
| Recall Items | Noise Abatement | Controlled Rest | Approach / Holding / Visual Requirements |
| Company Approach Procedures | Radio and Navigation Aids | Stabilised Approach | OCTA Operations |
| Flight Time Limitations | Radio Switching | Calls To Company | Customer Service Alert Calls |
| RFFS | Aircraft Loading | Maintenance System and Documentation | Flight with Unserviceabilities |
| Flight Deck Management | Flight Path Control In An Emergency | Rejected Take Off | Special Aerodrome Procedures |
| Flight Deck Cabin Emergency Signals | Categories of Emergency | Crew Incapacitation | Adverse Weather Operations |
| Flight In Turbulence | Role and duties during an Emergency | Emergency on Approach | Post Incident Actions |

*Data acquisition*

The preliminary investigations recruited four subjects in each expertise subgroup. This sample size was chosen based on advice in the literature. The knowledge concepts were printed on a series of cards. The cards were simply produced using heavy card stock and measured approximately 2.5 cm by 6 cm. All subjects carried out two distinct tasks. These can be described as *sorting* and *rating*. Using the attached script for instructions subjects were asked to firstly sort all of the cards into piles that were similar. They were told that piles could contain as many cards as they wished and that they could re-organise the cards as much as they wanted. The only requirement was that they had to name each pile at the completion of the sorting exercise. When this sorting task was completed and the cards collected and bagged for later data entry. The subjects were then given a fresh set of cards, identical to the first, and asked to isolate the ten most important and ten least important concepts to them. In particular, subjects were asked to prioritise their ratings given the need to train another pilot to do their own job.

Data were collected in the following ways. From the sorting task data was entered into a proximity matrix consisting of 3,136 data points or 1,512 data pairs per subject. This matrix was designed to have all 56 concepts along both the X and Y-axis. If a concept was sorted into a pile as another concept then the two nodes where these concepts intersected in the matrix showed a 1. Where they were not sorted into the same groups the nodes showed a 0. An example of part of this matrix is depicted below.

| Information is recorded about the Data Pairs. If placed in the same pile a one is recorded, if not then a zero is recorded. | Chain Of Command | Authority, Duties and Responsibilities | Operating Priorities - Safety, Pax Comfort, Schedule Economy | Licensing/Currency Requirements | Powers Of Arrest and Restraint |
|---|---|---|---|---|---|
| Chain Of Command | 0 | 0 | 1 | 0 | 0 |
| Authority, Duties and Responsibilities | 0 | 0 | 0 | 1 | 1 |
| Operating Priorities - Safety, Pax Comfort, Schedule Economy | 1 | 0 | 0 | 0 | 0 |
| Licensing/Currency Requirements | 0 | 1 | 0 | 0 | 1 |
| Powers Of Arrest and Restraint | 0 | 1 | 0 | 1 | 0 |

**Figure 13.1**
**An example Proximity Matrix**

Within each subgroup of New F/O, New Captain, Training Captain and Check Captain all data were summed. The proximity matrices were summed through each node or cell to produce a similarity matrix. This meant that each cell in the similarity matrix consisted of a figure between 0 – the minimum if no subject had placed those concepts together – and 4 – the maximum if all subjects had placed those concepts together. This matrix was then manipulated to give a measure of dissimilarity. All of the values in each cell were then subtracted from 5. The greater the subsequent value, the greater the distance between each concept and the less similar each concept pair is.[2]

Another matrix, in the form of a spreadsheet was used to collect information about the 10 most and least important concepts for each subject. Again a one was entered if one of the subjects had included this concept and the values were summed within each subject group for all 56 concepts. This gave a relative measure of importance, or lack thereof, to each subject group.

**Interim results**

Only preliminary analysis of the results has been completed. Caution must be applied when drawing conclusions from this dataset as more rigorous analysis using a larger sample size will need to be completed to ensure reliability and validity.

Initial analysis centred around the use of the chosen most and least important items. It was intended to use these ratings to reduce the number of declarative knowledge concepts selected for cluster analysis. However, examination of these items showed some interesting trends and results.

*Most and least important*

Although the primary intent of the rating task was to select knowledge concepts for cluster analysis, the rating exercise provided a variety of useful information in its own right. Simple frequency analysis was used to draw the following conclusions:

- All groups had a fairly similar spread of most and least important concepts within their group. This means that the group members appeared equally decided, or undecided about what comprised an important concept or not.

---

[2] For any number of subjects, n, the similarity matrix values should be subtracted from n+1 to give a value of dissimilarity. This technique is expanded in Seamster et al., 1997.

- All groups heavily biased their important concept selection towards generic crew management or generic standard company procedures.

- The F/O group showed the greatest agreement of any group about the importance of CRM concepts.

- The ratings appeared independent of actual duties performed. For example, F/Os are responsible for company radio inbound calls, however, they agreed with all other groups in listing this concept as not important for their own role.

- Some highly rated concepts from the organisation either rated poorly or were not considered important. For example the company customer service alert procedure is an important part of emergency response following an incident, however, all groups considered that important safety concept as not important. This particular finding had been supported during recent incident reports. The research was used to review the presentation of the procedure in manuals and initiate retraining of crews.

- Lastly the dispersion, spread or measure of agreement on the rating of the concepts by each expertise subgroup mirrored the results of the cluster analysis.

*Hierarchical Cluster Analysis*

The dissimilarity matrix was imported into SPSS for analysis. A hierarchical cluster analysis using single linkage method was carried out.[3] Interim analysis has concentrated on the knowledge concepts rated as most important. These concepts were somewhat arbitrarily selected based on the following criteria:

- chosen by twenty percent or more of all subjects, or
- chosen by fifty percent or more of any one group.

This technique attempted to cater for areas that were of more importance for one group while capturing a reasonable number for analysis.

After much trial an error it was found that increasing these percentages suddenly dramatically curtailed the concepts or decreasing the percentage required lead to a sudden dramatic increase in selected concepts. This technique elicited nineteen concepts for further analysis. These are listed in Table 13.2.

---

[3] This technique was used based on recommendations in Seamster et al., 1997.

127

**Table 13.2**
**Nineteen most important knowledge concepts**

| Knowledge Concepts Selected for Cluster Analysis[4] | | | |
|---|---|---|---|
| Concept | Abbreviation | Concept | Abbreviation |
| Flight Path Control in an Emergency | FLTPATH | Role and Duties in an Emergency | ROLEEMER |
| Flight Deck Cabin Emergency Signals | FLTCABSI | Recall Items | RECALLS |
| Tolerance Calls | TOLERANC | Approach/Departure Briefing | APDPBRIEF |
| Standard Calls | STDCALLS | Decision Making | DECISION |
| Flight Deck Management | FLTDECKM | Crew Management | CMANAGE |
| The Support Process | SUPPROC | Stabilised Approach | STABILIS |
| Fuel Requirements | FUELREQ | Operating Priorities | OPERATIN |
| Flight Planning | FLTPLAN | Aircraft Limitations | ACLIM |
| Terrain Avoidance | TERRAIN | Autopilot | AUTOPILO |
| Rejected Take Off | RTO | | |

---

[4] Many of these concepts refer to specific procedures in Ansett's policy and procedures manual. Ansett has SOPs covering specific requirements to do with flight path control in an emergency, stabilised approach requirements, operating priorities of decision making – safety, comfort time economy. The Support Process is an Ansett procedure that lays down expected behaviour and calls when normal flight manual calls are inappropriate and details the procedure to be followed that authorises another crewmember to take control of the aircraft and carry out a missed approach if necessary.

## Single linkage dendogram

A series of single linkage dendograms were constructed in SPSS. The following example is representative of the cluster analysis.

```
FLTPATH    8   -+
ROLEEMER  13   -+--------------+
FLTCABSI   6   -+              +-+
RECALLS   12   ---------------+ +---+
TOLERANC  19   ------------------+   I
APDPBRIE   2   ------------------+-+
STDCALLS  16   ------------------+ +-----------------------+
DECISION   5   -+                I                         I
FLTDECRM   7   -+--------------+  I                         I
CMANAGE    4   -+             +---+                         I
SUPPPROC  17   ------------------+                         +---
STABILIS  15   -------------------------------------------+
TERRAIN   18   -------------------------------------------+
FUELREQ   10   -------------+---------+
OPERATIN  11   -------------+         +---------------------+
FLTPLAN    9   ----------------------+                     +-+
ACLIM      1   -------------------------------------------+ +-
AUTOPILO   3   -------------------------------------------+
RTO       14   -------------------------------------------
```

**Figure 13.2**
**Example single linkage dendogram**

## Discussion

In general the findings agreed with the literature. As the accepted level of expertise increased the clusters tended to become more closely knit. This spread or dispersion of the clusters relates to intra-group agreement and the literature review predicted that the check captain group should be in more agreement than the new captain group. However, this general pattern was disrupted by the first officer group. This group is the least experienced and was expected to display the widest spread. Indeed, the literature suggests that this group should have more in common with the experts rather than each other. Further investigations revealed that this group displayed extremely close knit CRM related concepts.

The majority of this group had recently undergone indoctrination training upon entry to the airline. This training was heavily focused on this CRM issue and some degree of experiential training was given in the use and application of these CRM procedures. It may be that the characteristics that this group displayed reflected the proximity of this training, however, further research need to be conducted to remove the element of chance from this finding.

The literature also suggested that some form dimensionality may exist in the cluster analysis. This dimensionality is normally extracted through analytical techniques such as multi-dimensional scaling (MDS). Interim results supported that a dimension of management may be present in the data. Evidence for this dimension was strongest in the lower expertise groups of First Officer and Captain. This dimension is characterised at its extremes by concepts such as Crew Resource Management and Decision Making at one end while concepts such as Rejected Take-off and Autopilot Limits were on the other extreme. Interestingly, first officers in particular associated concepts such as Flight Path Control in an Emergency towards the *management* end of this spectrum while more experienced pilots placed it towards the more *procedural* end of the dimension. Again, caution needs to be exercised with the results, as final analysis is not yet complete. For example, this dimension may appear through bias in the selection of original concepts.

The literature suggests that a dimension of time urgency may become stronger with increasing experience. The trials results supported this notion. It may be that this dimension learnt through experience replaced the more taught style of management – procedure dimension exhibited by the less experienced groups. Conversely, the stronger presence of the management-procedure dimension in the less experienced group may be evidence of a greater acceptance of CRM training principles.

**Future initiatives**

These results were very encouraging and have fulfilled most of the aims of the trial. It must be remembered that the primary aim of the trial was for the researchers to gain experience in these methods. Ansett Australia has agreed to expand the number of subjects to double the sample size. It is hoped that this increase in sample size may remove some of the concerns over the validity of the findings. More detailed analysis is to be conducted on the results using MDS and pathfinder techniques. The interim results have already been used to review sections of policy manuals and the next study may incorporate a before and after training assessment to explore the notion of measuring training transfer of CRM related concepts.

# References

Chase, W.G., & Simon, H.A. (1973). The mind's eye in chess. In W.G. Chase (Ed.), *Visual information processing* (pp. 215-281). New York: Academic Press.

Chi, M.T.H., Glaser, R., & Rees, E. (1982). Expertise in Problem Solving. In R.S. Sternberg (Ed.), *Advances in the psychology of human intelligence* (Vol. 1, pp. 1-75). Hillsdale, NJ: Lawrence Erlbaum Associates.

Ericsson, K.A. (1996). The Acquisition of Expert Performance: An Introduction to Some of the Issues. In K.A. Ericsson (Ed.), *The road to excellence: The acquisition of expert performance in the arts and sciences, sports, and games* (pp. 1-50). Mahwah. NJ: Lawrence Erlbaum Associates.

Gordon, S.E., & Gill, R.T. (1997). Cognitive Task Analysis. In C.E. Zsambok & G. Klein, (Eds.), *Naturalistic decision making*. Mahwah, NJ: Lawrence Erlbaum Associates.

Olson, J.R., & Biolsi, K.J. (1991). Techniques for Representing Expert Knowledge. In K.A. Ericsson & J. Smith (Eds.), *Towards a general theory of expertise: Prospects and limits* (pp. 240-285). Cambridge: Cambridge University Press.

Richman, H.B., Gobet, F., Staszewski, J.J., & Simon, H.A. (1996). Perceptual and memory processes in the acquisition of expert performance: The EPAM Model. In K.A. Ericsson (Ed.), *The road to excellence: The acquisition of expert performance in the arts and sciences, sports, and games* (pp. 1-50). Mahwah. NJ: Lawrence Erlbaum Associates.

Seamster, T.L., Redding, R.E., & Kaempf, G.L. (1997). *Applied cognitive task analysis in aviation.* Aldershot: Ashgate.

**Annex 1**

**Ansett Australia CTA Trial
Biographical Details Form**

Identification Number =
(to be used on all envelopes)

Date =

Interviewed by =

Position =

Age =

Gender =

Total Flight Time =          (nearest 1000 hrs)

Total Command Time =          (nearest 100 hrs)

Years with Ansett =

Years in Current Position=

Current Aircraft Type =

Previous Ansett Types =

Experience Pre Ansett =

Career Synopsis =

Career Aims =

## Ansett CTA Trial
## Telephone Contact Script

Introduction

- Ask if they would be interested in participating in a research trial that would take approximately one hour of their time following normally scheduled sign - off at [LOCATION] on [DATE] at [TIME].
- The trial is completely anonymous and no data will be placed on flight department records or identified with them in any way.
- Only the interviewer will know who took part in the trial.
- The research trial is not an exam or test and would require the participant to sort or rate a series of cards.
- A crusader sign-on adjustment sheet will be entered to credit them with an appropriate amount of extra ground duty time following the exercise.
- The sign - on adjustment sheet will only indicate safety department briefing.
- If they are not interested = Goodbye.
- If they are interested =
- Explain that the survey will be examining the differences in the way that technical crew of varying experience relate many of the discrete areas of knowledge needed to perform their duties.
- It is hoped that they results will lead to changes in the way that training concepts are introduced and validated to new and upgrading crew members.
- Arrange and reconfirm [PLACE], [TIME], [DATE].

Questions or queries or change in roster please contact me at [NUMBER] =

Thank you.

### Telephone Contact Record

Name =
Contact Number =
Available PLACE =          DATE =          TIME =
Interested = YES / NO
AGREED PLACE =          DATE =          TIME =

**Ansett Australia**
**CTA Trial**
**Letter to Participants**

Thank you for agreeing to assist in the research trial. As we discussed on the telephone, the trial is being conducted to examine how crewmembers associate the wide range of information they are expected to know in order to fulfil their day to day duties. It is hoped that the results will lead to changes in the way that training concepts are introduced and validated to new and upgrading crew members.

The trial is completely anonymous and no data will be placed on flight department records or identified with you in any way. Only the interviewer will know who took part in the trial and once the data collected has been collated for analysis it will be deidentified. Your name will never be associated with any of the forms completed and only generic details will be kept. This generic information will consist of items such as; Check or training captain, years with company and experience. Other details that are collected on the day of the trial will only be used to place groups of pilots together with similar backgrounds and experience.

The research trial is not an exam or test and simply requires the participants to sort or rate a series of cards. It is expected that about one hour will be required to complete the trial. A crusader sign-on adjustment sheet will be entered to credit you with an appropriate amount of extra ground duty time following the exercise. The sign - on adjustment sheet will only indicate that you attended a safety department briefing.

At present I expect to meet you at the crewing counter at PLACE on DATE at TIME. If your schedule changes I would appreciate it if you could advise me on NUMBER.

Once again thank you for participating in this trial.


Signature block

 **ANSETTAUSTRALIA**
# CTA Trial
# Instructions to Participants

### Part A

You have in front of you about 50 cards that have been annotated with a variety of the Knowledge Concepts needed to fulfil your daily duties.

Your task is too sort the cards into piles that contain concepts that you consider to be closely related to each other. You may make as many piles as you wish and each pile may contain as many cards as you wish. You may rearrange the cards and piles as many times as you want.

There is no correct answer and this is not a test. Take as much time as you need.

When you have arranged the cards to your satisfaction, you will be asked to name each pile.

### PART B

The cards in front of you contains are a copy of the cards you have just sorted. Identify those cards that you believe contain the 10 most important and the 10 least important concepts required to fulfil your duties. Place them into three piles with one pile containing the 10 most important concepts, another containing the 10 least important and lastly a pile containing discarded cards.

You may rearrange the cards and piles as many times as you want.

There is no correct answer and this is not a test. Take as much time as you need.

When you have arranged the cards to your satisfaction, a list will be made of the choice you made of the 10 most important and 10 least important concepts.

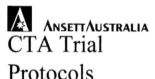 ANSETTAUSTRALIA

# CTA Trial
# Protocols

Needed:

- Two packs of cards for each participant.
- Envelopes prelabelled with the participant's ID number
- Crusader Sign-on adjustment sheet (Ask at crewing if you can not locate any)
- Data capture form for PART B prelabelled with the participant's ID number.
- Pens and paper for use by the participant if they desire it.
- Arrange to conduct the trial in a quiet area. Melbourne Airport has several debriefing rooms situated on the corridor between the entry and the crewing sign-on area.
- Collect the participant's biographical details and assess if they are suitable for the trial ie., not finishing a stressful day. Do not pass on any information about the study - if asked say that you will be quite happy to talk about it afterwards but you do not wish to influence them in any way.
- Once the participant is comfortable.

## PART A

- Place the pile of cards on the table and let the participant read part A of the instruction form.
- Explain that there is no time limit and no correct answer.
- Stay for a few minutes to answer any questions but only answer those that relate to the procedure to be used.
- Leave the participant alone and look in periodically.
- When Part A has been completed collect each pile of cards and place them into an envelope prelabelled with the participants ID number.
- Give each participant the envelop and ask them to label or name it.
- Continue until all piles have been sealed into an envelope and labelled.

PART B

- Let the participant relax and then give him Part B.

  - Place the pile of cards on the table and let the participant read part A of the instruction form.
  - Explain that there is no time limit and no correct answer.
  - Stay for a few minutes to answer any questions but only answer those that relate to the procedure to be used.
  - Leave the participant alone and look in periodically.

- To save on the use of cards it may be enough to record the 10 most and 10 least important concepts on a sheet of paper labelled with the participant's ID number.

# 14 GPS Training for General Aviation VFR pilots: To regulate or educate?

*Ross St. George, Civil Aviation Authority of New Zealand*
*Michael Nendick, The University of Newcastle*

## Introduction

*Climate.* The atmosphere or climate that evolves during the training must be mutually respectful and collaborative. The student must feel comfortable and safe to convey any attitude or ask any question. Individuals in the crew must not feel that they are being judged, evaluated or held up to ridicule. In short they must not feel threatened. They should feel that they are accepted as valid individuals of the crew, and that they are being listened to and understood. The instructor's role is to establish a supportive atmosphere where instructor and student act as a disciplined crew and not as individuals. For example, an instructor must facilitate a cockpit climate which is conducive to checklists and briefings being completed in a disciplined fashion.

From the research previously reported by Nendick and St. George (1996a, 1996b) it is clear that Global Positioning System (GPS) is well established in the general aviation (GA) Visual Flight Rules (VFR) environment as a primary navigation method. This is a global phenomenon, however to our knowledge no jurisdiction or aviation regulatory authority has yet mandated or attempted to regulate the use of this navigation method in the general aviation VFR environment. This approach may be driven by the position that only standard, visual navigation procedures are meant to apply, although there are already exceptions to this. For example, Australian VFR pilots can legally navigate the aircraft by means of approved radio navigation systems without visual reference to ground or water (Airservices Australia, 1997). Anecdotally the reality is that more and more GA pilots are using GPS as their primary, and often only, navigation procedure. GA pilots using GPS do admit to neglecting basic VFR operating procedures such as preparatory course plotting, and calculation of track, heading, distance, speeds and the like (Nendick & St. George, 1996b).

There may be a case for incorporating GPS technical and operational learning objectives into the theoretical and flight testing component of obtaining an initial pilots licence. We would anticipate resistance however, as there has not been a previous requirement to demonstrate competency using other radio navigation aids for an initial VFR pilot licence. In addition to 'historical' arguments, effecting regulatory change can be a slow process. Regulation is not necessarily the answer to safe flying with GPS. Nevertheless the rapid adoption of GPS as a VFR navigation and flight management tool suggests an urgent case for education about knowledgeable and safe GPS use for GA VFR operations.

In the absence of a regulated formal training and competency requirement in GPS use for an initial pilot licence, the adoption of education programmes by flight training organisations, aircraft owners and hirers, and even insurers is advocated.

Without a pro-active educational programme within the aviation community, calls to regulate are likely to develop if it becomes evident that inappropriate GPS use has been a contributing factor to incidents and accidents. A reactive regulatory 'solution' may prove to be far less palatable than an industry sponsored educational 'solution'.

The issue is not whether to train VFR pilots to use GPS, but how to best impart the required knowledge for pilots to fly safely and efficiently with GPS. This is due to the ubiquitous nature of GPS in the GA fleet, and because in the absence of well developed and organised GPS instruction pilots seek to self-instruct. Some will do so successfully and safely, others less so.

A 1994 survey found that VFR pilots were typically left to teach themselves from the user manual, or to obtain informal demonstrations from other experienced users (Nendick & St. George, 1996b). Over a third of the survey respondents considered that a formal training course was required to enable proficient use of GPS, and over half the respondents indicated that they would attend such a training course if it was available. This paper presents the concept of a generic GA-VFR-GPS education program to meet this need.

**Education perspective**

A GPS training programme has two components. These are a technical theoretical and procedural knowledge of the receiver; and an awareness of the operational issues related to using automated navigation equipment. The challenge is to impart an adequate understanding of GPS systems and operations, to encourage motivation to learn, and to apply this knowledge to maximise flight safety. The delivery process should place an emphasis on relevant content. An in-built evaluation method is required to assess the efficacy of both the training process and the training outcome.

Effort is also required to situate the learning in the context in which it will be used. Computer based training (CBT) can be a powerful tool here to assist in initial teaching, revision, and ongoing practice. CBT has the advantage of enabling student progress to be monitored and performance to be profiled. Inexpensive computer based flight simulator programs can be extremely effective in technical training delivery. They have immense potential for illustrating the operational and human factors issues involved through the creation of realistic scenarios with implications for subsequent consideration and reflection by the student. This has benefits for instructors and researchers evaluating effective new skill acquisition, application, and retention.

Traditionally, CBT methods have been available at the high end of the industry such as airline training. There is now a critical requirement to make similar structured training accessible at the entry end of the industry, for example, for the private pilot who is going to use GPS because it is readily available. CBT technology can display and present GPS for such training and education to competency. For example the Trimble 2101 Approach™ receiver has a procedural training program available for use on personal computers.

However, whether CBT instructional technology or more traditional instructional approaches are used (e.g., chalk, talk, demonstrate and display) there is an industry wide need for the appropriate courses to support the widespread use of GPS in VFR flight in general aviation.

**Current regulatory positions: Australia and New Zealand**

In Australia, an approved training program, flight testing and licence endorsement is required for GPS Instrument Flight Rules (IFR), but not VFR. Currently the industry GNSS Implementation Team (GIT) has provided a list of open recommendations for action by the Civil Aviation Safety Authority (CASA). The GIT recommended that GPS should be recognised as an approved means of navigation under the VFR, with certain conditions. One condition is that no specific licensing or training for day VFR operations is required, except that VFR flight above cloud should require similar training to radio navigation aids. A further condition is that advisory material dealing with issues which are not mandatory should be included in a Civil Aviation Advisory Publication (CAAP). It was recommended that the implementation of GPS navigation for VFR should be supported by a broad industry education programme incorporating pilot aid cards, magazine articles, amendments to the CASA GPS booklet, and safety seminars. A further recommendation was that CASA should begin planning for the inclusion of GPS in the Day VFR ground and flying training syllabus (Airservices Australia, 1996). Regulatory changes have yet to be implemented.

In New Zealand IFR GPS requirements have evolved through AIC-GENs 30/95, 5/96 and 2/98. The latter sets forth a GPS training syllabus in Appendix 1, which also contains the Civil Aviation Authority (CAA) Flight Evaluation Schedule for GPS IFR Approval (Civil Aviation Authority, 1998).

AIC-GEN 4/96 sets out the conditions for the installation of GPS equipment in New Zealand Aircraft registered for use in VFR operations. Clause 6 of this AIC GEN notes that the 'pilot in command will be responsible for ensuring that the flight path is monitored by traditional methods of navigation ...' (Civil Aviation Authority, 1996, p.11).

In January 1997 the Airways Corporation of New Zealand circulated a "GPS Information Bulletin" (ATS Operations Section, 1997). It noted that:

*"CAA does not see GPS being approved as a primary means of navigation for VFR operations. There will be too many varied types of equipment for formal certification. As we know, it will always be a very effective 'aid' (their emphasis) to navigation for the VFR pilot." (p. 10).*

**Current operational issues**

GPS units have proliferated in the GA environment. A recent survey of all Australian pilots (White & Frost, 1997) found that 34% of the more than 11,000 respondents owned their own GPS receiver. The situation in New Zealand is similar. Over 60% of GA GPS users surveyed in 1994 owned their own units (Nendick, & St. George, 1996a).

Equally it is clear from the popular aviation magazines available internationally that GPS use in various forms is widespread. The situation in regions with few or no reliable ground-based navigation aids, such as outback Australia, makes GPS 'essential', though probably not 'legal' for many flight operations.

Concerns about GPS knowledge and practice in GA VFR operations have been raised locally on the basis of flying experience and observation (O'Hare & St. George, 1994). Further confirmation of some of these concerns for GA continues with reports in the form of:

- Air space infringement reports where GPS use may have contributed.

- Accidents where GPS navigation reliance on VFR flights appears to have been implicated.

- GPS use and functioning difficulties stemming from 'finger-trouble', signal loss, power loss and inadequate competency with the technology (e.g., Nendick & St. George, 1996a; Nendick & St. George, 1996b; St. George & Nendick, 1997).

- Loss of primary VFR navigation knowledge and skills, and the failure to train (or learn) to integrate GPS navigation information into primary VFR navigation procedures such as fuel planning.

It is of little assistance to simply point out that GPS is not an 'approved' mode of primary navigation for VFR traffic and leave it at that. The trend in purchase and use is quite the opposite. Use is unlikely to diminish because it is not 'approved' in a particular flight mode. Pilots will purchase GPS receivers and try them without training. Some may be embarrassed by their mistakes and confusions, but there may also be unnecessary fatalities.

Trainers and educators in aviation can be the role models for a professional and knowledgeable approach in how to properly use GPS, even when *only* for a GA VFR flight. We should not wait until enough incidents or accidents force a regulation on the industry. If the flying club or flight training school has GPS equipped aircraft, students and licensed hirers should receive instruction or demonstrate appropriate competency. If a pilot is going to hire your aircraft and use a portable GPS the same standard can apply.

**Training structure**

It is essential that flying instructors are proficient with GPS equipment. Flight trainers need to provide courses or blend GPS use into their instruction in GA VFR operations. There are enough GA pilots getting into 'trouble' with GPS to motivate many to seek instruction. Courses offering GPS operational techniques and highlighting 'traps' for the unwary ought to prompt others to seek formal training.

A GPS training course should include sections on GPS theory, system components and principles of operation; navigation performance requirements; authorisation and documentation; errors and limitations; human factors of operation; and specific GPS navigation procedures and equipment checks. The human factors section should incorporate design ergonomics such as standardisation, controls and displays, and physical location; GPS operation; operational behaviour such as input errors, workload, mode awareness, monitoring, and cross-checking; hazardous attitudes such as over-reliance, complacency, over-confidence, and distraction; and specific model proficiency requirements. A certificate of competency appropriate to the instruction should be issued.

**Basic VFR GPS course**

From our research and industry comment the following basic GA-VFR-GPS course structure is presented. It sets out what we believe pilots should know about the nature of the equipment; simple, surface operations (the point where a lot of GA pilots get to); and complex, deep operations (memory intensive multi keystroke operations such as route building where menus and modes it can get difficult and confusing). VFR flight planning and operations in which GPS is integrated as part of the flight management are emphasised, but with options in support of basic VFR flight navigation requirements.

- Principles and components of the GPS system
  - System architecture and control
  - Aircraft GPS equipment
  - Triangulation, range measurement and position fixing
- GPS navigation system performance
  - Technical Standard Order (TSO) and non TSO units
  - Random Autonomous Integrity Monitoring (RAIM)
  - GPS errors and limitations
- GPS installation
  - Aerials, connections, mountings
  - Power: sources, integrity, back-up
- GPS operational procedures - introduction
  - Mode knowledge and access - (what is it, how do I get to it?)
  - Set up menus - (What are the options? What do I choose and why? Confirmation of choice. Initialisation checks)
  - Alerts - (What do they mean? How do I respond?)

144

- Simple GPS operations
  - Displays (What do they tell me?)
  - 'Go To' mode
  - 'Nearest' mode
  - Data entry and checks

- Complex GPS operations
  - Aviation data base and updates
  - User created data base (airfields, way points, position autostore)
  - Route creation and pre-flight route verification
  - Route selection and operation (activate, invert, edit etc)

- Integrated VFR flight planning and operations with a GPS
  - Standard VFR flight planning
  - Flight route entry into GPS
  - Standard VFR flight plan cross-checks with GPS
  - In flight VFR - GPS cross-checks (planned points)

- VFR-GPS assisted check flight
  - Flight plan for a standard VFR flight and integrate GPS route planning. (instructor sets a three leg minimum flight)
  - Preview VFR planning and GPS planning
    (check accuracy and competency)
  - Check knowledge of GPS principles, installation, unit modes and operation

- VFR-GPS assisted competency flight
  - Adherence to standard VFR navigation and operations requirements
  - Airborne use of simple and complex GPS functions
    ('Go To' route operations; route selection and manipulation)
  - Require a route reversal on a leg.
  - Selection of 'Nearest' navaid
  - Visual navigation cross-check of data
  - Introduce actual or simulated power/signal loss and check VFR primary navigation
  - Observe 'look-out' and standard VFR operational procedures - navigation and R/T
  - Check GPS data interpretations: CDI bar, track, heading, range, groundspeed, time etc
  - As appropriate confirm navigation with other navaids

- Issue VFR -GPS Competency Certificate
  - Dated, not IFR, issued signifying VFR - GPS competency check

## Conclusion

In the absence of a legislative or regulatory requirement for GA VFR pilots to formally learn to use GPS, we suggest that the industry develops suitable training courses for GA VFR operations, and actively encourage pilots to educate themselves appropriately.

While GPS is not the cornerstone of VFR navigation, its power and affordability encourages its primary use in GA VFR operations. While superficially simple to use, even the cheapest handheld models are complex enough to demand a high level of knowledge and understanding for safe and competent flying. The aviation training industry, can do better, we believe, in educating for the safer use of GPS in general aviation. We need not sit back and watch 'self- instruction' result in 'self- destruction'. If we do, the result will ultimately be regulation with enforcement and all that it entails.

## Disclaimer

The views expressed in this paper are those of the authors and do not necessarily reflect Civil Aviation Authority of New Zealand policy.

## References

Airservices Australia (1995). GPS set for introduction as Primary Means Navigation. *Aviation Bulletin, 4, (6)*, 1, 4-5.

Airservices Australia (1996). GIT 5 minutes. Canberra: GNSS Program Office.

Airservices Australia (1997). Navigation requirements (RAC 44). In *Aeronautical Information Publication Australia*. Canberra: Aeronautical Information Service.

Airways Corporation (NZ) Ltd., (1997). *GPS Information Bulletin*. Wellington: ATS Operations Section.

Civil Aviation Authority (1995). *Requirements for the use of GPS as an approved supplemental navigation aid when flying under IFR*. AIC-GEN A30/95. Wellington: Aeronautical Information Service.

Civil Aviation Authority (1996). *Conditions of installation of Global Positioning System (GPS) equipment in New Zealand registered aircraft for use in VFR operations*. AIC-GEN A4/96. Wellington: Aeronautical Information Service.

Civil Aviation Authority (1998). *GNSS IFR operations.* AIC-GEN A2/98. Wellington: Aeronautical Information Service.

Nendick, M., & St. George, R. (1996a). Human factors aspects of Global Positioning Systems (GPS) equipment: A study with New Zealand pilots. In R. Jensen (Ed.), *Proceedings of the Eighth International Symposium on Aviation Psychology.* Ohio State University: Columbus, Ohio.

Nendick, M., & St. George, R. (1996b). GPS: Developing a human factors training course for pilots. In B.J. Hayward & A.R. Lowe (Eds.), *Applied aviation psychology: Achievement, change and challenge.* Aldershot, UK: Avebury Aviation.

O'Hare, D., & St. George, R. (1994). GPS - (Pre). Cautionary tales. *Airways, 6*(2), 12-15.

St. George, R., & Nendick, M. (1997). GPS = 'got position sussed': some challenges for engineering and cognitive psychology in the general aviation environment. In D. Harris (Ed.), *Engineering psychology and cognitive ergonomics (Vol 1).* Aldershot: Ashgate, pp 81-92.

White, B., & Frost, R. (1997). *Survey of consumers of Airservices Australia's products and services.* Final Report. Sydney: AGB McNair.

# 15 Future airline training: What has been learned from pilots and instructors?

*Henry R. Lehrer, The University of Nebraska at Omaha, USA*
*Phillip J. Moore, The University of Newcastle, Australia*
*Ross A. Telfer, Instructional Research & Development*
*Pty Ltd, Australia*
*Aimee Freeman, The University of Nebraska at Omaha, USA*

## Background

This paper extends several earlier studies examining the ways in which learning is approached in the aviation industry. The theoretical underpinnings of this research lie in a long tradition of examining individual differences and focus on the different ways in which people approach learning. A number of researchers have investigated the field in non-aviation settings (e.g., Biggs,1987; Bowden, 1986; and Entwistle & Ramsden,1983) and there seems general agreement on the constructs of Surface, Deep, and Achieving approaches to learning (the designations to be used throughout this paper). Specifically, a Surface approach to learning might be typified by a desire to meet minimal standards by the use of rote-style memorisation; a Deep approach to learning is characterised by becoming intrinsically involved in learning for understanding, application and problem solving; and an Achieving approach to learning is grounded in a competitive desire to seek high grades and recognition. Additionally, a Surface approach tends to be somewhat lacking in structure, a Deep approach is well-organised and elaborated while the Achieving approach can interact with either Deep or Surface to produce well ordered outcomes. Research demonstrates quality outcomes from Deep-Achieving approaches (Biggs, 1987). While most of the approaches literature has focussed on school-university type settings, a number of studies have examined the construct in aviation. The next section of the paper addresses that research.

*Pilots*

The first aviation-related test of the relationships between approaches to learning and both ground school and flying performance was undertaken some time ago by Moore and Telfer (1990) using a sample of ab initio pilots. In brief, the ground school results showed that being Deep was helpful for learning while Surface was harmful. Further, those who reported deeper approaches to learning flew solo earlier than those who did not report such an emphasis. In that study, Moore and Telfer employed a slight modification of Biggs' (1987) Study Processes Questionnaire, a questionnaire originally designed for use with university level students.

A second study of some 350 airline pilots (Moore, Smith & Telfer, 1994; Moore, Telfer, & Smith, 1994) from five international airlines and a US aviation institute, surveyed approaches to learning using the Pilot Learning Processes Questionnaire (PLPQ) which was based upon the constructs of Deep, Surface, and Achieving but designed specifically for experienced pilot populations. The general trend from the experienced pilot study was for Deep scores to be higher than Achieving scores with Surface scores being substantially lower than Achieving scores, the respective overall means being 4.63, 3.93, and 2.74 (on a scale from 1 to 6). These data suggest that these pilots were keen on understanding, applying their knowledge, and learning in an organised fashion. The relatively lower scores for Surface suggests that they were not very interested in just passing the test and reproducing the information they had been given. Moore (1995) further showed that check and training captains held stronger Deep views of learning than those not in such training positions. Additional data have been secured from other airline pilots, substantiating these trends (e.g., Monfries & Moore, 1998).

*Instructors*

The research of Moore, Lehrer and Telfer (1997) is an extension of earlier studies with pilots but the emphasis has moved from pilots to instructors. Such a focus is important to aviation training because there is a need to examine the ways in which pilots, instructors and context influence both the processes of learning and the outcomes (Telfer & Moore, 1997). Instructors clearly influence their students' learning (e.g., Henley, 1995) and what an instructor believes about learning potentially influences how he or she presents information, encourages learning through appropriate feedback, sets expectations, facilitates self-directed learning and monitoring, and generally prepares pilots for an aviation career. There is a growing literature base demonstrating the important role of teacher beliefs in determining quality learning outcomes (see Moore, Lehrer & Telfer, 1997).

A question might be asked about instructors' beliefs about learning as a function of the type of training being examined. For example, do instructors in an airlines' training program have different views on learning from instructors in general aviation? Do instructors in university programs differ from the above groups? What of instructors in an academy whose essential purpose is to prepare candidates for airline entry? What of comparisons of instructors and pilots? We have argued elsewhere that understanding the relationships between what instructors and pilots think about learning is critical to aligned instruction (Telfer & Moore, 1997). Questions such as these guided the research reported below.

I.     Specifically, two null hypotheses were under investigation: There are no significant differences between the ways that specific instructor groups within the US aviation training industry approach learning.

II.    There are no significant differences between the ways that instructor groups within the US aviation training industry approach learning as compared to an earlier group of air carrier pilots.

## Methodology

*Subjects*

The subjects were 177 aviation instructors. They came from four different non-military US aviation training settings. Specifically, they were from the general aviation (non-air carrier) community, from a university aviation flight training program, from an aviation training academy that specializes in airline preparation, and from a major (over $1B per year revenues) air carrier's training department. These groups will be referred to in the following sections as General Aviation, University, Academy, and Airline respectively. These four different subgroups were identified and included since they are representative of the range of training in the US aviation community (with the exception of military instruction). It should be noted that it was not possible to make specific comparisons between instructors who were solely ground school and those who gave both ground and flight training.

151

The General Aviation subjects all attended a flight instructor refresher clinic in a Midwestern US state or were employed by the Airplane Pilots and Owners Association (AOPA), the sponsor of the clinic. The University subjects were employed as flight instructors in the flight training program of a large university in the Midwest. The Academy subjects were instructors at a flight training corporation located in the state of Florida and the Airline subjects were employed by a mature domestic/international air carrier headquartered in the Midwest.

*Instrumentation*

The survey instrument was the Pilot Instruction Process Questionnaire (PIPQ) of 30 questions consisting of 10 items related to Deep, 10 to Surface and 10 to Achieving approaches to learning (Moore, Lehrer & Telfer, 1997). The PIPQ was field-tested with a general aviation instructor sample group. This group was selected from a flight instructor forum group on the AOPA *www Flight Instructor Homepage*; minor modifications were made to only the format of the survey.

**Results**

The results are reported in two parts, demographics and PIPQ findings.

*Demographics*

The average age of the respondents was 33.95 years; the oldest were the Airline instructors with an average age of 42.67 years and the youngest group was University instructors who had an average age of 22.55 years. University and Academy mean ages were 22.55 and 28.81 years respectively. This average age is lower than the average age of the entire US instructor community which is 41.05 (General Aviation Manufacturers Association (GAMA), 1995).

The General aviation group had been instructing the longest (8.97 years), whereas the University group had been instructing an average of two and one-half years. In between were the Airlines (7.5 years) and Academy (2.9 years). The average for the group was just over five years. No US comparison data are available in this demographic category.

The sample was well educated with 62.94% of the respondents holding at least a Bachelors degree. Within the sample population, over 90% of the Airline instructors had earned at least a Bachelors degree, as had 78 percent of Academy, 50 percent of General Aviation and 9.7 percent of University instructors. Six respondents had a Masters degree and one respondent had a doctorate.

The population for this study was predominately male; one hundred fifty-five participants or 87.6% were male and twenty-two or 12.4% were female. However, this percentage of female instructors is greater proportionally than the 4,338 of 75,621, or 5.7%, female instructors in the US (GAMA, 1995).

*PIPQ Results*

Table 15.1 illustrates the descriptive statistics for each group on each measure of the PIPQ. Surface refers to the 10 PIPQ questions relating to that approach and Deep and Achieving to question in those constructs respectively.

**Table 15.1**
**Means and standard deviations for groups on PIPQ measures**

|  | General Aviation (n=34) | University (n=31) | Academy (n=63) | Airline (n=49) | Weighted mean (n=177) |
|---|---|---|---|---|---|
| Surface Approach | 3.31 (0.90) | 3.57 (1.06) | 3.49 (1.09) | 3.54 (0.94) | 3.48 |
| Deep Approach | 4.43 (1.13) | 4.49 (1.05) | 4.33 (0.98) | 4.40 (1.11) | 4.39 |
| Achieving Approach | 3.93 (1.23) | 4.17 (1.10) | 4.00 (0.98) | 3.91 (1.03) | 3.99 |

In order to address the hypothesis of differences between instructor groups on the three approach constructs, a series of one way ANOVAs (General Aviation, University, Academy, and Airline) was conducted with Surface, Deep and then Achieving scores entered as the dependent variable. These analyses revealed $F$ values of less than 1.00 indicating no reliable differences between the instructor groups on any of the approach measures. Consequently, in further discussions, the average weighted mean for each construct will be used.

Next, comparisons were made between the current instructor means for Deep, Surface and Achieving and the corresponding pilot results reported by Moore, Smith and Telfer (1994) and Moore, Telfer and Smith (1994). The means from the instructor group for Deep and Achieving are not within the range of means from the air carrier pilot study. Specifically, the pilot means for Deep ranged from 4.55 to 4.80 and the instructor mean was somewhat below at 4.39; the pilot means for Surface were 2.81 to 2.93 with instructor means quite a bit higher at 3.48 and finally, the means for Achieving of the pilots ranged from 3.64 to 4.35 and the instructor mean was solidly in the middle of those scores at 3.99. Several t tests using Welch's method were performed comparing the means from the instructor group with those of the pilot group. For Surface, Deep, and Achieving, the t values proved to be significant ($p<.05$), the emerging profile showing higher Surface and Achieving scores for instructors but higher Deep scores for pilots. Clearly, the second hypothesis of no differences between instructors and pilots is rejected.

**Discussion**

This approaches-to-learning research was guided by two basic hypotheses, one related to differences between instructor groups, the other related to differences between instructors and pilots.

The finding of no significant differences between instructor groups is interesting and may be attributable to a number of factors. One factor may be that instructor training places very little emphasis in general on issues such as learning, learning theories, and educational psychology and very little specifically on individual differences such as approaches to learning. Two, it also could be that instructor perceptions of regulatory authorities (their rules, examinations etc) encourage a more uniform rather than diverse view of how learning can be constructed, the focus is on the outcome not the processes that lead to such outcomes. Third, it also could be the case that the PIPQ is not sensitive enough to detect any differences that may reside between instructor groups. To address this issue, we will be conducting detailed reliability and validity checks on the PIPQ once we have extended the data base of instructors.

As for the second hypothesis, the finding of instructors reporting as being more Surface (and slightly more Achieving) but less Deep compared to pilots highlights potential alignment problems. While it is recognised that the instructors in this study were not involved in the training of the pilot sample used, it would be difficult to argue against the need for trainees, pilots and instructors to approach learning in a similar way. It is important that their priorities, attitudes, goals, and strategies match. At the individual level this can make the difference between passing a test and being a professional pilot in the fullest sense. Current human factors and CRM training is heavily dependent upon values and attitudes and while traditionally there has been a greater emphasis on skills and knowledge, there needs to be an emphasis on all aspects of learning. It is not likely that such attitudes, skills, and knowledge will be enhanced by a Surface approach. If the industry seeks to produce truly professional pilots by recognising that there is a difference between passing a test and understanding aeronautical information, then it is likely that instructor perspectives on learning and ways of testing that learning may have to be changed.

These differences can be seen to impact in three ways:

1) For individual pilots and instructors there is the probability of a conflict in values and approaches if the trainee is seeking depth of understanding and standards beyond those of the syllabus and examinations.

2) For organisations such as airlines, colleges and flying schools, there is the economic dilemma of whether they will pursue the expense of the possible ideal as opposed to the economies of the regulations.

3) For the industry and regulatory authorities, there is a need to recognise there is a qualitative difference between identifiable levels of approaches to learning.

These results were obtained from an instructional force with formal educational qualifications far higher than in countries such as Australia. A peripheral point is that they show that the professionalisation of flight instruction is occurring: it is becoming a career vocation with specialist preparation. More relevant for this discussion, though, is the question of how such a group was more surface and less deep than the airline pilots. One needs here to probe the nature of professional socialisation: how one takes on the values and particular attitudes of a particular group to which one belongs. On this point, several airlines have adopted train-the-trainer programmes which incorporate explicitly reference to approaches to learning, and provide manuals which espouse deep and achieving approaches (as well as appropriate applications of surface approaches). However, to date the tracking of the effectiveness of such programmes has not been undertaken.

This paper is based on work in progress. Clearly it has raised more questions than answers and we invite anybody interested in collaboration to contact us. General aviation flight instructors may now respond to the survey at an on-line version of the PIPQ at *http://cid.unomaha.edu/~unoai/acilpq* and that data will be added to the database. An additional major US air carrier and two other university flight schools have also indicated their willingness to work collaboratively with us on the project.

*Acknowledgment*: We wish to recognise the co-operation of the instructors and their organisations who participated in this project.
*Note:* Full statistical data can be obtained from the first author.

## References

Biggs, J.B. (1987). *Student approaches to learning and studying*. Hawthorn, Victoria: Australian Council for Educational Research (ACER).

Bowden, J.A. (1986). *Student learning: Research in practice*. Melbourne: Centre for the Study of Higher Education, University of Melbourne.

Entwistle, N.J., & Ramsden, P. (1983). *Understanding student learning*. London, UK: Croom Helm.

General Aviation Manufacturers Association. (1995). *General aviation statistical databook*. Washington, DC: Author.

Henley, I. (1995). *The quality of the development and evaluation of flight instructors in Canada and Australia*. Unpublished doctoral dissertation. The University of Newcastle. Australia.

Monfries, M.M., & Moore, P.J. (1998). Pilot selection procedures: A case for individual differences in applicant groups. *Paper presented at the Fourth Australian Aviation Psychology Symposium*, Manly, Australia, March.

Moore, P.J. (1995). Across airline differences in pilot learning: The roles of experience and qualifications. In N. Johnston, R. Fuller, & N. McDonald (Eds.), *Aviation psychology: Training and selection*. Aldershot: Avebury Aviation.

Moore, P.J, Lehrer, H.R., & Telfer, R.A. (1997). Instructor perspectives on learning in aviation. *Paper presented at the Ninth Annual International Symposium on Aviation Psychology*, Columbus, Ohio, April.

Moore, P.J., Smith. M.W., & Telfer, R.A. (1994). Learning for automation: generic versus specific approaches. In M. Mouloua & R. Parasuraman (Eds.), *Human performance in automated systems: Current research and trends* (pp. 307-313) Hillsdale: Erlbaum.

Moore, P. J., & Telfer. R.A. (1990). Approaches to learning: Relationships to pilot performance. *Journal of Aviation/Aerospace Education & Research, 1*(1), 44-58.

Moore, P.J., Telfer. R.A., & Smith. M.W. (1994). A comparative analysis of airline pilots' approaches to learning. *Journal of Aviation/Aerospace Education & Research, 4*(3), 17-23.

Telfer, R.A., & Moore, P.J. (1997) *Aviation training: Learners, instruction and organisation.* Aldershot: Avebury.

# 16 Stress in training transfer: Cognitive interference

*Heather J. Irvine and H. Peter Pfister*
*The University of Newcastle*

High fidelity simulators have become a fundamental component of pilot training in an effort to technologically assist man. Technology has ensured that these simulators behave almost identical to the actual aircraft. However, despite the sophistication of technology and current training between 85% and 88% of aviation accidents currently have their 'probable cause' attributed to 'pilot error' (Taylor, 1991). It is arguable that these technological advances have not reduced the number of global errors, but merely changed the type of errors that occur (Amalberti & Wibaux, 1995).

This is not to suggest that flight simulators have failed to expertly reproduce the technical demands, sensori-motor challenges and multitrack thinking required by pilots in operational flight situations, but they appear to have struggled with the replication of high physical risk and other psychological stress components inherent in the flying of an actual aircraft. (Taylor, 1991).

Such omissions become important if one considers more recent theoretical models for optimal conditions for training transfers which suggest that what accounts for transfer between practice and test situation or between two skills is the extent to which the cognitive processes required in the transfer task are similar to those present at the time of encoding (original learning/training) (Lidor & Singer, 1994).

The retrieval of cue-response relationships are dependent upon the reinstatement of the precise way in which the cue was encoded (Tulving, 1976). Thus under conditions of psychological stress, the retrieval of the cue-response relationship may be prevented because the cues failed to be reinstated in the precise way in which they were encoded. Hence, psychological stress may actually interrupt or distort the cognitive structures necessary for positive transfer.

Sells (1970) suggested that stress increased if the consequences of the failure to respond effectively to the task were important to the individual. Sells (1970) model has been modified as follows: $ES = C\,[(D + K) - A]$ where *ES* is experienced stress, *C* is the perceived consequences of meeting or not meeting the demand, *D* is the individual's perception of the severity of the environmental demand, and *A* is the individual's perceived ability to meet the demand. Controlling for perceived consequences, persons with high demand and low ability would receive the highest scores, and persons with low demand and high ability would receive the lowest stress scores. K equals the number of scale values that *A* can represent, such that inability to meet the demand of the performance criteria (i.e., overload) has a greater impact on expected stress levels than excessive ability to meet the demand criteria (i.e., underload).

It would appear from the research that stress does not limit the processing capacity *per se*, but rather that limitations in the processing of task-relevant cognitions occurs as a result of other variables such as stress that also demand attentional capacity in their own right. Indeed, Hamilton (1982) proposed stress should be regarded as a primarily cognitive event that if presented to the cognitive processing system whilst the system is engaged in another task, actually pushes the information processing capacity of the system to or beyond its limits. According to supporters of the parallel limited capacity system definition of human information processing, a stressor imposes its own share of processing demands thus drawing on a limited pool of attentional resources shared by a central task. Certain components of the central task subsequently suffer if the resources from which they partake fall below levels required for optimal performance (Fisher, 1986).

This study aimed to provide evidence for stress induced decrements in the performance of a training transfer task as a function of processing capacity limitations and motor control impairments associated with stress in a fine motor task.

**Method**

*Participants*

Twenty-four undergraduate male and female students, with normal or corrected hearing and vision, at the University of Newcastle participated in this study. They had no previous flight or flight simulator experience (not including arcade game type simulators). The sample consisted of 12 females and 12 males between the ages of 20 and 31 (mean = 22.5, *SD* = 2.5).

Controlling for gender, half the subjects were randomly allocated to the experimental group while the other half constituted the control group.

*Equipment*

*Flight simulator.* The simulator used was a NovaSim FT-1 fixed-base generic flight simulator, with a built in hand grip pressure sensor. Based upon the contention that muscles undergo various forms of contraction under states of stress (Calvo & Alamo, 1987) a hand grip pressure instrument (HGPI) was developed. When hand grip pressure is applied to the control yoke, which contains the sensor, pressure is transformed into signals which then are processed via a data logger and stored in a PC based microprocessor.

*The Perceived Consequences Questionnaire* (PCQ). Originally developed by Harris and Berger (1983) to assess the expected stress levels of individuals about to perform a potentially stressful task. This questionnaire was adapted for application to the present study. The seven point rating scale required respondents to indicate the perceived consequences of the task, the perceived demand of the task and their perceived ability to meet the perceived demand of the task.

*Procedure*

Participants viewed a 5 minute instructional video advising them of the intended task to be performed. They then completed 2 training approach and landings. Experimental subjects were then informed of a monetary loss of one dollar from their twenty dollar pay for mistakes made in their forthcoming flight, while control subjects incurred no penalty. Participants then completed the PCQ before completing their final transfer task. Performance levels for each subject were obtained according to the required altitude for each one-tenth of a nautical mile away from the center of the runway. Hand grip pressure measures were taken at 0.5 second intervals.

**Results and discussion**

*Perceived Consequences Questionnaire*

The following analyses present responses to the PCQ. The descriptive statistics for each section and total score is contained in Table 16.1.

161

Firstly, it was important to ensure that expected stress scores were not overtly influenced by differences in each group's perceived ability to meet neither the perceived demand nor the importance of performing all tasks well. Referring to Table 16.1, it becomes apparent that the control and experimental groups did not differ significantly on these variables. Any differences in PCQ (total scores) could thus be expected to reflect the importance of performing the flight task well. However, upon referring to the means values contained in Table 16.1, suggest that both groups did not differ markedly in the 'flight task importance' scores either. The PCQ total (expected stress) scores did not support the notion that the experimental group would report a higher stress score.

**Table 16.1**
**Descriptive statistics for sections and total scores for the PCQ .**

| Variable | M | SD | df | F | p |
|---|---|---|---|---|---|
| Demand - Ability | | | 1,222 | .23 | .53 |
| Control | 5.56 | 3.11 | | | |
| Experimental | 5.25 | 2.80 | | | |
| Flight Task Importance | | | 1,22 | 1.36 | .26 |
| Control | 4.92 | 1.24 | | | |
| Experimental | 4.16 | 1.85 | | | |
| All tasks | | | 1,22 | .77 | .38 |
| Control | 5.33 | 1.23 | | | |
| Experimental | 4.92 | 1.08 | | | |
| PCQ (total) | | | 1,23 | .06 | .81 |
| Control | 31.29 | 11.99 | | | |
| Experimental | 29.88 | 15.92 | | | |

The PCQ was utilised in this study primarily to ascertain whether incorporating monetary loss would elevate the subjects' total PCQ (expected stress) scores. The results obtained suggest that monetary loss (as defined in this study) did not impact upon the subjects' reporting of the importance of performing well on the transfer task to avoid this consequence. Given that the mean scores for both groups on other elements of the PCQ were not significantly different, performing well on the transfer task did not provide the predicted discriminating component for the control and experimental groups' total PCQ scores. This finding did not support the hypothesis predicting the experimental group would report higher scores on the PCQ than the control group.

*Hand grip pressure*

The results revealed the experimental group exerted slightly greater HGP than the control group throughout both the training and transfer conditions. The difference in HGP, however, reached significance during the transfer phase $(F (1,43) = 10.54, p <.01)$. To eliminate undue influence by non-contributing components the mean value of their transfer HGP was divided by their training HGP to establish a ratio score which is presented as a percentage. This indicated that the control group HGP actually decreased in the transfer task $(M = -7.1\%)$ whilst the experimental group increased dramatically $(M = 47\%)$. These changes are summarised in Figure 16.1. A one-way ANOVA provided statistical support for the hypothesis that the experimental group produced significantly greater HGP in the transfer condition than the control group $(F (1,22) = 6.12, p = .022)$.

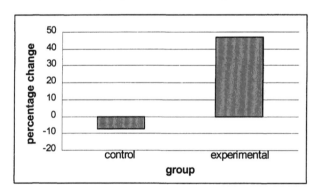

**Figure 16.1**
**Percentage change in handgrip pressure between training and transfer for experimental and control groups**

There was support for the hypothesis that imposing a consequence upon performance in the transfer condition would increase physiological indices of stress. While this did not contribute to performance decrements, it provides some evidence for changes in physiological states under threats of a deleterious consequence. Given these changes under relatively minor

163

threatening conditions, it may be expected that greater physiological reactions occur under greater stress. Just as pilots are trained on content-expertise to complete a task, providing maximum cue-response relationships might be ensured if pilots are trained to perform with the same muscle tension that occurs in the cockpit. In other words, if the retrieval of cue-response relationships is dependent upon the reinstatement of the precise way in which it was encoded (Tulving, 1976), then training under conditions of elevated muscle tension may produce greater transfer in the cockpit since cockpit performance is also likely to occur under states of muscle tension.

*Performance*

Overall, the mean error scores for both groups did not differ significantly for either the training or transfer conditions suggesting group similarity in terms of performance (Table 16.2).

**Table 16.2**
**Descriptive data for errors in the training and transfer conditions**

| Variable | n | M | SD |
|---|---|---|---|
| Training Error | | | |
|     Control | 12 | 7.34 | 1.66 |
|     Experimental | 12 | 7.83 | 5.37 |
| Transfer Error | | | |
|     Control | 12 | 7.37 | 2.71 |
|     Experimental | 12 | 6.20 | 3.50 |

However, contrary to the proposed hypothesis predicting the number of errors committed by the experimental group would increase in the transfer condition, the mean error for the experimental group actually decreased, the effect, however, was not significant. Whilst it may be contended that any improved performance reflected the subjects' steep learning curve, this seems unfounded given that the control group did not also perform better in the transfer condition.

Given that the experimental group reported significantly greater HGP than the control group, and muscle tension is an indicator of a stress state, which in turn is normally associated with performance decrements, these relationships would lead to an anticipation of poorer performance (greater errors). However, alternative explanations for the apparent contradictory direction of performance changes are also possible. Arousal produces muscle tension which prevents smooth motor movements, motor co-ordination and timing (Calvo & Alamo, 1987) with the greatest impact purported to be upon fine motor movement (Pargman, 1986). However, even for fine motor skills, some degree of arousal is associated with enhanced performance. The introduction of the HGPI as an experimental measure of stress prevents accurate knowledge of whether the significantly greater increases in HGP for the experimental group indicated low, moderate or high levels of stress. Considering the relationship between HGP and the low self reported stress scores, it might be suggested that the obtained difference in HGP measures indicated only a minor change in stress, perhaps from low to slightly higher than low. For a fine motor task, this minimal change would be sufficient to improve performance. However, the literature that suggests that physiological arousal should also reduce performance efficiency through the consumption of attentional resources fails to provide instances in which this consumption might actually increase performance efficiency, as was the case in the current findings. Perhaps further research in this area may discover that worry cognitions and fine-motor performance are also related in an inverted-U type function.

This study was the first to incorporate operator HGP as a non-intrusive measure of mid-performance stress. This has potential for the measurement of pilot physiological stress levels. This study has also reconceptualised existing models of stress. Previously, the models have focused on perceived demand and ability, without addressing the role of perceived consequences. This study has argued that a legitimate way of conceptualising performer stress is encapsulated in the formula $(ES = C [(D + K) - A)$. While considerable refinement and/or modification of this theoretical model is required, this study has given some limited encouragement to its potential usefulness.

This study confirmed that at least some level of physiological arousal can be induced in the simulator by imposing a potential threat. This finding suggests that aviation researchers should continue to investigate this apparent potential for creating greater simulated realism in the current training devices.

**Notes and acknowledgment**

1. The assistance from Warren Wilks and Lisa Duff is greatly acknowledged.
2. This research was in part supported by RMC grant 45/299/701.

# References

Amalberti, R., & Wibaux, F. (1995). Maintaining manual and cognitive skills. *Aviation Psychology, Training and Selection: Proceedings of the 21st Conference of the European Association of Aviation Psychology*, 333-346.

Calvo, M.G., & Alamo, L. (1987). Test anxiety and motor performance: The role of muscular and attentional demands. *International Journal of Psychology, 22,* 156-178.

Fisher, S. (1986). *Stress and strategy.* London: Erlbaum.

Harris, J.H., & Berger, P.K. (1983). Antecedents of psychological stress. *Journal of Human Stress, 9,* 24-31.

Hamilton, V. (1982). Cognition and stress: An information processing model. In L. Goldberger and S. Breznitz (Eds.), *Handbook of stress: Theoretical and clinical aspects* (pp. 105-122). New York: The Free Press.

Lidor, R., & Singer, R.N. (1994). Motor skill acquisition, auditory distractors and the encoding specificity hypothesis. *Perceptual and Motor Skills, 79,* 1579-1584.

Pargman, D. (1986). *Stress and motor performance: Understanding and coping.* New York: movement Publication.

Sells, S.B. (1970). On the nature of stress. In J.E. McGrath (Ed.), *Social and psychological factors in stress.* New York: Holt, Rinehart and Winston, Inc.

Taylor, R.L. (1991). *The command decision series Vol. 6: Human factors.* Pennsylvania: Belvoir Publications Ltd.

Tulving, E. (1976). Ecphoric processes in recall and recognition. In J. Brown (Ed.), *Recall and recognition.* New York: Wiley.

# 17 The impact of executive control on trainee commercial pilots' strategic flexibility

*Susan L. Cockle and Phillip J. Moore*
*The University of Newcastle*

To be effective operators, trainee commercial pilots require adequate strategic management to allow them to plan, monitor, and if necessary, modify their learning. This study addresses how differences in the executive control of novice pilots are reflected in their strategic flexibility. Within this context we review the literature pursuant of a learner's mindfulness when addressing the orchestration and control of learning.

## Conceptions of learning

Pivotal to this paper and the on-going research to which it is associated is the recognition that a learner's belief component is central to the instrumentation and regulation of learning. Parallel to the belief component are learning performance outcomes which in themselves are comprehensive of a learner's strategic management, working method, and set achievement goals. In this context the belief component may be viewed as one of mindfulness (Salomon & Globerson, 1987) inclusive of the conative dimensions of epistemology, motivation, and volition. The concept of mindfulness is referred to as the third-order of learning (Schoenfeld, 1987).

Viewed as a functional differentiation, the second-order of learning is characterised by metacognition - the *knowledge* of cognitive processes; and executive control - the *regulation* of cognitive processes (Lawson, 1984; Schoenfeld, 1987; Cantwell, 1994). Unless the essential processes of using strategy knowledge are stressed as central goals of aviation learning ecologies, higher-order thinking and its strategic management is likely to be neglected. We also run the risk that the knowledge transmitted to the learner may remain inert.

It is important to note that the majority of students view learning as gaining domain knowledge or facts; and memorising for future recall (Iran-Nejad, 1990). In the constructive framework as indicated, it would be expected that these learners' beliefs reflect a surface approach (Moore & Telfer, 1990; Moore, Farquharson & Telfer, 1997) to their learning in that the breadth and depth with which content is addressed remains superficial. Certainly, in terms of pilot performance, research (Hunt, 1997; Moore & Telfer, 1990) indicates that an adoption of the surface approach results in superficial learning strategies and less than optimum level ground and flight performance.

On the other hand, students who view learning as a structure of understanding hold a deep approach to their learning (Entwistle, 1988; Moore, Telfer & Smith, 1994). It would be expected that these students seek to be dynamic, creative, innovative, interpretative, powerful thinkers. However, less than one third of students view learning in this way (Iran-Nejad, 1990) but those who do seek mastery in their performance and achievement goals (Ames & Archer, 1988; Ames, 1992; Archer, 1994).

**The process of knowing and executive control**

The influence of beliefs, recognised as mindfulness, may be viewed within the executive control context. In this paper it is stated that executive control is considered to be the self-regulation of the metacognitive processes by the learner. The operation of that control is recognised in scales of strategic flexibility (Cantwell, 1994). For instance, a learner reflecting mindfulness of self-regulation or control effort represents an 'adaptive' predisposition in orienting, planning, monitoring and modifying learning decisions.

In sharp contrast are those learners whose mindfulness reflects a *somewhat* mindless, flawed conception of knowledge and beliefs. For example, success in learning is attributed to extraneous or distal measures and as such beyond the imagined control of the learner. These learners adopt a fixed approach to strategy management and are viewed as 'inflexible' (Cantwell, 1994). In further contrast, some students' understanding of the knowledge and processes of regulation or management results in a sometimes *overwhelming* loss of control of the learning situation. The extent of their inability to effectively regulate their learning effort is considered maladaptive. This maladaptive tendency is recognised as 'irresolute' (Cantwell, 1994).

Using Cantwell's predisposition scales of 'adaptive', 'inflexible' and 'irresolute' the on-going study addresses the concept of strategic flexibility and its relationship to aviation academic and operational performance. We assumed that by classifying students in terms of strategic flexibility tendencies any differences in aviation academic learning outcomes would be optimised. We further assumed, as indicated by prior research in nursing and education university faculties (Cantwell, 1994; Cantwell & Millard, 1994; Cantwell & Moore, 1996) that an 'adaptive' or flexible predisposition in learning would underlie optimum level aviation education, training and operational performance.

**Method**

*Participants*

A total of 46 Bachelor of Science (Aviation), trainee fixed wing commercial pilots volunteered to participate in the study. The Bachelor of Science (Aviation) is a three year undergraduate programme integrating flight training and university aviation academic studies. Subjects ranged in age from 17 to 31 with most volunteers being close to the mean age of 19.

The students were from two mutually exclusive groups defined by their enrolled first or second year level. Year one students majored in flight theory and training. The assessment included both Civil Aviation Safety Authority (CASA) and university aviation examinations. Year two students majored in a variety of aviation related subjects within the Department of Aviation and Technology. Assessments included both practical and examination components.

*Materials*

The strategic flexibility measure is a 21 question, 5-point Likert-type scale with response anchors ranging from never or only rarely (1) to always or almost always (5). In mixed placing, seven statements complete each of the strategic flexibility scales. Examples of the questions are included below.

"Adaptive" Scale

*I place a lot of importance on adjusting my study methods to meet the requirements of particular tasks.*

"Inflexible" Scale

*I find that I have one good way of going about completing my assignments and this is effective nearly all the time.*

"Irresolute" Scale

*I often find the ideas and methods I come across when preparing for an assignment more confusing than helpful.*

*Procedure*

All volunteers completed an identical strategic flexibility questionnaire at the beginning of each university designated semester. Time on task was not controlled, kept informal, and held post normal lecture times.

Semester one and semester two strategic flexibility scale group means and standard deviations were calculated and initial trends examined. Paired differential t-tests were performed on the strategic flexibility scale scores for semester one and semester two of each group.

**Results and discussion**

In order to examine the relationship between executive control of novice pilots' learning and their aviation academic performance, it was necessary to trace trainee pilots' strategic flexibility. Initial results from strategic flexibility scale individual percentage group means and standard deviations indicated that students began the year as "irresolute". Group one had a mean of 66.53% and group two a mean of 60.00%. In relation to the ecology of both years this is an understandable indication. For group one the year consisted of ab initio flight training which was completed off-campus at a flying training institution. For group two, once again the year began in a new environment where the context changed from training to higher education. T-tests indicated a significant difference between group one, semester one and semester two "irresolute" scales $t(27) = 2.47$, $p<0.05$ but no significant difference was noted for group two $t(15) = 0.57$, $p>0.05$.

Throughout the year group one students' adaptability increased slightly from semester one (mean 56.81%) to semester two (mean 58.06%). T-tests indicated no significant difference for group one $t(24) = -0.29$, $p>0.05$. The same was indicated for group two semester one (mean 57.14%) and semester two (mean 63.87%). Although a marked percentage difference is indicated, t-tests showed, due to size, no significant difference $t(13) = -1.37$, $p>0.05$.

We also noted that throughout the year, for both groups, inflexibility increased markedly. The means for group one were semester one (50.51%) and semester two (65.16%) and for group two semester one (56.14%) and semester two (66.89%). T-tests further indicated a significant difference for group one between semester one and semester two $t(22) = -3.03$, $p<0.05$. The same was indicated for group two $t(15) = -2.75$, $p<0.05$. The question arises as to why the students became more inflexible throughout a year of study. We believe that there are major implications for both the individual learner and the institutions that offer aviation related programmes.

## Conclusion

There is ample evidence to suggest that strategic flexibility and its integral metacognitive knowledge and executive control will play an important role in the future development and delivery of aviation education and training programmes. It may well be that the current industry view of what constitutes effective learning, education, and training may be prescriptive in its orientation towards skill acquisition. In effect this view undermines the multisource and potential creative nature of aviation learning. As a result operational performance will continue to be delimited in its domain to incremental procedures and regulations. Learning is not merely an additive process. Effective operational performance is not mechanistic. As such, given the ability to characterise the features that differentiate trainee pilots' performance a revised framework for education and training can be adopted. The progressive development of this thesis continues in our on-going research.

## Acknowledgements

The authors are indebted to the trainee pilots who participated so willingly in this study. Susan Cockle gratefully acknowledges Associate Professor Phillip Moore's doctoral supervision. Neil Macpherson's statistical lectureship is also gratefully acknowledged. This research, which constitutes one component of Susan Cockle's doctoral project, was supported in part by an Australian Postgraduate Award.

## References

Ames, C. (1992). Classrooms: Goals, structures, and student motivation. *Journal of Educational Psychology, 84*(3), 261-271.

Ames, C., & Archer, J. (1988). Achievement goals in the classroom: Students' learning strategies and motivation processes. *Journal of Educational Psychology, 80*, 260-267.

Archer, J. (1994). Achievement goals as a measure of motivation in university students. *Contemporary Educational Psychology, 19*, 430-446.

Cantwell, R.H. (1994). Executive control of learning: Its measurement and relationships to learning in education and nursing. Unpublished doctoral dissertation, The University of Newcastle.

Cantwell, R.H., & Millard, Y. (1994). The relationship between approach to learning and learning strategies in learning music. *British Journal of Educational Psychology, 64*, 45-63.

Cantwell, R.H., & Moore, P.J. (1996). The development of measures of individual differences in self-regulatory control and their relationship to academic performance. *Contemporary Educational Psychology, 21*, 500-516.

Entwistle, N. (1988). Motivational factors in students' approaches in learning. In R.R. Schmeck (Ed.), *Learning strategies and learning styles*, 21-51. New York: Plenum.

Hunt, L.M. (1997). Influences on the learning process and learning outcome: Practical implications for the instructor. In G.J.F. Hunt (Ed.), *Designing instruction for human factors training in aviation*, 17-27. Aldershot, UK: Avebury.

Iran-Nejad, A. (1990). Active and dynamic self-regulation of learning processes. *Review of Educational Research,* Winter, *60*(4), 573-602.

Lawson, M.J. (1984). Being executive about metacognition. In J.R. Kirby (Ed.), *Cognitive strategies and educational performance*, 89-109. Orlando, FL: Academic Press.

Moore, P.J., Farquharson, T., & Telfer, R.A. (1997). Automation and human performance in airline pilot training. In M. Mouloua and J. Koonce (Eds.), *Human-automation interaction*, 126-136. New Jersey: Erlbaum.

Moore, P.J., & Telfer, R.A. (1990). Approaches to learning: Relationships with pilot performance. *Journal of Aviation/Aerospace Education and Research, 1*, 44-58.

Moore, P.J., Telfer, R.A., & Smith, M.W. (1994). A comparative analysis of airline pilots' approaches to learning. *The Journal of Aviation/Aerospace Education and Research*, 17-23.

Salomon, G., & Globerson, T. (1987). The role of mindfulness in learning and transfer. *International Journal of Educational Research, 11*, 623-638.

Schoenfeld, A. (1987). What's all the fuss about metacognition? In A. Schoenfeld (Ed.), *Cognitive science and mathematics education.* Hillsdale, NJ: Erlbaum.

# 18 Does facilitated group work and independent study in undergraduate pilot education improve learning and foster team skills?

*Steven J. Thatcher*
*University of South Australia*

## Introduction

It has been suggested that 70% of accidents and incidents, worldwide are attributable to flight crew actions (Helmreich & Foushee, 1993). Investigations have shown that these flight crew actions, (loosely termed pilot error), are more likely the result of a breakdown in group processes such as team communication or co-ordination (Cooper, White, & Lauber, 1980; Murphy, 1980). Increasingly the aviation industry is recognising the importance of group processes to safe flight crew performance. In order to foster appropriate team skills in individual flight crew members many airlines have introduced crew resource management (CRM) courses. However, Hackman (1993) is concerned that CRM courses still tend to concentrate on the individual crew member rather than the crew as a whole. He suggests that if team skills are to be learned by the crew as a whole and positive outcomes achieved, a team-centred approach should be used. Team skills are only learned effectively in team situations.

I have suggested that both student-centred and group-centred approaches be adopted in Undergraduate Pilot Education (UGPE) (Thatcher, 1997). These approaches are a central feature of an adult or andragogical approach to teaching and learning, and should promote more assertive, team-focussed attitudes and behaviours. Because students assume responsibility for the group's learning, as well as their own, this approach should promote better learning. By adopting a crew-centred flight training (CCFT) curriculum students would learn in a supportive crew environment which demonstrated, in situ, appropriate team behaviours (Thatcher, 1998).

This paper examines a group-centred approach used in the first year undergraduate civil aviation program offered by the University of South Australia. Operating in parallel with the degree course is the University's flight training program. The flight program is offered at the University's flying school at Parafield Aerodrome, adjacent to the University's Levels Campus.

Aviation Physics is a one year course delivered in semester 2 of the first year (Aviation Physics 1) and semester 1 of the second year (Aviation Physics 2). In the past Aviation Physics has been taught using the traditional, pedagogical, approach of lecturers, tutorials and practicals. This paper discusses a new approach based on the successful and innovative student-centred approach of Berk and Younger (1996). Using this approach the subject was delivered by a structured mix of independent study and interactive, facilitated group work. This development is in line with the University's policy of encouraging strategies for student-centred learning and flexible delivery

*Student-centred learning and flexible delivery*

Research at the University of South Australia by Moore et al., (1996) has indicated that students are dissatisfied with the traditional lecture format. They found that students are bored and passive during lectures. They also found that students perceived that the lecturer spends too much time preparing lectures, while they spend too much time writing notes instead of listening and thinking. The student perception is that the lecture is not necessarily enjoyable for the lecturer or the students.

Flexible delivery enables students to learn in their own time and place, at their own pace, with their individual learning style, using a range of resources which suits them best (Berk & Younger, 1996). This independence encourages students to become self-disciplined and take responsibility for their own learning. Facilitated group work provides an environment where students can develop their communication skills and become collaborative learners. Group work enables students to develop their ability to critically evaluate their own and other group member's work. All of these skills are necessary if a student is to become a life-long learner. In addition, these skills are essential for effective CRM in flight operations (Thatcher, 1996).

**Method**

*Course design*

The new approach retained the traditional practical sessions (2 hr) but no formal lecturers or tutorials. Instead, students were given a weekly Independent Study Sheet to be used for self study and discussion in the weekly group session (2 hr).

*Independent study sheet.* The study sheet was issued weekly and detailed a structured reading program from the textbook. In addition, it detailed conceptual questions and numerical problems relevant to the reading. Students were expected to take notes and work through the questions and problems at their own pace. It was anticipated that students would complete the study sheet before the weekly group session. Unresolved problems and conceptual difficulties were raised during the group sessions.

*Group sessions.* Students were allocated to groups of 4 to 6 students, catering as far as possible for academic diversity and age. Students were encouraged as far as possible to solve their conceptual difficulties and numerical problems by interaction within their group. The lecturer facilitated this process, becoming a group member to answer problems that the group could not resolve, and to stimulate communications on conceptual issues. If the misunderstandings or problems were general to most of the class, the lecturer would clarify these issues with the whole class.

*Student assessment.* The final assessment was based on the following:

- 2 examinations (60%), one mid semester and one final
- Practical work (30%)
- Group work (10%), assessed on participation and attendance

*Student sample*

The study included all first year civil aviation students enrolled in second semester Aviation Physics 1 in 1996 (sample 1) and Aviation Physics 1 in 1997 (sample 2). Also included in the study were second year civil aviation students enrolled in Aviation Physics 2, in 1997 (sample 1). Aviation Physics 1 in 1996 (sample 1) was initially delivered using traditional lectures. Independent study was introduced half way through the semester.

Aviation Physics 2 in 1997 (sample 1) was delivered using independent study with some group work in class. However, with these students the study program was written on the board rather than on the independent study sheets. For the students in sample 2, Aviation Physics 1 was delivered using the Independent Study Sheets and structured, facilitated group work.

## Results

Final marks and survey results were taken as the evaluation criteria.

*Analysis of final marks*

Sample 1 second semester mean mark ($M = 56.9$) was significantly below the population mean ($M = 63.7$; $z = -2.12$; $\alpha = 0.05_{\text{2 tail}}$). Sample 1 first semester and sample 2 second semester mean marks ($M = 53.1$ and $58.1$ respectively) were below the population means ($M = 57.5$ and $63.7$ respectively) but were not significant ($z = -0.98$ and $z = -1.56$ respectively at $\alpha = 0.05_{\text{2 tail}}$). See Table 18.1.

**Table 18.1**
**Results for independent study and group work delivery method**

| Sample | Subject | Semester | Delivery Method | Mean | Z | Significant, $p = 0.05_{\text{2 tail}}$ |
|--------|---------|----------|-----------------|------|------|------------------|
| 1 | Aviation Physics 1 | Two | Traditional/ Independent study | 56.9 | -2.12 | YES |
| 1 | Aviation Physics 2 | One | Independent study/ Group Work | 53.1 | -0.98 | NO |
| 2 | Aviation Physics 1 | Two | Independent study/ Group Work | 58.1 | -1.56 | NO |

*Analysis of survey results*

Students in sample 2 were surveyed at the middle and end of semester. They were asked to evaluate the Independent Study and Group Work components of the subject. The students were asked three questions.

1.  Which aspects of the above components are you finding the most useful?
2.  Which aspects of the above components are you finding the least useful?
3.  What changes to these components would you like to see introduced?

*Mid-semester survey results.* On the whole students thought that the group work was useful. Comments include: "Explaining to other people is an excellent form of personal revision in this subject"; "Group work, because you can compare solutions"; "Group work because if you're stuck while your lecturer is not available, then you can get some help from your group"; "Group work has been found more useful by me because we come to know lots of points and different ideas from different minds and when they are put together the thing really works."

Students thought that independent study was less useful. Comments include: "Independent study because once you're stuck you have nowhere to go"; "Independent study sometimes the explanations in the text book are not enough to solve the questions and problems"; "The independent study because it is hard to go home and study Physics on top of the flying subjects which are more important."; "Independent study I would prefer we do note taking in class...so that the lecturer explains everything we are noting."

A few students thought that group work was least useful with comments such as:

*   "Group work sessions don't seem to be very productive leaving too much to independent study";
*   "Group work, as often little is learnt. Often the difficult problems encountered in independent study are not comprehensively reviewed during group work."

In response to what changes would you like to see introduced, two thirds of the students wanted the lecturer format reintroduced, while the rest wanted other things like text book and group structure changed.

*End of semester survey results.* Similar comments to the mid-semester survey were observed. However, the comments expressed in the answers to the third question, "What changes would you like to see introduced?" suggest a negative attitude towards group work and the subject in general. Comments include: "no group work"; "the teaching style - a lecture format may be more helpful"; "lectures by lecturer"; "More in-class lectures"; "Taught lectures"; "We need to be lectured and have things explained".

The level of frustration amongst the students had increased from the mid-semester evaluation and was seen in comments such as: "Scrap this subject", "Didn't really enjoy Physics." and "Hopeless - group study not effective."

*Mid semester and final examination results*

Compared with the Aviation Physics 1 general population results (Figure 18.1) the 1997 Aviation Physics 1 results indicate a bi-modal distribution of results (Figure 18.2).

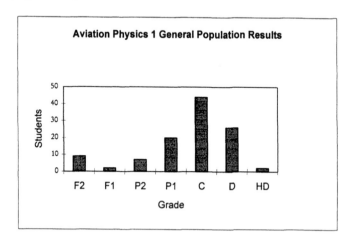

**Figure 18.1**
**Aviation Physics 1, general population results**

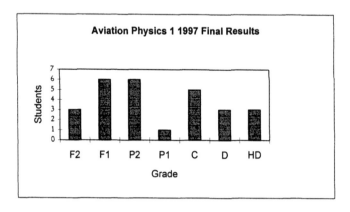

**Figure 18.2**
**Aviation Physics 1, 1997 final results**

**Discussion**

The sample results indicate that the use of a traditional lecture/tutorial delivery combined with independent study produced significantly poorer performance than the general population. When group work was combined with independent study performance was not significantly different from the general population results. This suggests that between student samples group work may have some beneficial effect. However compared with the general Aviation Physics population there was no significant difference. This tends to agree with research by Stephens (1967) (cited in Knowles, 1990) and Dubin and Raveggia (1968) (cited in Knowles, 1990) that the teaching method or instructional technique make no difference to college student achievement as measured by final marks.

One area for concern was the comments provided on the survey forms. Although the mid-semester survey revealed a positive attitude towards group work by the majority of students, the end of semester survey revealed a positive attitude by only a minority of students. These comments seem to suggest a certain level of frustration with the group work/independent study method of delivery which increased as the semester progressed. Students on the whole commenting that they preferred the traditional lecture/tutorial format. Students' perception was that they would perform better with the traditional format. The results (Figure 18.2) indicate that roughly equal numbers of students did better or worse than usual. It may be that some students were developmentally ready for this approach and performed better, while some students were not developmentally ready and performed worse. However, this perception about group work and the level of frustration amongst the students, is of concern due to the possible formation of negative group or team attitudes.

Care must be taken to assess a student's developmental level before using an andragogical approach. For some students in this sample this technique was introduced too early in their development and they would possibly have performed better with the traditional pedagogical approach.

**References**

Berk, M., & Younger, P. (1996, July). *Flexible delivery of bridging physics: Promoting lifelong learning.* Paper presented to the Higher Education Research and Development Society of Australasia, Adelaide, 8-11 July.

Cooper, G.E., White, M.D., & Lauber, J.K. (Eds.), (1980). *Resource Management on the Flightdeck: Proceedings of a NASA/Industry workshop. (NASA CP-2120).* Moffett Field, CA: NASA-Ames Research Center.

Foushee, H.C., & Helmreich, R.L. (1988). Group Interaction and Flight Crew Performance. In E.L.Wiener & D.C. Nagel (Eds.), *Human Factors in Aviation.* San Diego: Academic Press.

Hackman, J.R. (1993). New Directions for CRM Training. In E.L. Weiner, B.G. Kanki, & R.L. Helmreich (Eds.), *Cockpit resource management.* San Diego: Academic Press.

Helmreich, R.L. & Foushee, H.C. (1993). Why Crew Resource Management? In E.L. Weiner, B.G. Kanki, & R.L. Helmreich (Eds.), *Cockpit resource management.* San Diego: Academic Press.

Knowles, M.S. (1990). *The adult learner: A neglected species.* (4th Ed.). Houston: Gulf Publishing Company.

Moore, B., Willis, P. & Crotty, M. (1996). *Getting it right getting it together: Perceptions of student learning in The University of South Australia.* Adelaide: Flexible Learning Centre.

Thatcher, S.J. (1996, November*). What effect does ab initio flight training have on CRM?* Paper presented to the Australian Aviation Psychology Association, Melbourne.

Thatcher, S.J. (1997, April). *Flight instruction or flight facilitation: A foundation for Crew Resource Management.* Paper presented at the Ninth International Symposium on Aviation Psychology, Columbus, OH.

Thatcher, S.J. (1998). *Towards crew-centred flight training.* Manuscript submitted for publication.

# 19 Atmospheric science, air safety and essential weather briefing in student pilot training

*Skye Hunter, Martin Babakhan and H. Peter Pfister*
*The University of Newcastle*

Pilots must fully understand the characteristics and behaviour of the ocean of air in which they fly. Meteorology is the branch of science which deals with the earth's atmosphere, including the movement of air within the aviation environment. A central goal of atmospheric science is to learn about the winds, to understand why they come to life, develop, take the form and patterns they do, why they change, evolve and finally die in the birth of new winds.

Meteorological conditions play a significant role in air safety. It is, therefore, essential to develop a sound understanding of these factors in early formal pilot training. Most current pilot training programs appear to place little emphasis on understanding, interpretation and prediction of prevailing and/or impending weather conditions. Consequent to the increasing automation of weather information within the aviation industry, a greater burden is emerging for pilots to be able to conduct 'self briefings', effectively assess their own limitations and to make appropriate decision regards the safety of flight in certain weather conditions.

This study identifies adverse meteorological conditions and links these to accidents and incidents within aviation. It recognises voids within current teaching strategies, and provides solutions to this problem by compilation of weather briefing information appropriate to both the instructor and the pre-solo student pilot, the development of a program for inclusion into training manuals and suggests area of further research.

**Need**

In May 1997, the Bureau of Air Safety Investigation (BASI) created a statistical analysis from a variety of sources including the National Transport Safety Board (NTSB) accident data and NASA Aviation Safety Reporting System data. The examination focused on weather-related issues, over the period 1990-1996. The annual number of weather-related accidents and incidents is represented below on Figures 19.1 and 19.2 respectively.

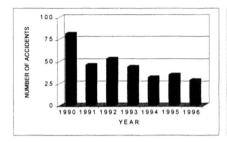 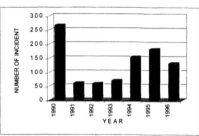

**Figure 19.1**
**Weather-related aircraft accidents**    **Figure 19.2**
**Weather-related aircraft incidents**

BASI showed that between 1988-1992, weather was a contributing or causative factor in 22% of these aircraft accidents. This clearly demonstrates the importance of weather in air safety, since more than one fifth of the accidents that occurred were caused or factored by weather phenomenon. These data are presented in Figure 19.3.

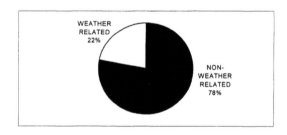

**Figure 19.3**
**Proportion of accidents related to weather phenomenon**

*Total aviation accidents*

Further analysis of the data revealed the weather related factors involved in GA accidents comprise the following components and magnitude; wind (42%), visibility/ceiling (24%), turbulence (8%), density altitude (8%) icing (8%), precipitation (7%), thunderstorm (2%) and windshear (1%).

The citings of weather conditions which were either causes or factors involved in GA accidents, requires further attention. Analysis of these data shows that wind is clearly the most significant single factor (42%) involved in all weather related GA accidents. Grouping both accidents and incidents shows that wind factors contributing to weather related GA accidents and incidents in the following ways (Figure 19.4).

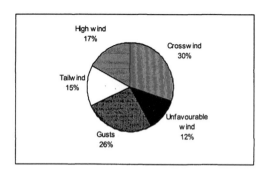

**Figure 19.4**
**Wind-related accidents and incidents**

Of notable interest here, is the fact that only 12% of the winds cited are regarded as "unfavourable", indicating that 88% may be regarded as "favourable" and yet have been involved in accidents or incidents which compromise or threaten air safety.

Thus, winds are poised to plague the pilot. This would indicate a stark need for a thorough knowledge of all factors relating to wind to be resident within the armamentaria of all pilots, so that they can better deal with this problem when it arises or, preferably, anticipate and avert the problem before it arises. Thus, the study of winds should be a major component in pilot training programs.

In comparing categories and individual weather factors, it is evident wind factors amongst instructional pilots (59%) is by far the largest single factor in GA weather related accidents (Figure 19.5). This highlights the need for more effective forms of education regards wind factors in early pilot training.

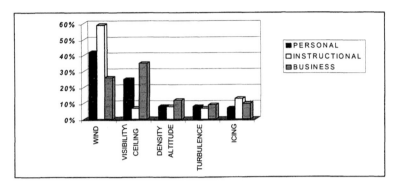

**Figure 19.5**
**Categories and weather-related accidents**

These data led to an analysis of the various ways in which information about weather is obtained for flights. The main division of weather-related accidents is distributed between three sources mentioned in Figure 19.6, which displays the aspect of weather briefing sources needed in aviation for flights.

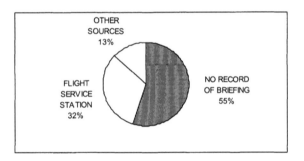

**Figure 19.6**
**Weather brief sources involved in weather-related accidents.**

The foregoing data, along with a review of the literature available, indicates a lack of awareness and appreciation for weather related factors, especially wind, amongst pilots generally.

Since wind and weather play an important role in air safety, it would appear prudent to develop an essential respect for these factors in early formal pilot education and training. Most pilot training programs appear to place little emphasis on understanding and interpreting weather factors. Along with the rapid growth in the aviation industry and the increasing automation of weather information, a greater burden is placed on pilots to conduct "self briefings" and to be able to effectively assess their own abilities and limitations as well as make decisions regarding flights in special weather conditions. The current methods of teaching weather related factors to pilots will now be discussed.

## Method

This research has clearly identified a need for improved pilot training in weather matters, since these contribute to a significant proportion of aircraft accidents and incidents. It also recognises a void in current teaching strategies, instructional resources and training regimes. It provides solutions to this problem by way of a weather briefing section for inclusion into an instruction manual. It proposes a program, designed to set new baseline standards of pilot education and training in weather related matters, by marrying existing resources with modern technology to create new frontiers in aviation training.

Wind is traditionally taught in separate dimensional aspects whereby horizontal motion may significantly effect flying. This is correct, however a third axis requires acknowledgment. Understanding and appreciation of wind needs to be studied in all three dimensions. Upward motions play a key role in the production of weather, namely clouds, precipitation in which create flight hazards, especially when low ceiling, visibility and icing is produced. Along with weather deterioration, aircraft capability is effected when the motions are large enough to cause injury, damage and loss of aircraft control. Student pilots should understand not only how vertical motions are produced, but also what the important effects of atmospheric stability are on these motions. Knowledge of the causes and characteristics of wind will be a great value to a student pilot, so they can examine "vertical motion, clouds and weather", and this is where the three-dimensional aspect of winds need further acknowledgment.

There is an obvious need for instructors to train student pilots in the practical aspect of taking and reporting aerodrome weather observations. To learn, understand and transform the weather observation into a complete mental picture is necessary to help determine the type of weather, which may affect flights. This may be achieved through aerodromes being equipped with instruments such as an Automatic Weather Station (AWS). The AWS system may assist pilots' understanding and prediction, and thus enhance safety.

A valuable extension of this AWS concept would be to connect all instruments to a computer terminal at each aerodrome, for pilots to readily access information prior to flights. This research could then be connected, on line, to a central database at the Bureau of Meteorology (BoM) or Flight

Service (FS) who would then have immediate and direct access to thousands of locations around the country, or perhaps the world.

The program with the following suggestions should be applied to aviation, which may increase the level of safety by allowing the pilot to understand weather at all stages of flight training.

**Program**

**Table 19.1**

**Program designed for improving safety**

| | |
|---|---|
| Pilot Observing Course | Help pass the message to outside<br>Weather wise increases safety<br>Fill the gap between the Bureau of Meteorology and the pilot |
| Interpreting Weather | Forming a mental model image<br>Pilot decisions, based on the weather impacting their flight<br>Pilot develops skills, to visualise complete weather situations |
| Self-Evaluation | Pilot ratings provides the most basic criteria for those decisions<br>Setting personal limitations is an important aspect of flight safety<br>Better understanding of weather than your predecessors |
| Training Aim | Weather manifestations can be awe-inspiring, so train pilots to operate with maximum efficiency, safety and confidence in all types of weather |
| Knowledge Value | Possibilities arise for pilots to plan flights to suit the weather and their experience by selecting; routes, altitudes, time of arrival and departures |

Benjamen Franklin is credited with the following adage, "Some men [sic] are weatherwise - most are otherwise". "Pilots do not really have to make a choice to become "weatherwise" - their very lives, and the lives of their passengers, may depend on it" (Green, 1994, p. 20). Pilots need to make themselves thoroughly familiar with the forecast weather conditions along their proposed route, at their destination and at any possible alternate destinations. A weather-wise pilot should always check weather information as part of the flight planning process, and should be able to recognise cloud formations, which may indicate particularly hazardous conditions.

Aviation weather forecasts are usually valid for a period of 12 or more hours and cover enormous volumes of airspace. The orientation of fronts, troughs or other features can change markedly. Thus both the forecaster and the pilot need to be aware that the actual conditions, which may develop over the validity period of the forecast may not be 100% reflected in the initial forecasts for all locations at any specific time, particularly when changes may occur later in the period. In addition, to the regular forecasts and observations a pilot is able to glean more information from a study of surface and upper air analysis and prognosis charts depicting the general weather pattern. A study of specific elements such as the prevailing wind regimes and or the topography over the planned route can help to make optimal decisions in the event of running into unfavorable weather. The pilot should be able to decide whether to change flight levels, divert left or right, land immediately, return to or to proceed.

As this study and program is directed to student pilots, the wealth of knowledge attained may store confidence and assist the decision-making process. As Wickson stated "To give a detailed weather prediction is a difficult task" (1992), however anticipation, understanding and application may support predictions which strengthen appreciation of weather.

**Summary**

"Flight instructor training, when it is formally taught, has changed very little since Major Smith-Barry first codified his principles of flight training in 1916" (Elshaw, 1993, p. 254). The richer the detail and the relevance of models used in pilot training, the greater is the prospect of enhancing the learning process by integrating each event into a structured plan rather than have it appear as a total surprise or an isolated factor.

Even before the student has flown, a 'mental model' may be formed as to what could happen. The student pilot should be trained to fully understand the weather information available and encouraged to interpret that into terms of air safety by translating it into possible consequences, through anticipation, prediction and expectation. With all due respect to student pilots, wind would have to be the most important weather phenomena, which may affect their flight. Knowledge such as time of day, area, terrain and aircraft capability must be considered.

Currently a variety of areas are covered in the training of pilots, but weather is not an individual component in any syllabus. Student pilot-instructor communication and current textbooks indicate there is a missing link in the training regime for pilots to become aware of the importance and effects, of weather. It appears prudent, that a program be developed, which is centered on the importance of weather-related accidents and incidents.

There is an obvious need for instructors to train student pilots in the practical aspect of taking and reporting aerodrome weather observations. To learn, understand and transform the weather observation into a complete mental picture is necessary to help determine the type of weather, which may affect flights. "One of the first hurdles confronting a student pilot who has learnt to control an aircraft has to do with the weather. Are the conditions suitable for flight? Can I continue my flight in the conditions ahead? These are the questions that all pilots should ask themselves on all flights, both at the planning stage and in flight" (Byron, 1996, p. 7).

In Australia, accidents involving weather factors, particularly on visual flight rules, occur with alarming frequency. The way in which a pilot handles decisions relating to weather is the main issue, rather than the physical characteristics of the weather itself. This view is supported by Byron and a recent BASI study of factors relating to accidents which showed that while 'pilot factors' featured in over 70% of fatal accidents, this figure includes accidents where decisions by the pilot in relation to weather conditions were the dominant factor rather than the nature of the weather itself (APAS, August 1996, p. 7). For those who fly, such statistics should reinforce the point that being able to make confident and safe decisions when faced with deteriorating weather is a very important survival tool.

Knowledge of minimum weather conditions should thus form part of every pilot's theoretical training and every pilot should have the minimum criteria for visual flight at their 'fingertips'. In the planning stages of a flight, it is imperative that a pilot should be able to compare the forecast weather conditions with the known minimum criteria. To effectively make safe decisions in relation to weather, pilots should be confronted with these situations as part of their training or development under supervision of an experienced pilot, normally their flying instructor. This type of supervised exposure would appear to be the best way to learn how to assess the suitability of weather and how to make crucial decisions such as to proceed, abort, divert or turn back.

A review of the instruction manuals currently available for pilot training indicates a lack of background information relating to wind and other important weather factors.

In summary, the current system of teaching weather-related issues to student pilots in the pre-solo phase is non-existent.

It was, thus, considered appropriate and important to develop a special section for inclusion into an instructor's manual, which catered for the needs of both the instructor, and the student pilot in teaching and understanding of weather related issues. In addition, to the manual, a practical approach such as instrumentation and equipment for weather measurements may reduce the accident and incident possibility due to the improvement of safety by increasing knowledge and understanding.

**Further research**

- Implement this program in the aviation industry as a weather-briefing insert into existing training manuals for instructors and pre-solo pilots.
- Develop more sophisticated 3-D models and engage electronic technology using audio, visual and animated components to produce videos, CD's and tapes for better pilot training.
- Extend the weather factors within this manual to include topics appropriate to the next phase of pilot training beyond the pre-solo phase, including thunderstorms, clouds, visibility/ceiling, fog and icing.
- Incorporate the proceeding resources into flight simulator programs to enhance appreciation of the influences of weather related matters in practical aviation.

**References**

Bureau of Air Safety Investigation. (1996, August). Human factors in fatal fixed wing aircraft accidents. *Asia-Pacific Air Safety*, *13*, 4-6.

Byron, B. (1996, August). Weather to fly, whether to fly. *Asia-Pacific Air Safety*, *13*, 7-9.

Elshaw, C. (1993). Preparing better flight instructors. In R.A. Telfer (Ed.), *Approaches to learning* (pp. 253-270).Aldershot: Avebury.

Green, E. (1994, October). Weatherwise or otherwise - your choice. *Aviation Bulletin*, *3*(9), pp. 20-21.

Wickson, M. (1992). *Meteorology for pilots*. Airlife: England.

# Part 3
# HUMAN FACTORS

# 20 Benefits and future applications of 3D primary flight displays

*Eddie L. Flohr*
*Leiden University and*
*The National Aerospace Laboratory NLR*

## Introduction

The predicted growth of civil aviation in the next 15 years is likely to double the number of aircraft movements on a global scale. Passenger traffic is expected to increase annually by 7-8% in East Asia and the South West Pacific area alone. Such growth would cause unacceptable delays in the current Air Traffic Management (ATM) system due to its limited capacity, while the necessary reduction in separation standards would increase the risks significantly. In densely populated areas the increasing number of takeoffs and landings would increase noise pollution, which may impair the political acceptability of aviation growth.

To facilitate the anticipated growth, new ATM concepts are currently under exploration as means of safely enhancing the use of the available airspace. These concepts will require pilots to fly their route with much greater accuracy and flexibility than today. Based partly on the results of an experiment with three-dimensional (3D) Primary Flight Displays (PFDs) at the National Aerospace Laboratory NLR, the potential benefits of perspective PFDs on performance and situation awareness (SA) in various future aircraft operations will be discussed.

## Future aircraft operations

In Europe, the Programme for Harmonised ATM Research in EUROCONTROL (PHARE) four-dimensional (4D) ATM concept is aimed

195

at increasing the capacity of the airspace. In this concept, aircraft will fly via Air Traffic Control-cleared flight plans in which aircraft altitude and position are specified in time, hence 4D ATM. The route will be a virtual "tube" and the required 4D position of an aircraft can be depicted as a "bubble" that moves through the tube as a function of time (see Figure 20.1).

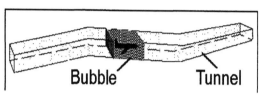

**Figure 20.1**
**The PHARE 4D ATM concept**

Separation will be assured as long as the aircraft stays in the bubble. A second prospective ATM concept that is currently under exploration on authority of the Federal Aviation Administration is Free Flight. In this concept, pilots will basically be free to decide via which route they will fly from their origin to their destination. In the Free Flight approach that is currently under investigation at the NLR, airborne separation assurance will be enabled by on-board systems which will provide the aircraft with information about the movements of other aircraft in the vicinity (Van Gent, Hoekstra, & Ruigrok, 1997). The aircraft's computers will determine for each individual aircraft whether or not it is a potential threat in the future. If so, certain algorithms will be used to calculate how this potential collision threat may be resolved, and a (two-way) resolution is then presented to the pilots. This resolution can consist of lateral-, vertical-, or speed changes.

Regardless of the ATM system, future economical and environmental demands will place a number of other operational constraints on aircraft:

• The ability to operate under low visability conditions must be increased to reduce the number of delays and airport evasions.
• The ability to operate independently of ground-based systems must be increased to improve landing capabilities on less equipped airports.
• Controlled-flight-into-terrain (CFIT) accidents must be prevented by improving the pilot's (vertical) awareness during low-altitude flight phases through new cockpit systems and display technologies.
• The level of noise pollution must be reduced by using more flexible curved arrival and departure routes instead of the current standard routes.

## Perspective primary flight displays

It is clear that in future aircraft operations pilots will be required to fly their conflict-free path, possibly specified by time constraints, with much greater precision and flexibility than today. This implies that pilots have to be informed about their required lateral and vertical position in time. Thus, the PFD will need to provide an indication of the current state, the required (future) state, and the actions necessary to achieve that state. One way to do this is by integrating information into a perspective PFD, of which two types can generally be distinguished: highway-in-the-sky displays, in which the future route is usually depicted as a 3D road made up from tiles, and tunnel-in-the-sky displays, in which the route is depicted as a 3D tunnel consisting of interconnected rectangles. Unlike the highway displays, tunnel displays also graphically present the altitude restrictions of the route, thus indicating the boundaries within which the aircraft has to fly. Although tunnel displays may consequently be more suitable for 3D precision navigation, there is hardly any empirical evidence to support this notion. It is therefore assumed that the benefits of perspective PFDs mentioned below apply to both highway and tunnel displays.

Perspective PFDs can have a number of benefits over conventional PFDs:

- By combining guidance information and a 3D image of the flight path in one display the pilot is able to anticipate the future trajectory, which may support performance on the integrated steering task.
- The high congruence with the real system may enable the pilot to form a better mental model, which will improve monitoring behaviour and support performance when the pilot switches from supervisory to manual control (Ballas, Heitmeyer, & Perez, 1991).
- The image of the future flight path in the 3D PFD can serve as a memory aid that relieves the pilot of memorising the future route on the navigation display, thus reducing mental workload, and enables him to anticipate the required actions.
- Based on Poulton's (1974) findings with *compensatory* and *pursuit* displays, a perspective PFD (a pursuit display since movement of both the path and the aircraft are displayed) will support flight path performance more than a 2D PFD (a compensatory display since only the error between the current and desired state is displayed).

Evidence of the advantages of 3D PFDs also comes from an experiment with the Research Flight Simulator at the NLR, described in detail by Flohr and Huisman (1997) and Huisman, Flohr, and Van Houten (1998). In this experiment a perspective PFD with graphically integrated bubble, an adapted conventional PFD, and a hybrid tunnel-PFD were compared in two autopilot (A/P) and two manually controlled curved continuous-descent approaches. In one of the manual flights the subjects had to land the aircraft after a display failure (the other manual flight contained no event), whereas in the A/P flights they had to take over control manually after a complete A/P and autothrottle failure in one case, and detect and correct a subtle A/P malfunction in the other case. This experiment demonstrated that route performance was much better with the two tunnel PFDs in most conditions. Only after the display failure, which basically degraded the displays to present-day PFDs, did performance with the 3D PFDs decrease to the level of the conventional PFD. Similarly, the eye fixation data of the subjects suggested that monitoring efficiency improved significantly with the 3D PFDs in all flights. Although pilots did not indicate any display difference in the subjective workload and situation awareness (SA) rating scales, their much faster detection and intervention responses to the subtle A/P malfunction when flying with the tunnel PFDs denoted that SA was higher with the perspective displays. With respect to pilot workload, the experiment did not reveal clear benefits of the tunnel PFDs. Indeed, the aileron input data under manual control showed that the superior route performance of the tunnel displays involved more physical workload. The cardiovascular measures that were taken indicated no clear differences between the displays in overall workload and mental effort, though there was some indication that taking over control after the A/P failure required the least mental effort with the 3D PFD with integrated bubble. Considering the fact that subjects received only very limited training with the displays prior to the experiment and that the approaches were quite complex, the observed workload effect may be attributed to unfamiliarity with the perspective displays. This conclusion is supported by the fact that 75% of the pilots indicated a preference for the perspective PFDs in most situations.

**Benefits of perspective PFDs in future aircraft operations**

Assuming that perspective PFDs have advantages over conventional PFDs, how can these displays be beneficial to the aforementioned future aircraft operations? First of all, the feasibility of the PHARE ATM concept will largely depend on the pilot's ability to accurately keep his aircraft in the bubble. The results of the experiment at the NLR clearly show that such performance can be improved with acceptable pilot workload by using 3D

PFDs. Similar findings have been obtained by Haskell and Wickens (1993) and Reising, Liggett, Solz, and Hartsock (1995), although the former study also found that the discrete task of maintaining a required speed profile is more difficult when the commanded speed is graphically integrated in the display. In Free Flight, airborne separation assurance will require a great manoeuvring flexibility when pilots deviate from their intended route to avoid traffic and resume their course after a conflict is resolved. This will place even higher demands on SA and route performance than in the PHARE ATM, because inaccurate path performance during conflict resolution may generate new conflicts. By displaying a trajectory preview of evasive manoeuvres on the PFD in the form of a tunnel, pilots can be provided with an integrated view of the required actions. This is likely to enhance both their SA and performance in a similar way as was found in our experiment. Moreover, Haskell and Wickens also found that identifying and making integrated judgements with regard to other aircraft improved with a perspective PFD.

Second, noise abatement procedures will primarily comprise curved approach and departure routes. Such routes will make it easier to avoid residential areas and reduce noise pollution through high-altitude approaches. This could also lower fuel consumption and emission, and reduce the overall approach time, particularly when approaches can be flown in continuous descent with idle throttles (Erkelens, 1997). Such complex curved continuous descent approaches were also used in our experiment, which demonstrates that they can be flown more precisely and with acceptable pilot workload with 3D PFDs. Furthermore, superior vertical track performance of 3D over 2D PFDs, found in both head-up (Reising et al., 1995) and head-down (Haskell & Wickens, 1993) displays, also indicate that steep-angle descents with idle throttles are more viable with perspective PFDs.

Third, since most CFIT accidents take place in mountainous areas it is imperative that pilots are able to accurately fly their planned routes in circumstances where the surrounding terrain is at the same level as that of the aircraft. Simultaneously, their SA must be enhanced to detect objects in the environment (e.g., structures, aircraft) and anomalies in their flight path (e.g., erroneous heading- or altitude commands). As argued above, these performance and awareness requirements are more likely to be met by 3D PFDs. Moreover, graphically incorporating terrain database information in the perspective PFD is likely to enhance terrain awareness considerably (Sutton, 1997). If in addition to this the perspective flight path would be made up from the FMS and mode control panel data, a perspective PFD could clearly show erroneous heading- or altitude commands by displaying that the resulting flight path would fly the aircraft into terrain. Lastly, it may be beneficial to project the 3D path with terrain information on a Head Up Display (HUD) because pilots are more likely to notice objects in the outside world with a the perspective PFD in such a location (Fadden & Wickens, 1997).

Fourth, to enable the pilot to operate under all weather conditions on both the ground and in the air, and to provide landing guidance without dependence on expensive ground-based guidance systems, current research focuses on the development of synthetic and enhanced vision systems (SVS/EVS) that provide an augmented image of the outside world. To perform such tasks the pilot will need an artificial representation environment based on reliable and accurate position information, terrain databases, and/or imaging sensors. This representation will have to include moving objects on the ground (e.g., for taxi operations) and in the air (e.g., for Free Flight operations). Perspective PFDs are likely to be more beneficial than 2D PFDs when combined with SVS/EVS by improving SA and performance in a similar way as mentioned in their application to CFIT prevention. Also, these benefits may be increased when the image of the outside world on the 3D PFDs contains more details and is displayed in a HUD position (Grieg, Shaw, & Lumsden, 1997). Moreover, if (moving) objects in the outside world are reliably displayed on the perspective display, it may even be possible to obtain Visual Flight Rules capabilities.

As suggested by Theunissen (1997), 3D PFDs may also be used to display flight envelope constraints and windshear threats, and to improve the pilot's knowledge of the A/P system. However, little research has been done on these issues so far.

## Conclusions

Based partly on the results of an experiment at the NLR, perspective primary flight displays (PFDs) proved to increase both lateral and vertical route performance in a variety of circumstances compared to conventional PFDs, and form a viable alternative in a wide range of future aircraft operations. An additional advantage of perspective PFDs is that they require only limited training due to their natural and intuitive format, which will curtail their implementation costs.

However, perspective displays also have drawbacks. First, there are intrinsic problems with distance, depth, and size cues when displaying three-dimensional information on a two-dimensional display that need to be considered in the design of perspective displays (see Wickens, Todd, & Siedler, 1989, for a discussion of these problems). An additional problem is that many display parameters like visual cues (depth, size), frame of reference (ego- vs. exocentric), field-of-view, refresh rates, terrain detail (low vs. high), and location (head-up vs. head-down) seem to be context dependent. For example, an egocentric frame of reference seems to be more appropriate for flight path guidance, while an exocentric frame of reference is more useful for navigational awareness. More research is needed to establish the best compilation of display parameters for each of the pilot's tasks. Because discrete tasks are not performed well if they are displayed in an integrated way (Haskell & Wickens, 1993), the amount of graphical integration of information should also be taken into account in the design. Other issues that need further attention are the format of predictor symbols in the display and the (dis)advantages of tunnel-in-the-sky over highway-in-the-sky displays.

Finally, some other factors will play an important role in the success of 3D PFDs in future aircraft operations. The application of tunnel PFDs as guidance and navigation tools (notably in SVS/EVS and CFIT applications) will strongly depend on the accuracy and reliability of (imaging) sensors, transmitters and receivers, terrain databases and precision navigation systems. This will be even more important if perspective PFDs are to be used for future surveillance (e.g., in Free Flight to monitor other aircraft) and separation (e.g., if another aircraft is landing on a converging runway and a 'ghost' of that aircraft is displayed on the 3D PFD) tasks. In addition, since flying with a 3D PFD requires different knowledge and skills than with today's PFDs, a structured design and certification approach must be developed.

## References

Ballas, J.A., Heitmeyer, C.L., & Perez, M.A. (1991). *Interface styles for the intelligent cockpit: factors influencing automation deficit.* AIAA-91-3799-CP.

Erkelens, L.J.J. (1997). Research on noise abatement procedures. *Proceedings of the 10th European Aerospace Conference on Free Flight.* Amsterdam, The Netherlands, 20-21 October.

Fadden, S. & Wickens, C.D. (1997). Improving traffic awareness with a head-up flight path highway display. Proceedings of the 9th International Symposium on Aviation Psychology. Columbus, OH, 27 April - 1 May.

Flohr, E.L., & Huisman, H. (1997). Perspective primary flight displays in the 4D ATM environment. *Proceedings of the 9th International Symposium on Aviation Psychology.* Columbus, OH, 27 April - 1 May.

Gent, R.N.H., van Hoekstra, J.M., & Ruigrok, R.C.J. (1997). Free flight with airborne separation assurance. *Proceedings of the 10th European Aerospace Conference on Free Flight.* Amsterdam, The Netherlands, 20-21 October.

Grieg, I., Shaw, G., & Lumsden, B. (1997). Augmented vision systems for the all weather autonomous landing guidance of fixed wing aircraft: An investigation of the key parameters by piloted flight simulation. *Proceedings of the 10th European Aerospace Conference on Free Flight.* Amsterdam, The Netherlands, 20-21 October.

Haskell, I.D. & Wickens, C.D. (1993). Two- and three-dimensional displays for aviation: A theoretical and empirical comparison. *International Journal of Aviation Psychology, 3*(2), 87-109.

Huisman, H. Flohr, E.L., & Van Houten, Y.A. (1998). *Tunnel-in-the-sky and conventional primary flight displays: A comparative flight simulator experiment.* NLR Contract Report. National Aerospace Laboratory NLR, Amsterdam. Manuscript in preparation.

Poulton, E.C., (1974). *Tracking skills and manual control.* New York: Academic Press.

Reising, J.M., Liggett, K.K., Solz, T.J., & Hartsock, D.C (1995). A comparison of two head up display formats used to fly curved instrument approaches. *Proceedings of the Human Factors and Ergonomics Society 39th Annual Meeting,* Vol. 1, pp. 1-5. San Diego, Oct. 9-13.

Sutton, O. (1997). New displays - Key to safer flying. *Interavia Business & Technology, Vol. 52,* no. 609, pp. 39-41.

Theunissen, E. (1997). Increasing safety through better navigation displays. In H. Soekkha (Ed.), *Aviation Safety* (pp. 743-762). VSP, Zeist, The Netherlands.

Wickens, C.D., Todd, S., & Siedler, K. (1989). *Three-dimensional displays: perception, implementation, and applications.* CSERIAC SOAR-89-01. Wright-Patterson AFB, OH.

# 21 Human factors issues in perspective display design

*Neelam Naikar*
*Defence Science and Technology Organisation*

## Introduction

These days considerable effort and financial resources are being directed towards the development of three-dimensional display technology. This paper identifies human factors issues that must be taken into consideration during perspective display design. First, the relative effectiveness of three-dimensional (3D) perspective displays and two-dimensional (2D) displays for supporting performance on different types of tasks (navigation, airspace awareness, and tactical awareness) is discussed. Then the selection of optimal settings for perspective display parameters, for example, frame of reference and perspective geometry, is considered. The paper emphasises the importance of the need to evaluate and understand job or task characteristics prior to display selection and implementation.

## Spatial awareness

Spatial awareness is an important component of situation awareness and refers to an operator's comprehension of the 3D geometry of the environment in which he/she is operating. Conventional visual displays for presenting flight and tactical information in the aviation and military domains are 2D in nature. A major limitation of this type of display is that it can only provide a spatial representation of two dimensions of space; the vertical dimension is usually encoded in a textual format. To obtain information about the vertical dimension of, for example an enemy aircraft in the environment, air defence operators are required to "hook" the symbol representing the aircraft on their display with a mouse or track ball and press a button to obtain textual read outs of altitude. To determine aircraft attitude, operators must monitor altitude read outs over time and observe changes. Operators are therefore forced to integrate textual with spatial information and mentally reconstruct the 3D nature of the visual scene. This process requires valuable cognitive resources and decision making time (Haskell & Wickens, 1993).

Three-dimensional perspective displays have the potential to reduce the limitations of 2D displays. Perspective displays can depict all three dimensions of space in a completely spatial format thereby eliminating the requirement to integrate textual with spatial information. Three-dimensional displays also provide a more natural representation of the real world (Wickens, Todd & Seidler, 1989).

**Perspective displays**

Perspective displays utilise the cue of linear perspective to create a 3D projection of an object on a computer screen. This is achieved by having straight projection rays, which emanate from the centre of projection (or station point) of the object, pass through each point of the object and intersect the projection (picture) plane or computer screen. A parallel projection is obtained when the centre of projection is at infinity and all the projection lines are parallel. A perspective projection is obtained when the centre of projection is at a finite distance. Perspective displays are popular because its 3D characteristics closely match the features of the human visual system (Yeh & Silverstein, 1992). However, the representation of 3D information on a 2D surface can create perceptual biases and distortions in the viewers' interpretation of the image.

**Two-dimensional versus perspective displays**

So just how effective are perspective displays compared to 2D displays? Research has shown that display effectiveness may depend on task. Wilckens and Schattenmann (1968) evaluated pilot performance on a simulated flight-path tracking task. Their results showed that a perspective display showed an advantage over a 2D display in the most difficult condition in their experiment in which the pilots were required to land the aircraft in a cross wind. In another study, Grunwald, Robertson and Hatfield (1981) showed that a perspective display allowed pilots to maintain better flight-path tracking accuracy on a landing task than a 2D display. Secondary task performance was also better with the perspective display indicating reduced workload.

Findings in favour of perspective displays have also been obtained in the area of airspace awareness. Ellis, McGreevy and Hitchcock (1987) found that compared to a 2D display, a perspective display supported improved avoidance manoeuvring by airline pilots: the pilots took less time to identify collision hazards and recommend a manoeuvre, fewer errors were made in selecting a manoeuvre, and pilots were more likely to achieve the required separation between ownship and the intruding aircraft. The pilots were also twice more likely to select a vertical manoeuvre with the perspective display.

Bemis, Leeds and Winer (1988) showed that for the task of detecting airborne threats and selecting the closest friendly aircraft to intercept a threat, naval operational personnel made fewer errors in detecting and intercepting threats with a perspective display than with a 2D display. The personnel were also quicker at intercepting aircraft using the perspective display. Survey results showed that 19 of the 21 personnel preferred the perspective display.

Tham and Wickens (1993), however, found negative evidence for the effectiveness of perspective displays. In their study, air traffic controllers, pilots, and novices performed better at making heading judgements, vectoring aircraft to specified locations, identifying the highest aircraft, and identifying the fastest aircraft with a 2D display. For the task of identifying potential conflicts in aircraft flight paths there was no difference between the perspective and 2D display.

One explanation for this discrepancy is that display effectiveness may vary for integration and focussed-attention tasks (Haskell & Wickens, 1993). Integration tasks require judgement or control that depends on the integration of information across the horizontal, vertical and depth axes. For example, for the task of flight control, pilots must integrate the three dimensions of location and rate of change along these dimensions. Focussed-attention tasks, on the other hand, require subjects to focus their attention on only a single or a pair of axes; for example the task of making precise readings along the vertical axis to determine the vertical separation of aircraft.

In a study evaluating this proposal, Haskell and Wickens found that a perspective display, which integrates all three dimensions of space in a single format, supported superior lateral and altitude flight-path tracking accuracy (an integration task) whereas a 2D display supported better airspeed tracking accuracy (a focussed-attention task). These results may explain why Tham and Wickens (1993) found that a 2D display supported better heading, altitude, and speed judgements than a perspective display.

205

The nature of the task must therefore guide the selection of a display format. Perspective displays may enhance performance for tasks requiring integrated judgements whereas 2D displays may be more effective for tasks requiring focussed-attention judgements. For tasks requiring both integrated and focussed-attention judgements one solution may be to provide the operator the flexibility to switch between the two display formats. However, the requirement for cognitive integration across the two display formats may create a high mental workload (Olmos, Liang & Wickens, 1997).

## Perspective display design issues

### *Frame of reference*

An important consideration in perspective display design is the frame of reference that should be provided to the viewer. Should the viewer be provided with an egocentric or exocentric view of the image? One proposal is that the frame of reference that is implemented should depend on whether the viewer is performing local guidance or global awareness functions. Local guidance refers to the task of remaining on a nominated navigation path through either 2D or 3D space (Wickens & Prevett, 1995) whereas global awareness refers to the knowledge of where objects are located in space, both in terms of one's momentary position and orientation (ego-referenced) and in terms of a stabilised coordinate system (world-referenced) (Wickens & Prevett, 1995). Several studies have shown that an egocentric frame of reference supports better local guidance and ego-referenced awareness whereas an exocentric frame of reference supports better world-referenced awareness (Barfield et al., 1995b; Wickens, Liang, Prevett & Olmos, 1996).

If the perspective display under design will be used to support a single function or two compatible functions (e.g., local guidance and ego-referenced awareness) then the decision as to which frame of reference to implement is an easy one. However, if two incompatible functions (e.g., local guidance and world-referenced awareness) are to be performed the decision becomes more difficult. The implementation of separate displays with different frames of reference may create a high mental workload (Olmos et al., 1997). One solution may be a single display that supports local guidance/ego-referenced awareness and world referenced awareness. There is some evidence that a 3D display with a mid-exocentric frame of reference (for example, a viewpoint location of 7500 m tethered to the aircraft) may meet this criterion (Wickens & Prevett, 1995).

*Geometric parameters*

The geometric parameters of a perspective display define the 3D nature of a geometric field of view (GFOV) angle, the eyepoint elevation angle (EPEA), and the azimuth viewing angle (AVA). The geometry that is used to define a perspective projection may influence the accuracy with which observers recreate spatial relationships from the display.

*Geometric field of view*

The GFOV angle refers to the visual angle that subtends the centre of projection of an object. The GFOV angle can be either veridical, telescopic (magnification of image), or wide angle (minification of image). A non-veridical GFOV angle can cause perceptual biases and distortions in the viewer's interpretation of the image due to the fact that the viewer's eye is not at the centre of projection of the display (Ellis, Tyler, Kim, McGreevy & Stark, 1985; McGreevy & Ellis, 1986). However, non-veridical GFOV angles are sometimes employed in displays to reduce or eliminate perceptual biases. For example, a narrow GFOV angle, which produces scene magnification, compensates for the tendency of pilots to perceptually minify a visual scene (Roscoe, Corl & Jensen, 1981).The necessity of using non-veridical GFOV angles makes it important to know its effects on viewers' accuracy at recreating spatial relationships from a perspective display.

Studies investigating optimal GFOV angle for making exocentric direction judgements, for example judgements of the azimuth and elevation angles separating two objects, have been inconsistent. For example, GFOV angles producing best performance include 60° and 90° (McGreevy & Ellis, 1986), 45° and 60° (Barfield, Lim & Rosenberg, 1990), and 55°, 70°, and 85° (Barfield, Hendrix & Bjorneseth, 1995). The results from tracking studies have also been inconsistent; Ellis et al. (1985) showed that only GFOV angles greater than 100° have a detrimental effect on tracking performance whereas Kim, Ellis, Tyler, Hannaford & Stark (1987) found that tracking performance deteriorated as the GFOV angle increased from 8° to 64°.

The inconsistency in the findings regarding the effect of GFOV angle on performance are probably largely due to differences in the viewer-eyepoint position employed in the studies. No general recommendations for optimal GFOV angle can be provided from this work except to say that biases in judging azimuth and elevation angles and detriment in tracking performance are likely when the viewer eyepoint is not positioned at the GFOV angle.

*Eyepoint elevation angle*

The eyepoint elevation angle (EPEA) is the elevation of the centre of projection of the display with reference to the ground plane. Studies investigating optimal EPEA for exocentric direction judgements and tracking tasks have produced several consistent findings (e.g., Barfield et al., 1995a, 1995b; Kim et al., 1987). First, EPEAs approaching extreme angles of 0° and 90° have a detrimental effect on performance due to compression along the depth and altitude axes, respectively. Second, optimal performance may be obtained at an EPEA of 45° presumably because it accommodates judgements along both the depth and altitude axes. Third, EPEAs ranging from 15° to 60° can also produce good performance. Within this range, lower elevations foster better altitude judgements whereas higher elevations foster better depth judgements. The selection of the EPEA of a perspective display should therefore be based on the relative importance of depth and altitude judgements to the viewer.

*Azimuth viewing angle*

The azimuth viewing angle (AVA) is the angle from which an object is viewed relative to a 0° (straight ahead) viewing orientation. Two studies have examined how AVA affects tracking performance (Ellis et al., 1985; Kim et al., 1987). These studies showed that best tracking performance occurs at an AVA of 0°; tracking is probably more difficult at AVAs other than 0° because of the rotation of the display frame relative to the viewer. Second, tracking performance starts to deteriorate at AVAs outside the range of -45° to +45°. Presumably it becomes more difficult for the subject to compensate for the excessive rotation of the display frame at these angles.

## Conclusion

Human factors issues in perspective display design should not be overlooked. First and foremost, the nature of the task should dictate the format that the display should take. There is evidence to suggest that perspective displays support better integrated judgements whereas 2D displays support better focussed-attention judgements. Second, having decided to implement a perspective display format, the choice of display parameters, for example frame of reference and perspective geometry, should also be dictated by the nature of the task. These observations emphasise the importance of having good knowledge about the characteristics of the task for which the display is being designed.

## References

Barfield, W., Hendrix, C., & Bjorneseth, O. (1995a). Spatial performance with perspective displays as a function of computer graphics eyepoint elevation and geometric field of view. *Applied Ergonomics, 26*(5), 307-314.

Barfield, W., Lim, R., & Rosenberg, C. (1990). Visual enhancements and geometric field of view as factors in the design of a three-dimensional perspective display. *Proceedings of the Human Factors Society 34th Annual Meeting*, 1470-1473.

Barfield, W., Rosenberg, C., & Furness III, T. A. (1995b). Situation awareness as a function of frame of reference, computer-graphics eyepoint elevation, and geometric field of view. *International Journal of Aviation Psychology*, 5(3), 233-256.

Bemis, S.V., Leeds, J.L., & Winer, E.A. (1988). Operator performance as a function of type of display: conventional versus perspective. *Human Factors, 30*(2), 163-169.

Ellis, S.R., McGreevy, M.W., & Hitchcock, R.J. (1984). Influence of a perspective cockpit traffic display format on pilot avoidance manoeuvres. In *Proceedings of the AGARD Aerospace Medical Panel Symposium on Human Factors Considerations in High Performance Aircraft* (pp. 16-1 to 16-9). Neuilly sur Seine. AGARD.

Ellis, S.R., Tyler, M., Kim, W.S., McGreevy, M.W., & Stark, L. (1985). Visual enhancements for perspective displays: perspective parameters. In *IEEE Conference on Cybernetics and Society* (pp. 815-818).

Grunwald, A.J., Robertson, J.B., & Hatfield, J.J. (1981). Experimental evaluation of a perspective tunnel display for three-dimensional helicopter approaches. *Journal of Guidance and Control, 4*, 623-631.

Haskell, I.D., & Wickens, C.D. (1993). Two- and three-dimensional displays for aviation: a theoretical and empirical comparison. *International Journal of Aviation Psychology 3*(2), 87-109.

Kim, W.S., Ellis, S.R., Tyler, M.E., Hannaford, B., & Stark, L.W. (1987). Quantitative evaluation of perspective and stereoscopic displays in three-axis manual tracking tasks. *IEEE Transactions on Systems, Man and Cybernetics 17*(1), 61-72.

McGreevy, M.W., & Ellis, S.R. (1986). The effect of perspective geometry on judged direction in spatial information instruments. *Human Factors 28*(4), 439-456.

Roscoe, S.N., Corl, L., & Jensen, R.S. (1981). Flight display dynamics revisited. *Human Factors, 23,* 341-353.

Tham, M.P. & Wickens, C.D. (1993). *Evaluation of Perspective and Stereoscopic Displays as Alternatives to Plan-View Displays in Air Traffic Control.* University of Illinois Institute of Aviation Technical Report (ARL-93-4/FAA-93-1). Savoy, IL: Aviation Research Lab.

Wickens, C.D., Liang, C.C., Prevett, T., & Olmos, O. (1996). Electronic maps for terminal area navigation: effects of frame of reference and dimensionality. *International Journal of Aviation Psychology, 6*(3), 241-247.

Wickens, C.D. & Prevett, T. (1995). Exploring the dimensions of egocentricity in aircraft navigation displays: influences on local guidance and global situation awareness. *Journal of Experimental Psychology: Applied, 1,* 110-135.

Wickens, C.D., Todd, S., & Seidler, K. (1989). *Three-dimensional displays: perception, implementation and applications.* Crew System Ergonomics Information Analysis Centre.

Wilckens, V. & Schattenmann, W. (1968). Test results with new analog displays for all weather landing. In *Proceedings of Avionics Panel Symposium "Problems of the Cockpit Environment."* Amsterdam.

Yeh, Y. & Silverstein, L.D. (1992). Spatial judgements with monoscopic and stereoscopic presentation of perspective displays. *Human Factors, 34*(5), 583-600.

# 22 Evaluation of workload during a diversion using GPS and VOR

*Benjamin Jobson and Michael Nendick*
*The University of Newcastle*

The relationship between pilot performance and operational workload has been the centre of major research emphasis in recent years as the level of technology and automation increases rapidly and the nature of aircraft operations changes to a greater systems monitoring role (Derrick, 1988; Harris, Hancock, Arthur, & Caird, 1995). The literature indicates that there is a clear relationship between operational workload and pilot performance (Bainbridge, 1987; Dorner, 1987), and that as relative pilot workload increases, pilot performance reduces, especially at the cognitive level (Laudeman & Palmer, 1995). Gawran, Schflett and Miller (1989) argue that system performance and safety are dependant on operator workload.

Workload can be defined as a cost to human operators of accomplishing task objectives (Hart, 1986). Kantowitz (1986) has further defined workload as being an intervening variable, similar to attention, that modulates or indexes the tuning between the demands of the environment and the capacity of the operator. Workload studies (Corwin, 1992; Derrick, 1988; Fadden, 1993) are important to both predict and assess workload, not only in terms relating to overall performance but in terms of the demands that may be imposed on the operators' processing resources (Stokes, Wickens & Kite, 1990). Simulation scenarios that impose predictable and objectively determined levels of workload on pilots are an essential element of research on current and future aircraft systems and procedures (Bortolussi & Hart, 1984).

Global Positioning System (GPS) is the most recent advance in aviation navigation systems. It is planned to replace traditional ground-based radio navigation aids such as Very High Frequency Radio Range (VOR) worldwide over the next 10 to 15 years in accordance with the International

Civil Aviation Organisation (ICAO) plan (O'Keeffe, 1996). GPS is approved in Australia as an aid to en route primary means navigation under the Instrument Flight Rules (IFR) (Airservices Australia, 1995). Its high level of accuracy and automation is intended to reduce pilot workload in flight. Therefore GPS should improve flight safety by allowing the pilot additional mental resources to cope with unusual or emergency situations.

A survey of general aviation pilots found that GPS was perceived to have significantly reduced pilots workload (Nendick & St. George, 1996), however, there has been little empirical data published to confirm this supposition.

This study is an initial part of a series designed to evaluate pilot workload using GPS. In this experiment, pilots were compared using a GPS and VOR receiver while conducting IFR enroute diversions in a Novasim synthetic flight trainer. The hypothesis under consideration was that pilot workload when conducting an in-flight diversion should be lower using GPS compared to using VOR as the primary navigation aid.

**Method**

*Participants*

Ten pilots volunteered to participate in the study. They were all male aged between 19 and 31 with a mean age of 22.7 years. Each pilot was required to hold a private pilot licence and to be familiar with the operation of the synthetic flight trainer, VOR, and GPS used in the experiment.

Participants had a mean of 414.1 ($SD = 740.1$) hours of total flying experience, with a mean of 71.7 ($SD = 151.4$) hours of experience using VOR as an aid to navigation, and a mean of 8.7 ($SD = 3.8$) hours using GPS as an aid to navigation.

*Apparatus*

A dual seat, fully enclosed Novasim synthetic flight trainer, configured as a generic fast twin-engine aircraft was used to conduct the instrument flight simulations. A generic VOR receiver formed part of the simulator instrument display. A Garmin 100 GPS receiver with an alphanumeric display screen was installed on the instrument coaming at eye level in front of the pilot. The flight instruments, including the altimeter and horizontal situation indicator (HSI) displays, were recorded with a video camera during each scenario.

*Procedure*

Four experimental scenarios were flown, two each using the GPS and VOR. Each flight scenario was identical with participants initially positioned over Amberley at 3,000 feet under simulated en-route IFR cruise conditions on the Brisbane VOR 222° radial. The simulator was then activated and the participants were required to maintain an altitude of 3000 feet whilst tracking to Brisbane. At 25 nautical miles from Brisbane the participants were asked to divert to one of three off-track alternates; Coolangatta, Maroochydore or Oakey. Response time and accuracy of the alternate bearing and distance calculations were recorded. Altitude and tracking performance prior to and during diversion were also recorded. Deviations were taken as a quantitative indication of pilot workload.

Participants were randomly allocated to one of two groups. Group A flew the GPS scenarios followed by the VOR with Group B reversed. This counterbalanced design allowed for the detection of learning effect as a function of repeated exposure to the simulator. Prior to conducting the scenarios participants were provided with the appropriate charts for the area of operation to familiarise themselves with the airspace and available alternates. Participants were told that there was a performance requirement to hold height accurately and when given, to rapidly complete the diversion calculations to the alternate. They did not know which alternate would be chosen. They were instructed to press the simulator hold button when satisfied that they had obtained the correct bearing and distance information to the alternate. The time to complete each task was recorded from the time the diversion was given until the time the participant pressed the simulator hold button. A practice scenario for both the VOR and the GPS was flown to provide familiarisation with the required task. Each participant was trialed individually with each trial lasting approximately 30 minutes.

On completion of the exercise participants were asked to complete subjective workload ratings for the scenarios using a series of seven-point Likert scales ranging from "extremely low" to "extremely high".

**Results**

The hypothesis tested was that there would be no difference between trials using GPS and VOR on any of the dependant variables. Objective workload for flying performance prior to and during diversion (altitude holding), and diversion calculations (response time and accuracy) were measured. Subjective ratings for the physical and mental workload involved, the ease

213

of operation of the GPS and VOR, the overall difficulty of the diversion calculations, and confidence in the calculations were obtained. Between-subjects and within-subjects repeated-measures paired *t*-tests were used to analyse the data.

*Objective findings*

*Altitude holding.* Mean deviation from assigned altitude for the VOR prior to the diversion was 25 feet (*SD* = 16.5), with a mean deviation during the diversion of 59 feet (*SD* = 32.5), a 118% increase. There was a significant difference between altitude holding prior to and during the diversion ($t(9)$ = 3.8, $p<.05$), suggesting that there was a relative workload increase when tracking on the VOR during the diversion.

Mean deviation from assigned altitude for the GPS prior to the diversion was 35.5 feet (*SD* = 34.5) with a mean deviation during the diversion of 54 feet (*SD* = 28), a 76% increase. There was no significant difference between altitude holding prior to and during the diversion ($t(9)$ = 0.112, $p >.05$), suggesting that there was no relative workload increase when tracking on the GPS during the diversion.

There was no significant difference for the mean deviation from altitude between the VOR and the GPS prior to the diversion ($t(9)$ = 1.618, $p >.05$), nor during the diversion ($t(9)$ = 0.716, $p >.05$). This suggests that relative workload between the navigation aids was similar for the scenarios.

*Response time.* Mean diversion task response time was 41.9 seconds (*SD* = 10.1) for the VOR, and 40.3 seconds (*SD* = 9.0) for the GPS. There was no significant difference between response times for the VOR and GPS ($t(9)$ = 0.371, $p > .05$).

*Accuracy* No errors were made for bearing and distance accuracy when using GPS. Two errors were made when using VOR. This equated to a ten per cent error rate using the VOR.

*Subjective finding*

*Physical workload.* Participants rated the GPS average (*Mean* =3.8, *SD* = 0.92) and VOR average (*Mean* = 3.8, *SD* = 0.92) with no significant difference for physical workload ($t(9)$ = 0.01, $p > .05$). This finding suggests that both navigation aids required similar physical effort during the diversion.

*Mental workload.* Participants rated the GPS slightly low (*Mean* =3.3, *SD* = 0.82) and the VOR average (*Mean* =4.4, *SD* = 0.70) with a significant difference for mental workload ($t(9)$ = 2.905 $p$ < .05). This suggests that GPS required less cognitive effort during the diversion.

*Overall difficulty.* Participants rated the GPS slightly low (*Mean* =2.9, *SD* = 0.74) and the VOR average (*Mean* =3.6, *SD* = 0.97) with a significant difference between the scenarios for overall difficulty ($t(9)$ = 2.689 $p$ < .05). This suggests that calculating the diversion information was perceived to be easier overall using the GPS.

*Ease of operation.* Participants rated the GPS slightly low (*Mean* =2.8, *SD* = 1.13) and the VOR slightly low (*Mean* =3.4, *SD* = 0.84) with no significant difference between aids for ease of operation ($t(9)$ = 0.111 $p$ < .05). This suggests that the perceived ease of operating both the GPS and VOR was similar.

*Confidence.* Participants rated the GPS moderately high (*Mean* =6.4, *SD* = 0.97) and the VOR moderately high (*Mean* =6.1, *SD* = 0.99) with no significant difference between aids for confidence in their answers ($t(9)$ = 1.406 $p$ < .05). This suggests that the confidence in the bearing and distance diversion calculations using the GPS and VOR was equally high.

**Discussion**

The findings supported the hypothesis that overall pilot workload on a given diversion task should be lower using GPS compared to using VOR. GPS was found to have a significantly lower relative increase in workload on the diversion measured by degradation of primary flight performance (altitude holding deviations), and to result in less diversion calculation errors than VOR. Participants perceived GPS to require significantly less mental workload and to significantly reduce overall difficulty of the diversion calculations compared to VOR. These results support previous research by Nendick and St. George (1995).

The simulated diversion task was designed to increase workload and the findings demonstrated that this occurred for each scenario. Degradation in flight performance was used as a measure of overall workload increase. Physical workload was perceived to be similar between GPS and VOR, however mental workload and overall task difficulty was perceived to be significantly lower using GPS.

The diversion scenario was relatively simple requiring only bearing and distance information to be calculated. Time taken to complete the task was similar for both the GPS and VOR, however pilots were more accurate using GPS. They made no errors using GPS compared to a 10% error rate using VOR, while being equally confident in their answers. Pilots perceived their mental workload and overall task difficulty to be greater when using the VOR. This suggests that the higher workload increased the potential for information processing errors thus reducing flight safety margins.

In summary, performance on the given task, a simple en-route diversion, was improved when using GPS in comparison to a traditional navigation aid, the VOR. If the results of this study apply to other phases of flight it appears that GPS is indeed an improvement on older technology, with positive implications for flight safety.

**Notes and Acknowledgments**

This research was supported in part by University of Newcastle RMC Grant 45/299/643.

**References**

Airservices Australia. (1995). *Requirements for the use of global positioning system as an approved primary means IFR navigation aid.* AIRAC H50/95. Australia: Airservices Australia Publication Centre.

Bainbridge, E.L. (1987). Ironies of automation. In J. Rasmussen, K. Duncan, & J. Leplat (Eds.), *New Technology and human error* (pp. 271-283). New York: Wiley.

Bortolussi, M.R., & Hart, S.G. (1984). Pilot errors as a source of workload. *Human Factors, 26* (5) 545-556.

Corwin, W.H. (1992). In-flight and postflight assessment of pilot workload in commercial transport aircraft using the Subjective Workload Assessment Technique. *International Journal of Aviation Psychology, 2,* 77-94.

Derrick, W.L. (1988). Dimensions of operator workload. *Human Factors, 30,* 95-110.

Dorner, D. (1987). On the difficulties people have in dealing with complexity. In J. Rasmussen, K. Duncan, & J. Leplat (Eds.), *New technology and human error.* New York: John Wiley.

Fadden, D.M. (1993). Workload assessment. In K. Cardosi (Ed.), *Human factors for operational personnel.* Washington, DC.: Department of Transportation/Federal Aviation Administration/Volpe National Transportation Systems Center.

Gawron, V.J., Schflett, S.G., & Miller, J.C. (1989). Measures of in-flight workload. In R. Jensen (Ed.) *Aviation Psychology.* United States: Gower Technical.

Harris, W.C., Hancock, P.A., Arthur, E.J., & Caird, J.K. (1995). Performance, workload and fatigue changes associated with automation. *The International Journal of Aviation Psychology, 5,* 169-186.

Hart, S.G. (1986). Theory and measurement of human workload. In J. Zeider (Ed.), *Human productivity enhancement: Training and human factors in systems design* (Vol. 1, pp. 396-456). New York: Praeger.

Kantowitz, B.H. (1986). Mental workload. In P.A Hancock (Ed.), *Human Factors Psychology.* Amsterdam: North Holland.

Laudeman, I.V., & Palmer, E.A. (1995). Quantitative measurement of observed workload in the analysis of crew performance. *The International Journal of Aviation Psychology, 5,* 187-197.

Nendick, M., & St. George, R. (1996). Human factors aspects of Global Positioning Systems (GPS) equipment: A study with New Zealand pilots. In R. Jensen (Ed.), *Proceedings of the Eighth International Symposium on Aviation Psychology,* Ohio State University: Columbus, Ohio.

O'Keeffe, B. (1996). The future air navigation system is here. *Navigation. Vol 3,* No. 10.

Stokes, A., Wickens, C., & Kite, K. (1990). *Pilot mental and physical performance.* Pennsylvania: Warrendale.

# 23 The investigation of cognition in NVG helicopter operations

*Peter F. Renshaw*
*University of Western Sydney, Macarthur*

## Introduction

Night Vision Goggles (NVGs) and, in particular, the helmet mounted Aviators Night-Vision-Imaging-System (ANVIS-6), has gained increasing importance and use in night-time military helicopter operations (Brickner, 1989; Ruffner, Grubb, & Hamilton, 1992). This increasing reliance on NVGs to enhance night flying capabilities, particularly at low-level, has also raised several safety concerns (Biberman & Alluisi, 1992).

The operational demands on military helicopter pilots are rapidly changing in accordance with ongoing developments in the utilisation and sophistication of night vision device (NVD) technology (Kaiser & Foyle, 1991). An understanding of the impact of NVGs on pilotage, therefore, needs to progress beyond perceptual issues and begin to more thoroughly explore the cognitive impact of NVGs on helicopter pilot performance (Ruffner et al., 1992).

United States Army Aviation accident data have indicated that night-aided (NVGs such as the ANVIS-6) flight crew errors were the result of a combination of operational factors such as inadequate planning, improper scanning by aircrew, reduced altitudes, restricted visibility, poor crew co-ordination, and spatial disorientation (Boyd, 1991; Crowley, 1990; Douglass, Braithwaite, Durnford, & Lucas, 1997; Fuson, 1990). More specifically, data from United States Army NVG operations has found that, on average, 70 per cent of rotorcraft night accidents occurred when NVGs were in use (Boyd, 1991).

## NVG accident data

According to Crowley (1990), the typical United States Army Aviation NVG accident involves a UH-60 Black Hawk helicopter on a training mission. Occupants of aircraft involved in NVG accidents are also more likely to be killed than occupants in day and unaided-night accidents (Crowley, 1990). Furthermore, the most common cause of fatalities in NVG accidents is midair collision (Crowley, 1990). DeLucia and Task (1995), for example, note that 'pilots have worn NVGs in 71 per cent of the Army's major midair collisions between 1985 and 1990' (p. 372).

On the basis of an analysis of 626 US Army rotorcraft accidents, Boyd (1991) classified the origins of crew-related NVG errors into eight types: improper scanning; aircrew inability to maintain/recover orientation; poor crew co-ordination; inadequate preflight planning; improper modifications to inflight planning; inaccurate estimates of closure rates; failures to detect hazardous conditions; improper diagnosis and responses to emergencies.

Boyd (1991) has proposed that these error types were related more to operational factors such as phase of flight, mission profile, and aircraft type, rather than the use of NVGs per se. Fuson (1990), however, has stated that the circumstances under which NVG missions are flown are reducing safety margins, thereby causing the resultant increase in NVG-related accidents.

Sixty nine per cent of the night helicopter accidents identified by Fuson (1990), occurred under the low-level NVG tactical flight regime and typically involved Black Hawk operations where pilots committed the following errors: improper scanning (attentional tunneling), inadequate crew coordination, inadequate procedures to maintain orientation and poor aircraft and terrain clearances (situational awareness). Restricted visibility and low illumination were the environmental factors that also contributed to these accidents (Fuson, 1990).

Friedman, Leedom, and Howell (1991) note that the categories used to designate human-error components implicated in United States Army aircraft accident analyses are subjective, sometimes imprecise, and may be of limited validity. Establishing the origins of such categories, therefore, requires a sound theoretical base from which to develop testable hypotheses that drive robust empirical outcomes which are designed to promote applied interventions (Friedman et al., 1991).

On the basis of the conclusions drawn from this research, it appears that the overall impact of NVGs on pilot performance is not fully understood (Biberman & Alluisi, 1992). Moreover, the majority of night vision device research has focused on optical sensory and perceptual problems, rather than the demands placed on the pilot's cognitive system (information-processing, decision-making, problem-solving) (Ruffner et al., 1992). As well, night vision research has only briefly referred to the inherently high workloads placed upon pilots (Brickner, 1989; Green, 1994; Stewart, 1997).

## Night vision goggles and helicopter operations

The most demanding task that a military battlefield transport helicopter pilot and crew faces is low-level and nap of the earth (NOE), night vision goggles (NVG) tactical formation flying in a hostile theatre of engagement (Brickner, 1989; Oldham, 1990; Sanders, Simmons, & Hofmann, 1979). According to Biberman and Alluisi (1992), Ruffner, Grubb, and Hamilton (1992), and Stewart (1997), there is likely to be an increasing emphasis on NOE night flight because of the inherent tactical advantages afforded by visual concealment from ground fire and enemy radar avoidance. Furthermore, pilots' level of anxiety, risk taking behaviour, and aggressiveness have all been shown to be affected by NVG flight (Harss, Kastner, & Beerman, 1991).

The additional workload imposed upon aircrew during terrain-following tactical NVG flight is, in part, due to the relative perceptual speeds at which terrain is traversed under limited illumination and field of view and the short periods of time in which pilots have to process navigational cues and ensure obstacle avoidance (Sanders et al., 1979). Consequently, co-ordination between the pilot, co-pilot, and loadmasters is critical in communicating and determining safe clearances between the other aircraft in a tactical formation (Fuson, 1990; Green, 1994; Ruffner et al., 1992).

The complexity of NVG helicopter operations and, in particular, the notion of pilot uncertainty, appears to be a recurrent theme throughout this type of applied research. Therefore, in order to understand and predict the impact of NVG operational complexity on helicopter pilot performance, it is important to delineate a theoretical model of complexity that can clarify and elucidate the cognitive difficulties imposed on pilots in NVG helicopter operations. Figure 23.1 presents the research approaches for examining the demands on pilots in NVG helicopter operations.

## Theoretical framework

Woods (1988) has proposed a model that maps the complexity of dynamic problem-solving domains, such as aviation, into qualitatively distinct dimensions.

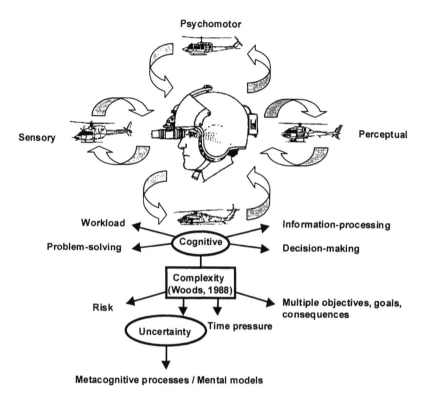

**Figure 23.1**
**An illustration of the research approaches for examining the demands on pilots in NVG helicopter operations.**

According to Woods (1988), a complex domain is one characterised by:

- a highly dynamic time-pressured event driven operational environment;
- an environment where one failure can have multiple consequences and where multiple objectives and goals often compete with, or limit each other;
- a high degree of uncertainty or unpredictability is apparent; and

222

- a level of risk, which is either a low probability-high consequence environment such as aviation, or may be characterised by frequent occurrences with less costly outcomes.

The current research investigates the impact of uncertainty on pilot performance in NVG helicopter operations and how it impacts upon cognitive skills such as situational awareness.

Lipshitz and Strauss (1996) have defined uncertainty as 'a sense of doubt that blocks or delays action' (p. 189). When uncertainty is high, the available information for problem-solving may be ambiguous, incomplete, or erroneous (Woods, 1988). The inferential value of information may also vary according to the operational environment context (Woods, 1988).

When a pilot's mental model of the operational environment and aircraft status becomes de-coupled from the actual state of the situation, errors of intention and execution may develop (Woods, 1988). Unexpected developments in the operational environment or aircraft state may facilitate this de-coupling. Moreover, uncertainty reduces a problem-solver's ability to anticipate and predict operational events and thereby revise operational assessments and implement functional tactical or strategic responses to rectify potentially hazardous situations (Woods, 1988). Furthermore, when uncertainty is high, problem-solvers may revert to heuristics, or a simple evidence-processing scheme which may have previously provided solutions to problems under most conditions (Woods, 1988).

Even though a more elaborate evaluation strategy may be necessary when confronted with uncertainty, pilots may revert to a reliance on familiar signs (Woods, 1988). This cognitive failure may also be induced by inadequate knowledge about the extent of the relationship between the questions and evidence that need to be collected and evaluated (Woods, 1988). To overcome this common problem, strategies for acquiring accurate data are required. Moreover, the data required for this situation assessment and information gathering exercise require organisational and individual effort and risk (Woods, 1988).

In the dynamic domain of military aviation, pilots still need to make quick, effective decisions in the midst of uncertainty (Svensson, Angelborg-Thanderz, Sjoberg, & Olsson, 1997). McCloskey (1996) has presented a model of uncertainty that codes both the sources and levels of uncertainty. This model is consistent with the framework developed by Cohen, Freeman, and Wolf (1996) and parallels Endsley's (1995) components of situation awareness. These classifications were developed from a broad research programme conducted by Klein and associates on uncertainty in United

States Marines Corps battlefield decision-makers. Under McCloskey's (1996) model, the four *sources* of uncertainty are:

i)  Missing information – Information is missing because the problem-solver or decision-maker does not have it or cannot find it when it is needed;

ii)  Unreliable information – Information lacks credibility or is perceived as unreliable;

iii)  Ambiguous/Conflicting information – Information is ambiguous or conflicting if there is more than one way to interpret it; and

iv)  Complexity – Information is complex when it is difficult to integrate into a coherent whole (pp. 194-195).

McCloskey (1996) has defined the three *levels* of uncertainty as follows:

i)  Data – This refers to uncertainty regarding elements of raw data such as troop locations and enemy strength;

ii)  Inference – Data becomes knowledge when inferences can be developed. A probable or most likely situation can be deduced from inferences; and

iii)  Projection – Inferences are synthesised into projections of the future, into diagnoses and explanations of events, or the identification of critical focal points in the mission or operation. Plans for action are then developed (p. 195).

Under the auspices of this model, McCloskey (1996) found that uncertainty in Marines Corps commanders was prevalent when the information received was incomplete or ambiguous. This created problems with inferences and subsequent projections. This research provides a means for manipulating uncertainty as an independent variable in the current study.

**Conclusions**

The current research is designed to develop practical training methods to support aircrew cognitive skill acquisition, improve the management of mental workload, enhance situational awareness, and devise mechanisms to assist aircrew to cope with uncertainty. Further research will need to address the distinctions between novice and expert pilot decision-making under uncertainty in NVG helicopter operations utilising the recognition/ metacognition framework proposed by Cohen, Freeman, and Wolf (1996).

# References

Biberman, L.M., & Alluisi, E.A. (1992). Pilot errors involving head-up displays (HUDs), helmet mounted displays (HMDs), and night vision goggles (NVGs). (IDA Paper P-2638). Alexandria: Institute for Defense Analysis.

Boyd, A. (1991). Crew error in night rotary wing accidents. (Briefing Documents from Research Analysis/Studies Branch). Fort Rucker, AL: US Army Safety Centre.

Brickner, M.S. (1989). *Helicopter flights with night vision goggles – Human factors aspects.* (NASA Technical Memorandum No. 101039). Moffett Field, CA: NASA Ames Research Centre.

Cohen, M.S., Freeman, J.T., & Wolf, S. (1996). Metarecognition in time-stressed decision making: Recognising, critiquing, and correcting. *Human Factors, 38(2),* 206-219.

Crowley, J.S. (1990). *Human factors aspects of helicopter accidents with night vision goggles in use.* US Army Safety Centre Special Report. Fort Rucker, AL: US Army Safety Centre.

DeLucia, P.R., & Task, H.L. (1995). Depth and collision judgment using night vision goggles. *The International Journal of Aviation Psychology, 5(4),* 371-386.

Douglass, P.K., Braithwaite, M.G., Durnford, S.J., & Lucas, G.C. (1997). The hazards of spatial disorientation in flight using night vision devices. *Aviation, Space, and Environmental Medicine, 68(10),* 958.

Endsley, M.R. (1995). Toward a theory of situation awareness in dynamic systems. *Human Factors, 37(1),* 85-104.

Friedman, L., Leedom, D.K., & Howell, W.C. (1991). A new approach toward diagnosing military aircraft accidents. *Military Psychology, 3*(2),113-126.

Fuson, J. (1990). Crew error in night rotary wing accidents. *Flightfax, 19,* 1-5. US Army Safety Centre.

Green, D.L. (1994). *Assessment of night vision goggle workload – Flight test engineer's guide.* (FAA/RD-94/20). Springfield, VA: FAA.

Harss, C., Kastner, M., & Beerman, L. (1991). The impact of personality and task characteristics on stress and strain during helicopter flight. *The International Journal of Aviation Psychology, 1*(4), 301-318.

Kaiser, M.K., & Foyle, D.C. (1991). Human factors issues in the use of night vision devices. *Proceedings of the Human Factors Society 35th Annual Meeting* (pp. 1502-1506). San Francisco, CA: Human Factors Society.

Lipshitz, R., & Strauss, O. (1996). How decision-makers cope with uncertainty. *Proceedings of the Human Factors and Ergonomics Society 40th Annual Meeting* (pp. 189-193). San Diego, CA: HFES.

McCloskey, M.J. (1996). An analysis of uncertainty in the Marines Corps. *Proceedings of the Human Factors and Ergonomics Society 40th Annual Meeting* (pp. 194-198). San Diego, CA: HFES.

Oldham, T.W. (1990). *Night vision and night vision goggles.* (USAF Air War College Research Report). Maxwell AFB, AL: Air University.

Ruffner, J.W., Grubb, M.G., & Hamilton, D.B. (1992). *Selective factors affecting rotary wing aviator performance with symbology superimposed on night vision goggles.* Fort Rucker, AL: Ancapa Sciences, Inc.

Sanders, M.G., Kimball, K.A., Frezell, T.L., & Hofmann, M.A. (1975). *Aviator performance measurement during low altitude rotary wing flight with the AN/PVS-5 night vision goggles.* (USAARL Report No. 76-10). Fort Rucker, AL: US Army Aeromedical Research Laboratory.

Stewart, J.E. (1997). The effects of the AH-64A pilot's night vision system on the performance of seven simulated maneuver tasks. *The International Journal of Aviation Psychology, 7(3),* 183-200.

Svensson, E., Angelborg-Thanderz, M., & Sjoberg, L., & Olsson, S. (1997). Information complexity – mental workload and performance in combat aircraft. *Ergonomics, 40(3),* 362-380.

Woods, D.D. (1988). Coping with complexity: the psychology of human behaviour in complex systems. In L.P. Goodstein, H.B. Andersen, & S.E. Olsen (Eds.), *Tasks, errors, and mental models.* London: Taylor & Francis Ltd.

# 24 Musculoskeletal pain in S-70A-9 aircrew: A survey approach

*David A. Foran and Anna M. Zalevski*
*DSTO, Aeronautical and Maritime Research Laboratory*

## Introduction

Air Operation Division of the Defence Science and Technology Organisation was tasked by Army Aviation Support Group to investigate health and safety issues on-board the S-70A-9 Black Hawk helicopter. Concerns have been raised regarding aircrew musculoskeletal disorders and their potential to affect aircrew performance and impact on mission effectiveness.

Survey data were collected from S-70A-9 aircrew (pilots and loadmasters) to permit the quantification of the incidence and impact of musculoskeletal symptoms within this population.

Musculoskeletal complaints in military helicopter aviators have been the subject of considerable research for several decades. While unique characteristics of helicopter piloting, such as a slouching or hunched posture with upper limb asymmetry have been identified as contributory to the development of back disorders (Bowden 1985; Reader 1986; Shanahan, Mastroianni & Reading 1986; Froom, Hanegbi, Ribak, & Gross, 1987), research examining non-piloting helicopter aircrew has been sparse.

## Method

*Subjects*

There were 60 participants in the study comprising thirty S-70A-9 loadmasters and thirty S-70A-9 pilots. Biographical data revealed statistically significant differences between pilots and loadmasters indicating that on average loadmasters are older than pilots, they fly more hours per week than pilots and had been at their present position longer than pilots.

*Survey instrument*

The S-70A-9 Workstation and Activity Survey was developed to assess the incidence, aetiology and impact on job performance of existing musculoskeletal discomfort symptoms among S-70A-9 aircrew. The questionnaire was developed from the Standardised Nordic Musculoskeletal Questionnaire (Kuorinka et al., 1987), and the Job Discomfort Survey (Stuart-Buttle 1994) and incorporated multiple choice and free response questions, and a reference body chart.

## Results

Data concerned with the incidence, intensity, and cause of the reported pain were obtained from aircrew responses to multiple choice questions requiring them to select answers relating to each of nine body regions.

Data concerning the impact of the reported musculoskeletal symptoms were obtained from multiple choice and free response questions. Multiple choice questions concerned the level of interference with work activities, while free responses addressed effects on job performance.

*Incidence of pain*

Across the nine body regions under examination, the most striking features of these data are the high proportions of loadmasters reporting pain in the knees (90%), lower back (83%) and neck (90%), and the high proportions of pilots reporting pain in the lower back (80%) and neck (67%).

*Intensity of pain*

Lower back pain was considered to constitute a significant problem for both aircrew populations with 72% of loadmasters and 54% of pilots rating the pain intensity as moderate or greater (see Figure 24.1).

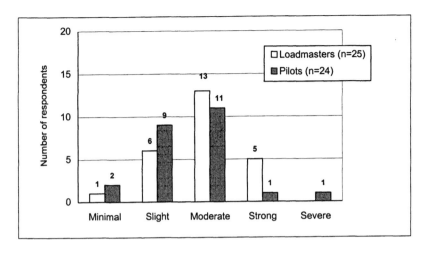

**Figure 24.1**
**Intensity of lower back pain**

Knee pain was also considered to be a major problem affecting loadmasters with 67% rating it as moderate or greater (see Figure 24.2).

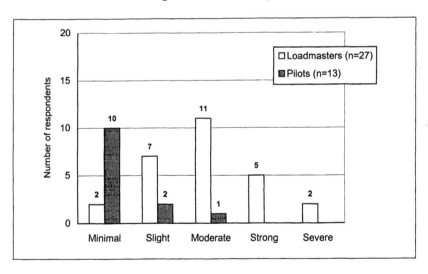

**Figure 24.2**
**Intensity of knee pain**

*Causes of pain*

For both loadmasters and pilots, of the five options available, 'Workplace Design' and 'Work-related Activities' were considered to be the main contributory causes of the symptoms they reported. Of the 198 responses given by loadmasters across all body regions, 193 (97%) cited either of these two factors. For pilots, this figure was 105 out of 120 (88%) responses. Remaining responses were distributed between the other categories of 'Sport', 'Accident' and 'Other'.

*Effect of pain*

*Interference with work activities.* Aircrew rated on a five-point scale the extent to which the reported pain was interfering with work activities . The five choices from which one selection was made were; not at all, slightly, moderately, strongly, and severely.

Across all body locations there was a total of 118 ratings provided by loadmasters about the level of interference of reported musculoskeletal pain. Of these, 34 (29%) considered the pain to interfere moderately or more so with work activities.

Pilots provided a total of 127 responses rating the extent of interference of reported symptoms. Of these, four (3%) considered the pain to interfere moderately. The remaining 123 responses were all rated as interfering with work activities slightly or not at all.

*Interference with job performance.* A free response question provided an opportunity for aircrew to identify specific effects of the reported symptoms on aspects of job performance. These data provided information about the mechanism by which aircrew tasks and functions might be affected. These responses were not specifically linked to a particular symptom but represent an integrated statement of impact that could involve combinations of symptoms.

*Mechanisms for interference.* Loadmasters provided 32 responses detailing the impact of the reported symptoms. Negative effects on concentration and distraction from the main task were the most commonly reported impact with 11 (34%) responses. Non-completion or decreased effectiveness of tasks were also cited, as were no or minimal effect and unspecified effects. Figure 24.3 contains a breakdown of loadmaster responses detailing the effect of reported symptoms on job performance.

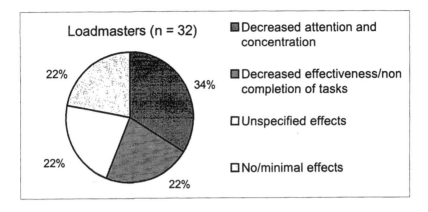

**Figure 24.3**
**Loadmaster responses detailing impact of symptoms on job**
**performance**

Pilots provided 23 responses reporting the effects of symptoms on job performance. While eleven (48%) of these identified no or minimal effect, the remaining 12 responses (52%) reported specific and general degradation of performance arising from the reported musculoskeletal symptoms (see Figure 24.4).

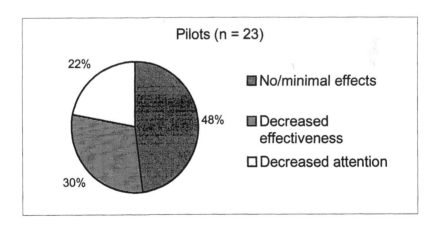

**Figure 24.4**
**Pilot responses detailing impact of symptoms on job performance**

**Discussion**

The results of this survey provide clear indications that musculoskeletal pain and discomfort associated with operating the S-70A-9 represent a significant problem that has the potential to compromise operator health and reduce operational safety and effectiveness. This situation was evident for both loadmasters and pilots; however, differences exist between these two groups with respect to incidence, severity, aetiology, and impact.

Of particular concern are the high incidence rates for pain reported by loadmasters in the neck, lower back, and knees, and by pilots in the neck and lower back and their corresponding severity.

Of further significance are the findings associated with the impact of the musculoskeletal symptoms on work activities and job performance.

While rates of incidence of pain and discomfort are useful in identifying potential problems for aircrew, the operational implications are perhaps even more significant. Pain related to job performance has serious health and safety implications, and as such demands close attention. The description of musculoskeletal complaints in terms of the extent to which they are considered to impact on job performance has great utility in that it provides a meaningful metric to evaluate the potential cost to mission effectiveness. Such a description has a further benefit of providing a means to evaluate remedial intervention programs.

**Conclusions**

This research has identified several issues regarding musculoskeletal pain and discomfort confronting S-70A-9 Black Hawk aircrew that have the potential to impact on mission effectiveness and operator health.

Of primary concern are the high rates of pain incidence reported by loadmasters in the neck, lower back and knees and by pilots in the neck and lower back. Further to these high rates, the severity and subsequent extent to which these symptoms were reported to impact on job performance raise concerns for the ability of crews to perform missions safely and effectively.

Concern stems primarily from the finding that the reported symptoms are caused by the performance of critical and essential functions and that it is these functions that potentially suffer from the pain and discomfort generated. Perhaps the most significant example the provision of clearance information by the loadmaster to the pilot.

While several options may prove useful in the short-term, the current mismatch between the functional demands of the loadmaster and the workstation design is only likely to be removed with an extensive redesign of the cabin interior. An alternative may be to redesign the tasks and functions performed by loadmasters and the possible inclusion of new technologies that limit the requirement to perform potentially injurious activities.

## References

Bowden, T.J. (1985). *Postural fatigue and backache in helicopters. DCIEM Report No. 85-R-30.* Ontario, Canada: DCIEM.

Froom, P., Hanegbi, R., Ribak, J., & Gross, M. (1987). Low back pain in the AH-1 Cobra helicopter. *Aviation, Space and Environmental Medicine, 58,* 315-318.

Kuorinka, I., Jonsson, B., Kilbom, A., Vinterberg, H., Biering-Sorensen, F., Andersson, G., & Jorgensen, K. (1987). Standardised Nordic questionnaires for the analysis of musculoskeletal symptoms. *Applied Ergonomics, 18,* 233-237.

Reader, D.C. (1986). Backache in aircrew. In *AGARD Backache and Back Discomfort Conference Proceedings, No. 378,* 29.1-29.6.

Shanahan, D.F., Mastroianni, G.R., & Reading, T.E. (1986). Back discomfort in US army helicopter aircrew members. In *AGARD Backache and Back Discomfort Conference Proceedings, No. 378,* 6.1-6.10.

Stuart-Buttle, C. (1994). A discomfort survey in a poultry-processing plant. *Applied Ergonomics, 25,* 47-52.

# 25 Active noise reduction in a helicopter environment

*Anthony J. Saliba and Robert B. King*
*DSTO, Aeronautical and Maritime Research Laboratory*

## Introduction

Over the past five years, the Air Operations Division (AOD) of the Aeronautical and Maritime Research Laboratory (AMRL) has conducted acoustic analyses of various helicopters. These analyses have revealed that aircrew are subject to extremely high noise levels during operational flying. There are two possible impacts that high noise levels have on the use of an aircraft. They may restrict the exposure times of aircrew, effectively resulting in the aircraft flying for shorter durations than required operationally. Conversely, the aircraft may be flown for operationally required flight times increasing the risk of noise induced hearing loss (NIHL).

Active Noise Reduction (ANR), a technique that cancels some noise before it reaches the ear, has also been investigated as a possible adjunct to the Advanced Lightweight Protective Helmet for Aircrew (ALPHA) currently worn by Australian military helicopter aircrew. The additional attenuation provided by ANR increases exposure times for aircrew, effectively enabling them to operate their aircraft for longer. This has the benefit of providing a safe working environment where the risk of NIHL is minimised.

ANR has a mixed history, with some early systems failing during use and providing variable performance. Recent systems are more reliable, some even include 'failsafes' (i.e., normal communications are maintained if the ANR system fails). The performance of a modern ANR system will be described and specific examples of application in the S-70A-9 Black Hawk helicopter provided. The integration of passive attenuation devices such as helmets will be discussed, highlighting the improved performance resulting from the combination of helmets or headsets with ANR. The current position of ANR in the market place is described and the future of ANR as a technology and a hearing protection device (HPD) is discussed.

**Passive attenuation devices**

Passive attenuation devices such as helmets and headsets are the most common HPD's worn by aircrew. They are relatively cheap, provide an additional safety component (in the case of a helmet) and generally attenuate low to mid intensity noise fields to safe levels.

Passive attenuation devices generally provide good attenuation at higher frequencies, although most do little to attenuate low frequency noise. The ALPHA helmet is a classic example (King & Foran, 1992). Attenuation provided at frequencies above 1 kHz is high, from 250 Hz to 1 kHz moderate and frequencies below 250 Hz minimal (see Figure 25.1).

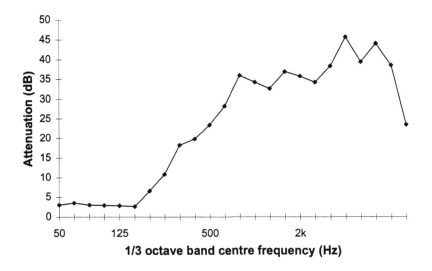

**Figure 25.1**
**Attenuation performance of an ALPHA helmet**

**Active noise reduction**

Unlike the passive attenuation provided by helmets, ANR cancels noise by generating a waveform that is (ideally) 180° out of phase with the noise inside the earcup and adding this "anti-noise" to the earcup. The destructive interaction between the original noise and the noise generated by the ANR system prevents some of the original noise from reaching the ear. The prospect of noise being cancelled before reaching the ear conjures thoughts of the fantastic, leading Defence Helicopter World to describe ANR as an "old science fiction idea that engineers had managed to make work" (1988, p. 22).

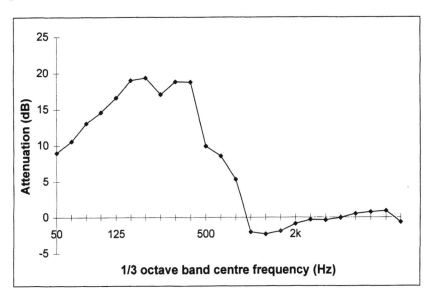

**Figure 25.2**
**Attenuation performance of a defence built ANR system.**

A feature of current ANR technology is that it effectively attenuates low frequency noise (<1 kHz). Attenuation performance of a Defence built ANR system incorporated into an ALPHA helmet is depicted in Figure 25.2 (King, Saliba, Brock & James, 1997).[1] High amounts of noise are cancelled at frequencies below 1 kHz, while little impact is made on noise at frequencies above 1 kHz. This makes ANR technology particularly useful in the aviation setting where aircraft commonly produce high levels of low frequency noise from aircraft vibration and propeller/rotor rotation. This characteristic also makes ANR an ideal partner to a passive attenuation device such as a helmet or headset. Where ANR cancels low frequency

---

[1] It should be noted that some ANR systems do perform better than others.

noise (and the helmet or headset does little), the helmet or headset attenuates higher frequency noise (where ANR does little). As an incorporated unit, ANR along with a helmet or headset provides excellent broadband attenuation performance.

ANR also improves speech intelligibility and reduces attentional demand associated with intercommunication system traffic (James & Harpur, 1990; Rogers, 1996; King et al., 1997). Chan and Simpson (1990) used a phonetically balanced word recognition task with intelligibility, clarity and attentional-demand rating scales to show that ANR improves speech intelligibility. It is generally accepted that ANR systems offer these benefits by reducing the upward spread of masking and adding speech pre-emphasis (Rylands, 1990).

Modern ANR systems are generally incorporated into an appropriate passive HPD such as a helmet or headset. The additional weight burden is low, and if the device is incorporated into the HPD, no comfort issues arise.

## ANR performance

In order to illustrate the influence of ANR on the helicopter noise environment, the effect of ANR on at-ear sound pressure levels (SPL) in the Black Hawk are used as an example. Like many rotary wing aircraft of its size, the Black Hawk helicopter can be a noisy aircraft. Evidence from anecdotal reports as well as scientific recordings indicates that noise levels exceed safety limits, even under a helmet (King, Saliba, Creed & Brock, 1996). Relevance to the civil world can be found in noise values reported for large civil helicopters (e.g., Howlett, Clevenson, Rupf & Snyder, 1977) and smaller military aircraft, of the size flown in general aviation, such as the Kiowa and the Iroquios (e.g., Cook, 1997). It is clear that the necessity for hearing protection is not limited to military aircraft but is required for many rotary wing (as well as propeller driven fixed wing) aircraft.

Noise levels produced in a typical flight condition[2] in the Black Hawk are depicted in Figure 25.3. The noise levels shown are measured either under an ALPHA helmet, or ALPHA helmet fitted with an ANR system (King, et al., 1997). As would be expected, the ANR system provides additional attenuation at frequencies below 1 kHz, while offering little reduction at higher frequencies. Attenuation peaks at 160 Hz, where 21 dB attenuation is provided over that provided by the helmet. The overall SPL is reduced from

---

[2] Measurements were taken from the pilot position during cruise, with the main door shut and loadmaster window open.

90.4 dB(A) under the ALPHA helmet to 77.7 dB(A) when the ANR system is added.

This particular condition was selected to illustrate a further point. Present military regulations allow a Permissible Daily Exposure Duration of 85 dB(A) for an eight hour day (Department of Defence, 1992). A pilot wearing only the ALPHA helmet while flying in this condition could safely operate the aircraft for 2 hours, 17 minutes, which is not an operationally viable time frame. The addition of an ANR system enables the pilot to operate the aircraft for operationally realistic durations of over 4 hours.

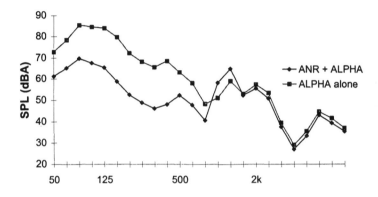

**Figure 25.3**
**At-ear noise levels at the pilot position for a typical flying condition in the Black Hawk helicopter, with pilot wearing (a) an ALPHA helmet and (b) an ALPHA helmet plus ANR system.**

The specific flight condition chosen here is not the highest noise level to which aircrew are exposed. Some recordings made outside the Black Hawk reached 114 dB(A) even under an ALPHA helmet, further highlighting the need for additional attenuation under some circumstances (King et al., 1996). Similar situations abound in other aircraft, including some civil aircraft.

It has been demonstrated here that ANR can be used in conjunction with passive HPDs, in this case a helmet, to provide an integrated attenuation factor which is far greater than the attenuation provided by either device used alone. This should act to reduce the potential for long-term hearing damage to aircrew flying helicopters and propeller driven fixed wing aircraft.

## Conclusion

Situations where hearing protection is required above that provided by a helmet have been presented and it has been suggested that these situations are not isolated to the aircraft presented. Helicopters typically produce high levels of low frequency noise - ANR impacts on just these frequencies. In conjunction with a passive HPD, ANR provides excellent attenuation across the entire frequency range. Evidence has also been cited showing that ANR improves speech intelligibility over communications channels, an enormous benefit in the helicopter environment where communication is often required between members in the front and rear of the aircraft. ANR can be incorporated into an existing helmet or headset and as such does not introduce weight or discomfort issues.

ANR systems rely on power and are therefore open to possible power failures. Most systems include power backup and communications failsafe however - therefore, at worst, the system will provide communications and attenuation not less than that provided by the passive HPD alone.

### The future of ANR

From the discussion presented above, ANR could be expected to be found in wide use within the aviation environment. However, this is not the case. The initial excitement over what ANR could offer has not translated into broad usage, nor abundant commercial production. In fact, it is disappointing to see the small technological improvement in ANR systems over the past decade. Industry has not taken up the challenge, presumably because of a hesitancy toward the desire represented in the market. Once usage increases, system cost will not only ultimately reduce, but system improvements will ensue. The introduction of digital ANR systems for instance would allow a broader range of frequencies to be attenuated; specific acoustic environments could even be 'tuned' into the system, where a defined frequency component is targeted by the user.

The development of ANR technology should be encouraged and present systems, that offer excellent attenuation characteristics and therefore protection, should be considered by current crews operating any helicopter or propeller powered fixed wing aircraft.

### References

Chan, J. & Simpson, C. (1990). *Comparison of speech intelligibility in cockpit noise using SPH-4 flight helmet with and without active noise reduction* (USAAVSCOM TR 90-G-1). Washington, D.C.: NASA.

Cook, R. (1997). *Acoustic characteristics of Kiowa, Iroquois and Black Hawk aircraft* (NAL commissioned report, No. 159). NSW, Australia: National Acoustics Laboratory.

Defence Helicopter World (1988). Turning noise around. *Defence Helicopter World*, Jun/Jul, 22-24.

Department of Defence. (1992). *Hearing conservation in the Australian Defence Force and the Department of Defence* (Defence Instruction (General) PERS 19-4). Canberra, Australia: Department of Defence.

Howlett, J.T., Clevenson, S.A., Rupf, J.A., & Snyder, W.J. (1977). *Interior noise reduction in a large civil helicopter* (TN D-8477). Washington, DC: NASA.

James, S.H., & Harpur, K.M.T. (1990). *In-flight assessment of a helmet-mounted Active Noise Reduction system in Sea Harrier FRS1* (TM MM33). Farnborough, UK: Royal Aerospace Establishment.

King, R.B., & Foran, D.A. (1992). *In-flight evaluation of noise levels and assessment of active noise reduction systems in the Seahawk S-70B-2 helicopter* (ARL-TR-9). Melbourne, Australia: DSTO, Aeronautical Research Laboratory.

King, R.B., Saliba, A.J., Brock, J.R., & James, S.H. (1997). *Assessment of a helmet mounted active noise reduction system in the Sikorsky S-70A-9 Black Hawk helicopter* (DSTO-TR-0574). Melbourne, Australia: DSTO, Aeronautical and Maritime Research Laboratory.

King, R.B., Saliba, A.J., Creed, D.C., & Brock, J.R. (1996). *Assessment of noise levels in and around the Sikorsky S-70A-9 Black Hawk helicopter.* (DSTO-TR-0300). Melbourne, Australia: DSTO, Aeronautical and Maritime Research Laboratory.

Rogers, I.E.C. (1996). *An assessment of the benefits Active Noise Reduction systems provide to speech intelligibility in aircraft noise environments* (DRA/AS/MMI/TR96015/1). Farnborough, UK: Defence Research Agency.

Rylands, J.M. (1990). *Assessing the efficacy of active noise reduction.* Paper presented at Defence Science Symposium, Ottawa, Canada.

# Part 4
# AIR TRAFFIC CONTROL

# 26  Just another typical pilot error

*Bert Ruitenberg*
*International Federation of Air Traffic Controllers'*
*Associations (IFATCA)*

## Introduction

One morning in October 1996, a TWR-controller at Schiphol Airport (Amsterdam, The Netherlands) observed that an inbound aircraft was deviating from the ILS localiser. This observation was done on an electronic Traffic Situation Display, for at the time the cloud base was around 200 feet AGL while the height of the tower is 300 feet - in other words, the tower was in IMC (Instrument Meteorological Conditions). The visibility (Runway Visual Range) was approximately 500 meters.

The TWR-controller notified the radar controller by intercom, and informed the pilot of the aircraft concerned by radiotelephony (R/T) that he was not on the localiser. The pilot acknowledged this by saying 'roger, continuing approach'. Another two or three transmissions of this kind were exchanged, until the point where the TWR-controller decided to instruct the aircraft to go around. The R/T-tapes later revealed that this instruction coincided with a transmission by the pilot in which he announced the execution of a missed approach.

On commencement of the missed approach, the aircraft (an Airbus 300, of a foreign operator) was some 0.6 Nautical Miles from the runway threshold, at an altitude of 200 feet. Next, instead of climbing to 2000 feet as specified in the missed approach procedure, the aircraft continued to fly at 200 feet or below, while drifting considerably to the left of the runway track. It overflew an aircraft at the holding point for the departure-runway, and also an extension of the terminal building where another aircraft was pushing back, at very low altitude. From both aircraft on the ground comments were made on the R/T-frequencies, and in both cases the pilots had identified the aircraft markings. Note that the cloud base was at 200 feet....

After passing the terminal building, the Airbus finally began to gain altitude and also corrected its track to the right (as per the instructions of the TWR-controller). It was subsequently given a new radar line-up for an ILS-approach, from which it landed without further complications.

Of this incident, an entry was made in the log at Approach Control. But since the TWR-crew realised that the aircraft had actually passed close to the tower, at an altitude that would have required them to look *down* to see the aircraft from the visual control room (tower cab) if the weather hadn't precluded that, the war-stories about the event began spreading among the ATC-staff real fast.

So, when a few days later it was my duty (as Supervisor) to follow-up on the entry in the log, I had already heard several versions of what had happened, and under what circumstances. The general view seemed to be that this was 'just another typical pilot error'. This inspired me to ask for permission from the Head of ATC Schiphol to conduct an internal investigation into the ATC Human Factors aspects of the case, if any. My boss readily agreed to it, provided I would coordinate my investigation with the department that was responsible for the 'traditional' investigation.

## The human factors investigation

Already at the initial stage of the investigation, it became apparent that the ATC-side was perhaps slightly more implicated in what had happened than they would care to be. Based on the then existing ATC-orders, the cold facts are that, at the time of the incident, the status (phase) of the Low Visibility Operation was incorrect; the use of two independent landing-runways for all categories of aircraft was incorrect; the choice of departure-runway was incorrect; and the tailwind-limit for the runway on which the incident occurred was exceeded.

So, the question I set out to answer in my investigation was: why had the ATC-crew (TWR and APP) been operating in violation of these safety-critical rules and procedures?

*Background: Rules and procedures*

The applicable rules and procedures were laid down in three different ATC-orders (internal documents, detailing how ATC Schiphol is to operate under various specific circumstances and/or conditions): ILS Operations, Low Visibility Operations, and Use of the Runway-system.

Ever since the first version of the Low Visibility Operations order had been created in the mid-eighties, it has been common practice at Schiphol TWR and APP to physically revert to the books, whenever the visibility and/or cloud base warranted the application of Low Visibility procedures. It was agreed and accepted that the rules and procedures were too complex for anyone to know by heart, and therefore controllers would simply look up the procedures to be used in the ATC-order when required.

The crews who were on duty that October-morning acted no differently: they had pulled the Low Visibility order from the bookshelves, and checked to find what procedure to use. The problem is, this gave them only about 25% of the rules and procedures they needed - without them knowing it!

At this point it is important to note that the mentioned three orders had recently been revised. The dates effective were: 7 January 1996 for 'ILS Operations', 1 April 1996 for 'Low Visibility Operations', and 15 August 1996 for 'Use of the Runway-system'. Remember that the incident occurred in October 1996 - on probably one of the first days when the weather-conditions were such that a low visibility operation was conducted on that particular runway-combination.

A thorough analysis of the three orders resulted in the following findings:

- the orders contained errors;
- the orders were incomplete;
- the orders were contradicting;
- the orders contained no cross-references;
- the orders contained multiple listings of conditions, without specifying how to act if those conditions were *not* met;
- allocation of responsibilities in the orders was unclear;
- the orders were unsuitable for use as 'checklist'.

For the ATC-crews on duty that morning this meant that they weren't even aware that they were supposed to also apply procedures laid down in the other orders. As usual, they had consulted the Low Visibility Operations order, and were handling the traffic to the best of their ability taking into account the items mentioned in that order.

Of the 'cold facts' listed above, the *incorrect status of the Low Visibility Operation* was a result of the unclear allocation of responsibilities in the order: half of the crew were under the impression that the correct phase was in force, the other half was under the impression that a conscious decision had been made to not declare that phase active since the weather was expected to improve any minute. This ambiguity could exist because the responsibility to determine and communicate the active phase was not clearly stated in the order. The *incorrect use of two independent landing-runways for all categories of aircraft* could occur because first of all the text relating to this procedure was only incorporated in the order Use of the Runway-system (without a reference to it in the Low Visibility Operations order), and secondly this text appeared to be wrong! It had been the intention, when writing the order, to allow the operation in the way it was performed that day in October - it's just that for some reason there was a text in the order stating the exact opposite.

With respect to the *incorrect choice of departure-runway*, this had a direct relation with the incorrect phase: in the phase where half the crew thought they were in, that particular runway can be used for departures. In the other phase, use of that runway in combination with the other two landing-runways is prohibited, but since none of the crewmembers of the other half were directly involved with the departures this wasn't seriously queried. Finally, the *exceeding of the tailwind-limit* is an example of practice overtaking procedure: the limits mentioned in the orders originated from the days when a totally different generation of aircraft dominated the skies. Today's generation is capable of accepting higher cross- and tailwind-limits than the earlier ones, but this fact had never been incorporated in the ATC-orders. The controllers of course were aware of the improved aircraft-performance, so they had long adopted the practice of offering the use of a runway with a high cross- or tailwind to pilots and then wait for the pilots' response to the offer - where no objection meant the wind was acceptable.

*Other factors*

Of course there also were other factors that contributed to the incident. Analysis of the weather reports from the meteorological office, and the forecasts issued by that same office, showed that the forecasts and trend-reports that morning had been continually too optimistic. The initial forecasts mentioned values for cloud base and visibility that would not have necessitated the use of Low Visibility procedures. When the actual weather-reports began to show a lower cloud base and a lower visibility than in the forecast, an amended forecast was issued which mentioned an expected improvement from the then current conditions. Subsequent actual reports showed that in fact a further deterioration occurred, even to below Cat. II limits. The worst conditions (in terms of cloud base and visibility) existed close to the time when the incident took place. Shortly after that moment, the forecasted improvement indeed began to materialise.

For the ATC crews on duty that morning, this meant that they never had a chance to anticipate the weather would deteriorate to the point where the limits for use of that particular runway-combination were exceeded. Even if a crewmember would have been aware that at a certain moment the cloud base or visibility was lower than authorised, the trend report and the forecast could have led him/her to believe that conditions would improve rapidly, thus perhaps discouraging him/her from taking any action to initiate a runway-change.

However, it is highly probable that each crewmember was concentrating on his/her task to the extent that they were too busy to maintain an overall view of the (weather) situation. Since the original forecast had not given cause to expect Low Visibility Operations, the number of aircraft inbound Schiphol was high as usual. The actual weather had necessitated Low Visibility Operations, which implies the application of wider separation-standards on final approach. This of course resulted in the landing-capacity being less than the demand. It became very busy in the airspace around Schiphol, and ATC was under considerable pressure to safely handle all the traffic.

Another factor that was identified, was that a malfunction had developed in one particular traffic light at the airport. This traffic light is one of a total of six sets of lights that can show either red or green, and is used to control tow-traffic (i.e., aircraft that are pulled by a truck or tow-vehicle) that needs to cross an active runway. Normally, the lights are red and when a towed aircraft needs to cross the runway, the truck driver requests the TWR to switch the light to green. The TWR-controller who is responsible for the runway involved subsequently decides when the tow can cross, and switches the light from red to green by means of a button on his console.

That morning, about half an hour before the incident, a malfunction occurred in the most-used traffic light for crossing the same runway where the Airbus would make its approach later. The immediate result in the field was that the lights remained red, so no tow-traffic could cross. The immediate result in the tower was a series of high-pitched electronic beeps that became audible, to alert the crew that a failure had occurred. Normally, such an audio-alarm could be reset to stop the beeping, but for some reason that morning the beeping didn't stop. Several of the TWR crewmembers commented afterwards that they considered those beeping sounds a real distraction and nuisance at a time when their concentration was required most.

Meanwhile, an ad-hoc solution was found to the problem of what to do with the tow-traffic that was waiting to cross the runway. A follow-me car, capable of maintaining radio-contact with the TWR, was dispatched to the crossing point, and would guide the tow-traffic across the runway after permission from the TWR-controller. At a suitable moment such permission was given, but to the surprise of the controller there was also a second towed aircraft crossing the runway, behind the car and the first tow. This forced the controller to instruct an aircraft on short final to make a go-around. (NB keep bearing in mind that the TWR was in IMC. The controller had to rely on radio-reports, and observations on his Surface Movement Radar and the mentioned Traffic Situation Display - a derivative of the Approach radar.)

Following the go-around, the controller needed to coordinate with the radar controller in order to inform him why the go-around was made, and to obtain instructions for heading and altitude for the aircraft involved, with a view to fit it in with the other traffic. This co-ordination took place at around the time when the Airbus 300 - the aircraft from the incident - reported 'established on the ILS' to the radar controller, and was transferred to the TWR-controller.

A last contributing factor has its origins in the relief-scheme used at Schiphol. The TWR-controller's duty began just 15 minutes before the incident. When he entered the tower, the Low Visibility operation on that specific runway-combination was already in full swing. Even if he had expressed his doubts regarding the appropriateness of the operation in relation to the actual weather, it would have been very difficult (and certainly: most inconvenient) to change to a more suitable combination. So, rather than strongly expressing his doubts, he relieved another controller and began working the runway on which the malfunction in the traffic light had occurred shortly before. The aircraft that he instructed to make a go-around, because of the unexpected crossing tow, was the second aircraft he handled that morning; the Airbus 300, deviating from the localiser, was his third. I guess any controller will agree that this is not quite the optimal start of a working-day....

All factors listed above relate to ground-based events. An investigation by the Dutch Civil Aviation Authority (CAA) however has yielded some interesting insights to what happened on the flight-deck of the Airbus, both before and during the incident.

*Meanwhile, in the cockpit*

Firstly, the crew had expected to be radar-vectored to a 'longer' final than they actually were given. Under Low Visibility conditions, it is normal for an aircraft performing an auto-coupled ILS-approach to first intercept the localiser (i.e. the electronic beam representing the extended runway-centreline) and then intercept the glidepath (i.e., the electronic beam representing the optimum descent-angle). In this case, the aircraft was vectored to a position where in fact the glidepath was intercepted *before* the localiser. Incredibly, what happened next is described in a 1994 NASA paper by Asaf Degani and Earl L. Wiener called 'On the design of flight-deck procedures':

> *When a glass-cockpit aircraft is intercepting the glide slope and localiser while HEADING SELECT mode is engaged, and subsequently selecting APPROACH mode before the 'localiser' and 'glide slope' are captured, there is a possibility for a false capture: the "glide slope" will capture and the plane will start to descend while maintaining the heading displayed in the HEADING SELECT window (and not the LOCALISER course). The concern is obvious -- the aircraft will descend, but not to the runway. The only feedback available to the flight crews is on the ADI: the LOCALISER symbol will be armed (white), as opposed to being engaged (green). This information can not be obtained from the mode control panel (MCP) -- because according to the MCP logic, once APPROACH mode is armed, the button is lit (regardless of whether the "localiser" has been captured or not).*

To put it in other words, as a result of flaws in the (design of the) aircraft automation, the crew was under the impression that they were correctly positioned on the ILS and therefore didn't act on the TWR-controller's message that they were deviating. Only when visual ground-contact was made (i.e. when breaking clouds at 200 feet) did they realise they were incorrectly aligned, and initiated a go-around.

Secondly, the crew was surprised by the strong tailwind during the approach. This tailwind gave them a high groundspeed, which meant they had less time than usual to perform their checklists. This may have caused them to devote less attention to the navigational instruments than desired.

Thirdly, the crew reported that the response of the throttles had been inexplicably slow after initiating the go-around. The (initial) CAA-report gives no further explanation for this phenomenon, but I would like to venture launching a theory about it. I submit that it is possible that, when activating the go-around lever, the crew inadvertently de-activated the auto-throttle by accidentally hitting a wrong lever located closely to the other one. This may have caused the aircraft to adopt a go-around attitude, without adding the required power for its climb. Only after the crew noticed that the aircraft was failing to gain altitude, power was added manually by pushing the throttles forward, and the aircraft began to climb.

(My theory is based on an accident that occurred at Fukuoka Airport, Japan, also with an Airbus 300, where the exact reverse happened in the cockpit: the crew intended to shut off the autothrottle, but accidentally activated the go-around mode. As the aircraft commenced its unwanted go-around manoeuvre, the crew literally fought it to the ground...)

## Results of the investigation

Returning now to the ATC-side of the incident, there are three points worth mentioning as a result of the investigation.

1. This incident has served to raise the awareness of all ATC-crews at Schiphol on the criticality of Low Visibility Operations. Indeed, since October 1996, several other instances were reported where controllers have taken decisive actions under similar conditions to avoid similar problems.
2. The Human Factors approach in my investigation has triggered a review of the ATC-internal incident investigation process.
3. A complete review of the Schiphol ATC-orders was conducted.

In the following paragraphs this last point will be explored in more depth.

Until the review, all ATC-orders for Schiphol were printed on green paper. This use of colour was historically intended to enable easy distinction between the Schiphol orders and those for the Amsterdam Area Control Centre (printed on blue paper), a facility located in the same building. Originally, the Schiphol orders even were on pink paper, but after an updating-exercise in the early nineties green paper was chosen to distinguish the updated orders from the older ones. Apparently at some point there had been a problem with the supply of green paper, for the first updated orders were printed on paper of a lighter shade of green than the orders that were revised in 1996, which were all printed on dark green paper.

In the review it was discovered that many controllers had experienced difficulties in reading the print on the dark green paper, particularly under low lighting-conditions (e.g., nightshifts). Since furthermore it was determined that the only place where the orders of Schiphol and Amsterdam ACC ever are physically close is the printshop, it was decided to abandon the colour-distinction and print the Schiphol orders on plain white paper.

A major step in the review was the decision to clearly distinguish Rules, Procedures and Explanatory text in the new orders. The distinction would be made visible by using different typographies for the three categories:

Rules are printed with a shaded background.
**Procedures are printed in bold font,**
*Explanatory text is in italics.*

At some point in the discussion it was considered to use colour to distinguish the categories, but in view of the cost involved with making copies of the orders (and the future amendments) for all controllers and assistant-controllers at Schiphol, it was decided to stick to black-and-white print. Purely from a Human Factors point of view however, using colourprint to differentiate between categories of information seems like a good idea.

The category 'Rules' comprises material from ICAO, regional aviation authorities, national aviation authorities, company rules and/or local rules. The one thing they have in common (for purpose of the ATC-orders) is that they are laid down somewhere in writing, which means that when a rule is quoted in the orders a reference to the source (or origin) of that rule can be incorporated. The method chosen at Schiphol is to use footnotes in the text whenever a rule appears, but other methods may be effective too.

A further (theoretical) attribute of 'Rules' is that they should be followed by a 'Procedure' in order to turn them into practices. This simple rule-of-thumb proved to be very useful when reviewing the orders, especially when determining the lay-out of (pages of) texts.

With each 'Procedure', care was taken to ensure that there was no ambiguity or doubt as to what it is for, and whose responsibility it is to carry it out. If a certain procedure could only be executed when certain conditions were met, specifications were included for how to act in case one or more of those conditions were *not* met, and whose responsibility this is.

Whenever texts in one order had a relation to another order, a clear cross-reference was made in both orders or the text was simply included in both. This also applies to individual orders: whenever something was mentioned in one section or paragraph that had a relation to another section or paragraph, the text was either repeated or a cross-reference appeared.

The review also achieved that existing errors and contradictions in and between the orders were eliminated. This may appear to be a simple task, but in fact it wasn't: many of the old texts were there for a historical reason (e.g. to counter an incident that had happened once), and it was very hard to retrieve or reconstruct such origins since little or no documentation about it was on file. So, as an aside, from the beginning of the review files were set up and kept for each order to record and document the rationale behind the Procedures and Explanatory texts. Where errors and contradictions were difficult to resolve, the philosophy governing the operation was redefined and used as a guideline to formulate new (or unambiguous) procedures.

In this way, most of the shortcomings in the orders as identified in the investigation were repaired. One that remained to be solved was how to deal with the complexity, and indeed sheer volume, of the new set of orders. Although they now were very comprehensive, it was foreseen they would not lend themselves easily for reference when needed during operational work, despite the fact they all contain an extensive list of contents at the first pages.

It was therefore decided to also produce a set of Quick Reference Charts and a series of Checklists, as companions to the orders. The QRCs contain an overview of the relevant procedures and conditions for each conceivable runway-combination, divided in procedures for good weather, marginal weather and low visibility. They do not contain all details of the procedures, but present the reader with the most significant points from the procedures, which are deemed essential to be able to perform the operation as intended.

The Checklists are meant as a memory-aid for the Supervisors, to ensure that all aspects of specific processes are covered, e.g., when changing from one operational mode to the next.

The new lay-out of the orders together with the main changes in the philosophy and content of the procedures were introduced to the controllers and assistant-controllers of Schiphol TWR/APP in five consecutive one-day classroom courses, held in the week preceding the date on which the new orders were to become effective.

**Summary**

In order for Procedures to be followed and adhered to, they should be well-designed and easily accessible. Accessible here means both *available when required*, and *understandable*. The way Procedures are presented to those who have to apply them in their daily work can make the difference between 'good' and 'bad' practices, and hence has a significant influence on flight safety. This is equally valid for the introduction of new or changed Procedures, which more often than not is done by just distributing the changes on paper rather than preparing a tailored introduction-programme.

- Procedures should be error-free
- Procedures should be unambiguous
- Procedures should be comprehensive
- Procedures should not contradict each other
- Procedures should be easy to understand and apply
- Procedures should clearly state who is responsible for their application
- When Procedures contain (listings of) conditions, it should be clear what is to be done and by whom in case any or all of the conditions are not met
- When a Procedure relates to a Rule, it should be clearly indicated what Rule it is and where that Rule is laid down
- Documentation about the rationale behind Procedures should be kept on file

# 27 Transition to the future: Displaying flight progress data in air traffic control

*Carol A. Manning*
*Federal Aviation Administration, Civil Aeromedical*
*Institute*

## Introduction

En route air traffic controllers in the United States are responsible for ensuring the safe, orderly, and expeditious progression of aircraft between controlled airports and the arrival and departure of aircraft entering or leaving uncontrolled airports. To accomplish this, controllers observe aircraft positions on a radar display and review flight plan information. One method of reviewing flight plan information involves the use of paper flight progress strips (hereafter called "flight strips.") A flight strip contains printed flight plan information about an aircraft (see Figure 27.1). A controller may review flight plan information by glancing at the flight strip or may access the information by using a keyboard to display either textual flight data on the Computer Readout Device (CRD) or a line showing the route on the Plan View Display (PVD).

Besides reviewing stored flight plan information, controllers also write information on flight strips. Certain information is recorded to remind controllers of tasks they have completed so they do not repeat them, such as transferring communications for a specific aircraft, or tasks they still need to perform, such as passing heading or speed assignments to the next sector.

Controllers may also use flight strips to anticipate possible conflicts, though the presence of an aircraft target on the radar display usually initiates conflict identification in a radar environment. However, in some cases, if an aircraft has not yet arrived at the sector, if radar coverage is not available, if aircraft are in hold status, or if aircraft are arriving at or departing from an uncontrolled airport, strips may be used more frequently to plan activities or anticipate possible conflicts.

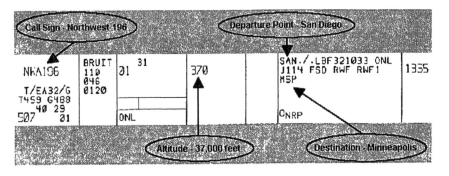

**Figure 27.1**
**Example of a flight strip**

The FAA has long been interested in eliminating the use of paper flight strips. The use of paper is not consistent with FAA's goal of transitioning to a fully automated environment. Information written on the paper flight strips cannot be transferred electronically to other controllers. Furthermore, the cost of flight strip printers and paper is high. A significant amount of effort is also spent identifying duplicate strips that are not necessary to view and ensuring that the strips that are displayed are updated with most recent versions.

The Initial Sector Suite (ISSS) system (U.S. Department of Transportation, 1989) was originally intended to replace and upgrade en route equipment and capabilities, including using electronic flight strips. The ISSS concept was replaced by the Display System Replacement (DSR, U. S. Department of Transportation, 1996). DSR is intended only to replace equipment and not provide additional functionality beyond what is included in the current system. Thus, electronic strips will not be included in DSR, and paper flight strips will be used. Eventually, software enhancements will be made to DSR, such as the Initial Conflict Probe (ICP), which will provide alternative electronic methods for displaying flight plan data, either through a graphic display or lists of aircraft with associated flight information. When such enhancements become available, paper flight strips should no longer be necessary.

In the meantime, the FAA faces a potential problem of how to transition to electronic flight data because most of today's controllers were trained to use and rely on flight strips. While some feel they can't control traffic effectively without strips, others say they use strips only because they are required to do so. To change the way they access flight data and record their activities, controllers will have to change a highly over-learned behaviour pattern.

Two lines of investigation are being conducted to address questions about this situation. The first examines controllers' perspectives about the need to use flight strips. The second examines the effects on controller performance and workload associated with various ways to reduce the use of paper flight strips.

## Controller perspectives

*Survey*

The first line of investigation has been to identify controllers' opinions about the need to use flight strips. A secondary purpose has been to obtain some preliminary ideas from field controllers about what methods might successfully replace the use of paper flight strips. To this end, an open-ended survey was conducted in June and July of 1997. Controllers were asked to describe circumstances that may make flight strips essential to sector operations, to name circumstances in which flight strips are currently required by regulations, but are not needed, and to suggest alternative methods for replacing flight strips. They were also asked to identify current strip marking procedures that can be recorded in different ways or replaced by other means.

Surveys were distributed to managers at en route field facilities, who then made them available to controllers and supervisors. Two hundred and twenty-three forms were completed and returned. Results of the survey are summarised here. Responses to Question 1, which dealt with circumstances making flight strips essential to operations, are shown in Table 27.1 below.

The rows in Table 27.1 show the categories of circumstances for which the responding controllers thought flight strips were needed. The highest percentage of circumstances requiring the use of flight strips were in the Record Information category (42%) with Planning (21%) and Display Information (17%) as the next most frequent response categories. These categories are described in the following paragraphs.

Information that controllers thought needed to be recorded included Wrong Altitude for Direction of Flight (WAFDOF) notations; passing heading and speed assignments; remarks; flight plan cancellations; amending proposed routes to conform to standard, non-published, preferential arrival and departure routes; pointouts; vectoring/sequencing notations; pilot requests; aircraft problems or emergencies; aircraft off course; recording departure clearances or approach information for aircraft at uncontrolled airports; weather deviations; transitioning aircraft; status of Military Operational Areas (MOAs); and holding information.

**Table 27.1**
**Circumstances that make flight strips essential to sector operations by suggested alternatives**

| | | CATEGORIES OF ALTERNATIVES | | | | | | |
|---|---|---|---|---|---|---|---|---|
| | | Deletion (non-usage)/ Reduction | Adapt Existing Procedures | Utilize Existing Software | Develop Written Alternative | Adapt Existing Software/ Electronic Alternatives | Not Applicable | *N* Responses |
| *CIRCUMSTANCES* | Strips Nonessential | 5 | 0 | 7 | 1 | 6 | 1 | 20 |
| | Display Information | 2 | 0 | 2 | 1 | 30 | 7 | 42 |
| | Record Information | 5 | 2 | 11 | 16 | 53 | 19 | 106 |
| | Planning | 5 | 3 | 1 | 7 | 31 | 6 | 53 |
| | Non-Verbal Communication | 0 | 0 | 0 | 0 | 3 | 0 | 3 |
| | Equipment Malfunction/ Maintenance | 3 | 0 | 1 | 1 | 8 | 3 | 16 |
| | Monitor Sector Workload/ Resource Management | 0 | 1 | 0 | 0 | 1 | 0 | 2 |
| | Non-Applicable | 6 | 0 | 0 | 0 | 4 | 0 | 10 |
| | *N* Responses | 26 | 6 | 22 | 26 | 136 | 36 | 252 |

Planning activities that utilize flight strips included non-radar and oceanic Air Traffic Control (ATC) in general, planning for crossing traffic entering the sector, sequencing aircraft with different performance characteristics, viewing multiple flight plans at the same time to choose the best option, sequencing during metering, anticipating future sector activity, and planning for arrivals and departures at uncontrolled airports.

The following activities, were noted as requiring display of information on flight strips: verifying destination/route of flight, examining more than one flight plan at the same time, determining aircraft type, identifying overdue aircraft, ensuring all activities regarding a flight are completed before it is handed off to the next sector, verifying altitude on initial call, determining if clearances have been issued, and verifying that flight plan changes are entered in the computer.

In Table 27.1, columns show the categories of alternatives that controllers thought might serve as replacements for flight strips in the circumstances where they were thought to be needed. Most of the suggested alternatives to flight strips involved adapting existing software or developing new software (54%). Some respondents (14%) said that no alternatives were applicable to the circumstances listed. About 10% said that strip usage could be eliminated or reduced, and 10% said that a written alternative to flight strips should be provided. About 39% of the suggestions regarding software modifications or improvements involved recording information, while 23% involved use of planning tools and 22% involved alternate ways to display information.

*Interviews*

After the surveys were collected and analyzed, we decided to collect more information about the way controllers use flight strips. Interviews with 22 controllers were conducted at four en route facilities. Participants were asked if they use the information in each field of a flight strip, if there are other ways currently available to obtain or record the same information, and if they could recommend alternative methods to display or record information that do not involve the use of flight strips.

The results of the interviews indicated that four fields on the flight strip provide information about the recency of the strips and the sector to which the strips should be delivered, and do not otherwise assist control operations. However, as long as paper strips are used, it is necessary to determine which strip is most recent and to which sector the strip should be delivered. If one printer per sector is available, delivery of strips should not be a problem, but some facilities have and will continue to use one printer to print strips that will be delivered to more than one sector. Another seven fields on the flight strip are used primarily for nonradar operations and are not necessary in a radar environment.

Information in ten other fields can be accessed on the computer. Controllers differed about whether they would prefer to look at a flight strip to obtain some of the information in the ten fields, or make the keystrokes required to access the information on the computer. Their preferences seemed to be based upon habits developed at their specific facilities. Most controllers at two of the facilities visited were comfortable making computer entries to obtain information, while controllers from the other two facilities preferred to glance at the strips instead of making a computer entry to obtain information.

Some controllers considered flight strips necessary to write information such as holding instructions and clearance information for aircraft arriving at or departing from uncontrolled airports. They thought other kinds of information such as speed and heading assignments might be recorded elsewhere, on a notepad, for example. Some controllers liked the idea of using a notepad to record information. Others preferred to use flight strips because they can be sorted, relevant information is already printed on them, and does not have to be written again.

The controllers were concerned about eliminating paper flight strips completely, based on the chance of a radar outage, considering both existing and future equipment. At the same time, many thought that much of the workload involved in controlling air traffic results from the requirement to maintain strip marking and posting. One controller said that twice as many controllers are needed to control traffic and manage the strips. Controllers typically noted that they work differently when part of the team than when they work alone, specifically with regard to the amount of information they write on flight strips. Some controllers thought that only about 10% of the information they write on strips is relevant to them, while the remaining 90% is written only because regulations require it. Many controllers thought they might be able to look at the strips when they are posted at the sector, then remove most of them from the bay once communications have been established with the aircraft. If an unusual circumstance arises, the strips could then be re-posted.

The controllers were then asked to speculate about how to display information currently contained on flight strips through another method. Two primary methods were suggested: adding information to the data block that tracks with the aircraft target across the situation display, and providing lists of flight data that would be located at the side of the situation display or on an adjacent monitor. When considering information that might be added to the data block, some controllers thought it might be valuable to include assigned headings and speeds, holding information, or aircraft type in a fourth line on the data block. Some preferred that this information be displayed in an extra line in the data block, rather than time-sharing it with information already present, because shared information would not always be visible. Other controllers were concerned about the data block being too big if an extra line were added. They thought that a larger data block would result in their having to move data blocks more frequently. Some thought that more than five or six aircraft in the sector could be difficult to manage.

Some facilities display aircraft destination in the data block. Ten facilities currently use a one-character destination patch that is displayed all the time and three others use a three-letter identifier that time-shares with ground speed. Because the one-character destination patch allows fewer than 30 airports to be displayed, an aircraft's destination is not always available in the data block. However, having the destination in the data block doesn't guarantee that the controller knows the route the aircraft will take. However, controllers generally said they use flight strips less frequently when the destination is in the data block.

Most controllers interviewed would be willing to obtain the information currently located on flight strips from some other source if they could glance at a list, for example, or bring up the information with only one keystroke. The lists available with the current software were considered inadequate because they do not contain necessary information. Controllers also considered it desirable to be able to examine flight plans for multiple aircraft at the same time, a capability not available in today's system. Controllers from a facility that is testing a prototype conflict probe system, the User Request Evaluation Tool (URET; McFarland, 1997) considered the flight list provided with that system valuable.

### Effects on controller performance and workload

It is necessary to conduct empirical studies about the effects of reducing the number of flight strips used, or changing the method for displaying flight progress data to supplement surveys and interviews of controller opinions. It is possible that controller opinions might overemphasize negative effects of such changes because the controllers who expressed those opinions haven't yet developed a strategy for working under different conditions. It is also possible that controllers might be overly enthusiastic about the effects of reducing the use of flight strips, resulting in unanticipated problems if changes are made in the operational environment without first testing their effects. Relevant research has been conducted over the past several years to examine the effects of alternative flight strip usage on controller workload

263

and performance. Another project, currently underway, is investigating a specific research question regarding the posting of flight strips. These two efforts are described below.

*Vortac studies*

From 1990 to 1995, several studies were conducted in support of the ISSS system development that assessed the effects on controller cognitive processing and performance of converting from paper to electronic flight strips. There was concern that implementing automated flight progress data could have unforeseen negative consequences. It has been noted in a variety of studies (Hopkin, 1990; Craik & Lockheart, 1972) that using multiple sensory modalities to process data, for example, examining the strips visually and touching them at the same time, could reinforce understanding of interrelationships between stimuli, in this case, aircraft flight paths. If the physical movement of flight strips, that is, initial placement, sorting, and offsetting, were eliminated because of the use of electronic flight strips, it might have a negative effect on controllers' ability to keep the "picture," that is, keeping track of what needs to be done to maintain separation between aircraft. Moreover, some proposals for display of electronic flight strips could increase workload and reduce understanding. For example, some proposals did not retain the history of flight plan changes. Others were not able to display all the electronic strips at the same time so if too many electronic strips were present, the controller might have to scroll through a list to view them all. With some proposals, controllers would have to learn many new number of computer entries to change information on the strip.

Because no capability was available that allowed simulation of electronic strips in a real-time ATC scenario, a series of studies was conducted that assessed functional equivalents of flight strips. The first two studies were conducted at the en route Radar Training Facility laboratory at the FAA Academy. En route Academy instructors served as participants. In the earliest of these studies (Vortac, Edwards, Fuller, & Manning, 1993), strip holders were glued together to prevent controllers from sorting the strips. Also, a flight strip containing reduced information was used, and controllers were not allowed to write on the strips. Controllers in this experimental condition granted more requests and granted them sooner than did controllers in the baseline condition, who controlled traffic normally using flight strips. Other cognitive measures, ATC-related activities, and performance were similar for the two conditions. However, controllers in the experimental condition averaged just one more route change remaining at the end of the scenario than did those in the control condition.

A second study (Vortac, Barile, Albright, Truitt, Manning, & Bain, 1994) examined the effects of two types of simulated electronic flight strips. One type of electronic flight strips was updated automatically and needed no involvement from the controllers (full automation). The other type of electronic flight strips could be moved, highlighted, and deleted by the controllers, but the information on them could not be updated (partial automation). Although the controllers preferred the paper strips to the electronic versions, use of electronic strips did not affect their performance negatively. Moreover, when controllers were in the full automation condition, they granted slightly more requests and granted them sooner than when they were in the normal strip condition.

A third study (Albright, Truitt, Barile, Vortac, & Manning, 1995) compared controller performance and workload when using flight strips normally and when no flight strips were present. By this time in the research program, it appeared that electronic flight strips were not going to be implemented with new en route replacement hardware. This study was conducted in the training lab at a field facility using operational controllers as participants. Not having flight strips had some effect on controllers. When they did not have flight strips, they took longer to grant pilot requests than when they did have flight strips. They also compensated for not having flight strips by using the Flight Plan Readout function more frequently than when they did have flight strips. At the same time, controllers not using flight strips looked at the PVD almost 5 minutes longer (out of a 25 minute scenario) than did controllers who used flight strips. Other performance measures were similar, and subjective workload assessments were similar for the two conditions.

A fourth study (Durso, Truitt, Hackworth, Albright, Bleckley, & Manning, in review) compared controller performance and workload when using standard-sized en route flight strips (1 3/8" x 8") and when using smaller (1" x 5") flight strips. Control of radar traffic was not affected but control of nonradar traffic was negatively affected by using the smaller strips. These effects were present for both the radar (R-side) and data (D-side) controllers. Management of the strips was also impaired by using the 1" x 5" flight strips. R-side controllers found working with the 1" x 5" flight strips to be more effortful and frustrating. In spite of the problems, controllers granted the same number of pilot requests and granted them in the same amount of time when using the smaller strips as they did when using the standard-sized strips.

265

These studies do not provide a definitive answer to questions about the role of flight strips in ATC. Some aspects of performance were affected, though control of traffic in a radar environment was not particularly impaired. Controllers compensated for a lack of strips by obtaining the information from the computer. Controllers spent more time looking at the Plan View Display (PVD) when they were not using the flight strips. Overall, it appears that reducing the information printed on flight strips, eliminating the requirement to write on flight strips, or eliminating flight strips altogether may not have a significant effect on controllers in a radar environment. However, these studies did not encompass many different sector types and did not test controllers over a long period of time. The main lesson to be learned from these studies seems to be that the dire circumstances that had been predicted to result if flight strips were automated do not seem likely to occur.

**Current research**

A study, currently underway, will provide information to enable management to make policy decisions about requirements for using flight strips. In preparation for the implementation and use of new air traffic planning and display tools, the Air Traffic Service wants to encourage controllers to rely less on paper flight strips. At the same time, safety cannot be compromised. A test is currently underway to assess the effects on controller workload and performance of reducing requirements to keep flight strips posted for all aircraft under their control. This test would allow flight strips to be removed from the strip bay when:

1) the handoff has been accepted,
2) transfer of communications is complete, and
3) no unusual circumstances, such as aircraft transitioning from radar to nonradar environment, aircraft requiring special handling, all nonradar flights, flights transitioning from automated to non-automated modes of operation, and when holding instructions are issued.

Controllers would not be required to remove flight strips. After a flight strip has been removed, if information is needed, the strip should be located and re-posted in the bay. Strips left in the bay can be marked as the controller team deems appropriate.

Data collection to assess this test procedure was conducted at one facility during the last week of February, 1998. Data will be collected from at least one other facility and possibly a third.

## Summary

While elimination of pieces of paper might seem to be an easy process, it has become a challenge for the FAA to do so. Use of those pieces of paper has become ingrained in much of the controller workforce, and now the FAA must determine how to change this behavior, so the workforce can transition to a paperless environment. Research has suggested that this is not an insurmountable problem because circumstances have been identified in which use of flight strips is not essential. So far, controllers have indicated that, if flight strips are no longer available, a replacement of some sort must be available to allow ready access to flight progress information and/or a way to easily document activities. They do not seem to be too particular about what form that replacement might take. Research may indicate that one method is more efficient, and may contribute to the identification of an effective replacement tool.

Research is currently underway that should provide information about whether it is appropriate for controllers to choose to reduce the number of flight strips posted in the strip bay. If approved, this would be one small step towards a paperless environment that will allow controllers to take advantage of new automated ATC tools.

## References

Albright, C.A., Truitt, T.R., Barile, A.L., Vortac, O.U., & Manning, C.A. (1994). Controlling traffic without flight progress strips: Compensation, workload, performance, and opinion. *Air Traffic Control Quarterly*, 2(4) 229-248.

Durso, F.T., Truitt, T.R., Hackworth, C.A., Albright, C.A., Bleckley, M.K., & Manning, C.A. (In review). Reduced flight progress strips in en route ATC mixed environments.

Hopkin, V.D. (1990). Automated flight strip usage: Lessons from the functions of paper strips. In *Book of Abstracts from the Symposium Challenges in Aviation Human Factors: The National Plan,* (pp 64-64). Vienna, VA: American Institute of Aeronautics and Astronautics, Inc.

McFarland, A.L. (1997). Conflict probe for airspace users and controllers. Air Traffic Technology International 1998: The international review of air traffic technology management (pp. 78-82). Surrey, U.K.: UK & International Press.

Vortac, O.U., Edwards, M.B., Fuller, D.K., & Manning, C.A. (1993). Automation and cognition in air traffic control: An empirical investigation. *Applied Cognitive Psychology, 7,* 731-651.

Vortac, O.U., Barile, A.B., Albright, C.A., Truitt, T.R., Manning, C.A., & Bain, D. (1994). Automation of flight data in air traffic control. In *Proceedings of the Third Practical Aspects of Memory Conference.* Hillsdale, NJ: Lawrence Erlbaum Associates.

US Department of Transportation, Federal Aviation Administration. (1989). *National Airspace System Plan: Facilities, Equipment, Associated Development, and other Capital Needs.* Washington, DC: Author.

US Department of Transportation, Federal Aviation Administration (1996). Display System Replacement (DSR) Overview. Washington, DC: FAA Enroute Domain Integration Team.

# 28 Development of Team Resource Management in European air traffic control

*Manfred Barbarino, Eurocontrol*
*Anne Isaac, Dédale*

## Introduction

In 1990 the European Civil Aviation Conference (ECAC) Transport Ministers decided to harmonise and integrate the European air traffic system in order to maintain and enhance safety and efficiency and to increase capacity. Forecasts of traffic increase in Europe indicated that existing procedures and systems could not cope with these demands. EUROCONTROL was asked to manage the project called EATCHIP, the European Air Traffic Control Harmonisation and Integration Programme, a four-phase programme utilising various domains with allocated objectives, specific tasks and individual implementation programmes for States.

The EATCHIP Human Factors project is concentrating on the development of a harmonised and integrated Human Factors methodology for current and future Air Traffic Management (including Air Traffic Services, Airspace Management and Flow Control Management) conforming to best practice and principles in the areas of human cognition, behaviour, capabilities and performance. The main objective of this work is to develop and apply human factors principles and methods for the best use of human performance and advanced technology.

At present many uncoordinated human factors related activities are carried out in ECAC Member States. Increased awareness and understanding of the benefits of common human resources activities and operational application in the ECAC area currently constitute the most important progress in this field. This includes the growing need for the application of human factors principles and methods in other EATCHIP domains and in particular in future European Air Traffic Management. The work so far has achieved a fundamental structure and processes for the development of a harmonised and integrated human factors methodology for ATS staff and equipment which has to be further developed and implemented in the operational environment in the coming years.

## Team Resource Management

Over the last 20 years, airlines have been increasingly successful in implementing the ideas of enhanced teamwork. Many airlines around the world apply the principles of Crew Resource Management (CRM) for pilots and other operational airline staff. The point has been made elsewhere that:

> *It is somewhat surprising that 'Controller Resource Management' did not develop in conjunction with Cockpit Resource Management (Helmreich, 1993).*

Although a great deal of effort and expertise is devoted to training individuals in the technical skills necessary for the air traffic control task, little, if anything, has been undertaken to train these individuals to function as team members . Incidents and accidents in which inadequate teamwork has been shown to be a factor indicate that more attention needs to be focused on this important area, and the adoption of the title "Team Resource Management" was intended to reflect the importance of the team in the safe and efficient conduct of Air Traffic Services (see also Eißfeldt, 1994; Haertel & Haertel, 1995; Helmreich; 1993; Hopkin, 1995; Mudge & Gidde, 1993; Ruitenberg, 1995; Tenney, 1993, Wickens, Mavor, & McGee, 1997)

## Teamwork in Air Traffic Services

In the past, human factors activities in ATC have been concentrated mainly on individual issues, although the work of the individual controller is very much dependent on teamwork reflected in communication and co-ordination with other operational staff such as flight crews, supervisors and adjacent controllers. The increasing complexity of ATC tasks requires a more structured approach to ensure Air Traffic Controllers have the opportunity to develop the appropriate attitudes, knowledge and skills for safe and efficient teamwork.

In ATC the attempt to define a team has been rather difficult. The term *team* is used in many European countries to describe the control staff or groups working physically together in one ATC unit such as Aerodrome, Approach and En Route Control (ACC). The criteria to describe a team ranges from controllers working in the same sector or controllers working in different sectors but belonging to one particular shift or watch. Controllers usually become members of a team after training and check-out, and stay in the team often for the rest of their career. Teams are often self-organised structures with specific cultures, rules and roles, and are highly protected from the outside world. It is also worth noting that, apart from ratings, once checked a controller has no further performance checks. Since explicit training of teamwork principles rarely exists, the acquisition of teamwork skills of the individual controller depends very much on the characteristics of his or her team. A few European countries have recently introduced individual shift rosters which no longer allow for these fixed team structures and it is interesting to note that the members of one ATC unit work in temporary teams based on the random allocation of work positions similar to the crew compositions of the airlines.

For the purpose of developing a concept for Team Resource Management it seemed necessary to concentrate more on teamwork processes rather than on team structures and to use a more generic definition of teams. Thus a team in ATS can be defined as "a group of two or more persons who interact dynamically and interdependently within assigned specific roles, functions and responsibilities. They have to adapt continuously to each other to ensure the establishment of a safe, orderly and expeditious flow of air traffic".

A wider scope of the teamwork concept is illustrated in Figure 28.1, depicting teamwork relations which a single operational controller might identify from their individual point of view. Firstly, controllers have safety-critical teamwork relations with the aircrews entering and leaving their sectors of responsibility. Amongst controllers the smallest teamwork cell can be described as those controllers and flight data assistants working physically together in the same operational unit. Teamwork relations also exist between controllers of adjacent operational areas and between controllers of different ATC units (ACC, APP, TWR). Teamwork aspects in a wider scope also occur between controllers and any other operational staff such as flow management, supervisors and ATM support staff. Even in the widest sense the ATC organisations and the whole air traffic world could be regarded as one big team.

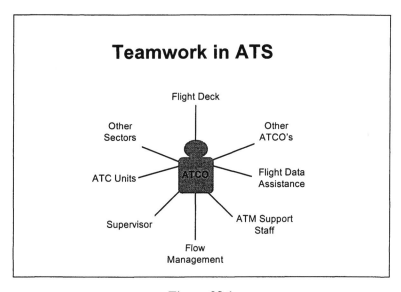

**Figure 28.1**
**Teamwork relations in ATM from the controllers perspective**

### The TRM approach

In July 1994, a Study Group was created to investigate the possible benefits of and requirements for a Team Resources Management (TRM) programme in the ECAC area. Within its scope the TRM Study Group carried out a literature survey concerning relevant CRM/TRM publications, a teamwork related ATC incident survey, a questionnaire survey to determine the attitude of controllers to teamwork in ATC and a TRM training survey to identify current team training activities in and outside the ECAC area. The results of these studies clearly indicated that failures in teamwork function contribute to incidents and often have a negative effect on the performance of controllers. This exercise supported the need for a TRM programme and in February 1995 the EATCHIP Human Resources Team (HRT) agreed to establish a Team Resource Management Task Force for an initial 12-month period.

The principal objective of the TRM Task Force was to produce guidelines for the development and implementation of Team Resource Management. A secondary objective was to foster the awareness of the benefits of teamwork in ATS, and to produce a draft syllabus on which TRM training courses could be modelled. The TRM Task Force, established in Summer 1995, included ECAC State representatives from Austria, France, Germany, Switzerland, the United Kingdom, Eurocontrol Headquarters and the Institute of Air Navigation Services, and IFATCA, a mixed team of active controllers, training staff and human factors experts. In February 1996 the TRM Task Force completed its mandate and the Human Resources Team approved the TRM guidelines as subsequently released in the EATCHIP document (EATCHIP, 1996).

## Guidelines for Team Resource Management

TRM in ATS is defined by the Task Force as: Strategies for the best use of all available resources - information, equipment and people - to optimise the safety and efficiency of Air Traffic Services. This is based on the principles that it should be developed by operational staff and human factors experts, linked to human factors incident and accident investigations and based on best practice from airline Crew Resource Management (Wiener et al., 1993).

The main expected benefits of TRM are considered to be reduced teamwork related incidents, enhanced task efficiency, improved use of staff resources, enhanced continuity and stability of teamwork in future ATM, enhanced sense of working as a part of a larger and more efficient team and increased job satisfaction.

However, in the effort to explain what TRM is, it is also important to make clear to them what it is not. TRM is not, for example, a substitute for inadequate training, nor is it intended to substitute for poor procedures and documentation, nor for inefficient management structures or loosely and inadequately defined organisational roles. TRM is not intended to be a replacement for technical training but should complement it.

## Guidelines for TRM Development

1. The practical benefits of enhanced team performance should be communicated as early as possible to both management and operational staff. This will encourage the necessary commitment to develop and reinforce TRM throughout the organisation.

2. The main objective of TRM for operational staff should be the development of attitudes and behaviour which will contribute to enhanced teamwork skills and performance. In turn this will reduce teamwork failures as a contributory factor in ATM related incidents and accidents.

3. The initial phase of TRM should concentrate on teamwork amongst air traffic controllers. At a later stage TRM could be extended to teamwork amongst other operational staff.

4. The development of the future ATM system should consider TRM principles in order to ensure continuity and teamwork stability.

5. TRM should comprise three phases: an introductory/awareness phase; a practical phase; and a refresher/reinforcement phase. Related training for operational staff should contain elements of TRM.

6. TRM principles should be mandatory elements in the selection, training and licensing of operational staff.

7. Teamwork, team roles, communication, situational awareness, decision making, and stress management should form the mandatory subjects of a TRM course.

8. Scenarios for facilitation purposes should be realistic, relevant to course participants and regularly updated. The provision of a simulation environment should be considered such that participants can practise and reinforce TRM skills in both normal and emergency situations.

9. TRM facilitation tools and methods should include lectures, examples, discussions, exercises, videos on team related errors, hand-outs, check-lists and simulator exercises.

10. The first phase of TRM should be provided both to operational controllers and supervisors and should later be extended to other operational staff in ATS.

11. TRM facilitators should be carefully selected and trained, and when possible should be current operational staff.

12. The benefits of TRM should be maintained by continuously evaluating the courses and the changes in attitudes and behaviour of operational staff in the work environment.

13. The reinforcement of TRM in the operational environment should be ensured by management backup and support, team and individual (de)briefings, visual reminders and feedback from incident investigations.

**Progress and current status of the TRM Project**

After the approval of the guidelines in February 1996 the TRM Task Force received a new mandate to prepare and coordinate the introduction, testing and evaluation phases of TRM. The Task Force was meanwhile joined by more States and today consists of members from Austria, France, Germany, Italy, Rumania, Switzerland and the United Kingdom, all of whom will probably run TRM prototype courses in early 1998. In the meantime the Task Force set up national working groups to promote TRM and to prepare the next phases within their respective States. This included the presentations and discussions with management, operational staff and staff associations to foster organisation-wide awareness of the TRM ideas. Some of the States had already identified controllers who could become TRM facilitators. However, the most important part of this phase was the communal development of a TRM prototype course.

*TRM prototype course*

Early in the process of the TRM concept the idea was to start with the harmonisation and integration procedure as early as possible and to develop a generic TRM prototype course on which the national administrations could build their own tailored courses (Figure 28.2). Harmonisation in this respect applied the 80:20 rule by which 80 percent contained common material and instructions for the facilitators and the remaining 20 percent was to provide sufficient scope for the States to be able to adapt it to their needs and to include their national examples, exercises and cultural influences.

Firstly a consultant was found (Dédale) with a proven record of developing CRM courses for airlines and associated areas. The development of the prototype course was based on the TRM guidelines, and was delivered in September 1997. This development was undertaken in close co-operation with a second TRM Task Force and members of the national TRM working groups to ensure a highly ATC specific product.

The course is a 3-day facilitation and instructional programme for operational controllers and covers the subject areas of teamwork, team roles, communication, situational awareness, decision making, and stress. These rather academic topics have been integrated in a highly practical way using day-to-day examples of the controller's work in the form of videos incident material and discussion. The prototype course also includes a set of evaluation materials which will allow a common assessment of the possible changes in course content, methods, opinions, and also allow an evaluation regarding the success of TRM itself and the cultural differences between the States involved.

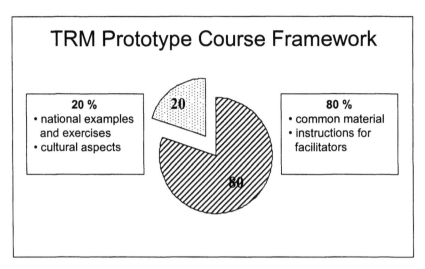

**Figure 28.2**
**The framework for developing the TRM prototype course**

*Customisation and testing*

The customisation of the course is happening at the present time. This process allows member States the opportunity to use State specific materials and content which is relevant to them. The customisation in some instances is being simultaneously run with facilitator training. In this way the ATS personnel who will be delivering the program have the opportunity to tailor the material to their own needs and at the same time become familiar with the content. After the customisation phase, a number of States (Austria, Denmark, England, Eurocontrol, France, Germany, Ireland, Portugal, Romania, Switzerland) will run the first "test" courses. Some of these should be completed by September 1998 which should allow the evaluation of the course and the opportunity to further improve the program for future delivery. After the assessment and evaluation of the testing phase the Task Force will issue recommendations for further implementation of the TRM concept. This will include advanced plans for implementation of TRM in all 35 ECAC States and its incorporation in selection, training and licensing of ATC staff.

## The future

After the initial implementation of TRM courses this concept is likely go through similar steps of evolution as CRM in the airlines. The target population will be extended to other operational staff in ATS and ATM. The whole TRM idea needs to be implemented in controller ab initio selection, training and licensing and in any form of controller upgrade and refresher training. Other areas such as incident and accident investigation need to fully consider teamwork related aspects in their evaluations and reports. The success of the development and introduction of advanced automation in ATM will partly depend on enhancing and supporting the teamwork culture both in controllers operations and on the flightdeck. The idea to train controllers and pilots in combined CRM/TRM courses may not be so far away.

## References

Barbarino, M. (1997). *Team Resource Management in European Air Traffic Services*. Paper given at the 9th International Symposium on Aviation Psychology, Ohio State University, Columbus, Ohio, USA.

EATCHIP (1996). *Guidelines for Developing and Implementing Team Resource Management (HUM.ET1.ST10.1000-GUI-01)*. Brussels: EUROCONTROL.

Eißfeldt, H. (1994). Team Resource Management Training - CRM-Training für die Flugsicherung. In H. Eißfeldt, K-M. Goeters, H-J. Hörmann, P. Maschke & A. Schiewe (Ed.), *Effektives Arbeiten im Team: Crew-Resource-Management-Training für Piloten und Fluglotsen DLR Mitteilung* (Vol. 94-09, pp. 97-114). Köln: DLR.

Härtel, C., & Härtel, G. (1995). *Controller Resource Management - What can we learn from aircrews?* (Vol. DOT/FAA/AM-95/21). Washington: US Department of Transportation.

Helmreich, R.L. (1993). Whither CRM? Future directions in Crew Resource Management training in the cockpit and elsewhere. In R.S. Jensen (Ed.), *Proceedings of the Seventh International Symposium on Aviation Psychology* (Vol. 1, pp. 543-548). Columbus, OH: Ohio State University.

Hopkin, V.D. (1995). *Human Factors in Air Traffic Control*. London: Taylor & Francis.

Mudge, G.W., & Gidde, M.H. (1993). Control Resource Management in Air Traffic Control. In R.S. Jensen (Ed.), *Proceedings of the Seventh International Symposium on Aviation Psychology* (Vol. 1, pp. 517-521). Columbus: Ohio State University.

Ruitenberg, B. (1995). CRM in ATC - is it feasible? In R.S. Jensen (Ed.), *Proceedings of the Eighths International Symposium on Aviation Psychology*. Columbus: Ohio State University.

Seamster, T.L., Cannon, J.R., Pierce, R.M., & Redding, R.E. (1992). *The analysis of en route air traffic controller team communication and controller resource management (CRM)*. (Proceedings of the Human Factors Society 36th Annual Meeting). Santa Monica, CA: Human Factors Society.

Tenney, D.P. (1993). Air Traffic Controller Resource Management. In R.S. Jensen (Ed.), *Proceedings of the Seventh International Symposium on Aviation Psychology* (pp. 817-820). Columbus: Ohio State University.

Wiener, E.L., Kanki, B.G., & Helmreich, R.L. (1993). *Cockpit Resource Management*. San Diego: Academic Press.

Wickens, C.D., Mavor, A.S., & McGee, J. (1997). *Flight to the Future - Human Factors in Air Traffic Control*. Washington, DC: National Academy Press.

# 29 Air Traffic Control Resource Management for new automation: Workload and workgroups

*Lisa Duff, Michael Nendick and H. Peter Pfister*
*The University of Newcastle*

Air traffic controllers work in a socially critical system transitioning to an increasingly sophisticated automation of work functions intended to close the widening gap between industry needs and provider capacities. Air traffic control (ATC) automation is moving beyond data gathering, data presentation, and simple analysis into automated problem solving and decision making. This has been made possible through advances in computer capabilities, and justified by the belief that the human is a limiting factor within a growing aviation world. It has been widely predicted that new technologies such as electronic flight strips and automated data links will produce substantial qualitative changes to the job of the air traffic controller. The aim of this paper is to highlight some specific operational changes and their ramifications for workgroups and ultimately workload within complex projects such as The Australian Advanced Air Traffic System (TAAATS).

## Overview

The purpose of ATC is to keep aircraft moving in a safe and orderly fashion through a given space. ATC may be described as a closed person-in-the-loop control system, concerned with the processing of frequently discontinuous information in an increasingly automated environment (Soede & Coeterier, 1971; Spring, 1991). The International Civil Aviation Organisation (ICAO) has stressed that automation is valid within ATC only to the extent that it assists controllers to carry out their responsibilities and that automation must not be designed in a way which could be detrimental to those responsibilities

(Fulton, 1995). United States aviation authorities have explicitly required that ATC automation upgrades reduce controller workload while concurrently increasing controller productivity (Murphy, Reaux, Stewart, Coleman, & Bruce, 1989).

## Air Traffic Control workload

Controller workload under time and task constraints has been extensively studied, in part due to the widely held belief that workload is linked to performance across several parameters including goal setting, remembering, perception, and judgement (Koonce, 1984; Hart, 1986; Zeier, 1994; Cardosi & Murphy, 1995). Although several studies have provided insights into the nature of controller errors, for example Danaher (1980), Morrison and Wright (1989), Stager and Hameluck (1989), Adams and Hwoschinsky (1991) and McCoy and Funk (1991), not all have been able to draw a clear relationship between workload and controller performance. However, it is likely that there is some optimum middle ground for error detection during the monitoring of an automated system over time, with exceedingly complex and simple tasks both producing detection decrements (Molloy & Parasuraman, 1996). By implication, new technologies should maintain controller workload somewhere in this midground, although it has proven particularly difficult to determine which factors increase workload and which decrease workload in systems involving vigilance and monitoring.

Not surprisingly, the number of aircraft under surveillance at any one time is a demonstrated determinant of workload (Sperandio, 1978). However as traffic has increased, controller ranks in general have not kept pace. In the United States, between 1,500 and 2,000 controller jobs were cut between 1981 and 1995 while air traffic there increased by 30 to 35%, resulting in mandatory six day working weeks at some major US airports (Jackson, 1995; Smolowe, 1996). The number of Australian controllers in pre-TAAATS 1998 hovers around 1,300, down from an historical high of 2,200, although the number may rise slightly when TAAATS becomes operational (Sean McNamara, Airservices Australia, personal communication, March 5 1998).

Analysis of US Aviation Safety Reporting System (ASRS) communication related controller incidents indicated that one-third of all reports referred directly to controller overload, with no correlation between errors and experience (Morrison & Wright, 1989). Morrison and Wright inferred that many controllers were handling traffic mixes that simply exceeded their cognitive abilities. Ground-to-air and air-to-ground communications may raise an individual's workload to the extent that handing an aircraft over to another controller is hampered (Porterfield, 1997).

An additional factor in controller workload has been the need to accommodate and work around system failures resulting from aging ATC equipment (Leopold, 1996). There is little argument over the benefits of replacing 1960s generation computer equipment. Controllers in the US have had to struggle through almost daily system outages (Anthes, 1996). Manual intervention, including the need to operate in backup mode due to system failure, has been shown to dramatically increase operator workload with no increase in job satisfaction (Hockey & Maule, 1995). However, any reduction in workload resulting from equipment upgrades is likely to be deferred until new technology achieves a stable and reliable platform.

**Emerging technology/workload issues**

An important information source for a controller has been the paper flight strip, physically passed from one individual to another (Stammers & Bird, 1980; Bashinski, Dunkle, & Lenorovitz, 1989). The future of paper flight strips is now under scrutiny. New Zealand ATC is moving towards the full implementation of electronic strips automatically transmitted between controllers for its oceanic control centers. TAAATS, which may become operational as a wholly developed system in 1998, will also implement electronic flight strips.

These changes are moving ahead despite some controller worries, especially since paper flight strips have been a proven and effective 'low tech' means of regulating workflow among controllers (Hamish Gray, NZATC, personal communication, July 20, 1997). A questionnaire developed by the US National Air Traffic Controllers Association (1997) asked users of paper flight strips if they felt that it would 'be feasible to transition to a stripless, electronic environment'. Particular concerns are that electronic flight strips will be unable to convey the subtle nuances possible with handwriting, will require more time to update, and may be affected by system failures. Citing such misgivings, controllers in the United Kingdom have successfully demanded that paper strips be maintained (Murphy, 1997).

The paper flight strip is not the only workplace feature which helps to ensure that the moment to moment workload of individual controllers is maintained within tolerable limits. The movement of the shift supervisor amongst the various work stations, together with the monitoring of radio communications, provides the supervisor with ongoing information on work capacity. This is similar to the party line effect whereby pilot/controller conversations are overheard by other controllers at adjacent work stations. Co-workers can estimate each others workload by interpreting nuances of speech. Irrespective of the potential of technologies such as the US Federal Aviation Administration's (FAA) Voice Switching and Control System to be applied to workload measurement (Porterfield, 1997), replacement of voice communication by automated datalinks may produce technological auditory isolation and limit the opportunities of supervisors and co-workers to identify when an individual is exceeding his or her safe working capacity (Midkiff & Hansman, 1993).

The design and test criteria for the emerging ATC systems appear to incorporate only modest appreciation of such human to human interactions within the operational environment. The research emphasis has instead been on the evolving human/technology interface, and especially on the computer/human interface (CHI). This type of approach is illustrated by the initial display capability assessments for the US Standard Terminal Automation Replacement System, or STARS, which will replace the Automated Radar Terminal Systems at the US Terminal Radar Approach Control facilities (Federal Aviation Administration, 1997). The 1991 tender documents for TAAATS had a similar orientation.

Even within the human factors framework relatively little emphasis has been granted to the human to human interface, and in particular how it may affect workload. This is despite the knowledge that controller workload has never been exclusively the function of the human/technology interface (Sperandio, 1978). For example, a study of computer-aiding on decision making (Whitfield, Ball & Ord, 1980) 'unexpectedly' found that controllers will resort to team sharing strategies in order to reduce individual workload.

## ATC as culture

Owen (1996) summarised five elements that provide evidence of organisational culture. These are specialised language and symbols, group values, myths and stories, artifacts, and group history and experiences. All these features are applicable to ATC and help to promote both professional identity and a safety culture. Therefore the controller world is more than a collection of individuals or even workgroups. It has been moulded into a unique organisational culture which serves to underpin the successful function of ATC as a whole.

One of the characteristics of an organisational culture is the existence of informal group norms. Although the official rules and norms of ATC imply individual responsibility, an approach echoed in liability laws, informal group norms help to reinforce collective solidarity and manage workload (Gras, Moricot, Poirot-Delpeche, & Scardigli, 1994). Within the controller community these self-imposed group norms permit individual variance as long as overall system safety is not compromised (Hopkin, 1971). Norms encourage familiarity within the group and the level of group familiarity is positively related to group productivity (Goodman & Leyden, 1991). The development of control systems which are inflexible when faced with informal group norms would not necessarily be an advance, no matter what the level of technical sophistication.

## Conclusion

The role of both the human-to-human interface and workgroup norms within ATC is known and appreciated by the controllers themselves. The challenge facing the designers of new systems should be to adopt technology which will enhance rather than degrade the humanity of the air traffic control environment. Otherwise the billions of dollars being spent worldwide on ATC system development and implementation might not in fact result in systems which are substantially more efficient or safer.

Overall workload is related to operational irregularities, and workload is moderated by operational group norms. Without a more rigorous emphasis and study of the impact of emerging ATC technologies on work norms, two non-exclusive outcomes are possible. First, estimates of work throughput based primarily on the human/technology interface may be inaccurate. Second, estimates of operational irregularities based on the chosen methods for system testing and acceptance may be flawed.

The limited attention currently awarded to workgroup issues may be even further reduced as new systems reach their implementation dates. When time and money begin to run out, oversight authorities may be tempted to jettison what may be perceived as relatively 'soft' issues. In such a scenario, any delivered system, albeit one insensitive to workgroup needs, may be considered preferable to no system at all.

The National Air Traffic Controllers Association announced (1998) an agreement with the FAA which will require comprehensive integration of human factors issues into all future STARS development. It may not be too late for a system such as TAAATS which is nearing implementation to follow suit and pursue rigorous testing of the effects its implementation will have on controller workload, workgroups, and work norms.

**Notes and acknowledgments**

The research was in part supported by University of Newcastle RMC Grant 45/299/701.

**References**

Adams, R., & Hwoschinsky, P. (1991). Information transfer limitations in ATC. In R. Jensen (Ed.), *Proceedings of the Sixth International Symposium on Aviation Psychology (Vol. 1)* (pp. 491-496). Columbus OH: Ohio State University Press.

Anthes, G. (1996). Ancient systems put scare in air. *Computerworld, 30* (30), 1-4.

Bashinski, H., Dunkle, D., & Lenorovitz, D. (1989). Defining man-machine interface requirements for air traffic control static information displays. In R. Jensen (Ed.), *Proceedings of the Fifth International Symposium on Aviation Psychology* (pp. 878-883). Columbus OH: Ohio State University.

Cardosi, K., & Murphy, E. (1995). *Human factors in the design and evaluation of air traffic control systems.* Washington DC: US Government Printing Service.

Danaher, J. (1980). Human error in ATC system operation. *Human Factors, 22* (5), 535-545.

Federal Aviation Administration (1997). *Standard Terminal Automation Replacement System: Early display capability initial diagnostic usability assessment.* Report Submitted to the Chief Scientific and Technical Advisor for Human Factors, December 18, 1997.

Fulton, N. (1995). Sensor based situational awareness as a hazard paradigm for optimisation of ATC systems design. In R. Otto & J. Lenz (Eds.), *Air Traffic Control technologies.* Bellingham WA: International Society for Optical Engineering.

Goodman, P., & Leyden, D. (1991). Familiarity and group productivity. *Journal of Applied Psychology, 76* (4), 578-586.

Gras, A., Moricot, C., Poirot-Delpech, S., & Scardigli, V. (1994). *Faced with automation: The pilot, the controller, and the engineer.* Paris: The Sorbonne.

Hart, S. (1986). Theory and measurement of human workload. In J. Zeider (Ed.), *Human productivity enhancement: Training and human factors in systems design* (Vol. 1, pp. 396-456). NY: Preager.

Hockey, G., & Maule, A. (1995). Unscheduled manual intervention in automated process control. *Ergonomics, 38* (12), 2504-2524.

Hopkin, V. (1971). Conflicting criteria in evaluating air traffic control systems. *Ergonomics, 14* (5), 557-564.

Jackson, W. (1995). Unions baulk at privatising FAA systems modernisation. *Government Computer News, 14* (12), 87.

Koonce, J. (1984). A brief history of aviation psychology. *Human Factors, 26* (5), 499-508.

Leopold, G. (1996). Will the air-control upgrade fly? *Electronic Engineering Times,* 925, 1-2.

Midkiff, A., & Hansman, R. (1993). Identification of important 'party line' information elements and implications for situational awareness in the datalink environment. *Air Traffic Control Quarterly, 1*(1), 5-30.

Molloy, R., & Parasuraman, R. (1996). Monitoring an automated system for a single failure. Vigilance and task complexity effects. *Human Factors, 38* (2), 311-322.

Morrison, R., & Wright, R. (1989). ATC control and communications problems: An overview of recent ASRS data. In R. Jensen (Ed.), *Proceedings of the Fifth International Symposium on Aviation Psychology* (pp. 902-907). Columbus OH: Ohio State University Press.

Murphy, E., Reaux, R., Stewart, L., Coleman, W., & Bruce, K. (1989). Where's the workload in air traffic control? In R. Jensen (Ed.), *Proceedings of the Fifth International Symposium on Aviation Psychology.* Columbus OH: Ohio State University Press.

Murphy, J. (1997). A tale of nats and bugs. *Computer Weekly,* April 10, 40-41.

National Air Traffic Controllers Association (1997, July 11) *NATCA Safety Survey* (Survey posted on the World Wide Web). Washington DC: Author. Retrieved February 16, 1998 from the World Wide Web:http://home.natca.org/natca/natca/central/safe/survey.html.

National Air Traffic Controllers Association (July 11, 1997). Controllers and FAA clear the path for progress in ATC modernization. (Press release). Washington DC: Author. Retrieved March 10, 1998, from the World Wide Web:http://home.natca/mediaandpublications/pressreleases/modernization .html.

Owen, C. (1996). Creating spaces for learning in air traffic control: Back to the future? In B.J. Hayward & A.R. Lowe (Eds.), *Applied aviation psychology: Achievement, change and challenge.* Aldershot UK: Avebury.

Porterfield, D. (1997). Evaluating controller communication time as a measure of workload. *International Journal of Aviation Psychology, 7* (2), 171-182.

Smolowe, J. (1996). Out-of-control tower. *Time, 147* (8), 52-53.

Soede, M., & Coeterier, J. (1971). Time analysis of the tasks of approach controllers in ATC. *Ergonomics, 14* (5), 591-601.

Sperandio, J. (1978). The regulation of working methods as a function of work-load among air traffic controllers. *Ergonomics, 21* (3), 195-202.

Spring, E. (1991). The human element in air traffic control. In R. Jensen (Ed.) *Proceedings of the Sixth International Symposium on Aviation Psychology (Vol 1)* (pp. 486-490). Columbus OH: Ohio State University Press.

Stager, P., & Hameluck, D. (1989). Analysis of air traffic control irregularities. In R. Jensen (Ed.), *Proceedings of the Fifth International Symposium on Aviation Psychology* (pp. 890-895). Columbus OH: Ohio State University Press.

Stammers, R., & Bird, J. (1980). Controller evaluation of a touch input air traffic data system: An indelicate experiment. *Human Factors, 22* (5), 581-589.

Whitfield, D., Ball, R., & Ord, G. (1980). Some human factors aspects of computer-aiding concepts for air traffic controllers. *Human Factors, 22* (5), 569-580.

Zeier, H. (1994). Workload and psychophysiological stress reaction in air traffic controllers. *Ergonomics, 37* (3), 525-539.

# 30 Air traffic control in a screen-based non-radar environment: A preliminary evaluation of human factors issues in TAAATS

*Greg Hannan, Phillip J. Moore and Ross A. Telfer*
*Unitas Consulting Pty Ltd, and*
*Claire Marrison and Geoffrey C. Ross*
*Airservices Australia*

## Background

The Australian Advanced Air Traffic System (TAAATS), due to be phased into operation during 1998, is to be a fully integrated air traffic management system making use of the latest air navigation technology such as ADS (Automated Dependent Surveillance) and CPDLC (Controller Pilot Datalink Communication). TAAATS will consist of two flight data regions and two major air traffic control centres in Brisbane and Melbourne, five additional terminal control units and nine radar control towers. Thomson CSF was contracted in 1994 to provide hardware and software ATC systems along with an AFTN switching system, voice communication systems, simulators and training support. TAAATS is to replace an ageing and fragmented system to facilitate Airservices Australia to continue to offer high quality air traffic management into the future in a diverse and very large airspace (Dunstone & Brown, 1994).

TAAATS is essentially an off-the-shelf purchase incorporating the Eurocat 2000 hardware with special software components for the particular requirements of Australian airspace. Dunstone and Brown (1994) argued that "procedures will be developed [for TAAATS] to take advantage of the system's strengths and work around its weaknesses." This paper outlines a research programme sponsored by Airservices Australia. The principal aim of the programme is to investigate the human factors issues involved in the use of screen-based operations for non-radar control, with particular emphasis to be given to the impact of the TAAATS Human-Machine Interface (HMI) and procedures on workload management and situation awareness (SA). The paper also discusses some of the issues associated with research in the workplace.

**Air traffic control in the non-radar procedural environment**

A significant feature of Australian airspace is the lack of radar coverage which requires procedural control methods to be used in these airspaces. In this environment air traffic controllers (ATCs) use multiple paper strips (manually delivered to the console) displaying each aircraft's flight details, which are placed on a flight progress board under common pilot reporting points. They can be arranged in time sequence in the posting bays and can generally be manipulated to facilitate the work of the ATC.

The strips serve several very significant functions and support important cognitive processes involved in maintaining SA and managing workload (Hopkin, 1988b). In the first instance, strips for a pending aircraft allow the ATC to quickly assess the impact of its passage through the sector on existing traffic by noting the estimated times at the fixes along the planned route and comparing these with the existing strips for other aircraft in the bays. Strips also allow the controller to keep a history of the flight by annotating the strips. This history of requests, actions and changes can be important in some cases in maintaining SA. Another significant function strips play is the capacity to use them as a memory prompt for future tasks. This can be achieved by annotations, or by cocking them to the left or right of the bay they are placed in, depending on the type of action required. ATCs have developed strategies for minimising the amount of information needed to be retained in short term memory storage by the efficient use of strips. Finally strips provide a means for controllers to quickly scan the flight progress board to determine pending actions and help prioritise them. Ross (1995) provided a useful model of these cognitive actions which are largely supported by strips in the procedural environment. In this model he asserts the cognitive processes are repetitive and cyclical. The key cognitive processes involved in ATC are:

- **identification** of actions required by the **recognition** of incoming information or by **scanning** existing information which comes principally from strips in the non-radar environment.

- **task recognition** is a process which results from the **synthesis** of information with the requirements of ATC procedures and objectives.

- **planning and prioritising** are the processes arising from task recognition in which the ATC coordinates information from various sources and determines a course of action from known strategies. These processes require a good level of infrastructure knowledge of airspace, patterns of traffic, procedures and optional strategies.

- **decision making** and **action** arise out of the above in that the controller, having recognised tasks, planned actions (and perhaps prioritised them), then commits to carrying out those actions.

The role of paper strips has been documented elsewhere by human factors researchers (Garland, Stein, Blanchard & Wise, 1992; Hopkin, 1992; and Vortac, Edwards, Jones, Manning, & Rotter, 1993). Garland, et al., pointed out that strips provide an active process of interacting with information that electronic strips do not facilitate. This occurs through mental interaction and "motoric enactment", a psychomotor process which they argued enhances encoding and subsequent recall of information. Strips, then, seem to play a vital role in the maintenance of SA and management of workload in the non-radar environment.

## Non-radar control in the TAAATS environment

The TAAATS environment has several significant changes for the procedural ATC. The most obvious of these is that the disposition of aircraft will be shown in a two dimensional visual display known as the air situation display (ASD). A single electronic strip for each aircraft is displayed in a window but these are not able to be ordered or manipulated. Information contained on these strips (such as altitude, ground speed, reported flight level and planned flight level) in TAAATS is also displayed on aircraft labels which also incorporates a text line ("opdata line"). Another feature of TAAATS in the non-radar environment is that the ASD is reliant on user entered information supplemented by automated data entry which is not always visible to the controller. This feature will require ATCs to accurately and efficiently enter information into the system using a combination of mouse, pull down menus and keyboard entry.

It is assumed that SA and workload will be facilitated by the ASD. It is also assumed that a range of graphic tools, such as bearing and range line (BRL) and the short route probe (SRP), will reduce the mental effort involved in calculations required for separation assurance. However, the removal of strips results in the loss of the capacity to notate actions, requests and changes to flight plans. It also results in the loss of memory prompts through strategies such as cocking strips and annotating them. While TAAATS may enhance overall SA and workload management in the ways suggested above, the nature and distribution of the cognitive resources required of the operators may change. For instance, although a decrease in overall workload may be observed in TAAATS, increased workload within specific domains may be embedded in new tasks and procedures.

Clearly TAAATS will result in significant changes in the way in which ATCs conduct their work and the strategies they will use to maintain SA and manage workload. The potential impacts of these changes in either reducing or enhancing SA or workload is unknown and therefore requires investigation to determine in what areas TAAATS operation in the non-radar environment may need special attention for software development, training emphases and/or procedures development. The remainder of this paper outlines the research programme being undertaken by Unitas Consulting, in cooperation with human factors specialists from Airservices Australia, and offers some discussion of the benefits and problems associated with action research in the ATC workplace.

**The research programme**

As stated earlier SA and workload are the central concerns of the research project. Accordingly, the project's main aim is to determine the impact of screen-based operations in a non-radar environment within TAAATS, on situation awareness and workload. Other aims are to investigate the human factors assumptions underpinning procedures and training.

To achieve these aims two studies have been proposed. The first of these is a quantitative comparative study in which ATCs' ratings of SA and workload in the current procedural environment will be compared with ratings in the TAAATS environment. The second study is a qualitative investigation in which ATCs will be tracked through their simulation training to determine if any aspects of the HMI and/or procedures are causing concern in relation to SA and workload. In addition, a series of observation sessions will be undertaken by the research team in which known human factors will be investigated, and cognitive interviews with ATCs conducted. These interviews will focus on the TAAATS environment and will examine:

- methods they are using to develop and maintain SA (such as scanning techniques, memory prompts);
- workload management strategies used to cope with new aspects of the HMI, including data entry requirements;
- adjustment to the new HMI;
- adjustment to new procedures resulting from the HMI.

**Methodologies**

*Study 1*

For the first study, two special simulation exercises, each of one hour duration have been developed for two non-radar sectors; one being a very large area containing many air routes, the other a much smaller sector but processing considerable volumes of traffic and containing a busy, medium size regional airport. The simulation exercises have been crafted to contain three distinct fluctuations in traffic volume and complexity. The first section starts with medium traffic volume and low complexity, building in the second section to high volume and complexity and easing in the third section to low levels of traffic volume and complexity. Twenty currently rated ATCs, who will be transitioning to TAAATS on these sectors, have volunteered to participate in the study. Testing in the procedural environment has been completed and provides baseline measures of SA and workload against which to compare the same ATCs on the same exercises in the TAAATS environment, after training on the TAAATS HMI.

Several measures of SA and workload have been chosen to provide both objective and subjective assessment. Endsley's model (Endsley & Rodgers, 1994) has been the basis of design in data gathering in relation to SA. This model suggests three levels of SA: Level 1 being the correct perception of elements and events in the environment; Level 2 the understanding of these elements in the scenario; and Level 3, the projection of these events into an understanding of the future status of the situation. The Situation Awareness Global Assessment Technique (SAGAT), proposed by Endsley (1987) involves freezing a scenario at multiple points and asking questions about

291

the situation. The original SAGAT tool for ATC involves locating the aircraft on a computer-based map that mirrors the radar screen, indicating details of nominated aircraft (such as callsign, level, ground speed and flight level). For this project the nature of SAGAT questions has been modified to suit the non-radar environment in Australia. Less emphasis is given to identifying specific aircraft callsigns and ground speeds, for example, and more given to the contents of controllers scanning, anticipation of events and separation priorities. Nevertheless Endsley's three levels of SA are accommodated.

In addition to the objective SAGAT measure, the Situation Awareness Rating Technique (SART) developed by Taylor and Selcon (Taylor, Selcon and Swinden, 1994), has been chosen as a subjective measure of SA. This instrument involves three dimensions: *demand* on attentional resources, *supply* of attentional resources by the operator, and *understanding* of the situation. These dimensions are rated by the operator on a twenty point scale are combined to provide a unitary measure of SA by the algorithm :

SA(calculated) = Understanding - (Demand - Supply).

Workload is being assessed principally by the Subjective Workload Assessment Technique (SWAT) developed by Reid, Potter, and Bressler (1989). SWAT involves the measurement of three workload factors: *time demand, mental effort* and *psychological stress load*, each assessed on a three point scale of high, moderate or low. Two subsidiary measures are also being used: number of, and time spent on calls as objective measures of controller workload (Porterfield, 1997); and heart rate, which may reflect more the psychological demand and threat the controller may be experiencing as a result of the task. Resting heart rate is taken prior to the simulation exercise.

During the course of the simulation runs, in both the current procedural environment and the TAAATS environment the following measures are taken.

- SWAT ratings (taken verbally without stopping the exercise) every five minutes.
- Continuous recording of heart rate using the Polar Vantage system.
- six staged stops for SAGAT enquires (four questions each stop).
- SART ratings at each of the six SAGAT stops.
- Continuous audio recording of controller transmissions.

These data will be used to compare ATCs' workload and SA in the three sections of the simulation exercise across the two platforms: procedural and TAAATS non-radar. In this way some tentative conclusions will be able to be made about the impact of TAAATS on ATC workload and SA, in three conditions of air traffic.

*Study 2*

The second study focuses on ATCs' adaptation to the TAAATS HMI and the procedures developed for the non-radar environment. It may also focus on human factors issues associated with sectors that contain a combination of flight plan tracks (non-radar tracks) and radar/ADS tracks. Two approaches to data gathering are being taken. The first involves ATCs completing a major questionnaire on completion of each their four simulation training programmes, while the second involves structured observations of ATCs operating TAAATS during simulation training. These observations are to be followed up with cognitive interviews aimed at tapping ATCs' progress in adjusting to the TAAATS environment for non-radar control.

The questionnaire contains 110 statements grouped in ten sections. The items are statements about particular features of the HMI and peripherals (displays, alerts, mice etc), the procedures, data entry requirements, as well as how the HMI and procedures facilitate SA and workload management. The items have been taken from the FAA's *Human Factors Checklist for the Design and Evaluation of Air Traffic Control Systems* (Cardosi & Murphy, 1995) as well as from issues raised in the initial Examination of TAAATS reports. ATCs will rate a statement such as *"scanning is aided by the way information is presented in TAAATS"* on a four point scale (strongly disagree, disagree, agree, strongly agree) or mark a box indicating that aspect has not yet been encountered in training. A section beside each item is provided for written comments and participants are encouraged (in the instructions) to use these sections, particularly if they disagree or strongly disagree with the statement. The data gathered from this four-stage process will enable the identification of problem aspects of TAAATS (as well as positive features) and those aspects which appear not to be improving with training. These data may also assist the training providers identify areas of training that may need additional emphasis or modification to existing approaches.

The second data gathering exercise involves observations of ATCs, in the latter stages of their TAAATS training, undertaking simulation exercises designed to introduce them to procedures and advanced functions of the system. Observations will be structured around information from the early questionnaire data which may identify problem areas. Interviews after the observations will focus on how controllers are progressing in relation to:

- building and maintaining SA and mental models in the new environment;
- developing alternative scanning techniques;
- developing workload management techniques;
- adjusting to the "paperless" environment, including strategies for memory prompting which previously relied on strips;
- adjusting to mouse and keyboard operations in a windows type environment.

At the conclusion of these studies it is expected that human risk and benefits involved in the TAAATS system would be identified, proposed procedures evaluated from a human factors perspective, training needs and emphases identified, and more generally, to have reached some conclusions about the impact of TAAATS on the key areas of SA and workload management. Finally it is anticipated that the project team would be in a position to make recommendations to Airservices Australia on human factors considerations for future system development and training.

## Research in the operational environment

The project is one in which the principal participants are currently rated controllers, working in an ATC workplace for an organisation involved in a very significant and complex transition. This situation poses some interesting, and at times, difficult problems. The purpose of this final section is to discuss the benefits and difficulties involved in this kind of research project. While the points are specific to this project they can be generalised to any research of a similar nature, conducted in the operational environment.

The main aim of this project is to evaluate the impact of a system which, during the time of the formulation of the research programme, was at an early stage of development. This situation, in itself, poses problems because until final versions of software are available and tested for stability, it is not possible to conduct vital aspects of the research. Detailed planning of research becomes problematic as changes to the system software, and the scheduling of implementation, invariably impact on research instruments such as questionnaires and observation checklists. One way around this problem is to plan a general framework and leave the specifics that may be affected by uncertainties to a later stage of development.

Another issue for the research team has been accessing the ATCs for the time needed to conduct simulation runs, interviews and questionnaires. In these circumstances it is vital to have contacts in the workplace who are committed to the project and who are prepared to organise the staffing needed to conduct the work, and generally promote the value of the project.

Control over the testing is far more difficult in an operational environment in which the researchers are guests rather than in control of a laboratory. Consequently, it has been important to trial testing extensively, not only to determine if the data gathering techniques can be used in the environment, but also to anticipate and therefore prevent, any factors that could compromise the data. For example, in a trial of the simulation exercises it was found that variation in the experience and ability of the pseudo pilots could be problematic. To overcome this a briefing sheet was prepared and one experienced pseudo pilot used throughout a testing block. This situation would not have been anticipated had an extensive trial not been conducted to reveal such a problem.

While control over testing in the operational environment can cause some problems of access and control, it is seen as more ecologically valid than testing staff in a more controlled training environment such as a college facility. Several studies in the literature draw conclusions based on research with groups of trainee pilots or ATCs (e.g., Mogford, 1997). While such studies may help illuminate the development of SA in novices, they have very little to say about SA in experienced controllers in the actual workplace.

## Conclusions

The project described in the pages above is due for completion (including reporting) by the end of 1998. At the time of writing testing for SA and workload for traditional procedural control was complete and work had started on the qualitative data gathering of controllers in training on TAAATS. Information on the project and results can be obtained from the second mentioned author.

## Acknowledgments

The research team wishes to thank Mr Stephen Angus of the Melbourne Air Traffic Control Centre for his organisation and commitment to the project, and the ATCs who have given their time to participate.

## References

Cardosi, K.M., & Murphy, E.D. (1995). *Human factors checklist for the design and evaluation of Air Traffic Control systems*. (DOT/FAA/D-95-3.1). Washington DC: FAA, Office of Aviation Research.

Dunstone, G., & Brown, R. (1994). *The Australian Advanced Air Traffic System: A project overview*. Paper presented to the 9th Annual Pacific Oceanic Airspace Conference.

Endsley, M.R. (1987*). SAGAT: A methodology for the measurement of situation awareness*. (NOR DOC 87-83). Hawthorn, CA: Northrop Corporation.

Endsley, M.R., & Rodgers, M.D. (1994*). Situation awareness information requirements for en-route air traffic control*. (DOT/FAA/AM-94/27), Washington DC: FAA, Office of Aviation Medicine.

Garland, D.J., Stein, E.S., Blanchard, J.W., & Wise, J.A. (1992). Situation awareness in the future air traffic environment. *Proceedings of the 37th Air Traffic Control Association Conference*, Atlantic City, New Jersey.

Hopkin, V.D. (1988b). Air traffic control. In E.L. Wiener & D.C. Nagel (Eds.), *Human factors in aviation*. San Diego, CA: Academic Press.

Mogford, R.H. (1997). Mental models and situation awareness in air traffic control. *International Journal of Aviation Psychology, 7*(4), 331-341.

Mogford, R.H., & Tansley, B.W. (1991*). The importance of the air traffic controller's mental model*. Paper presented to the Human Factors Society of Canada Annual Meeting, Canada.

Reid, G.B., Potter, S.S., & Bressler, J.R. (1989). Subjective workload assessment technique (SWAT): A user's guide. (AAMRL-TR-89-023), Ohio: Cseriac.

Ross, G.C. (1995). *The role of flight strips in supporting controller cognition*. Unpublished research report, School of Education, University of Tasmania.

# 31 A new approach to mental workload measurement in air traffic control

*Charmine E. J. Härtel, Graduate School of Management,*
*Andrew F. Neal and Graeme S. Halford,*
*Department of Psychology, and*
*Günter F. Härtel, Tropical Health Program*
*The University of Queensland*

## Introduction

Cognitive workload is one of the critical human factors in aircrew and air traffic controller performance (Härtel & Härtel, 1995; Härtel, Smith, & Prince, 1991; Prince, Härtel, & Salas, 1993). Error-proneness increases when mental workload exceeds an individual's cognitive capacity (Härtel & Härtel, 1997). For this reason, understanding and measuring cognitive workload is a fundamental aspect of aviation research programs around the world (cf. Wickens, Mavor, & McGee, 1997).

The measurement of mental workload is difficult because people use different strategies for managing their cognitive workload (Härtel & Härtel, 1997; in press), and because the effectiveness of such strategies depends not just upon the volume of the workload but also upon its complexity (cf. Halford, 1993; Halford, Wilson, & Phillips, submitted). Härtel's SHAPE model used together with Halford's metric of cognitive complexity provide a unique new way of assessing the likely cognitive workload at any given instance, and consequently the risk of error-proneness in cognitively-busy situations.

In this paper, we briefly describe the common approaches to mental workload measurement and prediction. Next, we review workload relevant aspects of the SHAPE model. Then we discuss the application of the

297

SHAPE model integrated with relational complexity to mental workload issues. We conclude with avenues for assessing and improving workflow design to reduce errors due to excessive workload.

## Approaches to workload measurement and prediction

Cognitive workload is human's cognitive experience of taskload: "the stimuli and behavioral demands placed on the system by the traffic flow, the environment, and sector specific requirements" (Stein, 1985, p.1). The problem of predicting and measuring workload is tied up in the operational definition of the construct. The literature is replete with views on operationalising workload (cf. Wickens, Mavor, & McGee, 1997). We briefly consider common theoretically and empirically derived operationalisations of workload before turning to the one advocated in this paper.

*Empirical approaches*

Computerised processes for providing quantitative estimates of ATC controller workload include the Relative Capacity Estimating Process (RECEP) and the Air Traffic Flow (ATF) model (Robertson, Grossberg, & Richards, 1979). RECEP uses a metric that looks at the frequency of specified activities performed within a defined time interval. This method provides a static measure of controller workload. In contrast, ATF provides a real-time continuous measure of controller workload in simulations of different system configurations of sectors or a centre.

RECEP and ATF permit the prediction of workload from system characteristics. However, because they are empirically derived models, they are only able to provide a model of outcomes, not of processes. Our theory-based model describes similar outcomes but emphasises the information processing strategies that lead to these outcomes. The advantage of this theoretical approach is that it provides an understanding of why overload and underload occurs, and it allows for the optimisation of the workload environment.

*Theoretical approaches*

Traditionally, cognitive workload researchers have drawn on information processing theories that focus on attentional resource limitations (cf. Wickens, Mavor, & McGee, 1997) or define workload in terms of number of items or units of information confronting human operators at any one time (cf. Wickens, Mavor, & McGee, 1997). These theories have contributed to the identification of some of the factors influencing workload such as stress, attentional demands from competing tasks and team-members, fatigue, and well-being (cf. Härtel & Härtel, 1997; Härtel & Härtel, 1996/1997). Consequently, workload measures focus typically on perceptions, observations, and physiological indicators of these factors (e.g., Stein, 1985). We argue that more sophisticated measurement of workload is being inhibited by the continued reliance on qualitative theories of information processing, quantitative theories using item or unit metrics (volume measures), and empirically derived models of controller workload. We propose that theoretical perspectives aimed at quantifying both volume and complexity of information processing are needed to advance workload measurement to the next level. We illustrate this point by discussing an alternative basis for approaching the problem of workload measurement and prediction, namely the incorporation of Graeme Halford's complexity metric with Härtel's SHAPE model addressing information processing strategies.

**The SHAPE model**

SHAPE designates both a theory of decision making and problem solving and a specific decision making algorithm (i.e., the acronym stands for Scrutinise, Hypothesise, Analyse, Perform and Evaluate). SHAPE was designed for cognitively busy decision-situations such as faced by air traffic controllers and aircrews. An essential feature of cognitively busy decision-situations is the requirement to deal with information in real-time within time-constrained environments. The workload measurement issue therefore is how to measure workload demands instantaneously, or in real-time.

Decision making involves cognitive processing of information in order to choose an alternative or action. Clearly decisions will vary in their complexity and cognitive workload demand. The complexity depends partly upon the information required to make a decision and the complexity of this information. Typically the amount of information involved in making a decision would exceed an individual's cognitive capacity. Therefore the SHAPE decision making strategy involves breaking the information processing into sequential or serial steps each of which is sufficiently small to not exceed or strain cognitive capacity (Härtel & Härtel, 1997; in press). Traditional decision making theory ignores this requirement, based on an unrealistic assumption of virtually infinite computing power (Simon, 1977).

The SHAPE strategy is a sequential and iterative algorithm that assists a decision maker in sequencing information processing and in managing cognitive workload (see Härtel & Härtel, 1996/1997; 1997; in press for more complete detail on SHAPE algorithm). For the purpose of this discussion the essence of SHAPE is that it assists workload management by having users generate decision alternatives one at a time rather than generating many decision alternatives and then comparing them. SHAPE also includes simple heuristics for assessing the suitability of each alternative. The alternatives are generated based on an expert's ability to recognise familiar situations and almost automatically retrieve a dominant response. The cognitive load on the individual while assessing a single alternative is simply retrieving known information about this alternative and assessing it relative to the current decision situation and objectives. Halford's methods can be used to assess the complexity in the mental load of such an individual step.

A key aspect of the SHAPE approach is the identification and analysis of the decision situation. This situation analysis includes identifying the cognitive workload and resources available to assist in workload management. SHAPE contends that it is necessary to understand the complexity of the information-processing environment in order to design effective environmental modifications and training interventions. We propose that an adaptation of this notion to the workload measurement issue may enable improved instantaneous measures of workload to be developed.

The SHAPE situation analysis is a way of seeing how complex information is in a given environment. We propose that the SHAPE situation analysis include Halford's relational complexity metric.

**Quantifying information processing load using Halford's relational complexity metric**

In the past information load has been quantified by assessing the number of entities that have to be held in short term memory. This has commonly been done by assessing memory span, which is the longest string of items that can be remembered after a single presentation. For example, adults can typically remember about 7 decimal digits, barely enough to dial a telephone number. The major drawback with span measures is that they assess the number of items stored, whereas the real need is to assess how much information can be taken into account in making a decision. Short term memory storage is at least partly independent of information processed, and a single task cannot be assumed to measure both. The distinction can be illustrated by considering the processing load imposed by adding two multi-digit numbers. For example, in adding 369 and 478, some information is stored for future processing, but this storage is distinct from using information to make a decision. So when adding 9 and 8, the digits are not simply being stored, but are being used to constrain the output. This is information processing rather than storage. Evidence that the two are distinct cognitive processes is provided by studies showing that decision making is not necessarily disrupted by concurrent short term storage of information (Klapp, Marshburn, & Lester, 1983). To investigate the workload of controllers it is necessary to devise a way of estimating processing, rather than storage, loads. This can be done using a metric based on complexity of relations that are being processed (Halford, 1993; Halford, Wilson, & Phillips, submitted - see world wide web access in reference list), as explained below.

One of the distinguishing features of air traffic control tasks is the large amount of information that controllers are required to process. Analyses of situation awareness (Endsley & Rogers, 1994) show that a very large amount of information may impinge on the controller's decision making at any one time. Previous work has helped define the type of information that is processed. Seamster, Redding, Cannon, Ryder, and Purcell (1993) identified three major sources of information that expert air traffic controllers attend to: sector management data, conditions, and prerequisite information. Sector management data includes information pertaining to present or anticipated sector traffic events, basic data about each aircraft in the sector, and the controller's plans for managing present and future traffic events. The conditions represent the contextual factors that the controller must attend to, which constrain the types of actions that the controller can take (e.g., weather factors). Prerequisite information relates to information stored in long term memory, and includes both sector-specific and general ATC information (e.g., airspace limitations, and ATC procedures). However information processing loads have not yet been adequately quantified. While most controllers and supervisors are well aware of the demands that the quantity of information makes on controllers, analysis of the problem in depth requires a scientific way to assess information processing load which has not previously been available.

There clearly is a need to quantify the amount of information that the controller must consider when making a decision, and to relate this to known human capacity to process information. Research on this question indicates that the best approach is to analyse the complexity of relations that must be processed. Any decision process can be expressed as a relation between entities or variables, and it turns out that complexity of relations that can be processed in parallel is the best way to quantify human processing capacity (Halford, 1993; Halford et al., 1994; Halford, Wilson, & Phillips, submitted). The essential idea is that a quaternary relation, or relation between four entities, is the most complex that adult humans can process in parallel. Thus human capacity is enough to keep track of about four interacting variables in parallel. This is a soft limit, so performance can be expected to decline gracefully, rather than catastrophically, when task complexity increases above this level, but increased error and longer decision times are to be expected.

## Segmentation and chunking

Many tasks are more complex than quaternary relations, and they can be handled by segmentation and conceptual chunking (Halford et al., 1994). Segmentation means that complex tasks can be decomposed into smaller segments that can be processed serially. The development of serial processing strategies permits complex tasks to be performed without exceeding limits on the amount of information that can be processed in parallel. The SHAPE algorithm provides a mental heuristic for facilitating this segmentation process.

For the controller, the development of serial processing strategies would mean that a situation could be segmented into a number of sub-problems that could be handled one at a time, returning periodically to a representation of the overall situation to check that decisions are not in conflict with each other. Situation monitoring can be viewed as a segmentation strategy. ATCs continually scan the situation display to identify changes in the environment and to update their situation awareness. The sequential nature of the scan suggests that the controllers are explicitly representing each relation, or a small subset of relations, in turn. Controllers focus on identifying the information within the display, developing an understanding of the present situation, and projecting the current situation forward in time (Endsley & Rogers, 1994). If situation monitoring is not carried out continually (e.g., because the controller gets distracted by a particular problem), then the operator's situation awareness quickly deteriorates, and errors can occur (Wellens, 1993).

Management of information processing load is an important part of a controller's expertise, and is a key aspect of ATC training. Seamster, et al. (1993), for example, found that expert controllers used a wider range of strategies for managing information processing load than novices. However there are limits to segmentation and chunking, and overload of processing capacity can occur, even for experts. The current model suggests that overload will reflect not only the quantity of variables that the controller has to attend to, but also the complexity of the relations between those variables. Accurate quantification of information processing loads, and assessment of the processing skills of controllers, could increase precision of job design and training, and lead to better prediction of error, controller stress, and personnel requirements.

**References**

Endsley, M.R., & Rogers, M.D. (1994). *Situation awareness information requirements for en route air traffic control.* Washington, DC: Federal Aviation Administration.

Halford, G.S. (1993). Competing, or perhaps complementary, approaches to the dynamic binding problem, with similar capacity limitations. Open peer commentary on paper by L. Shastri and V. Ajjanagadde, From Simple Associations to Systematic Reasoning: A connectionist Representation of Rules, Variables, and Dynamic Bindings using Temporal Synchrony. *Behavioral and Brain Sciences, 16,* (3), 461-462.

Halford, G.S., Maybery M.T., O'Hare, A.W., & Grant, P. (1994). The development of memory and processing capacity. *Child Development, 65*(5), 1338-1356.

Halford, G.S., Wilson, W.H., & Phillips, S. (submitted*). Processing capacity defined by relational complexity: Implications for comparative, developmental, and cognitive psychology.* May be accessed at: http://www.psy.uq.oz.au/Department/Staff/gsh/

Härtel, C.E.J., Härtel, G.F., & Barney, M.F. (in press). SHAPE: A scaffold for decision making and problem solving paradigms. *Training Research Journal.*

Härtel, C.E.J., & Härtel, G.F. (1997, September). SHAPE-assisted intuitive decision making and problem solving: Information-processing-based training for conditions of cognitive busyness. *Group Dynamics: Theory, Research, and Practice, 1*(3), 187-199.

Härtel, C.E., & Härtel, G.F. (1996/1997). Making decision making training work. *Training Research Journal, 2,* 69-84.

Härtel, C.E.J., & Härtel, G.F. (1995). *Controller Resource Management -- What can we learn from aircrews?* (DOT/FAA/AM 95/21). Oklahoma City: Civil Aeromedical Institute.

Härtel, C.E.J., Smith, K.A., & Prince, C. (April, 1991). Defining aircrew coordination: Searching mishaps for meaning. *Proceedings of the 6th International Symposium on Aviation Psychology.* Columbus, OH.

Klapp, S.T., Marchburn, E.A., & Lester, P.T. (1983). Short-term memory does not involve the "working memory" of information processing: The demise of a common assumption. *Journal of Experimental Psychology: General, 112,* 240-264.

Prince, C., Härtel, C.E.J., & Salas, E. (April, 1993). Aeronautical decision making and consistency of crew behaviors. *Proceedings of the 7th International Symposium on Aviation Psychology.* Columbus, OH.

Robertson, A., Grossbreg, & Richards, J. (1979). *Validation of air traffic controller workload models.* Report No. FAA-RD-79-83. Washington DC: US Department of Transportation Federal Aviation Administration, Systems Research and Development Service.

Seamster, T.L., Redding, R.E., Cannon, J.R., Ryder, J.M., & Purcell, J.A. (1993). Cognitive task analysis of expertise in air traffic control. *The International Journal of Aviation Psychology, 3,* 257-283.

Stein, E.S. (1985*). Air traffic controller workload: An examination of workload probe.* Report No. DOT/FAA/CT-TN84/24. Atlantic City Airport, New Jersey: Technical Center Library.

Wellens, A.R. (1993). Group situation awareness and distributed decision making: From military to civilian applications. In N.J. Castellan, Jr. (Ed.), *Individual and Group Decision Making* (pp. 267-291). Hillsdale: NJ: Lawrence.

Wickens, C.D., Mavor, A.S., & McGee, J.P. (Eds.) (1997). Workload and vigilance. *Flight to the future: Human factors in air traffic control.* (pp. 112-134). Washington, DC: National Academy Press.

# 32 Developing measures of situation awareness, task performance, and contextual performance in air traffic control

*Andrew F. Neal, Mark A. Griffin, Jan Paterson and Prashant Bordia*
*The University of Queensland*

## Introduction

An automated air traffic management system is currently being introduced within Australia. The Australian Advanced Air Traffic System (TAAATS) will represent a major change to ATC within Australia, particularly within sectors not under radar control. One of the major changes for controllers will be the replacement of paper flight progress strips with electronic strips, and the presentation of flight plan tracks and radar tracks on a common air situation display. There will also be significant changes to the way that flight data is processed, stored, and accessed, and there will also be major changes to the procedures used for managing traffic. In addition, a range of new functions (Automatic Dependent Surveillance, and Controller-Pilot Data Link) and traffic management tools (e.g., short route probe, route display) will be introduced.

The introduction of TAAATS, therefore, will have a significant impact on the job of an air traffic controller. One of the many challenges posed by the introduction of this new generation of technology relates to the measurement and management of ATC performance. The new technology will eliminate many of the behavioural cues that assessors have relied on to make judgements regarding the performance of controllers. In the past, assessors have been able to base their judgements of a controller's performance on a range of observable cues. Scanning technique, for example could be inferred by observing the way that the controller physically interacted with the strips (e.g., cocking and annotating strips). Furthermore, a history of the controller's actions was immediately available by reference to the annotations on the strips. In the new system, it will be much more difficult to assess factors such as scanning technique, because controllers will no longer be able to physically interact with the display in the same manner.

These changes are reflected across a range of industries where automated production technologies have been introduced. The introduction of these technologies poses a number of problems for traditional approaches to performance measurement (Hesketh & Neal, in press). Traditionally, the focus of performance measurement has been on behaviours that are under the control of the individual. The aim has been to isolate those aspects of performance that are directly attributable to the individual, and to select, train, and reward individuals on the basis of those aspects (Pulakos & Ilgen, in press). However, as can be seen from above, automation has reduced the behavioural component of jobs such as ATC. Performance measures now need to incorporate cognitive elements of performance, such as monitoring, planning, and problem solving and need to provide techniques for assessing them.

*Performance*

The current project aims to develop a set of ATC performance measures within this new environment. The measures are based on models of performance developed by Campbell, McCloy, Oppler, and Sager (1993) and Borman and Motowidlo (1993). Campbell et al. (1993) define performance as a set of behaviours that are relevant to the goals of the organisation. Performance can be distinguished from effectiveness, which is defined as the value of those behaviours for the organisation. Managing traffic, issuing instructions, and operating the workstation are elements of performance, since they are behaviours carried out by controllers. Effectiveness, however, is judged by the extent to which there is a safe, orderly, and efficient flow of traffic. Effectiveness can be influenced by both the performance of the individual, and the difficulty or constraints of the situation. Very little work has been carried out assessing the potential relationships that may exist between performance, situational factors, and effectiveness.

Existing research has focused on performance. Campbell et al. (1993) make a distinction between the components and determinants of performance. The components of performance represent the actual behaviours that constitute performance. The determinants of performance represent the human capacities necessary for individuals to produce these behaviours. Campbell et al. (1993) argue that there are only three determinants of performance: knowledge, skill and motivation. In relation to the components of performance, both Campbell et al. (1993) and Borman and Motowidlo (1993) make a distinction between technical proficiency (termed 'task performance' by Borman and Motowidlo) and other non-technical components of performance. Borman and Motowidlo (1993), for example, introduced the construct of contextual performance. Contextual performance relates to discretionary activities such as volunteering to carry out tasks, cooperating with coworkers, exerting effort, and promoting the organisation.

While the existing performance research represents a significant advance on previous conceptualisations of performance, these models are limited by their exclusive focus on the behavioural elements of performance. As noted above, many aspects of a controller's work are no longer directly observable. The project team, therefore, expanded the definition of task performance to incorporate cognitive elements relating to Situation Awareness (SA), such as perception, comprehension and projection (Endlsey, 1995).

A job analysis was carried out to identify the key elements of en route and TMA controller's jobs within the new system. The results of the job analysis are shown in Figure 32.1. The elements of situation awareness within the job include: scanning; interpreting and evaluating traffic events; and prioritising, projecting, and planning. The remaining behavioural elements of task performance include executing control actions, communicating, and operating facilities. The elements of contextual performance included teamwork, professionalism, and support for organisational objectives. The situational factors that were identified were traffic volume, traffic complexity, weather, abnormal situations, and pilot actions. The elements of effectiveness were orderliness and efficiency of traffic flow.

A set of behaviourally anchored rating scales was developed to assess performance on each of these dimensions. Given the difficulty in making judgements regarding SA in TAAATS, focus groups were run to identify the types of cues that assessors could use to make inferences for this component. Three types of cues were identified: the methods and

307

techniques used by the controller when managing traffic (e.g., the position of the mouse cursor may illustrate his/her scanning technique); observable outcomes (e.g., if the ATC is surprised by an aircraft call s/he may not have been scanning); and questions that can be used to assess awareness.

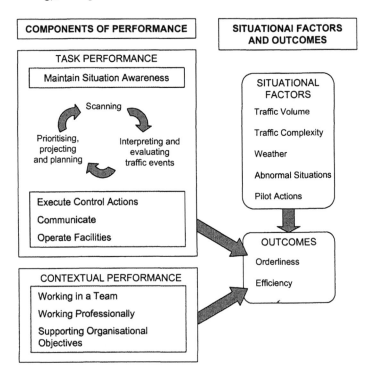

**Figure 32.1**
**Model of performance, situational factors, and outcomes.**

The current paper reports the results from a study examining the reliability and validity of the measures of task performance. Two videos were created to illustrate different levels of performance (barely competent vs. expert) in an en route sector. A group of team leaders was asked to rate the performance of the controllers in the two videos. Half of the team leaders had prior experience with the sector, while half did not. It was predicted that there would be significant variance in ratings due to the competence level of controller and the dimension being assessed. Any variance in ratings due to rater represents error. It was predicted that the variance due to rater would be lower in the experienced group than in the inexperienced group.

# Method

## *Materials*

A simulation exercise was videoed, using an en route sector in northern Australia. The exercise ran for 15 minutes. Two subject matter experts were selected to perform the exercise and to simulate different levels of performance. One controller was asked to simulate the minimum level of performance required to maintain their endorsement (simulation 1). The second controller was asked to simulate the performance level shown by an expert on that sector (simulation 2). A set of seven point graphic rating scales was used by the subjects to assess performance on three dimensions (*1= remedial training required, 4=minimum level expected of an endorsed controller, 7= best possible performance that an expert could be expected to show*). The dimensions were: situation awareness (SA: 7 items), executing control actions (ECA: 6 items), and communication (Com: 8 items). Specific behavioural anchors were provided for points 1, 4 and 7 on each scale, and summarised in an accompanying reference manual.

## *Subjects*

Eight team leaders participated in the study. All of the subjects in the experienced group supervised controllers in the en route sector shown in the video, or in adjacent en route sectors. Two subjects in the inexperienced group supervised TMA sectors, and two supervised tower controllers.

## *Procedure*

Subjects attended a workshop in which they received training in how to use the performance measures. Following the conclusion of the training, the subjects were shown simulation 1, and were asked to rate the performance of the controller. Following a break of half an hour, the same procedure was repeated for simulation 2.

# Results

Ratings from the eight assessors on the three performance dimensions for both simulations were first assessed for internal consistency. Alpha reliabilities for each dimension were consistently high (see Table 32.1). Intercorrelations of the dimensions were not higher than the internal consistency estimates indicating that multicollinearity of the dimensions was not a problem with the ratings. The correlation between situation awareness and communication was the only correlation that was not significant. The internal consistency results provided initial evidence that the dimensions describe distinct constructs amenable to rater assessment.

**Table 32.1**
**Means and intercorrelations of performance measures**

|  | Mean | SD | ∝ | SA | ECA |
|---|---|---|---|---|---|
| SA | 4.7 | 0.5 | .98 | | |
| ECA | 4.6 | 0.3 | .94 | .85* | |
| Com | 4.5 | 0.3 | .96 | .63 | .79* |

$* p < .05$

The next step in understanding the structure of the ratings was a variance components analysis of the performance ratings. The total variance in ratings can be attributed to variation between the two simulations, variation among the performance dimensions, and variation among the raters. In addition, interactions among these factors may contribute to variation in ratings. We found that most of the variation in ratings was between the two simulations ($F_{1, 276} = 320.1$, $p < .001$). This result demonstrates that the measures were sensitive to the experimental manipulation of performance levels. The mean performance rating for Simulation 1 was 3.56 ($SD = .47$) with the target value for the simulated task being 4.00. The mean rating for simulation 2 was 5.61 ($SD = .74$) with a target value of 7.00.

There was also substantial variation across raters indicating that there was not good agreement among the raters on the performance dimensions ($F_{7, 276} = 10.6$, $p < .001$). However, when raters were divided into those with experience in the sector and those without experience in the sector, we found that only the inexperienced group showed significant variance in ratings ($F_{3, 130} = 26.0$, $p < .001$). This result suggests that experienced raters were more accurate in assessing the level of performance in both simulations compared to raters without experience in the sector.

Across all ratings, there was no significant variation attributable to the three performance dimensions ($F_{2, 276} = 1.3$, ns). This result does not support the proposed dimensional structure of the measures. However, there was a significant interaction between the simulation and the performance dimensions ($F_{2, 276} = 6.2$, $p < .01$). Further inspection of these results indicated that there was little variation among the performance dimensions for the simulation that depicted minimum performance but that there was a difference for the simulation that depicted higher levels of performance ($F_2$, $_{130} = 4.6, p < .05$).

Overall, three key results were obtained from the variance components analysis. First, the differences between the two videos indicate that different levels of performance can be reliably distinguished using the rating dimensions. Second, raters with en route experience were more accurate in their assessments of performance. Finally, the performance dimensions were more distinct when the simulations depicted high levels of performance compared to simulations depicting mediocre levels of performance.

**Discussion**

Overall, the results provide reasonable support for the hypotheses. The performance measures had high internal consistency, and the assessors were able to reliably distinguish between good and average levels of performance. The results also demonstrate that the team leaders' ability to assess performance was critically dependent upon their prior experience. These findings reinforce the importance of prior experience and training when providing performance assessments.

The finding that subjects discriminated between performance dimensions when observing high levels of performance, but not when observing lower levels, was unexpected. There are a number of potential explanations for this effect. It may be the case that there is greater opportunity for experts to demonstrate variability across the different dimensions of performance. Novices may perform uniformly poor on all dimensions. Alternatively, these differences may simply be an artefact of the instructions given to the SMEs, or may reflect idiosyncratic differences between the SMEs that may not generalise to the population as a whole. Finally, it could be the case that the assessments of performance for the mediocre example simply reflected halo error. If this were true, then it also suggests that halo effects are weaker when assessing experts than novices.

The absence of a significant correlation between situation awareness and communication should be interpreted cautiously given the small sample size. However, it does make sense that this correlation should be lower than the others, as the key elements of situation awareness (e.g., recognising conflicts) are directly linked to control actions (maintaining separation). Similarly, the execution of control actions is dependent on the use of communication procedures. There is no direct link between situation awareness and communication.

311

The major limitation of the current study was the small sample size. The sample size limited the power of the between groups analyses, and precluded the use of confirmatory factor analysis to test the dimensional structure of the measures. Studies are currently underway using the performance measures to assess controllers in a field environment. These studies will allow us to test the factor structure of the measures, and the hypothesised relationships among performance, situational factors, and effectiveness.

*Practical implications*

One of the major practical implications of the current study is that rating scales can be used to reliably assess performance in ATC. Competency-based approaches to assessment, as promoted by the National Training Authority, do not allow for the grading of performance. Within a competency-based approach, performance is simply assessed as competent or not competent, and no attempt is made to assess the relative level of expertise of the worker. A critical objective for any organisation in a safety-critical area, such as ATC must be to encourage the development of expertise. This involves the development of performance management systems that track the performance of individuals from the time that they first apply for selection, through training, until they leave the job. This type of database provides an invaluable tool for the management of individual performance.

The practical value of performance management systems can be further increased by incorporating the types of variables shown in Figure 32.1. A database that links performance to situational factors and effectiveness can be used to identify the critical variables that influence effectiveness, and to monitor the effects of intervention programs aimed at modifying these variables. Linking selection and training data to the performance measures then allows the organisation to quantify the impact of selection and training programs on organisational effectiveness.

**Acknowledgements**

This research was supported by Airservices Australia. We are grateful to Ted Lang, Iain Burley, Christine Boag and Matthew Neale for their assistance.

# References

Borman, W.C., & Motowidlo, S.J. (1993). Expanding the criterion domain to include elements of contextual performance. In N. Schmitt & W.C. Borman and Asssociates (Eds.), *Personnel Selection in Organizations.* San Francisco: Jossey-Bass.

Campbell, J.P., McCloy, R.A., Oppler, S.H., & Sager, C.E. (1993). A theory of performance. In N. Schmitt, W.C. Borman and Associates (Eds.), *Personnel Selection in Organizations.* Jossey-Bass, San Francisco.

Endlsey, M.C. (1995) Toward a theory of situation awareness in dynamic systems. *Human Factors, 37,* 32-64.

Hesketh, B., & Neal, A. (in press). Technology and performance. To appear in D. Ilgen & E. Pulakos (Eds.), *The changing nature of work performance: Implications for staffing, personnel actions, and development.* San Francisco: Jossey Bass.

Pulakos, E., & Ilgen, D. (in press). *The changing nature of work performance: Implications for staffing, personnel actions, and development.* San Francisco: Jossey Bass.

# 33 The human-machine interface in air traffic control: Task analysis of existing ATC

*Hiroki Sato, Ministry of Transport (Japan)*
*David Rackham, International Christian University (Japan)*

## Abstract

Air traffic control is a very complex process that depends to a large degree on the human operator's capabilities and limitations. The design of an advanced and efficient Air Traffic Control (ATC) console for the future requires an understanding of the nature of the interaction between the controller and the four basic available sources of information: (1) aircraft pilot; (2) other controllers; (3) the radar display console; and (4) paper flight progress strip. A task analysis of the current en route ATC system in Japan was conducted by observing a radar controller/coordinator team over a 4,500 second observation period. Analyses indicated a very high work load for both members of the team as measured by work time and frequency of sub-tasks. The combined time spent on the eleven sub-tasks over the 4,500 second interval was 6,415 seconds for the radar controller and 6,244 seconds for the coordinator, indicating that two or more tasks were being performed simultaneously by team members. This paper also presents additional useful technical data related to both ATC console issues and future air traffic control working environments.

## Introduction

En route air traffic control exists to provide safe aircraft operation. Controllers are responsible for maintaining an adequate in-flight separation standard and air traffic flow as well as an orderly approach pattern to airports. Air traffic control is a complex process influenced to a large degree by the human operator's information processing capabilities and limitations (Hopkin, 1988).

Increasing air traffic volume has made the controller's work load more demanding. Too much information presented simultaneously or inefficiently can exceed the processing capabilities of the controller, increasing the chances for error. It is important to consider how future air traffic control systems can be enhanced in terms of the capabilities of the human operator. In designing the human-machine interface, it is not sufficient to design solely with machine engineering specifications in mind (see Sato, 1993; Sato, Rackham, & Yamazaki, 1997). Serious consideration must be given to providing a simplified operational procedure for the controller. We have been engaged in task analyses of the controller's job in anticipation of developing a new method for the presentation of critical information on ATC display consoles.

## Operations concept

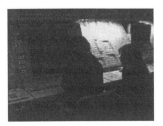

Figure 33.1. Air traffic controllers' working environment

Figure 33.1 shows the air traffic controller's working environment. The radar controller and coordinator work as a team to manage air traffic in their assigned sector. The radar controller is seated in front of the radar display while the coordinator is located to the right in front of the strip board. The radar controller and the coordinator team work with four basic sources of information: (1) they exchange information with the pilot (aircraft); (2) they coordinate with other air traffic controllers; (3) the radar display provides information about the status of individual aircraft and traffic flow; and (4) flight progress strips provide an ongoing record of individual aircraft data (see Figure 33.16, "present working environment").

## Task analyses of the present en route ATC working environment

In the face of increasing air traffic volume, it is necessary to understand more clearly the factors affecting the efficiency with which the radar controller/coordinator team perform their functions. Accordingly, task analyses of routine en route ATC functions were conducted as follows. Two

Sony Handycam Hi-8 mm video cameras (Model #CCD-TRV90 NTSC) were used to record the tasks performed by a radar controller/coordinator team during a routine course of duty. Radio and voice communication events and strip marking, handling and reading events were also recorded in terms of time and number of events. Computer input and output data records from the Flight Data Processing System (FDP) and the Radar Data Processing System (RDP) were also used.

**Results of task analyses**

Controllers' activities were divided into eleven sub-tasks as follows: (1) switching radio frequency; (2) radio transmitting; (3) radio receiving; (4) strip marking; (5) strip handling; (6) strip reading; (7) data inputting to RDP; (8) RDP display monitoring; (9) data reading on CRT from FDP; (10) coordination with controllers in other sectors; and (11) coordination with the controller in the same sector.

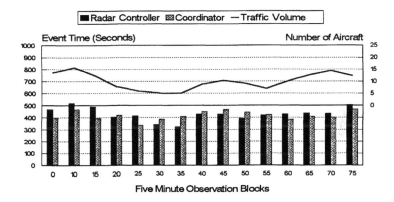

**Figure 33.2**

**Total work time summarised over 5-minute blocks of all sub-tasks for the radar controller and the coordinator, respectively, based on a total observation period of 4,500 seconds**

Figure 33.2 shows the total work time summarised over intervals of 5 minutes of all sub-tasks for the radar controller and the coordinator based

317

on a total observation period of 4500 seconds. Average air traffic volume over 5-minute observation intervals is also represented in Figure 33.2. It can be seen that work load tends to vary with traffic volume. A strong relationship was observed between air traffic volume and the amount of time taken by the radar controller to perform his tasks ($r = 0.834, p \leq .01$). There was no statistically significant relationship between air traffic volume and the amount of time taken by the coordinator to perform his tasks ($r = 0.369, ns$). This suggests that the radar controller's job is more tactical or immediate in nature while the coordinator spends more time anticipating and planning for the future traffic situation.

Figure 33.3 shows the total time taken to perform all episodes of each of the eleven en route ATC sub-tasks over a 4,500 second observation period.

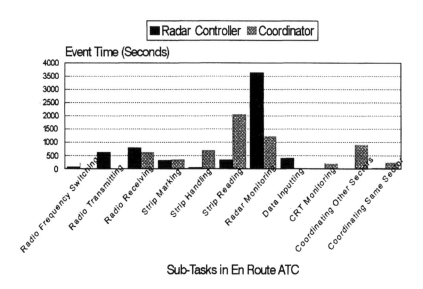

**Figure 33.3**
**Total time taken to perform all episodes of each of the eleven en route ATC sub-tasks over a 4,500 second observation period**

It can be seen that the radar controller spends the largest single proportion of his time on radar monitoring (80.4% of the 4,500 second observation period; 56.4% of the amount of time taken for all sub-tasks). This is followed by radio receiving and radio transmitting. In contrast, strip reading, radar monitoring and coordinating with controllers in other sectors are the most time intensive tasks performed by the coordinator. Overall, Figure 33.3 suggests that monitoring the radar display is the single most critical and time consuming task for the radar controller/coordinator team. Although the coordinator does not sit in front of the radar display, he nevertheless makes intensive use of the information available there to understand the present traffic situation and to anticipate future changes in air traffic flow.

Frequency histograms were developed for each sub-task on the basis of number of events and time taken to complete these events measured in one second intervals. Figure 33.4 shows the distribution of radio frequency shifting events for the radar controller. Radio frequency shifting involves looking up to the switch panel, selecting and pushing the appropriate button, and then looking down again to the radar display. The mean time taken to perform this task was 1.5 seconds, standard deviation of 0.74.

Figure 33.5 is a histogram of radio transmitting events for the radar controller. Radio transmitting is the primary responsibility of the radar controller and is normally integrated with the radio receiving task. The mean time taken to transmit instructions to pilots was 3.4 seconds with a standard deviation of 1.86.

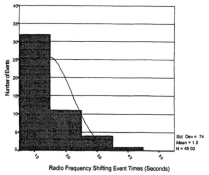

Radio Frequency Shifting Event Times (Seconds)

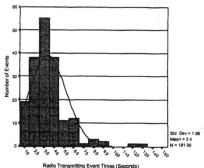

Radio Transmitting Event Times (Seconds)

**Figure 33.4**
**Radio frequency shifting event times for the radar controller**

**Figure 33.5**
**Radio transmitting event times for the radar controller**

319

Figures 33.6a and 33.6b are histograms of radio receiving events for the radar controller and coordinator. Radio receiving is done by both the radar controller and the coordinator. The mean time spent by the coordinator on this task is a little less than that of the radar controller because coordinating with other controllers is a higher priority task for the coordinator.

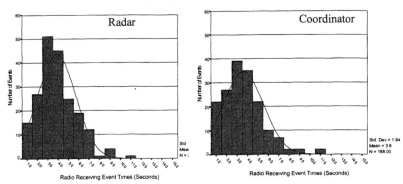

**Figures 33.6a and 33.6b**
**Radio receiving event times for the radar controller and coordinator**

Figures 33.7a and 33.7b show strip marking events for the radar controller and coordinator. The average time spent on strip marking was very short for both the radar controller and coordinator (2.6 and 2.7 secs. respectively). However, the standard deviation for the radar controller coordinator is considerably less than the standard deviation for the coordinator (1.20 vs. 1.94). This is likely due to the fact that the coordinator is recording information on the strips from a variety of sources as a result of his coordinating activities with other controllers in other sectors.

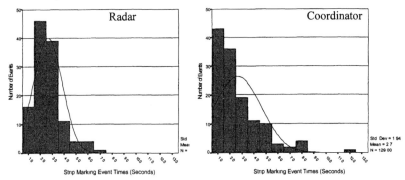

**Figures 33.7a and 33.7b**
**Strip marking event times for the radar controller and the coordinator**

320

Figures 33.8a and 33.8b are histograms of strip handling event times for the radar controller and coordinator. Strip handling is mostly done by the coordinator. The mean time and number of events for the coordinator are much larger than for the radar controller. The coordinator often reads the data on strips while in the process of handling them. It also takes a considerable amount of time to arrange the strips on the strip board.

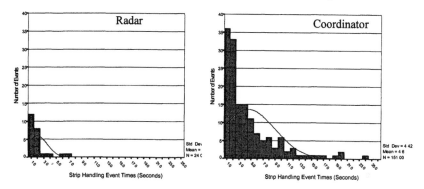

**Figures 33.8a and 33.8b**
**Strip handling event times for the radar controller and the coordinator**

Figures 33.9a and 33.9b show strip reading event times for the radar controller and coordinator. Strip reading is mostly done by the coordinator. The mean time for strip reading by the coordinator is twice as long as that for the radar controller. The radar controller is essentially looking at the strips while recording information on them because he has enough information available from other sources, particularly the radar display. The coordinator has to read and understand strip data to carry out his duties.

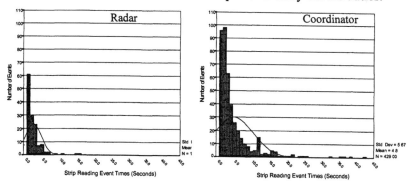

**Figures 33.9a and 33.9b**
**Strip reading event times for the radar controller and the coordinator**

321

Figures 33.10a and 33.10b show radar monitoring event times by the radar controller and coordinator. The time spent on radar monitoring by the controller is nearly three times as long as that for the coordinator (9.2 vs. 3.5 secs.). The time spent on radar monitoring by the controller and the coordinator together comprises the largest amount of time spent on a single task. However, the total number of monitoring events by the coordinator differs little from the number of monitoring events by the radar controller (347 vs. 393). This indicates that information on the radar display is very useful for both team members to understand the current air traffic situation.

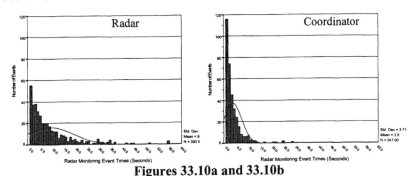

**Figures 33.10a and 33.10b**
**Radar monitoring event times for the radar controller and coordinator**

Figures 33.11a and 33.11b show times for entering data to the system. Entering data is mostly done by the radar controller but the mean time spent in this activity by the radar controller is very short (1.8 seconds). The radar controller normally enters data to the system when he issues instructions to the pilot. When instructions are being issued to the pilot, the air traffic situation tends to be more complex. The radar controller must pay close attention to changes in the situation after issuing his instructions.

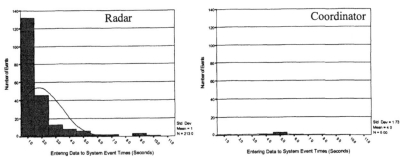

**Figures 33.1a and 33.11b**
**Entering data to system times for the radar controller and coordinator**

Figure 33.12 is a histogram of monitoring CRT event times by the coordinator. The CRT is located to the right of the strip board. Revised information from the FDP, mostly regarding revised estimated time of arrival and/or revised altitude, is displayed on the CRT. The coordinator is responsible for monitoring information on the CRT and transferring this information to paper strips as necessary.

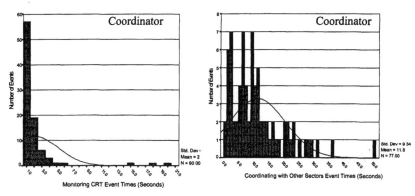

**Figure 33.12**
**Monitoring CRT event times for the coordinator**

**Figure 33.13**
**Coordinating with controllers in other sectors event times for the coordinator**

Figure 33.13 is a histogram of coordinating with controllers in other sectors event times for the coordinator. The coordinator has primary responsibility for coordinating with controllers in other sectors. The mean event time is quite long (11.8 seconds) and the standard deviation is also large (9.34). This indicates that coordinating with other sectors is a complex and time consuming task for the coordinator.

Figures 33.14a and 33.14b are histograms of coordinating with the controller in the same sector event times for the radar controller and coordinator. Since the radar controller and the coordinator are working in the same sector, the histograms have a very similar appearance. Mean times and number of events are very similar for both members of the team. Compared to the task of coordinating with other sectors, both the mean event time and the standard deviation are very small for both team members. If the radar controller and the coordinator had equal access to the same kind of visual information about the current traffic situation, this would enhance their ability to manage air traffic in their sector. Under present circumstances, the radar controller has much easier access to visual information than the coordinator as the radar display is situated directly in

323

front of him. The coordinator must orient to the left in order to have access to the radar display (See Figure 33.1).

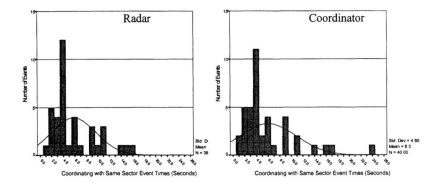

### Figures 33.14a and 33.14b
### Coordinating with controller in the same sector event times for the radar controller and the coordinator

## Summary and recommendations

To consider an improved working environment for the radar controller/coordinator team for en route ATC, it is necessary to have a clear understanding of the present working environment. The tasks analyses described above lead to a number of recommendations for future en route ATC developments.

Figure 33.15 summarises the sources of information used by the radar controller/coordinator team in terms of the amount of time working with these sources as recorded over a 4,500 second observation period. The controllers have to work with all four sources of information to properly fulfill their duties. Present operating procedures based on these sources of information are quite complex, especially under heavy traffic conditions. Lower priority tasks can often consume just as much time and effort as higher priority tasks. For example, when the radar controller recognises that instructions have to be issued to a pilot, he must follow a certain sequence of actions. The main priorities are determining the proper instructions to be sent to the pilot and then transmitting those instructions. If the traffic flow is heavy, these are very demanding tasks by themselves. However, he is also required to spend time writing those same instructions on a strip and to input data to the system. This increases the probability of controller error under heavy traffic conditions when he may have difficulty managing even the high priority tasks. There is an obvious need to simplify working procedures in order to reduce the controllers' work load and to minimise error rates.

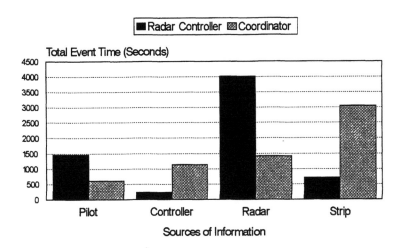

**Figure 33.15**
**Total time spent working with information from four basis sources based on a 4,500 second observation period**

The task analyses reported here suggest that an integrated radar display system should be developed which provides the same basic information to the radar controller and the coordinator, even though they may use this information in somewhat different, although overlapping, ways as they carry out their specific sub-task responsibilities. Such a display unit would reduce four sources of information to three as shown in Figure 33.16.

Figure 33.16 represents a possible future en route ATC working environment. In a proposed future working environment, four sources of information are reduced to three – the pilot, other controllers, and radar and flight information. In Figure 33.16, radar information and flight information, presently managed by two separate systems (radar display and strip board), would be combined into a single integrated display system

325

providing both radar and flight information (See Sato, Rackham, and Yamazaki, 1997). Such a display system would be provided to both the radar controller and the coordinator, helping them to synchronise their activities in managing their sector. Theoretically, such an integrated display could result in a significant reduction of the controller's work load. The benefits could appear in terms of an overall improvement in the efficiency of air traffic management. This, in turn, could result in a reduction in controller error rates with obvious implications for the overall safety of aircraft operations.

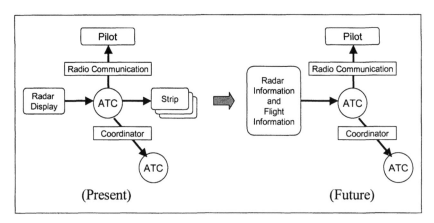

**Figure 33.16**
**Present and proposed future en route ATC working environments**

### References

Hopkin, V.D. (1988). Air traffic control. In Earl L. Wiener (Ed.), *Human factors in aviation*. San Diego: Academic Press, pp. 639-663.

Sato, H. (1993). Improving the man-machine interface in ATC displays: Changing ATC job characteristics. In *Proceedings of the 31ˢᵗ Aircraft Symposium*, Gifu, Japan, pp. 556-559.

Sato, H., Rackham, D.W., & Yamazaki, S. (1997). Future automated integrated display for en route ATC: Current developments. *Journal of Air Traffic Control, 39*(3), 51-55.

Wiener, E.L. (Ed.), (1988). *Human Factors in Aviation*. San Diego: Academic Press.

# 34 Making the link between human factors and organisational learning

*Christine Owen*
*University of Tasmania, Australia*

## Introduction

In this paper it is contended that the success or failure of a human factors related change may have nothing to do with the actual program itself, but may by influenced by a range of other organisational factors. Organisational factors break into two components: organisational structures and organisational cultures. Structures include: (1) physical resources and capability (e.g., the physical layout, as well as technologies used and their limitations, how busy the work gets); (2) work organisation (which includes hierarchies of authority, division of labour, career development paths); (3) policies and rules governing the organisation of work. For example, recruitment policies, appraisal and career development policies; rules of accountability (e.g., procedures for handling mistakes); (4) occupational roles performed and role expectations of the workforce.

## Organisational cultures

Organisational cultures are defined as the "habits, folkways and norms that shape action" (Westrum, 1992, p. 401) and the "set of understandings or meanings shared by a group of people" (Louis, 1986, p. 74). In organisations, both cultures and structures overlap. Both are sometimes visible to participants and at other times, invisible. So, for example, an organisation may have the best crew resource management training program in the world, with a sophisticated means by which to evaluate success or failure of training outcomes, but the program may still flounder because of internal organisational politics; it may not be supported by other divisions within the organisation because there is no readily identifiable link between the training program and the operational goals of the organisation; other policies or procedures may be in contradiction with the proposed change; or the program may initially succeed in some parts of the organisation, but then fail in others because of different cultural values, beliefs and social factors that may work against the change.

The claim developed in this paper is that we can advance the goals of the human factors project by drawing on perspectives that shed light on the influence of organisational context on the changes that we are trying to bring about. The perspective suggested to better understand the success or failure of human factors initiatives is organisational learning. Both human factors and organisational learning fields of practice are attempting to create conditions where learning is continuous (Westrum, 1992). Both express an interest in understanding the ways in which contextual elements (tools, structures, processes) influence work activity, and both acknowledge the importance of the role of the group in performance. The data used in this paper are drawn from the author's Doctoral research into learning in the ATC workplace and are used to show the ways in which organisational context influences human factors initiatives. This has been a three year qualitative study comprising 125 interviews across three ATC Centres.

What might a learning perspective bring to enable a better understanding of the ways in which contextual factors enhance or inhibit safety and efficiency? The purpose of this research has been to look at contextual influences in learning in the workplace in air traffic control. The contextual factors investigated have involved elements of organisational structure and culture. Some of the more important findings from this research include:

1. Organisational structures and cultures can be meaningfully classified in terms of the ways in which they enhance and inhibit learning.

2. Organisational change processes of recent years have fundamentally changed the ways in which people learn about the complex organisations and systems within which they work with both positive and negative results for learning. For example team work practices are modifying occupational identities from "lone rangers" to "team players".

3. Changes in work practice have narrowed the "band width" of work experience by removing a range of work activities with the consequence that reduced the opportunities to learn about the aviation system.

4. These changes increase the need to look for ways of spanning boundaries within and between organisations and functions to compensate for these changes.

5. In terms of cultures, story telling is a fundamentally important and under-stated component of learning in aviation organisations.

6. These stories are changing and access to them is diminishing due to the narrowing and splintering of functions, resulting in reduced capacities to learn from them.

7. Changes to structures and cultures combine to produce conflicting goals that result in tensions and contradictions within complex systems.

Themes that emerge from the organisational learning literature will be used to further develop some of these points. Within the organisational learning literature, information is re-framed as organisational knowledge and attention is given to how that "knowledge" is acquired, dispersed, interpreted and recalled. The following are identified as necessary within successful learning organisations:

1. rich and continuous processes aimed at the acquisition of knowledge (the term "knowledge" is used here in a broad sense to mean skills, understandings, attitudes),

2. densely interwoven patterns of knowledge distribution,

3. norms of behaviour where knowledge is interpreted and shared widely across the organisation, and

4. remembered through a range of strategies aimed at enhancing organisational memory.

*1 Knowledge acquisition*

How is knowledge acquired (formally and informally) within an organisation? In aviation organisations knowledge is acquired through pre-service and in-service training as well as through everyday work practice. In terms of formal pre-service training in ATC, recent changes in economic climate have led to a streamlining of course content with removal of "nice to know" material, with a subsequent reduction in time taken in training. Recruitment strategies have also changed with less reliance on individuals having an aviation background and a greater reliance on more sophisticated selection techniques (Hannan, 1996). These changes are leading to controllers being competent in job tasks and job performance, but who have less understanding than their older, more experienced counterparts, of the relationship between the controller's role and the roles others play within a complex system. The following quotation from an "old hand" summarises

329

concerns held about the level of background aviation knowledge held by newer controllers.

> We did a two year course and went out into the field and we did airline attachments and we did out-station attachments and we went to RAAF attachments and all sorts of things. We got to know about aviation. I already knew it because I had a pilot's licence before I joined. You got right into it and you met the pilots and you flew in the aeroplanes and you checked out the [aircraft] profiles and all sorts of things. There are guys up there now who have never even been inside the control tower. They have come out of the College and / they have never been inside a cockpit of a jet or anything else like that. They don't know what an aeroplane does. What it looks like. It is just a blip on the screen that goes so many knots. Then you have even got to tell them how fast they go. *'How fast does he really go?'* and you say *'well he does this, that and the other. The cockpit looks like this inside, visualise what's inside the cockpit. The pilot hasn't got a control panel, just a little stick on the side.' 'Oh has he?'* Just little things like that and get them to visualise what's going on. At the moment it's just a production line.

The narrowing of opportunities to learn about the aviation industry as a whole have also been expressed by others working in airline organisations. Recruitment and training strategies for pilots for example, have undergone similar changes. For example, in the past, many pilots learned to fly in aero clubs and flying schools whereas the new generation of pilot is being trained in universities. The processes by which people acquire knowledge as part of their everyday work practice have also undergone change. When individuals undertake their work tasks they learn not only about those tasks, but to some degree, about the ways in which those tasks impact on the work of others. In organisations where people move through various job roles, there is an increased likelihood that those individuals will gain a greater understanding of the "requisite variety" (Weick, 1987) within the system. The ways in which people acquire knowledge informally through work activity in air traffic control for example has undergone some dramatic changes in the five to ten years that reflect changes external to and within the organisation, and similar changes are found in other organisations. In Australia, for example, there has been a concerted effort across a range of industries to engage in:

- industrial development and technological improvement; the introduction of procedures in line with international practices; and the development of closer economic linkages between organisation and industry.

- work re-organisation and award restructuring, (the development of such change has been a major thrust of Australian government industrial reform). In air traffic control, this has lead to the closure of some services (e.g., flight operations), the reduction of services, the introduction of a new industrial award that involves multi-skilling; and the introduction of new accountability and decision making structures, (such as the introduction of teams) as well as changes to recruitment practices and career paths (such as "streaming" where controllers are recruited and trained to operate on one specialised stream of work such as approach or en route control).

Clearly these practices have been introduced for the betterment of the aviation system. And in most cases, this intention has been achieved. However, what these changes have also done has been to remove from the organisational system a variety of opportunities that employees have had in the past to learn about the aviation system and their impact on other actors operating within that system. The following quotation describing the impact of the closure of briefing offices in ATC illustrates this point.

At the stage that I first went to the [ATC Centre] we were running briefing offices at every general aviation aerodrome around the country. The purpose of the briefing offices [was] two fold. One is the provision of flight information for pilots/ like normal flight planning procedures. The second one was/ pilot education. It provided a link between air traffic services, air traffic controller flight service and the pilot. So that the pilot could go out, if flying around, [and] maybe not clear about something when they came back, they'd call in the briefing office and have someone clarify. Or maybe they did something wrong. Instead of a rather impersonal sort of phone call of whatever, it was quite common to ask a pilot to report to the briefing office so he could sit there and he could actually go through what the problem was and possible ways that they could solve that problem. It [was] an education tool. There's a huge advantage to this. That was our main interface with general aviation. We closed all our briefing offices around the country. / But immediately there was a noticeable difference to me. / you immediately lost that contact, face to face contact you had with pilots. Because everyone worked the briefing roster. You'd be over there, you might have to do one shift in 5 or 6 or something. But at least if you're in the briefing office you get to know the pilots as they're coming in, you talk to them. They know you, they recognise voices when you're talking to them on the radio./ So that went. It was a great loss to us.

Other structural changes occurring within the organisation, such as the introduction of teams produce counter tendencies to the "tunnel vision" described above, because (in many cases) these structures enhance requisite variety by enabling the experience that is distributed across the team to be pooled and shared. This of course, is only possible under certain conditions of team work (Beylerlein, Johnson & Beyerlein, 1997).

*2. Knowledge distribution*

How is knowledge distributed within an organisation? The ways in which knowledge is distributed will be determined by the type of "integrative mechanisms and lateral linkages" (Thompson & McHugh, 1990) built into organisational structures. The distribution of knowledge occurs when feedback loops are integrated into work activity within and between work groups and divisions. Programs such as crew resource management and team-building are aimed at enhancing the knowledge that is shared within groups. Greater attention however, needs to be given to how information is shared between, for example, flight operations and training departments, or in the case of air traffic control, between units such as safety and quality management and those involved in operational work. Within ATC, the increase in work complexity arising from the concentrations of work into two large Centres, has led the Southern District Office to develop a specific role within every team known as a "Team Training Specialist". This person's role is to span the boundaries between the team and the training annexe. Boundary spanning roles are important in complex organisations, as are processes which enable knowledge to be shared.

*3. Knowledge sharing and interpretation*

The cultural elements outlined at the beginning of this paper, that is, the collective beliefs, values and norms shape interpretation of experience, assist individuals and groups to make meaning of experience. The way individuals and groups make sense of their situations and their consequent strategies for action are bound up in "complexes of values" developed in relation to social or interpersonal situations. These elements all provide insights into how individuals and groups shape and interpret their experience and how they learn. Understanding something of a group's culture therefore, can play an important role in enhancing an organisation's reliability and its capacity to learn from mistakes by enhancing group understanding of shared meanings. Paying attention to the informal language used in a work place reveals how individuals and groups make sense of their experiences. The ways in which values and beliefs filter action is an important insight for anyone interested in introducing human factors related change or creating continuous learning environments.

One approach to investigating sense making and interpretation is to look for the metaphors people use to describe their experiences. Perhaps because of its history and still close association with the military, the language typically used by ATCs to describe their work and their learning is often combative.

Policies and procedures governing assessment of learning for example, are described as "rules of engagement". Assessors sometimes described themselves as being a "mine detector". In another instance a trainee referred to himself as a "time bomb". This provides information about values that either need to be supported and/or challenged in the process of a human factors implementation. Instructors do need strategies to "detect" hidden mines, but at the same time, if both parties - to extend the metaphor - view "training as war" then what are the implications of trainee's view the instructor as "enemy" (and vice versa), particularly, for creating environments when the trainee can feel comfortable about revealing what they do not know, so that they might receive help? Examining metaphor is also useful, because, as this example shows, the metaphor reveals a structural contradiction between the role of an instructor to facilitate learning, and the role of an instructor to be a gatekeeper, to ensure that people who cannot do the job, do not get through.

*4. Organisational memory*

Organisations have a variety of processes and structures in place for remembering important events and learning from them. Story telling is one means by which individuals share their experiences so that learning is in turn transferred to others. Within high-reliability organisations, stories are a particularly valuable means of sharing information since traditional means of learning such as trial and error are not available in these organisational forms. Sharing stories means that individuals can learn vicariously through the experiences of others. One of the most frequently used means of informal learning in ATC is through "war stories". War stories are the stories of a controller's experience where something dramatic happens, perhaps because of a controller's performance (or lack thereof), a system deficiency or an unexpected event. War stories are passed informally between controllers and across centres. Some of them are decades old, others are more recent. War stories are used to help illustrate both good and bad actions, right and wrong ways of operating. War stories have a dramaturgical quality. They often set up an "us-against-other" struggle or battle of some sort and therefore are well characterised as war stories. The "other" may be another controller, the technology, the environment, oneself and a combination of these elements.

Stories remind people of the key values on which they and the collective operate. When people share stories, they enhance the potential for requisite variety among participants. Stories are important, because they register, summarise, and allow reconstruction of scenarios that are too complex for logical, linear summaries (such as a set of regulations) would preserve (Weick, 1987, p. 125). According to Weick (1987), a system that values stories, storytellers and story telling will be more reliable than a system that derogates these forms of learning, "because people know more about their system, know more of the potential errors that might occur, and they are more confident that they can handle those errors that do occur because they know that other people have already handled similar errors" (p. 113). Telling stories assist individuals to make sense of the non routine. Through stories, group members accommodate the unfamiliar to their existing experience. Stories provide a means of collective remembering. They enable experiences of an organisational system to be shared vicariously.

There is some evidence that the structural changes described earlier in response to Australian industrial reform policies (centralising services to two locations) are having an impact on the ways in which stories are shared and transferred in ATC and hence on the understandings controllers gain from those stories, as the following quotation highlights:

> It amazes me that those sort of stories the younger guys haven't heard / I suppose the ones who have come into the room, if they don't know you because of the set-up that is up there now, if they don't know you, they haven't heard the stories about you. It's the likes of us who knew all the old-fellows-who-were-anybody years ago, and we have heard all their old stories. / There doesn't seem to be as many of the stories about people and we put it down to the fact that the room up there, you

could work up there and not know half the people in the room. Whereas, the way it was when I said there was approach, arrivals and two sectors, you knew everybody. When I first went to [name of Centre], I prided myself in what controllers were in [name of State] that I hadn't met or didn't know. / I knew everybody else in [name of State] or had met them or seen them or something. Now I couldn't because there is so many of them. I think that is part of the problem - you don't know the people any more.

Three recommendations flow from these observations:

1. Organisations should evaluate various forms of work activity in terms of the learning opportunities that that activity may provide, before changing or dismantling them.

2. A valuable area for research would be to investigate and understand the degree to which these changes in industry impact on work performance.

3. Attention needs to be given to the ways in which structures and cultures can be modified to substitute for any loss of understanding resulting from changes described above and to enhance learning about the interdependence of relationships that comprise the aviation system.

**Conclusion**

The aim of this paper has been to suggest that when attempting to implement a human factors related initiative, we need to widen the focus beyond the immediate goals of the program and to consider the ways in which organisational factors such as cultures and structures may enhance or inhibit the chances of success. Some of those contextual factors may not be immediately evident and may be external to organisational processes, such the implementation of national policy. Organisational change processes of recent years have fundamentally changed the ways in which people learn about the complex organisations and systems within which they work with both positive and negative results for learning. Changes to structures and cultures combine to produce conflicting goals which result in tensions and contradictions within complex systems. Changes introduced to manage in a turbulent environment often narrow the "band width" of work experience by removing a range of work activities with the consequence that opportunities to learn about the aviation system are reduced. These changes increase the need to look for ways of spanning boundaries within and between organisations and functions in compensation.

**References**

Hannan, G. (1996). Selecting air traffic controllers: Airservices Australia's ATC conversion course selection program. In B.J. Hayward & A.R. Lowe (Eds.), *Applied aviation psychology: Achievement, change challenge* . Aldershot: Avebury Aviation.

Louis, M.R. (1986). An investigator's guide to workplace culture. *Perspectives, 3/5*, 73-93.

Thompson, P., & McHugh, D. (1990). *Work organisations: A critical introduction.* London: Macmillan.

Weick, K.E. (1987). Organizational culture as a source of high reliability. *California Management Review, 29*(2), 112-127.

Westrum, R. (1992). Cultures with Requisite Imagination. In J.A.H. Wise & P. Stager, P. (Eds.), *Verification and Validation of Complex Systems: Human Factors Issues* (pp. 401-416). Berlin: Springer-Verlag.

# Part 5
# MAINTENANCE

# 35 Maintenance engineering training needs of the Pacific Islands commercial aviation industry

*Michael J. Terim, Air Safety Investigation Directorate,*
*PNG Office of Civil Aviation*
*H. Peter Pfister, The University of Newcastle*

Technology continues to reach levels where total failure of aircraft components and aircraft systems has become remote. However, human error has become increasingly significant in the course of events in aviation accidents and incidents (Maurino, Reason, Johnston, & Lee, 1995). The systematic and costly failures of such technology-based industries have recognised the significance of effective training systems in terms of the prevention of human error in the operational environment. Prevention may be too optimistic; however an analysis of underlying issues seem feasible. In this paper human error is introduced in an industrial (aircraft maintenance engineering) context and further current error taxonomies are explored to map aircraft maintenance engineering error.

Little advancement has been accomplished on human error related to the performance of civil aviation maintenance engineers as compared to pilot and air traffic controller performance. The first documented work on human error by aircraft maintenance engineers was provided by Hobbs and Williamson (1996), based on performance levels (skill, rule and knowledge). They categorised maintenance errors (anomalies) in an Asia-Pacific airline based on Rasmussen's Skill-Rule-Knowledge (SRK) taxonomy of errors. In that study rule-based anomalies showed an aggregate of 63% which equated to the highest contributing factor, procedural errors. Maurino et al., (1995) addressed failure modes by exploring the performance levels (skill, rule, knowledge based) of individuals in an "activity space" defined by situations and level of consciousness. The proponents thus postulated that errors are likely to occur at the knowledge-based performance level among other things. Kaplan (1995) further argues that large deficiencies can exist in knowledge and skill levels to those required for successful operation and maintenance of new technology, in an industrially undeveloped society. Edgerton (1994) noted that societies with limited technical traditions tended to use tools or technology universally, though the technology was meant for a specific application. The criteria for designing new techniques for specific problems at hand were never cultivated, largely due to lack of support services (Edgerton, 1994).

"The culture implicit in the design of the new technology can clash with the culture of the user (e.g., labour force)" (Peiro, 1992, cited by Kaplan, 1995, p. 607). One such possibility is cross-cultural impediments and/or cultural differences in Licensed Aircraft Maintenance Engineer (LAME) training and in post-training work performance. Enforcing practises and training too soon and quickly would not make matters any simpler in dealing with cultural impediments however. In Kaplan's (1995) view, adapting training to local practice where possible, were important in two respects: "(a) establishing the various levels of knowledge on which to build the newly required technical skills and (b) training the skills themselves".

The acquisition by airlines of the Pacific of "high tech" machinery requires appropriate training for LAMEs to maintain and sustain the local commercial aviation industry. The airlines of the Pacific Island countries rely heavily on overseas training for their LAMEs. The trend of sending indigenous trainees to Australia and New Zealand is still continuing. While the training offered by institutions overseas is ample to cater for the global commercial aviation industry, the authors of this paper share the view of moving away from the "one size fits all" concept. The rationale behind this approach is to have training (CRM or others) design, delivering and evaluation to be in line with national cultures as well as the type of organisation.

Hofstede's (1980) cultural dimensions have been considered in cross-cultural CRM training implications among flightdeck crew, and as such an extension to cross-cultural maintenance engineering training is advocated in this paper. Hofstede's (1980) cultural dimensions were classified as being: (1) power distance; (2) uncertainty avoidance; (3) individualism versus collectivism; and (4) masculinity versus femininity. Power distance was classified as the extent to which members of a society accept that power in institutions and organisations is distributed unequally. Uncertainty avoidance was identified as the degree of being uncomfortable with uncertainty and ambiguity by members of a society. According to Hofstede this leads to beliefs promising a sense of certainty and preserves the notion of maintaining institutions which call for conformity. Individualism is defined as:

(standing) for a loosely knit social framework in society in which individuals are supposed to take care of themselves and their immediate families whereas collectivism stands for a preference for a tightly knit social framework in which individuals can expect their relatives, clan, or in-group to look after them, in exchange for unquestioning loyalty (Hofstede, 1980, p. 336).

Masculinity represents:

a preference for achievement, heroism, assertiveness, and material success as opposed to femininity, which stands for the preference for relationships, modesty, caring for the weak, and the quality of life (Hofstede, 1980, p. 337).

Due to differences in technological development, economics, or even politics, people of one culture may perceive others in a way they are not in reality. On this basis, one should think twice before applying the norms of one person, group or society to another (Hofstede, 1995). While data on Pacific Islands region is not available, categorising the region as a third world region, would equate to salient dimensional scores of Hofstede's (1980) study of the third world countries. The third world shows a high power distance, high collectivism, medium to high femininism and weak to low uncertainty. The Australian and New Zealand data suggest a low power distance, high individualism, high masculinity and medium to high uncertainty avoidance. The aim of this study was primarily an exploratory approach towards eliciting cross-cultural maintenance engineering training needs of the Pacific Islands commercial aviation industry.

**Method**

*Source of data*

The data for this study involved 64 item questionnaire responses from representative airlines of the Pacific. Interview responses collected after questionnaire administration were also incorporated into the data set.

*Participants*

Sixteen apprentices (14 male, 2 female) aircraft maintenance engineers from three organisations participated. All were being trained in an Australian airline hangar for the OJT and attend the same technical training institution. Eleven participants were in the 21-30 years age group, 5 in the 15-20 years age group. The sample represented all four years of training.

*Questionnaire design*

The 64 item questionnaire was focused on identifying the effects and manifestations of Hofstede's cultural dimensions; (i) power distance, (ii) collectivism versus individualism, (iii) uncertainty avoidance, (iv) masculinity versus femininity, in the training environment. Further it attempted to highlight six training factors or areas of specific attention. These training factors were: (a) adequacy of technical training, (b) the type of graduate sought, (c) theoretical areas that need improvement, (d) levels responsibility, (e) resourcefulness, and (f) communication. Participants were asked to rank each questionnaire item on a five point likert scale. High integers meant strong disagreement and low integers meant strong agreement to the 64 questionnaire items.

*Data processing method*

Due to the small number of participants in the questionnaire returns, the data analysis used is purely descriptive. In order to analyse data descriptively, questionnaire items were grouped for each factor considered as well as for the cultural dimension measure questions, which were typical questions used by Hofstede. The questionnaire items were then orthogonally loaded in an activity space defined by Hofstede's cultural dimensions and the factors considered so as to determine the aggregate relationship or mean scores (responses) which give an indication of how responses rated each cultural dimension and the factors (training) considered. Some items were anticipated to load more than once and others were loaded independently.

**Results**

*Hofstede's cultural dimensions*

The results indicated changes in attitudes, possibly as a result of the training process. It can equally be postulated that value and attitude changes were due to exposure to different people and the differences in culture. In the study, the responses shifted towards medium power distance, high uncertainty avoidance, high collectivism and high masculinity.

*Training factors considered*

The mean responses for the training factors considered show that the participants viewed the training process at the host airline as adequate and that the apprentices were equipped to the expectations of their airlines. It was noted that practical skills were preferred more than theory. According to the responses there were areas that were observed to be deficient, which included approaches to learning, lack of prior knowledge and high expectations from instructors. Management skills were not taught and it was not known whether that can be included in current training programmes. Being resourceful and responsible were common attitudes or values maintained among the participants. Communication was also viewed as an important part in the performance of tasks.

**Table 35.1**
**Summary of mean score results**

| Hofstede's Dimensions | a | b | c | d | e | f | Non-Loaded Items | Mean |
|---|---|---|---|---|---|---|---|---|
| i | - | 2.4 | 2.3 | 2.2 | 2.3 | 2.1 | 3.4 | 2.5 |
| ii | 1.8 | 2.3 | 2.1 | 2.1 | 1.7 | 2.1 | 2.7 | 2.1 |
| iii | 1.9 | 2.4 | 2.2 | 2.0 | 1.7 | 2.1 | 3.1 | 2.2 |
| iv | 2.0 | 2.3 | 2.2 | 2.1 | 1.7 | 2.1 | 2.5 | 2.1 |
| Non-Loading Items | 2.0 | 3.2 | - | - | - | - | 3.1 | 2.8 |
| Mean | 1.9 | 2.5 | 2.2 | 2.1 | 1.9 | 2.1 | 3.0 | - |

Key: (i) power distance, (ii) uncertainty avoidance, (iii) collectivism versus individualism, (iv) masculinity versus femininity

(a) adequacy of technical training, (b) type of graduate sought, (c) theoretical an practical areas that need improvement, (d) levels of responsibility, (e) resourcefulness, and (f) communication

*Non-loading items*

The responses to items which did not load on Hofstede's Dimensions indicated a trend towards the desire for managerial skills. There was disagreement among apprentices that maintenance engineers should be overlooked for managerial posts. The overall results indicated a high level of enthusiasm and motivation among apprentices. For management positions during their career. The changes in value and attitudes were evident, when participants indicated neutral responses on items which asked directly on cultural dimensions. Table 35.1 summarises the results as loaded orthogonally.

**Discussion**

The data provide limited support for Hofstede's cultural dimensions. Some dimensions were contaminated due to the exposure of standard requirements of maintenance engineering. The dimension of power distance was neutrally rated, however it was evident that the status of a licence or certificate meant much in terms of social recognition (which is power). Even being trained overseas carried in itself a sense of achievement and implied certain status. Power in some cases was seen as a necessity while others did not care much as there was someone more powerful than themselves on whom they could rely.

In terms of collectivism versus individualism, responses indicated the type of group one belonged to. Group cohesion was important and that relationships prevailed over task at hand. The sense of belonging to a group and being recognised as a member was a significant view held by the group.

Masculinity and uncertainty mean scores were rated highly. That trend may have been the result of training or exposure. Even then, the apprentices believed in the need for assertiveness, being heroic and for self actualisation. Those characteristics typify a strong gender based approach where the male is required to possess such qualities even in a traditional femininist society both in the family, and at the professional work life.

In terms of being stringent with rules, it was seen that the desire for rules and standard procedures was overwhelming. That dimension, in the authors' view was contaminated. Interview responses indicated a trend where rules and standardisation seemed too pragmatic and it interfered with their personal lifestyle. The results suggest that rules can be broken and are meant to be broken. Rules communicated in written or spoken form were appreciated. Again, it can be argued that the apprentices saw the significance of rules and standard operating procedures in a heavily regulated industry.

Learning for apprentices meant the imitation of task performances by LAMEs. Then after a period of trial and error, the apprentices are expected to become skilled. Learning facilitation of theory subjects was unconducive in terms of the environment. This could imply that there was no integration of theory and practical skills at the OJT. Thus, a need for rigorous cognitive analysis of technical problem solving skill is required.

Differences in cultures of apprentices and host airlines and training institutions pose the need to analyse culture-specific training packages. Learning has shown to be deficient in cultures with limited technical traditions. Prior learning was based on being shown by a master how to do things and not based on trying to find out how to do something for themselves (Edgerton, 1994). The apprentices expressed that more time was required to absorb subject matter and preferred more practice than theory. This could be attributed to the fact that the apprentices were not able to understand the abstract nature of theory.

There was consensus among apprentices that theory was less stimulating; task oriented instruction was preferred. This can be a manifestation of rote learning tendencies among apprentices. Expert problem-solving skill transfer can only be brought about if apprentices have a sound knowledge organisation and effective mental model generation capability. Therefore fundamental theory and spatial thinking need to be addressed to a greater degree.

Career development is therefore based on skilled performance. Skilled performance in this instance means the speed, efficient manipulation of tools and efficient component assembly or dismantling, with minimal understanding of the principles of operation. It was demonstrated that the apprentices need to be made aware of cultural contexts before their entrance to the overseas training facility. Written and unwritten communication was viewed as a significant part in task performance. Cultural impediments, may hinder effective communication, but the results indicated a strong desire for effective communication methods.

The findings support the view of Edgerton (1994) that diagnosis of learning strengths and weaknesses of students is essential in analysing the maintenance engineering training needs of the Pacific Islands commercial aviation industry. The key conclusion that can be drawn was the need for a proactive approach to system safety as postulated by Maurino, et al., (1995). To minimise the chances of human error in less developed aviation systems or where there is less technical tradition the cultural impediments be vigorously attacked. It is also noteworthy that cultural values cannot be changed overnight. Therefore, cross-cultural understanding and CRM principles need to be incorporated before training, during training and post training for a generative approach to efficient skill and knowledge transfer.

**Summary**

This study has provided an indication that an in depth analysis of maintenance engineering training needs of the Pacific Islands commercial aviation industry is needed. The next phase should then be devoted to fully develop the current questionnaire as an instrument to address specific issues. One of the first questions of interest that can be envisaged is to derive how apprentices from the Pacific Islands commercial aviation industry are taught in the school system. This should address how students are taught and how they learn. It should also highlight whether students are taught to develop inquisitive minds or to memorise and regurgitate. Similarly, mechanical or electrical exposure and learning aspects should be addressed. The second topic of interest is to have a complete understanding of the objectives of LAME training in the host institutions. This should address whether learning how to perform tasks is important or whether learning how to learn is. This will provide an avenue to marry client airlines' requirements with LAME training objectives together to provide a tailored training package.

**References**

Edgerton, R.H. (Dec, 1994). Developing engineering education programs for students from cultures with few technical traditions. *Inspiring integration: Futures in engineering education in Australasia.* Institute of Engineers Australia Conference Proceedings. 5-10.

Hobbs, A & Williamson, A. (1996). Human factors in airline maintenance. In B.J. Hayward & A.R Lowe (Eds.), *Applied aviation psychology. Achievement, change and challenge.* Proceedings of the 3rd Australian Aviation Psychology Symposium. Aldershot: Avebury Aviation.

Hofstede, G. (1980). *Culture's consequences: International differences in work related values.* California: Sage Publications.

Hofstede G. (1995). The business of international business is culture. In T. Jackson (Ed.), *Cross-cultural management.* Oxford: Butterworth-Heinemann Ltd.

Kaplan, M. (1995). The culture at work: Cultural ergonomics. *Ergonomics, 38*(3), 606-615.

Maurino, D.E, Reason, J, Johnston, N., & Lee, R.B. (1995*). Beyond aviation human factors: Safety in high technology systems.* Aldershot: Avebury Aviation.

# 36 Maintenance human factors: Learning from errors to improve systems

*Alan Hobbs*
*Bureau of Air Safety Investigation*

Maintenance errors can have a significant impact on the safety and financial performance of airline operations. It has been estimated that an air turn-back of a Boeing 747 with the need to accommodate passengers overnight can cost in the order of $250 000 (Innes 1998). While no firm figures are available, Marx (1998) has estimated that in the US, maintenance error may cost airlines one billion US dollars per year.

The English word "error" is related to the Latin *errare*, meaning to wander or stray (Macquarie Dictionary 1991). Despite the fact that the concept of human error is far from new, there is still much to be learnt about the nature of maintenance errors and the circumstances in which they occur.

This paper begins with a brief summary of recent Bureau of Air Safety Investigation (BASI) research which has led to the development of a simple cognitive model of maintenance error, and then considers the repetitive nature of some maintenance errors.

## BASI research into maintenance error

Interviews and a questionnaire were used to gather information on maintenance errors. One hundred and four errors were reported during structured interviews with maintenance engineers following a format outlined elsewhere (BASI 1997a; Hobbs & Williamson 1996). An additional 23 errors were reported by maintenance personnel who responded to BASI's regional airline survey (BASI, 1998).

Errors were first categorised with a modified version of the error categorisation system developed by Boeing (1994). The errors are summarised in Table 36.1.

**Table 36.1**
**Summary of maintenance errors reported in BASI research**

| Error | f | Error | f |
|-------|---|-------|---|
| System operated in unsafe condition | 16 | Material left in aircraft or engine | 3 |
| Towing event | 11 | Vehicle driving (not towing) | 2 |
| System not made safe | 10 | Pin or tie left in place | 2 |
| Incomplete installation | 9 | Warning sign or tag not used | 2 |
| Degradation not found | 7 | Not properly tested | 2 |
| Falls and spontaneous actions | 6 | Safety lock or warning removed | 2 |
| Improper installation or adjustment | 6 | Contamination of open system | 1 |
| Work not documented | 6 | Equipment not installed | 1 |
| Person entered dangerous area | 5 | Panel installed incorrectly | 1 |
| System not reactivated/deactivated | 5 | Required servicing not performed | 1 |
| Person contacted hazard | 4 | Unable to access part in stores | 1 |
| Vehicle/equipment contacted aircraft | 4 | Wrong fluid type | 1 |
| Did not obtain or use appropriate equipment | 4 | Wrong orientation | 1 |
| Unserviceable equipment used | 4 | Unable to access part in stores | 1 |
| Access panel not closed | 4 | Wrong fluid type | 1 |
| Verbal warning not given | 3 | Wrong orientation | 1 |
| Wrong equipment/part installed | 3 | (Total: 127 errors) | |

## A model of maintenance error

A useful model of human error should not only give labels to various classes of unsafe acts, but should also help to explain why errors happen, predict where or when they might occur and point to corrective action.

A model of maintenance error was developed by drawing on elements from existing human error taxonomies, in particular Reason's GEMS model (Reason 1987), the model proposed by Rasmussen (1982) and Norman's distinction between slips and mistakes (e.g., Norman 1988). To facilitate categorisation, the current model describes errors in plain English, in terms which might have been used by the person if they had become aware of their error. Describing errors in this way not only gives a clearer picture of what the person was thinking at the time, but also points to interventions which could prevent future errors.

The eight types of error in order of frequency were:

*1. Memory lapse: 'I forgot'*

Twenty four percent of the errors could be classified as memory lapses. In many cases, the lapse could be directly related to an interruption or a distraction.

> Being the only person on shift, I was responsible for both hangar and line maintenance. There was a fuel quantity problem on a __, I had to move fuel plumbing to gain access. I was distracted from my task by heavy commitments with line defects. I forgot to check the tightness of the "B" nuts causing the aircraft to develop a potentially disastrous fuel leak. (*De-identified incident report.*)

*2. Work-arounds: 'I know it is not the right way, but I thought it would be okay this time'*

> 'Work-arounds' accounted for 23% of the reported errors and were present in many incidents which could be described as relatively minor, such as performing a task without all the necessary equipment, or performing a task in a more convenient manner than that specified in the maintenance manual. There were also cases where, faced with time pressure, workers decided not to document their actions or failed to perform all the necessary steps in a task. The picture which emerges is consistent with the findings of recent European research, which found that in 34% of cases, maintenance technicians reported not following official task procedures (Eggerling 1998).

*3. Situational awareness: 'I didn't notice that the situation was unusual'*

A typical situational awareness error was where the person carried out familiar actions in a situation which was subtly different to normal, such as where a mechanic activated hydraulics without noticing that cockpit controls had been moved while the hydraulics were off. These errors generally stemmed from mistaken assumptions. Situational awareness errors comprised 18% of the reported errors.

*4. Expertise: 'I didn't know how to do it properly'*

Ten per cent of the errors could be classified as errors of expertise. As might be expected, errors of expertise tended to involve less experienced workers.

> An apprentice was spraying solvent to clean an engine with the aircraft power on. Solvent ignited over engine and into oil soaked drip tray. The apprentice had never been told of the dangers of solvent cleaning. *(De-identified incident report.)*

*5. Action slips: 'I didn't mean to do that'*

Action slips, in which the person unintentionally performed an action or sequence of actions, were relatively rare, accounting for only 9% of errors. Such errors (which have been described extensively by Reason (1990) and Norman (1981), typically involve skilled workers acting in familiar situations.

> An AME accidentally put engine oil into the hydraulics system of the aircraft. Oil and hydraulic fluid are stored in identical tins in a dark storeroom. *(De-identified incident report.)*

*6. Work practice: 'I always do it that way'*

The error type 'work practice' refers to circumstances in which the worker's routine work methods led to a difficulty, typically when the situation was non-routine. The persons' actions were not necessarily prohibited by rules or procedures and they typically did not consider that they were engaging in risk taking behaviour. Seven per cent of errors were of this type.

> The 'hot cup' water heating system of a Boeing 747 had been reported U/S. The LAME usually tests these systems by switching them on and then dipping his hand into the water to see if it is warming up. On this occasion the water was live and the LAME received an electric shock until the circuit breaker tripped.
> *(De-identified incident report.)*

*7. Technical inaccuracy: 'I tried to do it the right way, but couldn't'*

Six per cent of errors were of the kind where the person knew what they had to do, but was unable to complete the task with sufficient precision or skill.

> An aircraft was towed into a hangar crookedly. The driver's attempts at straightening the aircraft only resulted in it getting more out of line. Eventually the aircraft received minor damage when it contacted a hangar door. *(De-identified incident report.)*

*8. Perceptual difficulties: 'I didn't see the fault'*

Five per cent of the errors involved failures to see a fault, which was subsequently detected by another person. This figure almost certainly underestimates the frequency of perceptual difficulties, as there would have been an unknown number of additional cases in which no-one detected the fault.

> An experienced LAME carrying out an inspection failed to detect a damaged flight control cable, although aircraft maintenance manual and several service bulletins drew particular attention to the required inspection procedures. *(De-identified incident report.)*

*Predisposing factors*

Of course, errors do not occur in isolation, but happen in the context of systems and reflect the organisations in which they occur. Some of the human factors issues which are of current concern in maintenance are: sleep deprivation and the effects of shiftwork; the effects of pressure and haste on work quality; communication and coordination; shift hand over; and the documentation of work. These factors will not be discussed in the current paper, but are outlined in greater detail elsewhere (e.g., BASI 1997).

**Repetitive maintenance errors**

When participants in the BASI study were asked whether the incident had happened before, nearly 60% indicated that it had. Furthermore, it is not difficult to find published reports of maintenance-related accidents or quality lapses which stem from repetitive (and hence predictable) maintenance errors. While it can be difficult to predict the errors that may occur with a new or untried procedure, it should be possible to identify repetitive quality lapses arising from current procedures or equipment. Examples of such situations follow.

*L1011 O rings*

In May 1983, a US operated L1011 lost oil from all three engines in flight. Two engines stopped and a third was shut down and subsequently restarted by the crew, who were able to make a successful one engine landing.

The investigation revealed that on all three engines, master chip detectors had been installed without O rings, allowing oil to leak from the engines in flight. Over a period of 20 months, the airline had experienced 12 separate incidents involving in-flight engine shutdowns and unscheduled landings due to problems with O rings seals and master chip detector installation problems. However, the airline failed to recognise that these errors were repeating manifestations of a systemic problem (NTSB, 1984).

*Chicago DC10*

In May 1979 a DC10 crashed shortly after taking off from Chicago. During the takeoff run, the number one engine and pylon broke away from the wing, severing hydraulic lines. As hydraulic fluid was lost, the outboard slats on the left wing retracted, while the slats on the right wing remained extended. The aircraft rolled to the left and descended into the ground

The engine pylon had failed as a result of a fracture that was attributed to maintenance practices at the airline. Although the manufacturer specified that the engine and pylon should be removed separately, two US airlines had developed a one-step maintenance procedure in which the engine and pylon were removed as one unit. This not only saved about 200 person hours of labour but was also considered safer as it reduced the number of fuel lines, hydraulic lines and wiring which needed to be disconnected.

In the year before the accident, another airline using the same procedure had damaged engine pylons, yet the damage had been blamed on "maintenance error". The cause of the problem was not fully investigated and the damage was not reported to the FAA (NTSB, 1979).

*GE CF6 fuel filter*

During the fitting of a high pressure fuel filter housing on a GE CF6-80 C2, an apprentice and a licenced engineer did not adequately torque two nuts which are in a difficult to reach position. The omission was not detected during an engine run. As the aircraft took off, a fuel leak became apparent on the engine. The airline subsequently experienced a second very similar incident. During follow up action with the manufacturer, it became apparent that this error had occurred at least twenty times at other airlines around the world (BASI, 1997a).

*747 Aileron cables*

Whilst the Boeing 747-300 was taxiing for departure, the crew selected the flaps to the take off position. As the flaps extended, the left outboard aileron deflected to the full down position. The aircraft was returned to the gate where a maintenance inspection revealed that one aileron cable was broken and another was badly frayed. The cables had been misaligned on a cable drum. BASI investigators discovered that two decals which provide guidance on cable routing had been placed in a reverse sense. Since the incident occurred, at least three other B747 aircraft have been found with misrouted cables and misplaced decals have been found on eight aircraft from various operators (BASI, 1997b).

*Learning lessons from errors*

All systems need feedback to permit improvement and adjustment to new conditions, yet the occurrences described above each involved a maintenance organisation which failed to learn from errors, whether their own or those of others.

The Major Defect Reporting (MDR) system in operation in Australia and its equivalent in other countries focuses on technical defects such as metallurgical problems. In a typical year in Australia, the MDR system receives approximately 2000 reports, however, fewer than 10 % of the reports concern human errors.

It is well established that human factors are one of the most significant contributors to accidents and incidents (e.g., Hawkins, 1993), yet remarkably, there is no internationally coordinated system to monitor the human failures that occur in maintenance.

## Conclusions

In order to address the problem of human error in maintenance, the nature of maintenance error must be understood. The cognitive error model presented in this report provides a simple taxonomy of maintenance errors, which may assist in selecting the interventions necessary to address each form of error. For example, memory lapses may require one preventative strategy while situational awareness errors may call for a different approach.

Errors in aviation of course, are not generated in isolation, but reflect the systems in which they occur. Understanding the types of errors committed by workers is merely a first step in addressing system issues in maintenance. Perhaps one of the most pressing system wide challenges in airline maintenance is the lack of an international human error database that would permit repetitive error types to be identified and addressed.

## References

Boeing (1994), *Maintenance error decision aid.* Boeing Commercial Airplane Group, Seattle.

Bureau of Air Safety Investigation (1997a). *Human factors in airline maintenance: A study of incident reports.* Canberra, ACT: Author.

Bureau of Air Safety Investigation (1997b). *Air Safety Interim Recommendation IR970138.*

Bureau of Air Safety Investigation (1998). *Regional airlines safety study, Project overview.*

Eggerling, U. (1998). Airbus Industrie, *Human factors in maintenance: The need for dialogue and feedback.* Paper Presented to Association of Asia Pacific Airlines Maintenance Human Factors Conference, Sydney February 1998.

Hawkins, F.H. (1993). Human Factors in Flight, Aldershot, Ashgate.

Hobbs, A., & Williamson, A. (1996). Human factors in airline maintenance. In B.J. Hayward & A.R. Lowe (Eds.), *Applied aviation psychology: Achievement, change and challenge.* Aldershot: Avebury.

Innes M. (1998) personal communication.

Macquarie Dictionary (1991). Macquarie University.

Marx, D., (1998) *Learning from our Mistakes: A review of maintenance error investigation and analysis systems.* Prepared for the FAA by Galaxy Scientific Corporation.

National Transportation Safety Board (1979). *Aircraft Accident Report 79-17, American Airlines, DC-10.*

National Transportation Safety Board (1984). *Aircraft Accident Report 84/04 Eastern Airlines, Lockheed L1011.*

Norman, D.A. (1981). The categorization of action slips. *Psychological Review, 88* (1) 1-15.

Norman, D.A. (1988). *The psychology of everyday things.* New York, Basic Books.

Rasmussen, J. (1982). Human errors, a taxonomy for describing human malfunction in industrial installations. *Journal of Occupational Accidents 4,* 311-333.

Reason, J. (1987). Generic Error Modelling System (GEMS): A cognitive framework for locating common human error forms. In J. Rasmussen, K. Duncan, & J. Leplat (Eds.), *New technology and human error.* John Wiley and Sons, Chichester.

Reason, J. (1990). *Human error.* Cambridge, Cambridge University Press.

# Part 6
# SITUATIONAL AWARENESS

# 37  Situation awareness or metacognition?

*Graham Beaumont*
*Qantas Airways Limited*

## Introduction

This research into situation awareness (SA) was initiated as a result of an unacceptability high failure rate in command training programmes at a large Pacific rim carrier. Traditional aptitude and intelligence quotient tests have been unreliable in predicting potential success in training at this level (Beaumont, 1997). Additionally, check and training personnel at the same carrier nominated SA as second only to manipulative skills in frequency of use as an indicator of command performance (Beaumont, 1997).

Accordingly, the focus of this research was directed towards the discriminatory potential of aspects of SA. To do this, it would be necessary to identify facets of this dimension within the target population and measure their consistency as objective predictors of performance within the group. Grounded SA training development was also high on the agenda. But, the existence of so many definitions of SA and the belief of the respective authors in the validity of their approach (Dominguez, 1994) made it very difficult to settle on an 'off the shelf' approach.

Add to this the distinction being made between SA, the state, and situation assessment, the process (Endsley, 1995; Adams, Tenney, & Pew, 1995) and it is not difficult to conceptualise the magnitude of the initial problem from the practical standpoint. It has been proposed that research and development in the field is in danger of assuming a circular life of its own by ignoring the underlying principles which enable the process (Flach, 1995). Therefore, it was necessary to identify the factors which underpin the different approaches to SA definition and consider them in relation to this line of research.

## Developmental influences

Examination of the many definitions in existence reveals that each was formulated within a specific context by persons of identifiable academic or industry leaning (e.g., Sarter & Woods, 1991; Adams, Tenney, & Pew, 1995). These factors appear to have influenced the definition of the mechanisms involved in SA development and maintenance.

### Context

The primary step in understanding the context within which agents must develop and maintain SA is to clearly understand the agents' task. The role of the fighter pilot in aerial combat (Endsley & Smith, 1996) is quite different to that which the same pilot assumes in mission navigation (Amalberti & Deblon, 1992). The SA emphasis and the means of developing it are very different. Similarly, both of these expressions of SA can be seen to be different to scheduled regular public transport pilot SA (Tenney, Adams, Pew, Huggins, & Rogers, 1992) since the acceptable risks and desired outcomes are identifiably different.

Therefore, it is not hard to imagine that researchers working with one such group will develop a different answer to that proposed by a colleague working with another group. This argument runs along the same lines as the cultural argument which has influenced the development of CRM training for differing cultural settings (Merritt, 1997).

### Researcher background

There is an emergent pattern to the focus of SA definition that runs in parallel with the focus and level of academic qualification. The practitioner will quite rightly try to explain what it is that she/he does in easily understood practical terms so that other practitioners can understand and implement the procedures which have been found to work in the field (Jensen, 1995, p. 89). An academic using pure psychological theory (Charness, 1996) would be expected to analyse the topic in quite different terms to an equally qualified academic working within an applied environment (Endsley, 1988).

### Research processes

Understanding how the client group develops and maintains SA is fundamental to any attempt to improve skill levels in the area through selection and training. Group membership may be defined by cultural similarity (Merritt, 1997), outcome requirements (Tenney et al, 1992) or role classification (Beaumont, 1997). To this end, techniques such as the cognitive task analysis (Seamster, Redding & Kaempf, 1997), quantitative data collection and analysis (Endsley, 1988) and discriminatory instrument development (Pew, 1996) have their place in the process.

Using such techniques, it is unlikely that identical processes will be identified for the various aviator client groups. While parts of all such processes may be transportable across group boundaries, the mechanisms involved must be critically examined for contextual fit. The key to effective SA training and measurement would seem to hinge on being able to accurately identify what the concept means to the client group.

## Research

Having arrived at the point where more information needed to be sought from the client group, a mixed method approach (Brewer & Hunter, 1989) was adopted in the ensuing research. Most importantly, the emphasis in this research was directed towards tapping the knowledge of the clients (Strauss & Corbin, 1990) using the existing literature as a framework rather than as a definitive approach.

### Focus groups

Carrying on from the finding regarding the frequency of use of SA as a command readiness marker (Beaumont, 1997), three focus groups were convened for check and training personnel. They were initially asked to record what they believed SA was and how pilots developed and maintained this state. Plenary discussion on the topic was then facilitated. During this discussion, key words, phrases and concepts were recorded. The written responses were also analysed for key words, phrases and concepts. A composite definition was formulated incorporating the concepts. The process descriptors were then assigned to the primary conceptual processes contained within the definition.

The resultant definition was:

"Within the context of airline operations, flight crew can develop and maintain situational awareness by the continuous *acquisition, retention, analysis* and *application* of knowledge of events, conditions, data and variables."

The process descriptors were:

- *acquisition*: perceiving; questioning; listening; sharing; being vigilant; maintaining recency; tapping overall experience; increasing sensitivity; being systematic; aiming for continuity; self-discipline; delegating; empathising; maintaining open-mindedness.

- *retention:* memorising; diagram constructing; associating; listing; imagining; modelling; vocalising; repeating; chunking; rote learning; structured planning; developing mnemonics.

- *analysis:* deducing; categorising; assessing; sifting; prioritising; comparing actual with required state; assessing potential influence; considering internal and external influences; modelling; comparing with previous experience; comprehending; considering implications; cross-checking validity; resolving ambiguity.

- *application:* predicting; maintaining overview; controlling; gauging appropriateness; judging timing; ensuring safety; optimising; reassessing; remodelling; reviewing goals; assessing efficiency; worse case scenario planning; identifying present and future requirements; looking beyond the obvious; considering normal and non-normal conditions; revising the plan.

When all aspects of the definition are considered, the breadth and depth of the meaning of SA to this target population begins to take shape. The difficulty of developing an assessment tool also becomes apparent.

*Quantitative data*

A collection instrument based on the Situation Awareness Global Assessment Technique (SAGAT) model (Endsley, 1988) was devised and data collected from 120 pilots endorsed on the B747-400. This simulator exercise was designed to collect data on some of the component dimensions of the developed contextual definition where discriminatory differences might reasonably be seen to exist. In particular, elements of perception, vigilance, memory, modelling, deductive reasoning, ambiguity identification, and prediction were targeted. This same group of pilots completed a questionnaire which tested the validity of the developed contextual definition and the attendant concept processes.

## Results

This process has yielded a vast amount of both quantitative and qualitative data. Subsequently, only an overview of the results and provisional conclusions can be recorded here.

The contextual definition was endorsed by all but one of the of the 120 respondents. The rejection rate of each of the component processes averaged less than 0.5%. With regard to the establishment and maintenance of SA, analysis of the quantitative data resulting from the simulator exercise has revealed no discrete discriminatory SA dimension. Similarly, no correlation was found between developed SA and the age, experience or rank of the respondents.

### Further research

The results of the research process to this point dictated that the research take a new tack. A cognitive task analysis was initiated to try to identify discriminatory areas.

### *Cognitive Task Analysis*

Using the grounded and quantitative research, a protocol was developed to record the processes which pilots believe they employ in the development and maintenance of SA. To date this protocol has only been applied to experienced airline pilots. In order to tap the core processes, these subjects were asked to consider how they develop and maintain SA on unfamiliar routes.

The results of this analysis at the trial stage are significant. When faced with an unfamiliar task, experienced airline captains report that in order to develop and maintain SA they:

- employ a sector template to control their acquisition of data;
- break the sector into manageable sections (if necessary) for the purpose of data acquisition;
- construct a prototypical model of the sector (or section of sector) with large amounts of data amassed pre-flight and applied to the sector template;
- use this prototype as the executive script for the sector until novel, updated or conflicting data is acquired;

- use a potential impact hierarchy to determine the changes which need to be made to the prototypical model;

- consciously control the operation to achieve the most successful result possible given all the circumstances and;

- learn about this new route operation by active reflection.


**Discussion**

This summary is the distillation of a large amount of amplifying qualitative data. It does suggest that a formal cognitive task analysis should be conducted. Much of the process described is supported by contemporary literature. Templates have been proposed as instrumental in the mastery of chess (Gobet & Simon, 1996). Chunking as a method of storing related data has been explored by many researchers (e.g., Kiernan, Friedland, & Arad, 1991) and equates to the segmentation of the sector.

Prototypical modelling is suggested by several authors in the field of SA (Endsley, 1995; Amalberti & Deblon, 1992) as the principal method of expectation development used by pilots. The proposition that this prototypical model becomes the initial executive script is supported by Endsley and Smith (1996) who note that "avoiding the need to make on-the-spot decisions in stressful situations through anticipation and advanced response development can be seen as an effective strategy for coping with the demands of this environment" (p. 234).

While the differing temporal nature of tactics and strategies has not been explored by Endsley (1995), the acknowledgement of their use in SA maintenance is significant. When the initial inquiry level is added to these planning tools, a potential impact hierarchy is established. Reflective mechanisms will determine the potential impact of any episode and dictate the response required.

Exploring the concept of control with these pilots has given new direction to the research. Their idea of control is not allied to the chain of command and their position as head of the hierarchy. This concept of control is closely aligned with self-initiated influence over the operation, the ability to track their thoughts about "where they are, where they need to be and how best to get there". This process contains many components of metacognition as described by Nelson and Narens (1994, p. 11).

Investigation of the relationship between awareness and metacognition reveals the third-order factor of self-regulation (Hong, 1995) which adequately defines the concept of control identified by this cognitive task analysis. Further, Hong (1995) supports the link between self-regulation and metacognition. Gott, Lajoie and Lesgold (1991) also identified self-regulation as a component of metacognition.

In turn, metacognition is a product of awareness, cognitive strategy, planning and self-checking (Hong, 1995). These concepts exhibit an excellent 'goodness of fit' for pilots. Schraw and Dennison (1994) contend that metacognitive abilities cannot be predicted by aptitude or domain knowledge. This finding is supported by the lack of relationship between measured aptitude and command potential (Beaumont, 1997) where the latter has been shown to be largely dependent on self-regulatory skills.

These pilots indicated that they would consciously review the sector (often including the rest of the crew) to define the aspects which they should explore for future reference. This reflexive process is integral to transformative learning (Mezirow, 1991) and contributes to the experience bank which will facilitate SA development and maintenance should they operate the sector again.

## Conclusion

With qualification, Frederico (1997) has been able to show that metacognitive modelling of situation assessment is predictive of task performance. Hong (1995) has demonstrated an ability to measure self-regulation and attendant metacognitive attributes. While the state/trait relationship of self-regulation is yet to be fully investigated, these findings also indicate predictive capabilities. The measurability of pilot metacognitive abilities and their consistency as predictors of performance in the domain of airline command warrant investigation as a possible solution to the originating problem statement.

## References

Adams, M.J., Tenney, Y.L., & Pew, R.W. (1995). Situation awareness and the cognitive management of complex systems. *Human Factors, 37(1)*, 85-104.

Amalberti, R. & Deblon, F. (1992). Cognitive modeling of fighter aircraft process control: A step towards an intelligent on board assistance system. *International Journal of Man-machine Systems 36*, 639-671.

Beaumont, G. (1997). What attributes do pilots really need? In M. Wiggins, I. Henley, & P. Anderson (Eds.), *Aviation education beyond 2000* (pp. 13-24). Campbelltown: University of Western Sydney Printshop.

Brewer, J. & Hunter, A. (1989). *Multimethod research: A synthesis of styles.* Newbury Park, CA: Sage.

Charness, N. (1996). Expert performance and situation assessment. In R.D. Gilson, D.J. Garland & J.M. Koonce (Eds.), *Situation awareness in complex systems,* (pp. 35-42). Daytona Beach, FL: Embry Riddle Aeronautical University Press.

Dominguez, C. (1994). Can SA be defined? In M. Vidulich, C. Dominiguez, E. Vogel, & G. McMillan (Eds.), *Situation awareness: Papers and annotated bibliography* (pp. 5-15 Report AL/CF-TR-1994-0085). Wright- Patterson Air Force Base, OH: Air Force System Command.

Endsley, M.R. (1988). Design and evaluation for situation awareness enhancement. In *Proceedings of the Human Factors Society 32nd Annual Meeting* (Vol 1). Santa Monica, CA: Human Factors Society.

Endsley, M.R. (1995). Towards a theory of situation awareness in dynamic systems. *Human Factors, 37*(1), 32-64.

Endsley, M.R., & Smith, R.P. (1996). Attention distribution and decision making in tactical air combat. *Human Factors, 38*(2), 232-249.

Flach, J.M. (1995). Situation awareness: Proceed with caution. *Human Factors 37*(1), 149-157.

Frederico, P.A. (1997). An empirical examination of metacognitive models of situation assessment. *Human Factors, 39*(1), 149-157.

Gobet, F., & Simon, H.A. (1996). Templates in chess memory: A mechanism for recalling several boards. *Cognitive Psychology 31,* 1-40.

Gott, S.P., Lajoie, S.P., & Lesgold, A. (1991). In R.F. Dillon & J.W. Pellegrino (Eds.), *Instruction: Theoretical and applied perspectives.* New York, NY: Praeger.

Hong, E. (1995). A structural comparison between state and trait self-regulation models. *Applied Cognitive Psychology, Vol 9,* 333-349.

Jensen, R.S. (1995). *Pilot Judgement.* Aldershot, UK: Ashgate Publishing.

Kiernan, G., Friedland, N., & Arad, L. (1991). Chunking and integration: Effects of stress on the structuring of information. *Cognition and Emotion, 5* (2), 133-145.

Merritt, A. (1997). *Replicating Hofstede: A study of pilots in eighteen countries.* Aerospace Crew Research Project. The University of Texas, Austin, Texas.

Nelson, T.O., & Narens, L. (1994). Why investigate metacognition. In J. Metcalfe & A.P. Shimamura (Eds.), *Metacognition* (pp. 1-26). Cambridge, MA: The MIT Press.

Pew, R.W. (1996). The state of situation awareness measurement: Circa 1995. In R.D. Gilson, D.J. Garland, & J.M. Koonce (Eds.), *Situation awareness in complex systems* (pp. 7-15). Daytona Beach, FL: Embry Riddle Aeronautical University Press.

Sarter, N.B., & Woods, D.D. (1991). Situation awareness: A critical but ill-defined phenomenon. *The International Journal of Aviation Psychology, 1*(1), 45-57.

Schraw, G., & Dennison, R.S. (1994). Assessing metacognitive awareness. *Contemporary Educational Psychology 19,* 460-475.

Seamster, T.L., Redding, R.E., & Kaempf, G.L. (1997). *Applied Cognitive Task Analysis in Aviation.* Aldershot, UK: Ashgate Publishing.

Strauss, A., & Corbin, J. (1990). *Basics of qualitative research: Grounded theory procedures and techniques.* Newbury Park, CA: Sage.

Tenney, Y.J., Adams, M.J., Pew, R.W., Huggins, A.W.F., & Rogers, W.H. (1992). A principled approach to the measurement of situation awareness in commercial aviation. *NASA Contract Report 4451.* Hampton, VA: Langley Research Centre.

# 38 Individual differences in situational awareness and training for complex tasks

*David O'Hare and Kerry O'Brien*
*University of Otago*

## Introduction

The task of the operator of any complex system involves searching and monitoring relevant information, assessing opportunities, setting priorities, and maintaining performance under stress. The term 'situational awareness' (SA) has become widely used to refer to this constellation of characteristics (Adams, Tenney, & Pew, 1995; Sarter & Woods, 1995). Situation awareness has been studied in a variety of domains, including aviation (Endsley & Bolstad, 1994), anaesthesiology (Gaba, Howard, & Small, 1995) and automobile driving (Gugerty, 1997).

As Roscoe (1980) has pointed out, aviation psychology "deals largely with the complementary processes of behavioural engineering and the selection and training of personnel" (Roscoe, 1980, p. 3). On the one hand, it is incumbent upon designers of aircraft cockpits and systems intended for use in aviation to consider the impact of system design and interface characteristics on operator SA. On the other hand, it is important to consider the selection of personnel with the greatest potential to achieve high levels of SA and the appropriate strategies for training operator SA. The present paper is concerned with these latter issues.

It is well known that traditional pilot selection batteries are better at predicting initial flying training performance than in predicting performance at more advanced levels (Roscoe & North, 1980). If as suggested above, high levels of SA are required for successful performance in complex systems, and if traditional test batteries measure only underlying component abilities (e.g., perceptual speed, working memory capacity etc), then it is hardly surprising that much of the variance in advanced performance remains unpredicted.

## The WOMBAT-CS Situational Awareness and Stress Tolerance Test

The WOMBAT-CS test was developed (Roscoe, 1993; Roscoe & Corl, 1987) to provide a measure of an individual's ability to "search for, evaluate, and integrate information about all relevant events, conditions, and resources, quickly assess changes in situational priorities, and allocate attention accordingly (Roscoe, Corl, & LaRoche, 1997, p. 31). The WOMBAT-CS test requires the coordinated performance of a set of tasks involving pursuit tracking, pattern recognition, mental rotation, and working memory.

The individual tasks were designed to be relatively easy to learn and to show no positive transfer from previous real-world tasks such as flying or computer use. Further details are given in the method section below.

In a recently published study (O'Hare, 1997) we found that although initial performance on the WOMBAT-CS test was influenced by previous computer game experience and by pattern-recognition ability, neither of these variables was a significant predictor of WOMBAT-CS performance after sixty minutes of testing. In fact, none of the demographic (e.g., age) or ability measures was a significant predictor of performance on the test at this stage. These data support the premise of the WOMBAT-CS test as a measure of some higher-level ability which is not confounded with previous experience.

In comparing WOMBAT-CS scores obtained from eight elite pilots at the World Gliding Championships with scores obtained by other highly experienced pilots and with a group of matched controls, a clear association between elite pilot performance and score on the WOMBAT-CS test was demonstrated. It would appear then, that the WOMBAT-CS test offers some promise as a test of an individual's long-range ability to reach high levels of performance in tasks that are particularly demanding of situational awareness.

The study reported here was undertaken as part of a series of studies designed to contribute to a better understanding of the nature of the abilities measured by WOMBAT-CS. The study compared the predictive abilities of WOMBAT-CS versus a standard measure of IQ in relation to performance on a complex task demanding high levels of SA. The task chosen was the TRACON (Wesson International, 1991) air traffic control simulation. This is a highly realistic PC-based simulation of a terminal radar approach control facility. The programme allows the experimenter considerable control over the task, thus making it highly suitable for use in laboratory testing.

## Method

*Participants*

Twenty males were recruited from a local student job centre during the University summer vacation. The mean age of participants was 25.5 years (*SD* 5.4 years) ranging from 17 years to 35 years old.

*Materials*

*WOMBAT-CS task.* Testees interact with WOMBAT-CS (V4.0) by means of a console containing two joysticks and a 13-button keypad. The keypad consists of 10 numeric keys (0-9), left and right arrow keys, and a key labelled "bonus". The right-hand joystick contains a trigger switch that is used to engage an automatic tracking function. The left-hand stick controls the horizontal movement of a pair of parallel vertical lines with fore and aft movements of the joystick. The right-hand stick controls the position of a small cross on the screen (see Figure 38.1).

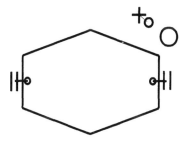

**Figure 38.1**
**The WOMBAT-CS tracking task**

Both sticks operate in either of two control modes. In the velocity control mode, the lines and the cross remain stationary until the sticks are displaced from their spring-centered positions, and the rates of movement of these symbols are proportional to the amounts of control displacement. In the acceleration mode, the symbols move at constant rates when the controls are centered, and the stick displacements determine the changes in their existing rates of movement.

371

In either mode, the task is to track the vertical sides of an expanding and contracting hexagon with the pair of parallel lines controlled by the left stick, while simultaneously tracking a target circle with the cross controlled by the right-hand stick. The control mode (velocity or acceleration) changes according to an adaptive logic. If the targets are tracked accurately, an automatic tracking function can be engaged with the right-hand joystick trigger. This continues to track the targets with frequent failures. When the "autotrack" fails, it does not disengage, but results in loss of tracking performance and a flashing of the integrated tracking performance display. This display must therefore be carefully monitored while the testee is engaged in other tasks.

There are three "bonus" tasks that must be attempted as frequently as possible. Each task is available for a 60-sec period. If the task is completed within that period, the display freezes until the full period has elapsed, thus allowing the subject to take a short break.

*Digit cancelling*: A succession of digits is displayed at several-second intervals. After the third presentation, the task is to press the button on the keypad matching the digit displayed two-back in the sequence.

*Quadrant location*: The numbers 1 to 32 are distributed across four quadrants of the display, eight in each quadrant. The task is to find each number in ascending order and press a button on the keypad that corresponds to the quadrant in which it lies. This deletes the number.

*3-D figure rotation:* Two three-dimensional figures (derived from Shepard & Metzler, 1971) are displayed side-by-side. Either figure can be selected and rotated about all three axes using the two joystick controls. The task is to determine as quickly as possible whether the figures are identical, mirror images, or otherwise different. Testees are also asked to indicate a degree of confidence in their answers. Maximum points are scored for a "certain" correct answer.

Testees received sufficient practice on all tasks to assure near asymptotic tracking performance and a clear understanding of each of the bonus tasks.

*Ravens Progressive Matrices.* This is a non-verbal test requiring testees to determine which of six or eight alternative patterns provides the best match to a target pattern. Anastasi (1968) notes that this test is regarded by many as the best available measure of "Spearman's $g$".

*Tracon Simulation.* The participant is seated in front of a standard PC running the TRACON (Wesson International, 1991) software. A simulated radar screen depicts the airspace around a major airport (in this case, Los Angeles) including other airports, airways, VOR navigation beacons, intersection fixes, and ILS approaches. Aircraft status is shown on electronic 'flight strips'. Communication between aircraft and controller can be heard via the speakers, and all dialogue is shown in a text box on the screen. Commands are issued via 'pull-down' menus. There are three types of flight: overflights, departures, and arrivals. If an arriving aircraft is not at the correct height and speed to intercept the ILS approach it will not be 'accepted' by the tower and will execute a 'missed approach'. Participants are scored on their performance with points deducted for errors in handing off, missed approaches, and separation conflicts. The TRACON test session was recorded on VHS video tape for subsequent analysis.

*Procedure*

There were two testing sessions. In the first session participants completed the timed Australian version of the Ravens Progressive Matrices test. They were then given an overview of the WOMBAT-CS test and a step-by-step hands-on practice session covering every element of the WOMBAT-CS test. When this was completed, they were given a ten-item test of the WOMBAT-CS instructions. Any errors were corrected before proceeding to the test. The testing session lasted 60 minutes.

On the second session, participants were given a general overview of the TRACON task and hands-on practice with three short scenarios containing one aircraft overflight/arrival/departure and then a fourth scenario containing three aircraft of mixed types. A 15-item checklist was then used to determine if there were any errors in the participants' understanding of how to operate the programme. Any misunderstandings were corrected before proceeding to the test. The test session involved eight aircraft of mixed types. The actual length of the test scenario depended on how well the aircraft were handled, and ranged between 20 and 40 minutes.

**Results**

*Bivariate analyses*

The product-moment correlations between WOMBAT-CS score, IQ score, TRACON score, and several demographic variables showed that age was negatively correlated with both WOMBAT-CS ($r = - 0.52$, $p < 0.02$) and TRACON ($r = - 0.6$, $p < 0.005$) scores. IQ was positively correlated with both WOMBAT-CS ($r = 0.73$, $p < 0.002$) and TRACON ($r = 0.5$, $p < 0.025$) scores. The WOMBAT-CS and TRACON scores were significantly correlated ($r = 0.48$, $p < 0.04$).

*Multivariate analyses*

Stepwise regressions were performed using both TRACON and WOMBAT-CS scores as the predicted variable. The $R^2$ values were 0.64 and 0.72 respectively. The stepwise regression models were used to estimate the unique proportion of variance in each predicted variable accounted for by given predictors. This controls for the variance that each predictor shares with other variables (Hatcher & Stepanski, 1994). Whilst TRACON scores were best predicted by age (10.5% unique variance), WOMBAT-CS scores were best predicted by IQ (28.4% unique variance) with age accounting for only 4% of the unique variance in WOMBAT-CS scores.

The bivariate correlation between age and WOMBAT-CS scores noted above is thus rather misleading. The multivariate analysis shows that this correlation is largely accounted for by other correlated variables. As might be expected however, WOMBAT-CS (but not TRACON) taps into a substantial pool of variance commonly associated with general intelligence or '*g*'.

*Errors in TRACON performance*

In addition to the overall performance scores used in the above analyses, a more detailed breakdown of performance in the TRACON task was obtained from the video tape of each session. A record was made of the number of incorrect speed and altitude commands, missed approaches, separation conflicts and missed handoffs in the test session. Of these, the missed approaches, caused by failing to get the aircraft correctly positioned at the start of the approach, and missed handoffs in which an aircraft leaves the sector without being handed off to the next controller, were of greatest interest.

The product-moment correlation data showed that there were no significant associations between the missed-approach errors and any of the other measured variables. In contrast, the handoff errors were positively correlated with age ($r = 0.6$, $p < 0.005$) and negatively correlated with IQ ($r = -0.5$, $p < 0.02$) and negatively correlated with WOMBAT-CS score ($r = -0.6$, $p < 0.005$).

## Discussion

The results of this study show that the WOMBAT-CS test of SA predicts early performance on a task which appears to require high levels of SA to perform successfully. In particular, scores on the WOMBAT-CS test show a high correlation with handoff errors involving a lack of awareness of aircraft situation. A reasonable proportion (28%) of variance in WOMBAT-CS test scores can be attributed to general intelligence ('$g$'). It is important to bear in mind however that the relatively low number of participants may limit the validity of conclusions derived from multiple regression analysis (Tabachnik & Fidell, 1996).

In combination with previous findings (O'Hare, 1997), the results suggest that the WOMBAT-CS test is able to predict aspects of both laboratory and real-world performance which are related to SA. I have found no evidence that test scores are dependent on age or experience with computers or computer games. I have also found no evidence that WOMBAT-CS scores are dependent on any specific underlying abilities but have found a sizeable overlap with general intelligence ('$g$'). It is important to note however, that nearly three-quarters of the variance in WOMBAT-CS scores is not shared with general intelligence as measured by a conventional static test.

We are currently investigating the nature of the differences between high and low WOMBAT-CS performers using a training paradigm. Participants are again trained to perform the TRACON task. One group is given 'emphasis-change' training (Gopher, 1993) in which they are forced to explore their attention control strategies. We have predicted that this rudimentary manipulation should have little effect on participants with already good attention awareness and management strategies (high WOMBAT-CS scores) but should improve the performance of low scorers. In a preliminary study involving eleven participants we have found the predicted interaction ($p < 0.05$) between training condition (control versus emphasis change) and ability (high versus low WOMBAT-CS scores).

In conclusion, our studies offer preliminary support for the notion that the WOMBAT-CS test measures an aspect of SA 'beyond basic intelligence and motor skills' (Roscoe et al., 1997, p. 11) which may be related to the efficiency with which the individual can manage and control their attentional strategy.

## References

Adams, M.J., Tenney, Y.J., & Pew, R.W. (1995). Situation awareness and the cognitive management of complex systems. *Human Factors, 37*, 85-104.

Anastasi, A. (1968). *Psychological testing (3rd edition).* Toronto: Macmillan.

Endsley, M.R., & Bolstad, C.A. (1994). Individual differences in pilot situation awareness. *The International Journal of Aviation Psychology, 4*, 241-264.

Gaba, D.M., Howard, S.K., & Small, S.D. (1995). Situation awareness in anesthesiology. *Human Factors, 37*, 20-31.

Gopher, D. (1993). The skill of attention control: Acquisition and execution of attention strategies. In D.E. Mayer & S. Kornblum (Eds.), *Attention and performance XIV*. Cambridge, MA: MIT Press.

Gugerty, L.J. (1997). Situation awareness during driving: Explicit and implicit knowledge in dynamic spatial memory. *Journal of Experimental Psychology: Applied, 3*, 42-66.

Hatcher, L., & Stepanski, E.J. (1994). *A step-by-step approach to using the SAS system for univariate and multivariate statistics*, Cary, NC: SAS Institute.

O'Hare, D. (1997). Cognitive ability determinants of elite pilot performance. *Human Factors, 39*, 540-552.

Roscoe, S.N. (1980). *Aviation psychology*. Ames, IA: The Iowa State University Press.

Roscoe, S.N., & Corl, L. (1987). Wondrous orginal method for basic airmanship testing. In R.S. Jensen (Ed.), *Proceedings of the fourth international symposium on aviation psychology* (pp. 493-499). Columbus: The Ohio State University.

Roscoe, S.N., Corl, L., & LaRoche, J. (1997). *Predicting human performance*. Pierrefonds, Canada: Helio Press.

Roscoe, S.N., & North, R.A. (1980). Prediction of pilot performance. In S. N. Roscoe (Ed.), *Aviation psychology* (pp. 127-133). Ames, IA: The Iowa State University Press.

Sarter, N.B., & Woods, D.D. (1995). How in the world did we ever get into that mode? Mode error and awareness in supervisory control. *Human Factors, 37,* 5-19.

Tabachnik, B.G., & Fidell, L.S. (1996). *Using multivariate statistics (3rd edition).* New York: HarperCollins.

Wesson International (1991). *TRACON for Windows.* Austin, TX: Wesson International.

.

# 39 Decision-making under time constraints

*Mark Wiggins and P. Anderson*
*University of Western Sydney, Macarthur*

## Introduction

The nature of the aviation environment is such that there are a number of competing demands on flight crew to manage information, and ensure an appropriate outcome to a flight. In many cases, however, the management of task-related information is constrained by the environment and, in particular, the time available in which to evaluate various options. Anecdotal evidence arising from aircraft accidents in both the airline and general aviation environments, suggest that time constraints impact significantly upon the decision-making behaviour of flight crew. This study is part of a larger program of research that is designed to examine the impact of time constraints on the process of decision-making amongst experienced and inexperienced pilots.

### Time stress and decision-making

The relationship between time stress and decision-making performance has been examined in a number of contexts, including fire fighting and missile warning systems (Cohen, Freeman, & Wolf, 1996; Cooke, 1990; Kaempf, Wolf, Thordsen, & Klein, 1992; Klein, 1989). Collectively, the results suggest that time stress initiates a 'recognition-primed' approach to decision-making, particularly amongst more experienced practitioners. This is usually characterised by the serial evaluation of options and is based upon the notion that the decision-maker 'recognises' the situation and implements a response almost immediately.

Recognition-primed decision-making is consistent with the notion that experts proceduralise or chunk information pertaining to a particular event and therefore, they tend to respond to classes of problems, rather than examine each new problem on its individual merits (Anderson, 1987).

379

Moreover, this evidence has led directly to the development of a number of training strategies, designed to facilitate the development of recognition-primed decision processes amongst novice practitioners (Means, Salas, Crandall, & Jacobs, 1993).

The difficulty with the recognition-primed approach to decision-making is that, although it may describe the type of decision strategy employed by experts within a particular environment, it is not necessarily descriptive of expert performance when the cognitive demands of the situation are altered. In the aviation environment, for example, there is considerable evidence to suggest that expert decision strategies differ according to particular characteristics of the task involved (Wiggins & O'Hare, 1995; Wiggins & Henley, 1997). Despite the evidence to support the notion of proceduralisation, experts may undertake a more analytical approach when the consequences associated with a decision are severe, and/or the level of time constraint is relatively low (Wiggins & Henley, 1997). This paper presents some preliminary data which examines the extent to which the decision strategies employed by both experts and novices differ in response to systematic changes in the cognitive demands associated with pre-flight decision-making.

*Pre-flight decision-making*

Pre-flight decision-making is a task in which the consequences of a poor decision can be severe. According to Kirkbride, Jensen, Chubb, and Hunter (1996), for example, errors in pre-flight decision-making contribute to the majority of aircraft accidents and incidents in the US. From a research perspective, however, it is also an operational task in which the cognitive demands may vary, depending upon the reliability of the information, and the time available in which to formulate a decision. Furthermore, it has the facility to be represented in a computer-based format which enables the sequence of information acquisition to be tracked and recorded.

**Participants**

The participants comprised five experienced and seven inexperienced pilots, ranging in age from 20 to 55 years ($\overline{X}= 38.25$). Experienced pilots were defined as those participants who had completed at least 250 departures involving cross-country operations ($\overline{X}= 1659$, $SD = 2484$), while inexperienced pilots were defined as those participants who had accumulated between 2 and 249 departures involving cross-country operations ($\overline{X}= 110, SD = 75$).

*Stimuli*

A computer-based program (Wiggins, Taylor, & Connan, 1996) was designed to simulate the process of pre-flight decision-making, and incorporated a series of information menus through which participants progressed to acquire information (see Figure 39.1). The menus included text and graphic information that would normally be available to pilots prior to a cross-country flight, including the relevant maps, maintenance documentation, and meteorological information. All the information was presented in the format in which the participants would receive the information within the operational environment.

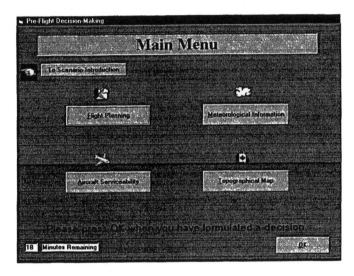

**Figure 39.1**
**An example of the main menu screen from the computer program**
**Pre-Flight Decision-Making**

The computer program comprised three sections: an introductory section; an information acquisition section; and a decision-making section. The introductory section included a brief description of the flight including the estimated time of departure and the way-points along the route. Having completed the introductory section, participants progressed to the information acquisition section in which they were asked to access the information as they would, within the operational environment. The

381

program recorded both the screen accessed and the response latency between entry and exit from the screen. Having completed the information acquisition phase, participants were asked to indicate whether or not they would conduct the flight on the basis of the information they had acquired. The validity of the computer program had been tested previously within the operational environment (Taylor & Wiggins, 1997).

*Procedure*

Once participants had been informed of the nature of the study, they were asked to enter their personal details into the computer. A practice scenario was initiated subsequently, and participants were encouraged to access each information screen to become familiar with its location and the information available. A time limit of twenty minutes was imposed during the practice scenario.

The study consisted of two experimental scenarios, the first of which was limited to four minutes, while the second was limited to two minutes. Following the completion of each scenario, participants progressed to the decision phase in which a dichotomous response was required as to whether or not they would authorise the flight under the circumstances. In addition, they were asked to indicate their level of confidence in the decision and rate, from 1 to 12, the relative importance of each piece of information to the decision-making process.

**Results and discussion**

Consistent with prior research in this area (see Wiggins & Henley, 1997), the process of data analysis was divided into three components according to an information processing approach to decision-making. The three stages: *situation assessment, information acquisition*, and *response selection/ excution*, form the basis of a tripartite model of information processing described by Wickens and Flach (1988). It should be noted the preliminary nature of the data precludes the application of inferential statistical analyses at this stage.

*Situation assessment*

Situation assessment was examined in terms of the duration spent reviewing the route, prior to the information acquisition phase. Preliminary analyses indicate that both experienced and inexperienced pilots spent less time examining the introductory information during the four minute scenario ($\overline{X}$ = 37.26, $SD$ = 17.06) than during the two minute scenario ($\overline{X}$ = 24.65, $SD$ = 15.69). This suggests that a learning effect may have been evident, in which participants became more confident during the second scenario, following the completion of the first scenario.

*Information acquisition*

The process of information acquisition was examined from a number of perspectives including the frequency of information screens accessed, the time spent examining the information screens, and the preference for particular types of information.

Comparisons between the mean frequency of separate information screens accessed indicates that inexperienced pilots accessed fewer screens than experienced pilots during the four minute scenario, although this relationship was reversed during the two minute scenario (see Figure 39.2).

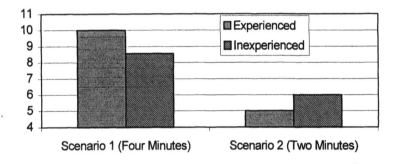

**Figure 39.2**
**Mean frequency of information screens accessed by experienced and inexperienced pilots during the four minute and two minute pre-flight decision scenarios**

Consistent with the data concerning the number of information screens, a comparison between the mean time (in secs.) spent examining the information screens indicated that experienced pilots spent more time examining the information during the four minute scenario, than their inexperienced counterparts (see Figure 39.3). Approximately the same amount of time was used by both groups of pilots during the two minute scenario. This suggests that the rate at which information was acquired was relatively consistent amongst both experienced and inexperienced pilots.

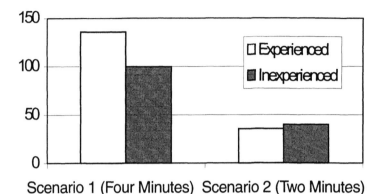

Scenario 1 (Four Minutes)  Scenario 2 (Two Minutes)

**Figure 39.3**
**Mean time (in seconds) spent examining information screens by**
**experienced and inexperienced pilots during the four minute and two**
**minute pre-flight decision scenarios**

Following the completion of each scenario, participants were asked to rate, from 1 to 12, the relative importance of various types of information during the decision-making process. The aim was to determine the extent to which experienced and inexperienced pilots differed in terms of their perception of the relative significance of task-related information. Median ratings were calculated for each type of information across each of the scenarios. For each scenario, the type of information was identified which yielded the greatest distinction between the ratings of experienced and inexperienced pilots.

The results indicated a relatively consistent pattern across both scenarios, with the greatest distinction emerging for the flight plan, and the maintenance release. In the case of both types of information, the relationship was consistent across scenarios, with experienced pilots rating the flight plan as relatively less important and the maintenance release as relatively more important during the decision-making process.

This suggests that experienced pilots may have been applying a rudimentary information acquisition procedure across both scenarios. Given the variability amongst the other responses, however, there is also evidence to suggest that pilots were responding to the particular characteristics of the scenario, rather than applying a universal procedure.

*Decision*

The majority of inexperienced pilots decided against the flight in both scenarios. In comparison, the responses amongst experienced pilots were more evenly distributed with three of the five pilots electing to conduct the flight in scenario one, while two pilots elected to conduct the flight in scenario two. Of particular interest, however, is level of confidence expressed in the appropriateness of the decision. Despite the decision against the flight by the majority of inexperienced pilots, the mean level of confidence was not particularly high in comparison to experienced pilots (see Figure 39.3). This suggests that inexperienced pilots may be electing against the flight in the absence of sufficient information to formulate a reasoned response. This suggests that a 'floor effect' may have occurred for inexperienced pilots in which the two minute time limit failed to provide sufficient information to formulate a reasoned decision.

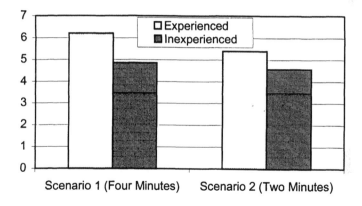

**Figure 39.4**
**Mean level of confidence in the appropriateness of the decision for experienced and inexperienced pilots during the four minute and two minute pre-flight decision scenarios**

**Conclusion**

The results of this preliminary analysis provide some important indications concerning the impact of time constraints on decision-making behaviour. In particular, it appeared that inexperienced pilots were less able to cope with the increase in time pressure than were their experienced counterparts.

Evidence for this assertion can be drawn from the decision to take the route of least risk, but express only limited confidence in the accuracy of this decision. This has important implications from a commercial perspective where the decision-making process is dependent upon calculated risks.

## References

Anderson, J.R. (1987). Skill acquisition: Compilation of weak-method problem-solutions. *Psychological Review, 94,* 19-210.

Cohen, M.S., Freeman, J.T., & Wolf, S. (1996). Metarecognition in time-stressed decision making: Recognising, critiquing, and correcting. *Human Factors, 38,* 206-219.

Cooke, N.J. (1990). Modeling human expertise in expert systems. In R.R. Hoffman (Ed.), *The psychology of expertise* (pp. 29-60). New York, NY: Springer-Verlag.

Kaempf, G.L., Wolf, S.P., Thordsen, M.L., & Klein, G. (1992). *Decision-making in the Aegis combat information centre* (Naval Command, Control and Ocean Surveillance Centre Report N66001-90-C-6023). San Diego, CA: Klein Associates.

Kirkbride, L.A., Jensen, R.S., & Chubb, G.P., & Hunter, D.R. (1996). *Developing the personal minimums tool for managing risk during preflight go/no go decisions.* Washington, DC: Federal Aviation Administration (NTIS DOT/FAA/AM-96/19).

Klein, G.A. (1989). Recognition-primed decisions (RPD). *Advances in Man-Machine Systems, 5,* 47-92.

Means, B., Salas, E., Crandall, B., & Jacobs, T.O. (1993). Training decision makers for the real world. In G.A. Klein, J. Orasanu, R. Calderwood, C.E. Zsambok (Eds.), *Decision making in action: Models and methods* (pp. 306-326). Norwood, NJ: Ablex.

Taylor, S.T., & Wiggins, M.W. (1997). The validation of a computer-based program for the development of pre-flight decision-making skills amongst pilots. In R.S. Jensen & L.A. Rakovan (Eds.), *Proceedings of the Ninth International Symposium on Aviation Psychology.* Columbus, OH: Ohio State University.

Wickens, C.D., & Flach, J.M. (1988). Information processing. In E.L. Wiener & D.C. Nagel (Eds.), *Human factors in aviation* (pp. 111-155). San Diego, CA: Academic Press.

Wiggins, M.W., & O'Hare, D. (1995). Expertise in aeronautical weather-related decision-making: A cross-sectional analysis of general aviation pilots. *Journal of Experimental Psychology: Applied, 1,* 305-320.

Wiggins, M.W., & Henley, I. (1997). A Computer-Based Analysis of Expert and Novice Flight Instructor Pre-Flight Decision-Making. *The International Journal of Aviation Psychology, 7,* 365-380.

Wiggins, M.W., & Taylor, S., & Connan, N. (1996). *Pre-Flight Decision-Making.* (Version 1.0). [Computer-Based Training Program]. Newcastle: Author.

# Part 7
# DEVELOPMENTAL
# WORKSHOP
# REPORTS

# 40 Air traffic control developmental workshop report

*Bert Ruitenberg, IFATCA*
*Anne Isaac, Eurocontrol*
*Carol Manning, FAA*
*John Guselli, Airservices Australia[1]*

## Introduction

The purpose of the workshop was to discuss human factors issues associated with new air traffic control technologies. The workshop considered new technologies in air traffic control from four perspectives: reasons for technology replacement (with paper vs. electronic flight progress strips being considered as an example); communication; information display; and system functionality.

Members of the ATC workshop also visited The Australian Advanced Air Traffic System (TAAATS) simulation facility at the Air Traffic Services Center at Sydney airport. This new system was observed and discussed in detail as an example of new ATC technology. A representation of the TAAATS workstation configuration is presented at Figure 42.1.

## Large-group discussion

The workshop divided into four groups which then discussed each issue independently. The groups then reconvened and presented their findings. While some issues were specific to each group, some common themes emerged. Concerns were expressed in more than one group about the

---

[1] The following participants also assisted with facilitation of this workshop: Robert Mason, Airservices Australia, and Don Hamilton, Airways Corporation of New Zealand.

possibility that new ATC technologies may produce information overload, reduce situation awareness, and result in problems recognising alarms and alerts. All groups recognised the need for extensive initial and refresher training for both controllers and pilots on the new technologies. Another issue that was identified by all groups was the need to achieve a backup if a system failure occurs.

Additional discussion among the full group identified additional issues:

- Selection of future controllers –will the job change enough to require changes in selection tests?
- How will new technologies change the roles of controller team members?
- Presently, controllers are experts. Who will be an expert when the transition to a new system occurs? (How does a controller achieve certification if no one is an expert?)
- How should ATC procedures be changed to accommodate new technologies?
- How will introduction of new technologies affect strategic thinking and teamwork?
- How will new technologies affect the role of the supervisor?
- How will new technologies affect service to the customer?

**Small-group discussion of specific issues**

**1. Technology replacement**

Replacement of paper flight progress strips with their electronic equivalent was chosen as a specific example for discussion.

Problem: The accuracy of displayed data depends on the controller constantly updating it. If a paper flight strip is used, the controller can write on it for his/her own purposes, but this does not support the rest of the system.

The primary purpose for replacing the paper flight strip with an electronic equivalent of some sort is to ensure the accuracy of flight data in the system that is displayed to subsequent controllers. It is presumed that it would be too workload-intensive to both type in computerised data and write notes on a paper flight strip. It is also assumed that if the paper strip is eliminated, then controller workload will also be reduced.

Issues:

- Flight strips serve a function besides containing information necessary for control:

  - Presence of strip in certain part of bay indicates runway is occupied;
  - A controller can sequence strips to anticipate the order of aircraft coming into a VFR airport;
  - The number of strips anticipates near-term busyness of a sector;
  - History of events on a paper strip may trigger recollection of event (e.g., that a pilot requested an altitude change due to turbulence);
  - Cocking/offsetting strips to highlight information;
  - Provides reminder that controller completed activity or that information was read back;
  - Provides reminder that separation was evaluated for an aircraft;
  - Physical reliance (tower);
  - Degraded modes – what information does controller have, not have?

- Some of these functions can be addressed electronically and all should be considered:
  - Display lists of incoming aircraft to anticipate busyness;
  - Highlight strips or extend data block to replace cocking/offsetting;
  - Sort or re-order electronic strips to indicate sequencing;
  - Use a notepad to supplement displayed data (sequencing of aircraft into or out of airport, holding information);
  - Conflict probe function may replace need to scan strips to evaluate separation.

- Other flight strip functions cannot be accommodated by current version of ATC automation:
  - Flight plan data not displayed in non-radar towers;
  - No history retained for electronic flight data;
  - No information available for non-radar aircraft.

393

- What to do if degraded operations occur?

  - Paper flight strips provide tangible reminder that a non-radar aircraft is in flight.

- How much should a controller rely on the currency and accuracy of information displayed electronically?

  - When are flight data updated/to whom is information sent?

  - Remote sites are vulnerable to losing flight data if processing occurs in off-site location

  - How are FDP data updated after system goes down and comes back up?

  - Sequence of updating flight data if have one planner for multiple en route controllers?

- Changes in controller roles at the same time paper strips are eliminated may produce unexpected problems (if planner has to monitor more than one sector, may not be the "second pair of eyes" for the en route controller, and, thus, may fail to identify problems that would not occur if paper strip were present).

- Transition training is necessary to train controllers accustomed to using strips alone, or a combination of strips and a radar display, to working with an electronic display alone.

- Will elimination of paper strips result in a more tactical, and less strategic, ATC operation?

  - Identify problem by looking at radar alone?

  - Less time, fewer options for recovery if problem occurs.

- Amount of head-down time (feeding the elephant).

## 2. Communication issues

- Aviation systems are becoming global, so new systems must take global interactions into account.

- It is necessary to look at the aviation system as a whole (ATC has had little attention).

- Future projections suggest that the ATC system is becoming closer to the pilot environment.

Four types of communications issues were discussed:

- Management of technology
  - Attempts to fight tomorrow's war using yesterday's tactics will be unsuccessful;
  - Systems development forces global commonality (can't afford not to recognise efforts of other nations);
  - International communications to agree on problems and work solutions;
  - Operator training must occur while still working through engineering solution;
  - Human factors must be considered up front – if consider early, then developers will pay once. If don't consider HF early, they will pay for redesigns over and over.

- Air/ground communications
  - Human voice changing to data link;
  - Customer communications affected by move of ATM facilities off airports;
  - 767/747-400 produces change to ground operations;
  - AIRCAT, TAAATS produce change to air operations;
  - For effective and safe operations, both pilots and controllers should be involved in development – need to understand each others' perspective;
  - Potential problems/concerns:
    - Loss of SA for both controllers and pilots;
    - Need to provide pilot refresher training about changes to ATC operations;
    - Only use the technology designed to do the job;
    - Only use the technology that works;
    - Fit the mode of communications to the situation (e.g., Data link in TMA);

- There must be voice backup in case of failure.

- Sector/sector or controller/controller communications:

  - Occurring at a local level

  - Resulting in a workplace changes, such as:

  - Physical: mouse, keyboard, strip loss (evaluate what is being lost, whether replacement assists cognitive functioning);

  - Also increases physical separation from other controllers;

  - Other changes: computerised voice, overloading visual system, increased amount of data;

    - All changes will require training (both HF and technical).

- Human-machine interaction (HMI), or controller/machine communications:

  - End stage – need a careful assessment of modes;

  - Physical environment (increased use of mouse, keyboard);

    - May change locus of pain from back to arm/hand/wrist.

  - Visual changes (windows, colour, amount of information that can be displayed);

  - Audio (emergency, AIS);

  - Requirement for training in new communications methods.

### 3. Information Display

There is concern about information overload with regard to the amount and type of information displayed to controllers. Recommendations about the amount of displayed information follow:

- Information must be sufficient on a continuous basis to:

  - maintain relevant situation awareness;

  - make and revise traffic management plans;

  - provide access to other information when necessary.

- Information must be sufficient on a task-specific basis to accomplish tasks while avoiding breakdown in separation, violation of SOPs, and unnecessary aircraft manoeuvering.

- It must be possible for the controller to manage (vary) the amount of information tasks require.

- System warnings must alert, inform, and direct controller to the situation.

- Excess information will degrade the maintenance of situation awareness and non-specific information (e.g., common colors, similar tones) will cause task triggers to be missed. Examples:

  - Colour of tracks: built in change for conflict;

  - Flight strips: Only display that information which is needed.

## 4. System functionality

- Alarms/alerts (problems):

  - Too many, too often? HF consideration;

  - False alarms and tolerances of alarms may result in ignoring hazardous situations:

    - Alerts may be displayed to those not responsible for taking action.

  - Establish priority of sound/visual cues:

    - One alert noise for all warnings – can't tell where sound originates.

  - Alerts at present are second generation automation and are aimed at providing more defences for the system;

  - Alerts may be confusing or not observed:

    - If occur within wrong window;

    - May not see or hear alert unless sitting in exact position;

    - Hard to silence.

- Probes and tools:

  - Automatic aids can add in achieving situational awareness, e.g., route monitoring probe;

  - Communications systems (start hand-offs);

  - Tactical/strategic - may result in erosion of strategic planning skills;

  - Future system requirements should be aimed at providing decision making aids for controller, however these should not take decision making away from the controller;

  - Automation should be aimed at reducing controller workload but should not leave the controller in a monitoring role;

  - Automation tools may lead to controllers relying on the tools to the limits. Training and performance monitoring should be used to ensure this does not come to pass.

- Training

  - Degraded modes (42 modes, 80 transitions).

**Conclusions**

The group arrived at the following conclusions:

- System acquisition should include a detailed concept of operations (how will controllers work with this system?).

- System development should be complete before training commences (don't fix problems after training has begun, requiring re-training).

- Extensive systems experience should precede implementation (someone should be an expert).

- Global compatibility and integration should be ensured.

And finally,

- Would you commence training a line pilot to fly an aircraft that has yet to complete its first test flight?

- ...and would you want to fly in it?

**Figure 40.1**

**Model of The Australian Automated Air Traffic System (TAAAATS)**

# 41 Aircraft maintenance developmental workshop report

*Nick McDonald, Trinity College Dublin, Ireland*
*Alan Hobbs, Bureau of Air Safety Investigation, Australia*
*Michelle Robertson, University of Southern California*

## Overview

The workshop set out to overview the systems approach to the role of human factors in aviation maintenance. A number of issues resulting from the systems approach were outlined, in particular three human factors models incorporating system elements were used to analyse an incident. Finally the move from short term "fixes" to system "solutions" was discussed.

## Human factors models

Three models were used to help analyse the Nationair DC-8 accident at Jeddah on 11 July 1991. The models were:

- The SHELL Model (see Hawkins, 1987 for further information)
- Reason's model (See Reason, 1997 for further information)
- the Organisational Safety System self-audit model (McDonald, see Annex A).

## System issues

Applying these models resulted in the identification of a number of issues which were seen as system dysfunction rather than individual "error". These are listed below:

- Poor communication (ineffective communication)
- Lack of technical knowledge (technical training)
- Lack of assertiveness (between the cockpit, ramp and maintenance)
- Attitude problems
- Lack of procedures
- Lack of supervision
- Perceived pressure (self and company)
- Poor teamwork (between the cockpit personnel and maintenance personnel)
- Lack of resources (tools and location)
- National culture differences
- Physical environment (hot weather)
- Fatigue and shift-work issues
- Stress
- Norms
- Lack of safety culture
- Chain of events.

Following this a number of goals for the overall safety management system were identified. Regulations should be simple and accurate. The organisation should promote a culture that values the role of every individual who contributes to safety while having a commitment from the top of the organisation down.

**Elements of a good safety culture**

What constitutes a good safety culture? The elements of a good safety culture were identified firstly in the organisation and secondly in the individual. A company can demonstrate a good safety culture through having a safe environment; having effective monitoring and reporting systems; providing training; facilitating the dissemination of information and providing channels for communication; ensuring motivation to be safe; providing effective supervision; and having procedures for evaluation of performance and feedback to all levels in the system.

Individual expressions of a good safety culture were seen as: using the environment safely; participation in safety initiatives; only doing what you are trained to do; taking personal responsibility; and taking pride in work - being professional.

**What do we want to address?**

An example of the kind of issue that may need to be addressed in an organisation was identified and a number of issues surrounding this was discussed. The "can-do attitude" or the "can we get away with it" approach was identified as being particularly prevalent in the aviation maintenance domain and presented particular problems for safety. The issues around this included:

- Knowing how to do it - but also knowing how to do it safely
- Knowing who draws the line
- Which is valued more - Safety or Performance
- Sharing responsibility - teams
- Recognising warning signs and alerting others
- Professional discretion vs. firm limits
- Saying "no", proposing alternatives.

**Achieving "system" solutions**

To achieve an environment in which such problems can be addressed effectively, an organisation must learn to develop rather than change. Development is different to change in that it emphasises the positive aspects of improvement without the negative connotations of change which focus on what is wrong. Aids to development include continuous improvement programs, creating a receptive environment to new approaches, and recognition of "different ideas".

In achieving system solutions it was emphasised that there should be firstly an assessment of external factors, the existing culture and current performance levels using objective baseline measures. Then one should establish your mission and goals, instigate the employee participation process (non jeopardy) all the while having full management commitment.

A full time human factors position needs to be established to co-ordinate the program. Communication strategies need to be formulated (images and symbols) and information dissemination mechanisms put in place - e.g., tracking of component failures, publication of incident reports and tracking of organisational performance. The organisation can introduce reward and incentive team programs; educational/training programs (team; management; technical skills); and a biennial maintenance review throughout the organisation which reinforces the company philosophy, aids "re-calibration" and deals with documentation and technical issues.

The organisation should introduce and internal feedback system, and encourage voluntary informal communication opportunities (e.g., social gatherings). It is important to establish accountability for implementing change, both top down and bottom up, and establish an effective measurement and evaluation process. The implementation of a human factors safety system should also be carefully monitored to identify potential bottlenecks.

**Summary**

The workshop on human factors in aircraft maintenance, using an applied example, identified the advantages of a "system" approach to human factors interventions. Based on a development approach the workshop identified key areas of concern in the implementation of system solutions to human factors problems in aviation maintenance.

**References**

Hawkins, F.H. (1987). *Human factors in flight*. Aldershot, UK: Gower Publishing Company.

Reason, J. (1997). *Managing the risks of organizational accidents*. Aldershot, UK: Ashgate.

**Annex A to**
**Aircraft Maintenance Workshop Report**
**Organisational safety system self-audit**

*Nick McDonald*
*Department of Psychology, Trinity College Dublin.*

The following informal organisational self-audit covers some of the critical features of a self-regulatory safety system. Please use your knowledge of your organisation (or an organisation familiar to you) to answer the following questions. Try to think of examples which will illustrate or justify your answer. If you don't know, say so.

## Policy

How important is safety compared to other goals in your organisation?

## Standards

How do you know how safe your organisation is?

## Organisation and planning

How often does it happen that the resources necessary to perform an operation satisfactorily (personnel, tools equipment, parts, environment) are not available when required?

## Normal operational behaviour

Does the way in which work is carried out conform to the way in which it is planned and documented? Is the official way of doing things different from the actual way?

## Auditing

Does your organisation audit performance (what actually happens), or just the documentation?

## Quality reporting

How well does your quality system generate relevant reports on safety problems?

## Incident investigation

How well does incident investigation identify appropriate preventative measures?

## Feedback

How effectively is information about safety and safety performance communicated to those who can use it?

## Change

How consistently does your organisation change its human systems and processes in response to identified (non-technical) defects, deficiencies or problems?

# 42 Situation awareness developmental workshop report

*Simon Henderson, Ansett Australia*
*Mica Endsley, SA Technologies, USA*
*Brent Hayward, Dédale Asia Pacific, Australia*

## Introduction

This Situation Awareness Developmental Workshop was the fourth in a series of developmental workshops conducted by the authors and colleagues in Australia, the USA and the UK since 1995. The first of these was held at the Fourth Australian Aviation Psychology Symposium in November 1995 and is reported in the proceedings of that event (Taylor, Endsley & Henderson, 1996). The second was held at the Ninth International Aviation Psychology Symposium at Columbus, Ohio in 1997 (Hayward, Endsley, Taylor & Henderson, 1997). The third was held at the British Psychological Society Occupational Psychology Conference at Eastbourne in January 1998 (Taylor & Henderson, 1998).

The first workshop set out to combine the group's research based theoretical knowledge of situational awareness (SA; see Endsley, 1995, 1996; Jones & Endsley, 1996; Taylor, 1990; Taylor, Selcon & Swinden, 1995) with operational experience from military and civil aviation environments to produce a useful applied training experience for operational personnel. Subsequent workshops have built on this model and have all included experiential exercises with operationally oriented linkages.

## Objectives

The aim of this fourth interactive/experiential SA workshop was to provide participants with a heightened awareness of the concepts of SA and their relevance to successful individual and multi-crew operations, together with an introduction to practical skills for use in guarding against the loss of SA during critical periods of operation. The simulation exercise involved in this workshop was also extended to include a larger operational team.

Some of the questions the co-chairs set out to answer for participants were as follows: What is Situation Awareness? Can we define and describe it? More importantly, can we measure and assess it, and can we train for improved SA? How does individual SA differ from team SA? How does the introduction of new technology affect SA? What of the role of information processing, memory, stress, fatigue, workload, personality, previous training and experience?

**The workshop**

*Structure and conduct*

This workshop, as with others in the series, was designed to provoke interest in further development of team or distributed situation awareness training techniques. The co-chairs were able to test and trial a variety of simulation techniques and then encourage panel discussion about their applicability and relevance to the training of operational personnel.

The workshop program included the following segments:

- Summary of previous workshops;
- Theory applicable to situation awareness training;
- Goals and aims of the simulated exercise;
- Separate pre-training for the roles of either technical or cabin crew;
- The simulation exercise itself;
- Debrief and relationship of observations to theory; and
- Participant's review.

In an advance on previous exercises, this workshop set out to directly simulate the interaction between cabin and technical crew engaged in a flight that suffers a malfunction requiring diversion. Crew pre-training and indoctrination, pre-flight duties and all phases of flight were simulated.

*Team SA principles*

As a basis for this workshop, a model of team SA was provided for building an understanding of the factors that can effect team SA (Endsley & Jones,

1997). Examining SA as it exists within teams and between teams in the aviation setting is important for identifying the causes of break downs in SA and for developing strategies to prevent them. The teams involved in aviation operations include the cockpit crew, the cabin crew, ATC, maintenance crews and ground/ramp personnel. SA is needed by each person on each team, to a level as required for that person's job. Team SA has been defined as "the degree to which every team member possess the SA required for his or her responsibilities" (Endsley, 1995). In aviation, even one person having poor SA can result in negative consequences for the operational team.

The degree to which team members possess a shared understanding of the situation with regard to their shared SA requirements is an extremely important aspect of team SA. Shared SA is defined as "the degree to which team members possess the same SA on shared SA requirements" (Endsley & Jones, 1997). Shared SA can be depicted as the shaded area in Figure 42.1, where each circle represents the SA requirements of each team member. It is the zone where these requirements overlap that constitutes the need for a shared understanding of the situation within a team. Similarly, where the SA requirements overlap between teams, a shared understanding of this information is equally important for the ability of the teams to achieve their goals.

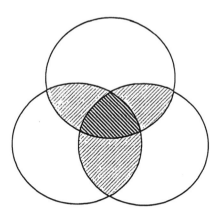

**Figure 42.1**
**Shared SA requirements**

Developing shared SA within a team and between teams can be extremely challenging, especially where those teams are distributed in terms of space, time or physical barriers, as may be the case in many of the teams found in aviation. The factors effecting shared SA within and between teams has been described in the model of team SA as a function of four components (Endsley & Jones, 1997):

1.  Shared SA Requirements - the degree to which the team members know which information needs to be shared, including their higher level assessments and projections (which are usually not otherwise available to fellow team members), and information on team members' task status and current capabilities.

2.  Shared SA Devices - the devices available for sharing this information, which can include direct communication (both verbal and non-verbal), Shared displays or a shared environment. As non-verbal communication and a shared environment are usually not available in distributed teams, this places far more emphasis on verbal communication and technologies for creating shared information displays.

3.  Shared SA Mechanisms - the degree to which team members possess mechanisms, such as Shared Mental Models, which support their ability to interpret information in the same way and make accurate projections regarding each other's actions. The possession of Shared Mental Models can greatly facilitate communication and co-ordination in team settings.

4.  Shared SA Processes - the degree to which team members engage in effective processes for sharing SA information which may include a group norm of questioning assumptions, checking each other for conflicting information or perceptions, setting up co-ordination and prioritisation of tasks, and establishing contingency planning among others.

5.  In the workshop we examined the effect of these components on the SA of team members in a simulated team exercise. This allowed workshop participants to experience first hand the factors that effect team SA and build an understanding of how to prevent breakdowns in team SA.

**The simulation exercise**

This exercise was designed to encourage the breakdown of team situation awareness by including factors that are found in typical aviation settings:

(1) little shared understanding of the SA requirements of other teams; (2) limited shared SA devices between teams; (3) poor shared mental models between teams; and (4) poor shared SA processes. This exercise, as with its predecessors, set teams in competition with each other to encourage rivalry and some degree of risk taking. The simulation was designed so that the "big picture" could become obscured by trivial and relatively inconsequential activities. The researchers believe that using a scored competition in this way allows participants to identify where and how they lost situation awareness. We also used typical team management gaming strategies such as providing different team members with unique information embedded within a similar format and setting up deliberate red herrings for teams to follow to no avail.

In this simulation exercise, technical and cabin crew were provided pre-training in normal and emergency procedures with regard to the flight of a regular public transport aircraft. The simulated flight took place within the surrounds of an international hotel. Conference rooms were used for pre-flight, the foyer was used for the airport ground areas, and differing floors of the hotel used as cruising flight levels. The scene was set to explore whether or not team SA within these small groups could be manipulated by the use of the artificial barriers.

*What really happened*

All teams were given similar instructions and training. All received the same general information regarding objectives and points scoring. However, Technical and cabin crew were given slightly differing operational information. Additionally, only captains were given the flight plan and route information while First Officers received some checklists, including the correct responses to cabin crew emergency procedures drills. The cabin crew's sheets included some essential technical information, which was to be passed to the flight deck in the event of an emergency.

The exercise commenced with a simulated pre-flight routine, where teams were required to be roped together in a certain order and Captains were provided with the flight planning information. Teams were allowed to "taxi" after this pre-flight activity was completed. After completing an information gathering exercise, they were instructed to call Air Traffic Control, via mobile phone, for take-off clearance.

Teams were assigned differing floors of the hotel and a planned route taking them to each end of the corridor to gather information. After completing the route on that floor they could call ATC to request an "altitude change", and then repeat the route on several floors of the hotel, as they made their way to the passengers' planned holiday destination – the rooftop pool. During the flight, an in-flight emergency was simulated and the "aircraft" was to divert to a safe destination. The route was simple and the entire exercise could be walked through slowly in five to six minutes. Teams were given 20 minutes to complete the exercise. Time penalties were to be awarded for late completion of team tasks.

Teams were accompanied by a Marshall (observer), who recorded progress, made notes and applied penalties as required by the rules. Observers' checklists were used to keep track of each team and a roving video camera recorded events for debrief purposes and posterity.

*Experimental design*

The event was designed to encourage the formation of barriers within the flight deck and between the technical and cabin crew, which are common impediments to team SA. Artificial barriers (see Chute & Weiner, 1994) were introduced to these airline crew teams in the following ways:

- Throughout the simulation the technical crew and cabin crew were required to play different kinds of games to simulate routine in-flight duties. These games were not complex and served to simply place all crew members under some form of cognitive load. However, they were designed to segment the aircraft crew into two separate teams playing separate games with an inflated belief in the importance of their own game to the success of the overall mission.

- Workload peaks were manipulated so that the technical crew members were busiest during the simulated take-off and landing phases, while cabin crew were busiest during simulated cruise. Emergency conditions were simulated by a transition by both technical and cabin crews to more complex games.

- Crew training was conducted separately and both technical and cabin crew role players were given information indicating that their own game was the most important. This information was not designed to be difficult to follow or to be secretive. It was freely available to all team members.

- Although crews were roped together at the start of the exercise, an extra length of rope was required to be kept tight between the technical crew and cabin crew. This simulated the flight deck door and meant that the flight deck and cabin crew had to make an effort to communicate. This was supported by training in a common "sterile flight deck policy" and the requirement for the technical crew to adopt a slightly different flight profile when in direct conversation with a member of the cabin crew.

All of the rules were designed to simulate normal airline operations. A free play threat environment was introduced to simulate the hazards encountered during normal line operations including weather avoidance. Crews all commenced their tasks at the same time. They were encouraged to rush the pre-flight stage and be first to obtain clearance. This simulated time pressure and competition between crews and subtly encouraged them not to pre-brief and establish a unified team at the beginning, common problems in commercial aircraft operations.

*Observations*

During the de-brief conducted following completion of the exercise, the participants were able to identify many areas of their performance which were not optimum, relate them to the SA theory that had been presented, and in many cases suggest solutions or strategies to overcome them. The following observations are particularly noteworthy:

- The physical barrier between the technical and cabin crews, although small and mainly symbolic, proved quite effective. Many of the cabin crew role players (mostly pilot CRM instructors) complained of feelings such as: being along for the ride; feeling unimportant; not knowing what was going on; and being unable to voice concerns when they believed the mission was going wrong. One such occurrence was neatly captured on video:

  *One team entered a lift and was intending to go up to a higher level. Unfortunately, the lift went down instead. This went unnoticed by the technical crew, who were busy with other tasks. The video captured the look of confusion and bewilderment on the tech crew role players' faces as they realised they had egressed the lift into the hotel foyer, when they had expected to exit at the sixth floor. Several of the cabin crew role players later commented that they thought they were going the wrong way, but didn't feel able to voice their concern.*

413

- Many of the role players never realised that their "vitally important" individual games were worth nearly nothing in the overall scheme of the simulation and continued to play them to the detriment of overall team performance and cohesion, rather than effecting team strategies which included the whole crew.

- Few first officers realised that they had the key to the flight attendant's emergency procedures (a game involving the round robin call-out of countries, animal or cities in alphabetical order). In general, needed information was not shared across teams.

- Most of the teams that had to wait for clearance because they were slower with their pre-flight procedures did not use the extra time to either brief or consolidate information between the two sides on the team.

- The teams were often slow or deficient in picking up on critical cues. The team members did not really understand all of the other team member's roles and did not understand which information it was important to pass on.

- Most teams did not enlist the aid of ATC as a team member with useful information, but rather thought of ATC only as a constraint.

*The participants' reports*

Participant debriefs consistently cited the following points:

- They may not have a deep understanding of SA but they certainly experienced the problems associated with its loss.

- They were united in the belief that good team SA requires some degree of heightened individual SA within the team.

- The role of the captain is vitally important. If the captain falls into an "SA black hole" then all may follow.

- There is no place for blind trust or an attitude like "they know what they are doing".

- Always provide a thorough briefing so that the Captain's mental model can be compared with other members of the team.

- Briefings should be structured and standardised with opportunity for cross-checking.

- Mistakes and some loss of SA are inevitable. Therefore, procedures should be designed to assist in recognising SA loss and recovery. In particular participants focussed on procedures that enhanced the ability of crews to question their beliefs about the current situation rather than merely confirm them.

- Joint training of technical and cabin crew is essential to build team work and gain appreciation of each other's task and role.

- Standardised and agreed cues, such as unfinished sentences or tasks, may be a valuable guide to deterioration in SA.

**Summary**

The simulated exercise proved to be quite successful and the researchers believe that it is possible to train for team situation awareness through the manipulation of workload, tasks and information sharing that is directly mappable to standard operating procedures. Participants left the workshop armed with the knowledge that loss of SA was a real problem. Several participants also managed to identify strategies or work practice changes they could implement to improve team SA.

*The future*

This workshop supported the findings of previous exercises and reproduced previously reported results. These general results have also been supported by the follow-up work of Taylor, Finnie and Hoy (1997) on cognitive rigidity. The simulation exercise reported here once again usefully highlights several key team processes and behaviours that impact on the ability to develop sufficient team SA to perform the task. These key behaviours are listed in Table 42.1.

There is considerable academic and industry agreement that these positive behaviours need to be encouraged and negative ones eliminated to improve crew SA. The gaming simulations undertaken in this series of workshops have consistently shown that poor or good SA behaviours can be manipulated and controlled with a variety of techniques. These techniques demonstrate the negative effects of such poor behaviours as:

- the setting of an incorrect mental model;
- information hoarding;
- task mis-prioritisation;

- confirmation bias;
- task fixation;
- overload and poor workload management;
- poor team cohesiveness; and
- failure to either self-check or cross-check.

**Table 42.1**
**Team SA processes**

| Ineffective teams' characteristics | Effective teams' characteristics |
|---|---|
| Fell into SA Blackhole:<br>• One member would lead others off | Self-checking:<br>• Checked against others at each step |
| Didn't share pertinent information:<br>• Group norm | Co-ordinated:<br>• To get information from each other |
| Failure to prioritise:<br>• Members went in own directions<br>• Group lost track of main goal | Prioritised:<br>• Set-up contingencies<br>• Re-joining |
| Relied on expectations:<br>• Unprepared to deal with false expectations | Questioning as a group:<br>• Group norm |

Participants from a wide range of aviation related disciplines are able to draw on the experience gained during the exercise to develop their own strategies and techniques to counter loss of SA. Operational personnel were consistently able to draw parallels between their workplace and the simulated exercise. An obvious extension of this workshop is to implement the positive strategies developed by participants in an environment that encourages poor behaviours.

The challenge facing our industry is to take the lessons learnt and techniques trialed during this series of developmental workshops and produce sound training packages for the operational community. A further extension of these workshops is required to investigate the transfer of SA-maintenance strategies to operating procedures and policies and their application to real-world operating environments.

**References**

Chute, R.B., & Weiner, E.L. (1994). Cockpit cabin communication: A tale of two cultures. In *Proceedings of the Eleventh Annual Aircraft Cabin Safety Symposium*. Long Beach, CA: Southern Californian Safety Institute.

Endsley, M.R. (1995). Toward a theory of situation awareness. *Human Factors, 37*(1), 32-64.

Endsley, M.R. (1996). Situation awareness in aircraft. In B.J. Hayward & A.R. Lowe (Eds.), *Applied aviation psychology: Achievement, change and challenge* (pp. 403-417). Aldershot, UK: Avebury Aviation.

Endsley, M.R., & Jones, W.M. (1997). *Situation awareness, information dominance, and information warfare (AL/CF-TR-1997-0156)*. Wright-Patterson AFB, OH: United States Air Force Armstrong Laboratory.

Hayward, B.J., Endsley, M.R., Taylor, R.M., & Henderson, S. (1997, April). *Situational awareness information and training (SAIT)*. Training Workshop presented at the Ninth International Symposium on Aviation Psychology, Columbus, Ohio.

Jones, D.G., & Endsley, M.R. (1996). Sources of situation awareness errors in aviation. *Aviation, Space, and Environmental Medicine, 67*(6). 507-512.

Taylor, R.M. (1990). Situation awareness rating technique (SART): The development of a tool for aircrew systems design. In *AGARD CP 478, Situation Awareness in Aerospace Operations*. Neuilly-sur-Seine: NATO AGARD.

Taylor, R.M., Selcon, S.J., & Swinden, A.D. (1995). Measurement of situational awareness and performance: A unitary SART index predicts performance on a simulated ATC task. In R. Fuller, N. Johnston, & N. McDonald (Eds.), *Human factors in aviation operations*. Aldershot, UK: Avebury Aviation.

Taylor, R.M., Endsley, M.R., & Henderson, S. (1996). Situational awareness workshop report. In B.J. Hayward & A.R. Lowe (Eds.), *Applied aviation psychology: Achievement, change and challenge* (pp. 447-454). Aldershot, UK: Avebury Aviation.

Taylor, R.M., Finnie, S., & Hoy, C. (1997). Cognitive rigidity: The effects of mission planning and automation on cognitive control in dynamic situations. In R.S. Jensen & L. Rakovan (Eds.), *Proceedings of the Ninth International Symposium on Aviation Psychology.* Columbus, Ohio: The Ohio State University.

Taylor, R.M., & Henderson, S. (1998). *Situational awareness workshop,* conducted at the Occupational Psychology Conference of the British Psychological Society. Eastbourne, UK, 7 Jan 1998.

Printed and bound by CPI Group (UK) Ltd, Croydon, CR0 4YY

23/10/2024

01777674-0016